Israel/Palestine in Wo

"Lurking behind, between, and arou
century-old religious claims. Whose P............ ...., ... peting narratives are intertwined, then deftly untangles them to assess their roots, interactions, and crucial contemporary impact. A spellbinding, innovative, and crucial revelation for consumers of religion and politics, Israel Studies, and Middle East affairs."
—Ron Hassner, Chancellor's Professor of Political Science, Director of *Helen Diller Institute for Israel Studies, U.C. Berkeley*

"Ilan Troen's latest book is a beam of light into the darkness of the present. He argues coherently and cogently that theological traditions of Judaism, Christianity, and Islam cannot be divorced from the more recent secular Israeli and Palestinian nationalisms. This religious echo from the past has not been marooned there but continues to shape the cultural reflection of the Israel-Palestine conflict even if framed in terms of modernity.

Ilan Troen is a pioneer of Israel Studies internationally and this work *Israel/Palestine in World Religions: Whose Promised Land?* unpeels the many layers that history and belief have laid down onto this still ongoing tortuous conflict."
—Colin Shindler, Emeritus Professor, *SOAS, University of London*

"*Israel/Palestine in World Religions – Whose Holy Land?* offers a much-needed analysis of the place and role of Israel/Palestine in the Abrahamic religions. This is an unprecedentedly comprehensive and brilliant study, which anyone interested in religious beliefs and their power to shape attitudes will read with great interest. Likewise, students of Israel/Palestine in global opinions should embrace the book. Ilan Troen has done a heroic job in writing this is a fascinating and rich text. I recommend it wholeheartedly."
—Yaakov Ariel, *University of North Carolina*, author of *An Unusual Relationship: Evangelical Christians and Jews* (New York University Press, 2013)

"The conflict over Israel/Palestine is generally understood as a clash of contending national, political, and territorial claims. It is that in large part, but it also has deep-seated theological and doctrinal dimensions. In setting these forth in such clear and incisive ways, Ilan Troen's book could not be more timely and necessary. It is essential reading for anyone who wishes to understand the full complexity of this ongoing, hugely consequential, and still unresolved struggle."
—Alvin Rosenfeld, Director, *Institute for the Study of Contemporary Antisemitism*, Irving M. Glazer Chair in Jewish Studies, *Indiana University*

"This excellent book traces the secular and religious conflict over Palestine from its Biblical and primordial roots. The principal question is: 'Whose Promised Land'? The answer lies in a masterly account of the conflicting Jewish, Arab, and Christian interpretations of the historical creation of the state of Israel."
—Wm. Roger Louis, Kerr Professor, *University of Texas*, and Honorary Fellow, *St. Antony's College, Oxford*

"Ilan Troen has written what is perhaps the single most effective analysis of the relationship between secular and religious forces in the Israeli-Palestinian conflict. Most authorities have devoted their efforts to describing one or the other of these factors but not covered both, let alone their intersection. Troen has thus contributed an essential study of this central, internationally important topic. And he has made it as fair and objective as one could imagine."
—Cary Nelson, Jubilee Professor of Liberal Arts and Sciences at the *University of Illinois at Urbana-Champaign*, former president of the American Association of University Professors, author of *Hate Speech and Academic Freedom: The Antisemitic Assault on Basic Principles*

"Ilan Troen has made an important contribution by tearing down the proverbial Berlin Wall that often separates the treatment of powerful religious and secular forces underlying the Israeli-Palestinian conflict. Troen looks at the nexus between them. Indeed, the profoundly enduring impact of religion upon competing nationalist claims explains the hold of this conflict upon so many inside and outside the Mideast."
—David Makovsky, Director, *Koret Project on Arab-Israel Relations, Washington Institute for Near East Policy*

"This is the first "serious history" that I know of, dealing comprehensively with the Israel/Palestine question not from the regnant overused "secular national narratives" purviews, but from an often ignored but imperative religious millenarian angle. In this learned, exhaustive, deeply searching volume, Ilan Troen brings to the fore of the Israel/Palestine discussions neglected religious foundations without which all attempts at understanding remain deficient, risking our current century of misunderstanding ushering in another century of more-of-the-same in our future."
—Franck Salameh, *Professor of Near Eastern Studies at Boston College*, Editor-in-Chief, *Journal of the Middle East and Africa*

S. Ilan Troen

Israel/Palestine in World Religions

Whose Promised Land?

S. Ilan Troen
Brandeis University (USA)/Ben-Gurion
University of the Negev (Israel)
Beersheva, Israel

ISBN 978-3-031-50913-1   ISBN 978-3-031-50914-8 (eBook)
https://doi.org/10.1007/978-3-031-50914-8

© The Editor(s) (if applicable) and The Author(s), under exclusive license to Springer Nature Switzerland AG 2024
This work is subject to copyright. All rights are solely and exclusively licensed by the Publisher, whether the whole or part of the material is concerned, specifically the rights of translation, reprinting, reuse of illustrations, recitation, broadcasting, reproduction on microfilms or in any other physical way, and transmission or information storage and retrieval, electronic adaptation, computer software, or by similar or dissimilar methodology now known or hereafter developed.
The use of general descriptive names, registered names, trademarks, service marks, etc. in this publication does not imply, even in the absence of a specific statement, that such names are exempt from the relevant protective laws and regulations and therefore free for general use.
The publisher, the authors and the editors are safe to assume that the advice and information in this book are believed to be true and accurate at the date of publication. Neither the publisher nor the authors or the editors give a warranty, expressed or implied, with respect to the material contained herein or for any errors or omissions that may have been made. The publisher remains neutral with regard to jurisdictional claims in published maps and institutional affiliations.

This Palgrave Macmillan imprint is published by the registered company Springer Nature Switzerland AG.
The registered company address is: Gewerbestrasse 11, 6330 Cham, Switzerland

Paper in this product is recyclable.

*We remember
our daughter, Shachar Deborah Troen-Mathias, and son-in-law,
Shlomi David Mathias,
murdered by terrorists while defending their family
Kibbutz Holit on the Gaza border
Shabbat morning, 7 October 2023
and celebrate
their lives and commitment to mutual understanding and
accommodation*

*Carol and Ilan Troen
Omer, Israel*

Preface

The struggle over Israel/Palestine is not just another contest by competing peoples, nationalisms and interest groups, or another instance of geopolitical competition. It may be some or all of these, but it is also about control of sacred territory that is deeply rooted in different theological traditions. This is evident in names still used to designate the Holy Land: *Eretz HaKodesh*, *Terra Sancta*, and *Al'ard Almuqadasa*. Moreover, this contest is more complicated than in places where two faith communities have been in conflict, such as the Indian subcontinent (Hindu and Islam); Cyprus (Greek Orthodoxy and Islam); Northern Ireland (Protestant and Catholic). Here the struggle involves local Jews, Muslims, and Christians, and worldwide faith communities with their own interests and stake in what transpires. These beliefs and interests were not suspended by defeat, exclusion, or absence. Over centuries, Judaism and Christianity anticipated that God's promises would be fulfilled at some undetermined time in the future. For Islam, from 636 C.E. with the conquest of Palestine by the Umayyad Caliphate and through World War I, fulfillment appeared to be self-evident and incontrovertible. Except for two centuries of intermittent rule by Christian Crusaders, Islam controlled the territory and has resisted change in its dominance.

Throughout the centuries of Islamic rule, theology concerning the Holy Land was largely dormant. The status quo was not disrupted until the end of the nineteenth and early twentieth century with the return of Jews and the sudden and unanticipated dissolution of the Ottoman Empire through the intervention of European Christian states that challenged the foundations of regnant theologies. Each had to reformulate traditional religious claims in secular terms suitable to the new reality and the discourse of the contemporary world.

In the twentieth century, terms held to be universal apparently superseded particularistic religious beliefs. Arguments are made in secular language when debating national rights before international institutions and in the public square. Such formulations appear to replace citations from Scripture and arguments based on Divine promises. Categories such as the right to self-determination, historical precedence, indigeneity, purchase, treaties, human rights, and international law commonly employed in the academy and particularly in the social and political sciences and in law are the substance of the new public discourse. It was hoped that this universal common language would lead to shared understanding and perhaps even mitigate if not resolve conflicts. That hope has not materialized in Israel/Palestine.

Despite the expectation that modernity would inexorably lead to secularization, religious culture retains its power. The present project highlights that contending theologies echo over millennia and continue to influence cultural memory, identities, and politics of both devout adherents and the avowedly secular. This observation may apply to many societies, but it is poignantly pertinent to the nature and longevity of the Arab/Israeli conflict over territory sacred to all. Resistance to Jews as a presence in Palestine, let alone to Jewish sovereignty, is anchored in secular as well as theological discourse. A similar mix has been employed to justify the Jewish state. Examining these multiple and opposing possibilities provides the substance of *Israel/Palestine in World Religions—Whose Holy Land?*

This book does not frame the evolution of the conflict chronologically. It does not focus on individuals, political events, or wars. It does not exhaustively explore many other events, claims and complaints. Rather it demonstrates that theological belief systems coexist with secular discourses concerning ownership privileges, rights, and injustice. It focuses on the century-long tangle of secular and theological debates about the legitimacy of the Zionist project and the right to reestablish a sovereign Jewish state on sacred land. It makes evident that purportedly secular debates are no less contentious than religious disputations.

The story told here is complicated since there are multiple secular and theological justifications for all sides in the conflict over Israel/Palestine. The tangle is both within these discourses as well as between them.

For example, both Israelis and Palestinians are granted legitimacy by contemporary concepts of nationalism. Both can claim the privileges that accrue from being indigenous; and both expect other historically based rights. Moreover, both invoke universal rights that are couched in the terminology of international law and principles of justice. Israel came into being in 1947 through a United Nations resolution that established both a Jewish and an Arab state in Palestine in recognition of national rights, a concept that gave legitimacy to the multitude of nation states that emerged in the course of the last century. However, in 1948, the UN promulgated its Universal Declaration of Human Rights. Rights of historical groups do not always mesh with abstractions accorded to humankind as a whole or as individuals. Both Jews and Arabs reference both national and universal rights. Which has priority over the other is a subject of potential contention.

There are other complications. The most contested issue in the early decades of this conflict is the dispute over the economic absorptive capacity of Palestine. Could the country absorb a significant influx of Jews without displacing Arabs? Jews said there was room for all with even higher standards of living than then existed. Arabs argued it could not. Their political pressure pushed the British to renege on the commitment to a Jewish state with disastrous consequences for potential refugees from European antisemitism and without avoiding violence between Jewish and Arab communities. Yet this territory now supports 20 times the population as a century ago and at an unimaginably higher standard of living. This is a rare example when the validity of a claim and counterclaim can be factually tested. Most arguments over the last century are not subject to concrete proof and remain to be aired in philosophical and theoretical terms.

Yet, even as the public square is replete with secular claims, theological positions persist. There is continuity of long-held beliefs such as supersessionism. There is also remarkable adaptation to new circumstances. Although there has been far greater variance in Christianity, Islam has also evolved to developed diverse positions on the place of a Jewish entity in territory it has dominated for centuries. An account of where, why, and how all three related monotheistic faiths have responded to new circumstances is a singular contribution of this book.

Mapping these phenomena is crucial to demonstrating that secular and theological positions may be maintained simultaneously and are often interwoven. For example, the idea of supersessionism or replacement theology has informed both Christianity and Islamic belief in their own exclusive priority and that Jews no longer have an active role in history. Entailed is that there is no basis for Jewish claims to Palestine/Holy Land. There is no divine or historical right of return. This religious belief parallels a secular version of supersessionism: the charge that Zionism is colonialism and labels Israelis as colonial-settlers, Europeans carrying out imperial aims in a foreign land. According to this dogma, it is the Palestinian people who have a unique, deep, historical, and unsevered connection to the land. The Jews established a state at the Palestinians' expense, and that using violence to expel them is legitimate.

The present war between Israel and Hamas in Gaza is a jarring illustration of the blending of secular and theological discourse to justify murderous attacks on civilians. *Hamas*, a translation of the *Islamic* Resistance Movement, is not a traditional national liberation movement. Hamas accepts nationalism as integral to Islam, but not in modern western formulations. Amin al-Husseini (1895–1974), the most significant early opponent of Zionism, was the Grand Mufti of Jerusalem. By definition, al-Husseini was a religious leader, not a cosmopolitan contemporary intellectual engaged in post-Enlightenment thought. Preaching the obligations of faith, he mobilized Muslims inside Palestine and beyond. Hamas emerged from this tradition in an extreme variant all too common throughout the Middle East and portions of Africa such as Al-Qaeda, Taliban, Boka Haram, Islamic Jihad, Al-Shabab, and Islamic State/ISIS.

The objective of Hamas is declared in the 1988 Hamas Covenant and a mass of subsequent pronouncements: "to obliterate it [Israel], just as it obliterated others before it" *(Preamble)*; "The Day of Judgment will not come about until Moslems fight Jews and kill them." (Article 7); and "There is no solution for the Palestinian problem except by *Jihad*. Initiatives, proposals and international conferences are but a waste of time, an exercise in futility." *(Article 13)* Moreover, even if an agreement is apparently reached for a suspension of hostilities—a *hudna* in Islamic tradition—it is merely temporary and war may be resumed at the discretion of Hamas. Thus, Hamas has engaged in intermittent attacks between formal armistices sending projectiles over a fence/security barrier and digging attack tunnels underneath it.

Peace with a Jewish state is not a theological possibility. Another round of fighting must follow until the foe is vanquished.

Defenders of Hamas ignore divine injunctions to massacre Jews and destroy their state. They invoke international law to label residents of Gaza victims of Israeli war crimes. Israel invokes international law to justify its right to self-defense, including when this results in civilian deaths. Imprecise terms exacerbate the shrillness of debate. There is no precise formula for quantifying justifiable collateral damage. "Proportionality" has no agreed definition. And who is responsible for injury to civilians used as human shields?

Such contrary views, based on diverse and irreconcilable sources of authority, have already produced the infamous Goldstone Report in the wake of the 2008–2009 conflict, termed "Operation Cast Lead" by Israel and "The Gaza Massacre" by Hamas. Its prime author, Richard Goldstone, ultimately reconsidered and recanted his position. The call to condemn Israel is now being repeated. Again, the public shouts slogans and ignores the theologically based command to slaughter Israelis. Again, Israel references rights granted in international law and practice, citing the experience of other states in similar circumstances.

It is not true that theology makes conflict and violence inevitable. My point is that there are the many strands that we have to untangle to understand conflict over the Holy Land in the modern period. I do not hold to determinism. As a historian I can try to offer a sensible interpretation of how matters came to be and how beliefs evolved, but I am limited to retrospective logic. At many points in the history of events, choices are made. Future paths lead in different directions and these include accommodation and respect for the beliefs and needs of others. Leading figures in modern Judaism, Christianity, and Islam have departed significantly from long established theological principles to validate a Jewish state, partition of the territory, and a commitment to peaceful coexistence. This, too, is part of my story. There are many moving parts to this history, and they indicate currents flowing in different directions.

Mutual understanding demands that we probe and interrogate the complexity of contrary claims on different levels. In the first part of the book, I explain when and how secular discourses achieved apparent priority over the theological in the public square. The next two major parts analyze the modern, secular discourse and the theological. The question of "whose Promised Land" comes to a head in the decades of the British Mandate and shortly after it ended. The third part is an effort to disentangle some of these strands into the present. Throughout, I comment on the ways secular and theological positions are interwoven. Readers will surely add others independently once the reasoning and method are appreciated. Although the analysis may be incomplete, I hope I have made readers aware of the intricate patterns of secular and religious beliefs embedded in the complex context underlying the question: Whose Promised Land?

Omer, Israel   S. Ilan Troen

Acknowledgements

The underlying insight that lead to this book crystallized into a research strategy when I participated in two nearly simultaneous, multi-year international seminars. The first was at the Institute on Culture, Religion and World Affairs (CURA) at Boston University, founded and led by the late Peter Berger, a pioneering and influential sociologist of religion. Those extended sessions were an extraordinary learning experience. Ongoing exchanges with scholars from across the globe probing the relationship between religion and secularization stimulated my desire to plumb the relationship between the two as applied to the Israel/Palestine conflict and century-long contentions regarding Israel's legitimacy. The second was an extended seminar that brought together diverse scholars and clerics. This was chaired by Philip Cunningham, a distinguished professor of theology at St. Joseph University in Philadelphia, who is active in Christian-Jewish relations and has headed the International Council of Christians and Jews. I am particularly grateful to Ruth Langer of Boston College who brought me into their discussions. Exchanges with the participants in these forums resulted in rethinking what I thought I knew and in developing new questions and insights. Several preliminary articles explore the interconnectedness of the religious and secular. I am grateful to the many colleagues in both seminars.[1]

Although I had parallel training in public and Hebrew institutions from elementary school through my first university degrees, my formal and systematic research into the study of Israel began through regular seminars I initiated when appointed academic director of the Ben-Gurion Institute for the Study of Israel and Zionism and its Archives in Sde Boker and later, at Brandeis University, as first incumbent of the *Karl, Harry, and Helen Stoll Chair in Israel Studies and* founding director of the Schusterman Center for Israel Studies. Moreover, as founding editor of *Israel Studies* (Indiana University Press) for a quarter of a century I was privileged to encounter numerous submissions and the work of more than six hundred scholars who published at least one article in the journal. This exposed me to a wide range of ideas, insights, and positions that have animated and aggravated the study of Israelis and Palestinians and the communities with which they are associated. This exposure informs my approach to a century of conflict and understanding of numerous topics in a multitude of settings. I have also learned much from graduate students, particularly at Brandeis, where I was able to participate in mentoring talented young people in topics related to Israel from the perspective of the varieties of monotheism. They include Zeynep Civcik, Rachel Fish, Rimah Farah, Eric Fleisch, Randy Geller, Mostafa Hussein, Ari Moshkovski, Jason Olson, Shay Rabineau, Joseph Ringel, Gangzheng She, and Amber Taylor. *Sayings of the Fathers* well expresses that wisdom may be gleaned by learning from others (*Pirkei Avot*, Chap. 4).

It is also a pleasure to acknowledge specific debts to individuals who reviewed this manuscript in whole or in part. I am especially glad to thank publicly colleagues notably the late and beloved David Ellenson, Donna Robinson Divine, and Natan Aridan who commented and suggested corrections on an early draft and raised questions for further inquiry. Natan also shared his extensive knowledge of sources and their locations. Arieh Saposnik provided an invaluable line-by-line critical review. I am also indebted to an anonymous reader who critiqued an earlier draft. I very much appreciate the contribution of other colleagues, notably Jacob Lassner and Noam Stillman, who offered information, expertise, and guidance on discussions of Islam. I identified and acquired material through the web especially during the Covid epidemic. However, I am especially grateful to the librarians at the Ben-Gurion Research Institute and at Brandeis University, where most of the work was carried out, for their expert advice for which there is no substitute.

Thanks are also due to my literary agent, Peter Bernstein, for wise and patient counsel during crucial stages in preparing and presenting the manuscript. It is gratifying to acknowledge Philip Getz, former editor at Palgrave Macmillan, who published an essay out of which this manuscript developed and who provided the support and encouragement in bringing this greatly enhanced product to the attention of this publisher. With the departure of Philip to another assignment, I was very fortunate that Victoria Peters, the Humanities Editor for Palgrave Macmillan, undertook to ensure that the project would reach a successful conclusion. Her wise advice and sympathetic interventions have been essential. Thanks, too, to Arunaa Devi for superintending the process or creating a book from the manuscript.

Finally, I want to publicly express my appreciation to Carol Troen, my partner in life, mother of our children, an academic, and an artist. She has shared her knowledge of subjects treated in this book and beyond as well as her extraordinary talents in critical thinking and language. This book is the product of our often-intense professional collaboration. It also bespeaks our shared desire to inform our children and their children about how we have tried to understand the complexities and challenges we face as Israeli Jews. We are witnessing the completion of only the first century of a local and international conflict that has accompanied the creation of a Jewish state and appears likely to continue for some undeterminable time. We cannot offer a path to a solution, we hope this book contributes a measure of insight to light their way forward. Carol and I originally intended to dedicate this book to them—Lisa, Aron, Joshua, Deborah, Judah, and Abraham—with all our love. In the aftermath of the murder of Deborah and her husband, Shlomi, defending their home at Kibbutz Holit on the Gaza border on Shabbat morning, 7 October 2023, we remember and celebrate their commitment to life and to mutual understanding and accommodation among peoples.

Omer, Israel   Ilan Troen

Note

1. Ilan Troen, "The Roles of Theology and History in Claims to Palestine-Israel," in *Enabling Dialogue about the Land: A Resource Book for Jews and Christians*, ed. by Philip A. Cunningham, Ruth Langer, and Jesper Svartvik (New York: Paulist Press, 2020), 107–128; with Carol Troen, "Theological and Secular Discourses in Validating a Jewish State," in *Secularization, Desecularization and Toleration; Cross-Disciplinary Challenges to a Modern Myth*, eds. Vyaheslav Karpov and Manfred Svensson (New York: Palgrave Macmillan, 2020), 191–214; Ilan Troen, "Multiple Modernities; The View from Jerusalem," in *Social Science and Modern Society*, 51:2 (March/April 2014), 145–151 and "Secular Judaism in Israel," in *Social Science and Modern Society*, 53:2 (March/April 2016), 153–162.

Contents

1 From Theological to Secular Claims 1
   Background 2
      Claiming Territory 4
   From Religious to Secular Arguments 6
   Structure of the Book 9
   Part I 10
   Part II 12
   Part III 15

Part I Secular Claims 19

2 Conquest, Treaties and Self-Determination 21
   Introduction 21
   Unusual Claimants 23
      The Jewish Narrative 25
      The Arab Narrative 30
   Competing Legal Principles 32
   Contrary Legal Views 33
      Henry Cattan 34
      Julius Stone 37

3 From Discovery to Rediscovery: The Economic Absorptive Capacity of Palestine 43
   Prejudice and Rights 48
   Evidence from Experts 49
   Debating the Economic Absorptive Capacity of Palestine 50
   Archaeology and Politics 51
   Testimony of Foreign Experts 54
   Institutionalized Zionist Research 56

4	**Possession and Dispossession Through Labor and Purchase**	65
	Introduction	65
	Labor	66
	Sanctification of Labor	68
	Background to Land Ownership in Palestine	75
	Jewish Land Purchases	78
	Dispossession	78
	Attempts to Alleviate Dispossession	81
	Arab and Jewish Land	82
5	**History as Legitimacy**	87
	Claims Derived from History	87
	The Significance of Being "First"	88
	Defining "Indigeneity"	90
	Secular History	94
	Modern Palestinians and Antiquity	95
	"Indigenous" Bedouins	97
	Further Misapplication of the Colonial-Settler Paradigm	99
	Conclusion	103

Part II	**Theological Claims**	109
6	**Judaism's Claims: A Multiplicity of Interpretations**	111
	Introduction	111
	Ultraorthodoxy: Waiting for the Messiah	113
	Engaged Ultraorthodoxy	114
	Religious Zionism	116
	Reform Judaism	122
	The Religious Basis for a Bi-National State	125
	Summary Observation	128
7	**Christianity's Claims: A Kaleidoscope of Theologies**	131
	Introduction	131
	Catholicism	134
	Protestant Alternatives	137
	Evangelicalism	137
	James Parkes: An Anglican Theologian	140
	Niebuhr: An American Theologian	141
	Interim Observation	143
	Palestine's Christians	145
	Concluding Reflection	149
8	**Islam: Encountering a Contemporary Challenge**	157
	Introduction	157
	The Significance of Religion in the Arab State and Politics	158
	Jews in the Qur'an	162

	Treatment of Jews in Islamic Societies.	164
	Mobilizing the Islamic Past	165
	Khaybar.	165
	Jews as Crusaders	167
	Jerusalem.	168
	Radical Islam	171
	Accommodation with Israel: An Alternative Islamic Path	173
Part III	**Concluding Reflections**	183
9	**Concluding Reflections**.	185
	Section A. Persistent Categories, Modified Applications	187
	Conquest	187
	Rediscovery and the Economic Absorptive Capacity of Palestine . . .	188
	Labor and Purchase.	189
	History.	190
	Contesting Sacred Land: Internal Debates	192
	Christianity	193
	Islam	195
	Section B. Modes of Contemporary Criticism	195
	Criminalization	195
	The United Nations as an Arena of Hostility	197
	UNGA Resolution 3379	199
	Lawfare: NGOS in the Work of the UN	200
	Occupation	202
	Imperfect Paradigm: Binationalism	205
	Section C. Towards the Second Century.	211
	Complications of the Present	211
	Final Observations	213
Selective Glossary.		223
Select Bibliography.		237
Index		247

Chapter 1
From Theological to Secular Claims

The legitimacy of establishing a Jewish state in Palestine has been disputed since at least the Balfour Declaration in November 1917, when the British Cabinet announced that it viewed "with favour the establishment in Palestine of a national home for the Jewish people."[1] Since the emergence of Zionism towards the end of the nineteenth century, Jews themselves have debated the desirability of an independent Jewish state within the portion of the Ottoman Empire they had always considered their ancient homeland. Many were content to remain in the Diaspora until the arrival of the Messiah. Others advocated integrating as citizens within the newly established democratic states. A determined and growing minority nevertheless persisted and ultimately succeeded in seeking sovereignty in their historic homeland. Israel's establishment has not ended internal dissention over the wisdom and legitimacy of that achievement.

The Balfour Declaration placed this initially internal debate as a contested topic on the international agenda. The question of Israel's legitimacy was not resolved by the League of Nations' endorsement of the Balfour Declaration in 1922, the British Mandate for Palestine, nor by the United Nations' decision in November 1947 in favor of establishing a Jewish state. Even after winning multiple wars in the seventy-plus years since independence, achieving membership in the OECD and recognition by a growing number of countries, including a growing number of Muslim Arab states, Israel's legitimacy is still disputed in the academy, in the polemics of the public square, and in religious settings. Challenges to its status, composition and identity remain part of the international agenda as the dispute over a Jewish national home in Palestine enters its second century.

The intention here is not to recount the history of the Arab-Jewish or the Palestinian-Israeli conflict. Rather, I propose to analyze the secular and theological discourses that interrogate, affirm, and challenge the legitimacy of Jewish sovereignty. Debates over the land considered holy by the three streams of monotheism have a long history. I trace the way they have shifted from arguments rooted exclusively in the authority of divine promises to arguments couched in avowedly secular discourse aspiring to ostensibly universal principles of international law and justice. Nevertheless, theological issues remain inextricably linked to disputations about Palestine/Israel, the "Holy Land" to Jews, Christians, and Moslems whether as *Eretz Hakodesh, Terra Sancta,* or *Al-Arḍ Al-Muqaddasah.* My aim is to disentangle the secular from the theological arguments that at times appear to be separate and discrete, or interwoven, or to intersect, and even complement one another. The underlying question is how the territory of the Holy Land is claimed. It is the diverse strategies disputants mobilize to legitimate their claims for the same territory that informs the structure of this book and the content of its chapters.

The focus in Part I is on the debate as it developed primarily between the Balfour Declaration of 1917 and the United Nations resolution in 1947 that partitioned Palestine into a Jewish and an Arab state with an international condominium around Jerusalem. The arguments that led to this by now familiar two-state solution still resonate in the twenty-first century as do the arguments made during that initial thirty-year period. In examining this basic frame, both earlier and contemporary articulations are featured and interrogated. Ultimately, I hope to provide current readers with a means to comprehend the discourses of the past and how they are carried on in the present.

Background

The land now called Israel/Palestine has been a venue for conflict and competition by numerous tribes, nations, and empires for millennia. The Old Testament is replete with this history. Subsequent sacred texts and secular histories continue the narratives of conflict and conquest. A partial list of rulers includes Canaanites, Hebrews, Egyptians, Assyrians, Persians, Greeks, and Romans in the ancient period and followed by Byzantines, various Muslim empires—Umayyads, Abbasids, Seljuks and Fatamids—before Crusaders arrived in Jerusalem on Christmas Day in 1100 and were finally driven out from Jaffa nearly two centuries later in 1291. They were followed by Muslim rule by Mamluks, and in 1516, by the conquest of Ottoman Turks who brought nearly 400 years of relative stability and a large measure of quiescence. Competition returned in the aftermath of World War I when the Ottoman Empire collapsed and much of the Middle East, including Palestine, was replaced by a system of Mandates established by the League of Nations.

It was expected that these temporary Mandates would nurture the territories during the transition to independent statehood. However, the Middle East, as restructured primarily by the British and French, was in disarray for the second half of the twentieth century and has certainly remained so through the first two decades of the twenty-first. Internal tensions, violent revolts, and warfare have beset the former Mandates of Iraq, Syria, Transjordan, Lebanon, and Palestine. Planned borders have proven fluid and ill-conceived; rulers and governing bodies have been subject to assassination and revolution. Outside powers—proximate ones like Turkey, Iran, Egypt, Saudi Arabia, and the more distant, especially the United States, Britain, France, the Soviet Union/Russia and recently China—are still vying for power and trying to shape and reshape the remains of the Ottoman Empire.

It is critical to situate the story of Palestine/Israel within this ever-changing kaleidoscope. What was originally intended as the British Mandate for Palestine at the end of World War I has been divided into Jordan (initially only Transjordan), Israel, and Palestine, with the latter further divided into separately governed areas of the West Bank and Gaza. All are afflicted with tensions within and between. The future portends much the same for a region beset with potentially new claimants seeking to redraw boundaries.

Israel is an anomaly in its success at achieving statehood and avoiding the upheavals of most of its neighbors. Nevertheless, seventy-plus years after the United Nations recognized its independence and numerous wars later, its borders are still contested as, indeed, is its very legitimacy as a sovereign state and how it is conceived. And despite President Trump's 2019 decision to move the U.S. embassy to Jerusalem, most of the 160-plus members of the United Nations that do recognize Israel's legitimacy do not accept its claims over Jerusalem as its capital. In addition, Israel's provocative encroachment into what was intended as a state governed by and for Palestinian Arabs invites continuing opposition, violence, and criticism.

In the huge literature devoted to the pathologies of the modern Middle East, this book offers a singular analysis of how modern claims to this much cherished territory have been made and rebuffed. Rather than focus on the military, political, and diplomatic history of selected events or the conflict as a whole, I describe the cultural and legal contexts and the theological and secular discourses in which claims are made. To understand claims to land considered holy by Judaism, Christianity, and Islam, I examine the filter through which believers view this sacred territory. Their theological positions have been complicated by the impact of Enlightenment thought and secularization and attendant changes in the evolving discourses of claims and arguments in the last two centuries.

Theological discourse has credibility within communities of adherents and is intended to reach them. In contrast, secular discourse is intended for the public square where ideas and principles contend with one another. It is geared to justifying positions towards outsiders. Contemporary debates about legitimacy are not limited to synagogue, church, and mosque. They are argued in international forums, the courts, the academy, and in the media where arguments are more likely to be cast in universal and secular terms. Nevertheless, what is fascinatingly complex about the case at hand is that these two discourses—the theological and secular, the parochial and universal—may appear to be distinct and separate but are often inextricably intertwined. They may also complement one another.

Claiming Territory

For most human history, until the end of the 18th century, claims to territory rested on appeals to divine sanction. Rashi (**Ra**bbi **Sh**lomo **I**tzhaki, 1040–1105), a medieval French rabbi and commentator, wrote a classic text that captures this historic perception both as a general principle but particularly as applicable to the Jewish connection to Canaan/Palestine. Questioning why *Genesis* begins "When God began creating the heaven and the earth," he observed that this declaration stipulates that it is the Creator who apportions the earth and grants legitimacy to claimants for portions of it. As Rashi explained,

> If the nations of the world should say to Israel, "You are robbers because you have seized by force the lands of the seven nations (i.e., Canaan)," they (Israel) may respond: "The entire world belongs to the Holy One, Blessed be He. He created it and gave it to whomever it was right in His eyes. Of His own will, He gave it to them, and gave it to us." (*Yalkut, Exodus* 12.2)

This interpretation was formulated many centuries earlier and expressed in a host of verses throughout the Old Testament that promised the ultimate return of Jews to *Eretz Yisrael* [The Land of Israel], their Promised Land. These texts, that had been understood as reporting the word of the Lord, validated the special Covenant that began with Abraham and his descendants, became more specific with Moses, and then reiterated through the judges, prophets, and kings, especially through David and his progeny. These covenants came to viewed as permanent but requiring Jews to fulfil divine commitments. If they did not, their entitlement to the inherited land could be temporarily revoked, though with the promise of eventual redemption and return. The Promised Land, then, was a gift of the deity to the Children of Israel although tenure was conditional and susceptible to interruption. Even though the borders of the promised territory were subject to fluctuation through contraction and expansion, the basic principles remained fixed in the triadic formula: God, the People, and the Land.[2]

The belief that the Lord is the ultimate disposer may be the oldest and most consistently used argument of how territory may legitimately be held. Claims to this same territory have been upheld by Jews and then by Christians and Muslims. All agreed the Land of Israel was once assigned to Jews, but Christianity and later Islam held that God's favor has transferred it to believers of faiths that superseded Judaism. In Part II, I explore views that developed within the three monotheistic faiths regarding the contemporary preeminence of Jews in the land all consider holy. As we shall see, an extraordinary variety of positions produced remarkable combinations of traditional theological and modern secular views through which the Israel/Palestine conflict may be perceived.[3]

The notion that God assigns territory to his favorites extends beyond monotheism. Even in modern secular societies, the Divine remains a vital source of legitimacy for how societies are organized. Monarchs claim legitimacy through "divine right." Human interactions are regulated by rules and values derived from Revelation or other ways of ascertaining divine will. Legitimacy and proper behavior are often viewed and evaluated through a religious prism. Hence the ubiquity of such expressions as *God willing* [*im yirzeh ha-Shem*], *deo volente* or *inshAllah*. These formulaic expressions are so deeply embedded that they are still much in use today despite the apparent secular character of the contemporary world and the behavior of secular moderns.

In other words, claims to Israel/Palestine that are publicly made in secular terms often resonate with traditional religious beliefs, whether explicitly or implicitly, deeply embedded or merely superficial. The analysis of this phenomenon is informed in large measure by the idea of civil religion that originated during the French Enlightenment with Jean-Jacques Rousseau. Robert Bellah used it to understand the American experience in the 1960s.[4] Charles Liebman and Eliezer Don-Yehiya applied Bellah's work to Israel in the 1980s. They pointed out that religious values abound in modern Israeli nationalism and are expressed through public rituals, symbols and ceremonies, "sacred" days, and sites. Importantly, they demonstrated the strong undercurrent of religion in Israeli nationalism, however avowedly secular.[5]

I also draw on the late Peter Berger's work that reverses his earlier certainty that secularity will inevitably overtake religion during the course of modernization.[6] His insight, that I relate to both Palestinian and Jewish claims, is part of a growing appreciation that modernization and secularization do not supplant or eliminate religion. Both may exist independently but as I suggested above, may also merge in supporting or rejecting a given cause.

Finally, Michael Walzer's recent *The Paradox of Liberation; Secular Revolutions and Religious Counterrevolutions* (2015) is usefully provocative. Walzer analyzes the Zionist experience within the context of three national liberation movements—Algerian, Indian, and Zionist. He might have added the Turkish, also an explicit model for Ben-Gurion, and Yasser Arafat, initially a secular revolutionary committed to national liberation on the Algerian model, who came to use symbolic Islamic elements even as a sector of secular Palestinian nationalism came to include Islamic fundamentalists.[7] In each of these cases, the first generation of revolutionaries was secular in a "Western" mold. This was true of Ben Bella's FLN (National Liberation Front), Nehru's Indian National Congress, and Ben-Gurion's Labor Zionists. Their movements rejected foreign rule and religious culture—whether Islam, Hinduism, or Judaism as a defining element in the societies they hoped to build. Yet, all made compromises of some sort along the path to power. Most importantly, their influence was never complete or permanent. The religious worldview they ignored or expected to supplant reasserted itself, and they were forced to accommodate to traditional religious power centers and traditions. The promise and premise of a total secular transformation was never achieved. Even when distinctions between secular and religious were attempted, Walzer indicates it has proven difficult to sustain them. Lurking beneath the surface and usually deeply embedded, religion and religious elements reassert themselves to assume significance if not dominance.

In sum, I suggest that in argumentation over claims to territory, the secular and the religious, are not hermetically sealed or necessarily antagonistic to each other. They can coexist. The well-known dictum of Hugo Grotius, *etsi deus non daretur*, is instructive: one can discern and formulate principles based in natural law "*as if* God did not exist." Grotius, a deeply religious Christian, sought principles that derived from alternative epistemologies. Among his followers was John Locke who provided a means for claiming territory based entirely in secular concepts rooted in Natural Law but without contradicting traditional religious beliefs. Indeed, even in Locke's writings, the secular and religious elements can be considered complementary as Locke draws on human experience, including that which is recorded in the Bible.

From Religious to Secular Arguments

Secular political claims originated in the eighteenth century in the context of the European Enlightenment and were further elaborated in the nineteenth century with the rise of the modern state. The example of British colonists in North America illuminates the process. They established a state without making explicit reference to the sanction of a deity.[8] How this came about and the course this revolutionary idea took is paradigmatic for how modern claims are made elsewhere. The United States' Declaration of Independence refers to God only in general language as a source of rights; neither it nor the Constitution mentions Jesus or Christianity. This is not to claim that church and state have been or are separate as formal American political thought might suggest in the well-known principle of separation of church and state. American coinage maintains that "In God We Trust" and that phrase has been established as the official motto of the United States.[9] Which God is not specified. Tensions of greater and lesser magnitude between commitments to religion and secularity have been a permanent feature of American society throughout its history, as certainly evidence in contemporary American politics. Severance of one from the other has never been complete. Nevertheless, a novel system developed in which a revolutionary category of referencing only secular principles came to predominate in the public square. It is in detailing the controversial application of such principles that came to become widely adopted into defined categories that will concern us as we examine their relevance to the case of Palestine.

By 1776, the authority for the creation of this society derived from the will of the people. Transplanted Europeans would come a long way since the Mayflower Compact of 1620 that incorporates the traditional assertions of Divine authority, declaring:

> Having undertaken, for the Glory of God, and advancements of the Christian faith and honor of our King and Country, a voyage to plant the first colony in the Northern parts of Virginia, do by these presents, solemnly and mutually, in the presence of God, and one another, covenant and combine ourselves together into a civil body politic …[10]

The contrast with the Constitution's opening assertion is marked and crucial:

We the People of the United States, in Order to form a more perfect Union, establish Justice, insure domestic Tranquility, provide for the common defence, promote the general Welfare, and secure the Blessings of Liberty to ourselves and our Posterity....

There were many European claimants to the New World across the Atlantic. Americans, who had denied the Divine right of kings and had declared disassociation of Church from State, invoked the abstract concept of Providence to legitimate their nation's movement across the continent without recourse to a national church. As citizens of an avowedly secular state, they developed novel theories of legitimacy that allowed them to claim vast territories from the Atlantic coast to the Pacific. These were a means of rationalizing their own rights, not only in opposition to the indigenous Indians and Mexicans, but to their European competitors—particularly France, Spain, Great Britain and even Russia.

Applying natural law in asserting claims to territory was revolutionary. John Locke did so in his *Second Treatise on Government* through the Labor Theory of Property where he proposed that by adding value through labor, one could gain title to land.[11] This landmark secularized a principle that was rooted in religion. To appreciate its significance, I can briefly trace the evolution of thought on the subject from Puritan encounters with America through Jefferson's assertions about the agrarian democracy that was to transform the United States in the nineteenth century.

The first English settlers in New England in the 1620s commented on the paucity of the local population in contrast to the superabundance of natural resources. They argued that it was "lawful now to take a land which none useth and make use of it." Under the leadership of the Calvinist Governor of the Massachusetts Bay Colony, Jonathan Winthrop, in the 1630s, they articulated the theory of rightful settlement that echoed a Christian interpretation of the Bible. Basing himself on Genesis, chapter 1, Winthrop wrote:

The whole earth is the Lord's Garden and he has given it to the senses of men, with a general Condicion: Increase and multiply, replenish the earth and subdue it.... And for the [Indian] Natives of New England—they inclose noe land, neither have any settled habitation nor any tame cattle to improve the land by, and so have none other but a natural right to those countries. So as if we leave them [land] sufficient for their use wee may lawfully take the rest, there being more than enough for them and us....[12]

Blending biblical and Lockean arguments in his writing in 1802 of the natives' rights, John Quincy Adams, the future President, commented that native Americans must have, by right, "a space of ample sufficiency for their sustenance, and whatever they have annexed to themselves by personal labor." But there were lands over which they did not have rights. Thus: "Shall he forbid the wilderness to blossom like the rose? Shall he forbid the oaks of the forest to fall before the ax of industry and rise again transformed into the habitations of ease and elegance?"[13]

In like manner, twenty years later, President James Monroe observed: "The hunter or savage state requires a greater extent of territory to sustain it, than is compatible with the progress and just claims of civilized life, and must yield to it..." And: "The earth was given to mankind to support the greatest number of which it is capable, and not tribe or people have a right to withhold from the wants of others more than is necessary for their own support and comfort."[14]

From the present vantage point, these rationalizations are paternalistic at best. But they emphasize that although rights over land could be acquired by conquest, the American settlers primarily had recourse to purchase or treaty to claim territories for cultivation. In the course of this process of acquisition, truths rooted in revealed religion were overlaid by references to the principles of Natural Law. Winthrop justified settlement as a biblical mandate in the seventeenth century; by the eighteenth century John Locke justified settlement by Natural Law, reasoning that the right to property is vested in one who works the land and makes it productive. Labor, rather than mere residence, whether occasional or long-term, endowed ownership.

This Lockean version of the social contract was the principle behind Jefferson's yeoman ideal used to justify the United States' expansion across the continent and to establish a legal system grounded in the protection of individual rights, including the right to property. The earliest Zionist pioneers at the end of the nineteenth century drew on and adapted the same fund of ideas that had spread throughout the Western world since the eighteenth century. These ideas were shared by the Zionist Right and by Socialist Labor, that privileged the "conquest of labor" to "redeem" land in Palestine. They were rooted in the precedent that territory could legitimately be acquired by investing their own labor to make it productive.[15]

Locke's and Jefferson's theories found their way into a series of court cases in the 1820s and 1830s that have since served as precedents in litigation between settlers and natives throughout the world. The most frequently cited were disputes between the Cherokee Indians and white settlers over land rights in Georgia, Indiana, and Illinois. All were adjudicated in the United States Supreme Court of Chief Justice John Marshall, perhaps the most important early theorist of American liberties and institutional arrangements. Marshall authored a series of opinions that synthesized legal theory and practice inherited from the Enlightenment and the British colonial system. He accepted the validity of the traditional concepts of *discovery* and *conquest* as legal bases for claiming territory, but argued that *purchase*, *treaties* and making proper use of land through *improvement* and *cultivation* were the relevant categories for adjudicating the rights of natives and of settlers. Although the imposition of these principles in the exercise of European colonialism in displacing traditional native rights is subject to contemporary criticism, the categories detailed in Marshall's judgements indicate the legal, political, and philosophical principles in which controversies over land have been conducted. Even though contemporary critics may view them as inappropriate or unjust instances of conquest through law, they delineate the debates that are the subject of this book. A telling indicator of the present popular reassessment of European colonization is expressed in the phenomenon of supplanting Columbus Day with Indigenous Peoples Day in numerous American states and venues.[16]

In the aftermath of the Balfour Declaration, Jews and Arabs made fulsome reference to accepted international principles and attempted to interpret and apply them to their advantage. Jews, Muslims and Christians necessarily referenced Marshall's categories and other modern principles, rather than draw solely on traditional beliefs, anchored in their respective cultures, in order make their case over the disposition of Palestine. Indeed, the Arab side was so successful in doing so that by the White Paper of 1939 it had significantly derailed the explicit intention of the Balfour Declaration to transform Palestine into "the national home for the Jewish people."

Marshall's thought provides a coherent and systematic theory of primary and secondary rights in land ownership. Natives have rights as nomads or cultivators, but they do not have the right to claim unused territory or lands they have only occasionally or inefficiently used. His conceptualization has achieved such authority that even today courts in Australia and Israel hearing claims from peoples as distant and distinct as Australian Aboriginals and Negev Bedouin may argue that their lands are "*terra nullius*," that is, open to possession by others because they have not been or are not currently being used effectively by contemporary standards. Australian courts have granted considerable rights to the indigenous Mabo in what is termed "Native Title" legislation.[17] Israeli courts have found Bedouin claims of indigeneity unsubstantiated in terms of the historical record and lacking the documentation modern governments generate and require regarding land ownership. In general, as in the recent case of the Dakota pipeline, contemporary courts may be sympathetic to the rights of indigenous peoples to protect their culture, but not to their right to control territory and challenge state sovereignty and authority. Discussion of indigenous rights follows in the chapter that treats the use of history to support claims in the Israeli/Palestinian conflict.

A clutch of secular principles beyond Divine favor have been used to legitimate claims to land: *discovery, conquest, treaties, labor, purchase* and *history*. I analyze these terms singly or in various combinations including the ways in which God's favor is implied and alleged. I also evaluate how other modern concepts such as *self-determination* and concerns for the *dispossessed* and *indigenous* fit in or clash with these principles. This book is focused on how these categories are applied by the contending parties as givens within an established framework that shaped debates before international forums and in the public square. They also inform the organization of this book.

Structure of the Book

The structure of the book follows from the foregoing analysis. I decided not to adhere to the historic order, beginning with the theological followed by the secular. Instead, I begin with the present secular arguments and work back towards the fundamental theological and persisting positions of Judaism, Christianity, and Islam. I examine first the contemporary challenges to Israel's legitimacy that are largely formulated in international legal principles and political debates expressed in secular terms, but which rarely reference theological concepts although protection of religious institutions and believers is significant. On the other hand, theological discussions often favor perspectives grounded in secular discourse. This sequence should make for a more coherent and logical analysis. I aim to demonstrate the tangled connections between these arguments and the secular ones detailed in the first section. I conclude with observations on how these complex interrelationships are implicated in contemporary contentions over Israel's legitimacy.

Part I

Chapter 2 examines how Zionists and Arabs related to two of Marshall's categories—conquest and treaty—in the period following World War I. Both sides took it for granted that because they had aligned with and supported the British war effort they were entitled to a share of the spoils as the Ottoman Empire was divided and reconstituted. When I reconsider these claims in relation to "self-determination," a concept that was formulated nearly a century after Marshall developed his categories, I find that the expectations of Grotius's followers that international law would be universally applicable to resolving conflicts were overly optimistic. It is extraordinarily difficult to apply universal principles to the Israeli/Palestinian conflict. For example, the right to self-determination opposes the right of conquest and the validity of treaties that derive from them. Moreover, rights are not necessarily equal in merit. How one prioritizes or even denies an alternative right is another part of our puzzle. Finally, the relative weight of rights changes over time. Thus, the rights that accrued to the victor at the end of World War I are not be similarly privileged in the post-World War II period. This further complicates applying principles immutable in theory to changing perceptions and realities of a real, long-term, festering conflict. It would be correct to suspect that the apparently secular choices made by the disputants over the same territory are informed by value systems and cultural preferences other than mere positions cogently presented before secular international forums.

Chapter 3 considers rights that come from "rediscovery." I use this term because Palestine has been imagined and known for thousands of years. Unlike the New World in the age of Columbus and subsequent explorations, Palestine was "known" by the West and beyond. "Discovery" would not be exact and appropriate. Ancient maps often placed Jerusalem and the Holy Land at the center of the world. In the modern period the kind of knowledge implicit in "knowing" has been redefined. In today's secularly constructed maps, Palestine has moved from the center to the periphery, although in maps focusing on the conflict, it remains central. Rediscovery also indicates that new kinds of knowledge would be sought and utilized to legitimate the political aspirations of contending sides.

Not only were "science" and scientific evidence not conclusive in adjudicating conflicting claims to Palestine, but they also added to the tangle. Some findings of modern scientific discovery were used to restrain Jewish settlement, if not deny its legitimacy entirely. Arab opponents claimed that Palestine had no room for Jews; their presence was incompatible with the rights of the Arab majority already resident in the land. This position had significant political success for a time, but ultimately the science developed by those who favored the establishment of a Jewish state won out. Palestine's potential was explored, cultivated, and, in the process of re-discovery, shown to be far greater than claimed by those who doubted Palestine's economic absorptive capacity. A century after the Mandate for Palestine was created, the same territory on the western side of the Jordan River supports more than 14 million people or twenty times the 700,000 who then lived there.[18] This is another instance where arguments that appear neutral and objective in the abstract are ineffective in adjudicating complex realities where the choices of adherents to opposing claims are based in unexpressed preferences.

Chapter 4 considers the Lockean idea of improvement through Labor and the rights that accrue to purchase and to working the land. In the New World, the Dutch purportedly purchased Manhattan from local Native Americans in the early seventeenth Century, while a century and a half later, Thomas Jefferson famously purchased what became a large portion of the United States from France. From its beginnings at the end of the nineteenth century, when the Zionist movement set out to restore Palestine to its Biblical status as "a land flowing with milk and honey," it too resorted to purchase, and engaged in massive fund raising to reclaim land in Palestine with that intention. Not being an instrument of Britain or any other foreign empire, Zionists did not use force of arms to acquire title to territory until the 1948 War of Independence and the 1967 Six-Day War, when additional land was acquired through victory in defensive wars. In keeping with the significance Locke placed on labor, Zionist ideology sought to improve both the land and with it the Jewish workers through their own labor, even though the pioneers had to be paid higher wages than local Arabs. Zionism has been charged with being just another colonial settler movement, but as I will demonstrate, the Zionist settlement project was markedly different. Nevertheless, the issues around taking possession of the land are tangled. *Purchase* may appear neutral, but it displaced Arab peasants although not to the extent often alleged. And although it was decidedly not the sole or major cause for the transformation of the Palestinian countryside and demographic change, the very success of Zionist settlement did alter the Palestinian economy and even improvement disrupted patterns of land holding and the regional ecology. Although Zionists believed the benefits of improvement would be shared and would assuage the Arabs, the modernization and progress the Zionists achieved could not counteract fundamental differences, inequality, and hostility. Here, too, competing demands could be both justifiable and irreconcilable. A single right advanced legitimately could compromise other rights such as uprooting long-term residents. At the same time, denial of rights to European Jews who were desperate for refuge as well as the opportunity to work and purchase land, contributed to an enormous human catastrophe. Here, too, agendas articulated in the public square are made in terms appropriate to the time and setting and reflect traditional cultural perspectives.

Chapter 5 turns to History, a category Marshall did not consider, that became hugely significant with the rise of nationalism during the twentieth century. It is currently a particularly rich and contested topic used by all sides of the conflict to legitimate their territorial claims. The Middle East is a region where the past remains present in numerous layers of narratives in texts, in the evidence of physical remains, and in collective memory. The Bible, reputed to have been the most widely read book in human history, was certainly central when the Mandate for Palestine was established. Contending parties referred to Biblical narratives to substantiate their claims to the land, alluded to and cited different texts, and used the same or altered verses to argue conflicting rights.

Since mid-twentieth century, a fascinating new application of history emerged in the category of "indigeneity." Claims to being the sole authentic descendants of original inhabitants complicate questions of legitimacy as real, distant, attenuated and even invented origins are invoked to endow claimants with special rights, privileging the indigenous in contemporary law, and bringing calls for recognition to public attention. Clearly, appeals to history are found in all the previous chapters. But legitimating claims to the Holy Land where multiple contestants have deep roots, whether real or imagined, necessarily brings both theology and history to bear. Weighing one right against another when different historical claims to legitimacy are asserted from within both secular and religious frameworks has proved a daunting task.

Part II

Chapter 6. Theology is a natural extension of the discussion on History, and I begin Part II with Judaism, the oldest of the three monotheistic faiths. Most streams in Judaism share a commitment to the central significance of *Eretz Yisrael* [Land of Israel]. While a contemporary Jewish minority hold that Judaism is or should be separate from Jewish peoplehood, most endorse that they are inextricably intertwined. This perception derives from the biblical history of Covenant. God made a promise to Abraham and his descendants, the Children of Israel, culminating with a contract [*brith*] with his chosen people [*am*—nation] expanded and made explicit at Mount Sinai as the people made their way to the Promised land. Adherence to this covenant was carried into the Diaspora, and over a period of two millennia Jews regularly remembered the exile and read about and prayed for their pledged return to the Promised Land. Disagreements remain over the boundaries of the promised territory, *when* the time for redemption might come, and by whose *agency* and *how* the return should be accomplished. That is, does God intervene in history and how? Can Jews hasten the arrival of that moment through their own actions? And, are there moral requirements conditioning how the land may be repossessed? Moreover, there is an acrimonious dispute with serious political ramifications about whether and which of the borders described in the Old Testament apply to the modern State and to legitimate claims to land in the present.

Since the 1967 War, when Jerusalem and areas of the West Bank or Judea and Samaria came under Israeli control, these questions have been not merely theological and theoretical but increasingly practical, and they have generated numerous thoughtful and conflicting responses. Delineating and analyzing these issues reveals how often secular and theological positions are interrelated, complementary, and contradictory.

Chapter 7. Christianity has had to confront and define its relationship to Judaism and Jews since its beginnings. What becomes of God's Covenant with the Jews after the Coming of Jesus? Does it continue to confer rights to the Promised Land to Jews in the present and the future? Did a New Church replace the Old or could there be multiple Covenants? Have Jews lost their role in history or have they returned? Put another way, does God still speak to the Jews and, if so, what does He say? The answers to these theological questions bear directly on whether Zionism's arguments to reclaim a Jewish homeland in Palestine are seen as legitimate and whether the international community was and is justified in endorsing a Jewish polity. Moreover, they lead to further questions as to what role, if any, Christians should play in either facilitating or denying the Zionist project. The range along these views is extraordinary.

Christianity is composed of large and ancient ecclesiastical groups. While these are relatively limited, there is a very large number of denominations within Protestantism. The latter are particularly pertinent to our discussion since decisions over Jewish claims are often debated in the Western Christian world. Christian concerns are further complicated by the need to protect their sacred sites and by the fact that there are communities of Arab and Palestinian Christians who largely oppose Israel. Dual Arab and Christian identity has compounded opposition and complicated deliberations on the legitimacy of the Jewish state. Yet many American Evangelicals are sympathetic to Jews as a fellow *dhimmi* community who are unfairly challenged by contemporary Arab nationalism, especially by those with an extremist Islamic component that threatens Christians as well as Jews.

In reviewing this enormously large and complex story, the analysis runs from early Christianity's adoption of replacement theology or supersessionism during the period of Constantine and St. Augustine through Catholicism's apparent but limited revision with Vatican II's *Nostra Aetate* in 1965. Changes in Protestantism derive from largely different sources as Evangelical thought developed over the last two centuries to produce Christian Zionism and its critics. Then, too, the emergence of Liberal Protestant sympathy for Israel at mid-twentieth century in Britain and the United States as well as the recent critique of this movement illustrate how dynamic and perhaps even tentative is the contemporary Christian approval of the Jewish state. In more recent decades, an emerging Palestinian Liberation Theology voices the struggle of indigenous Palestinian and Middle Eastern Christians to redefine Christian positions that have hitherto been largely representative of the views of European and American theologians. Finally, there is some sympathy for Israel among some local Christians who have come to discover that, in the face of the threat from Arab and Islamic extremism, a shared fate with Israel is an option worth exploring rather than affirming a shared "Arab" identity.

Chapter 8. Israel has been confronted by Arab states whose populations are overwhelmingly Moslem. For these states Islam is a defining characteristic of national identity and, in varying degrees, infused in their legal structure. Consequently, theology has an extraordinary impact on positions in the Arab-Israeli conflict in parallel to the secular discourse adopted to attack Israel's legitimacy before the international community.

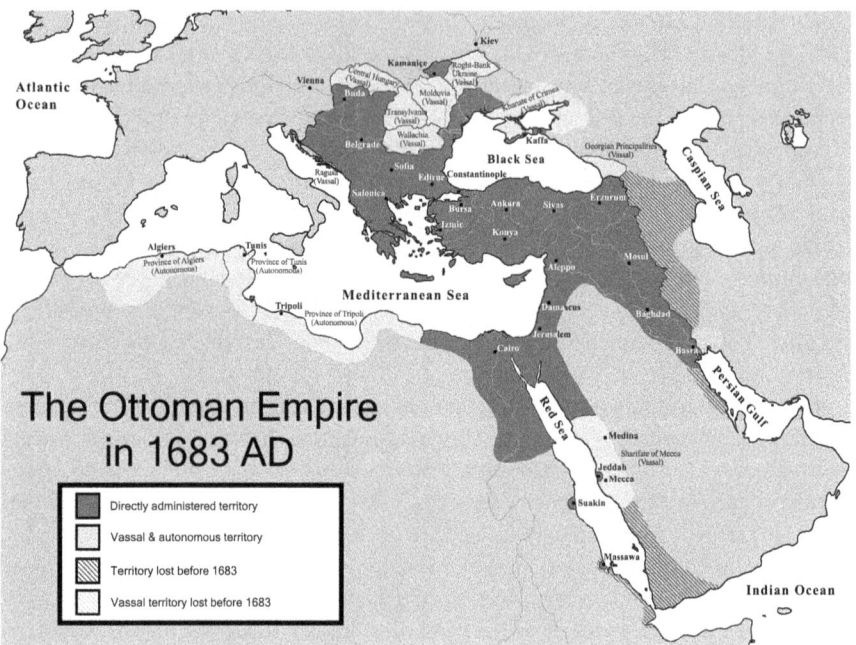

Map of the Ottoman Empire at its greatest extent before its defeat near Vienna in 1683. The Ottomans ruled territories in three continents, extending across southern Europe from the Balkans to portions of present-day Hungary, Bulgaria, Romania, Ukraine, Russia and Crimea, around the Mediterranean basin from Greece to include all of Turkey and portions of Georgia, Armenia, Azerbaijan, Iran, Iraq, Syria, Lebanon, Israel/Palestine, Saudi Arabia, states on the Persian Gulf and on the Indian Ocean to the Red Sea, then up to Egypt and along the shores of Mediterranean in North Africa to Morocco. Significant retrenchment took place in the nineteenth century until final dissolution through defeat in World War I

According to classical Islam, establishing a sovereign Jewish state in the Moslem heartland should not have been possible. Many maintain that, as in the struggle against the infidel Crusaders, Zionism must be resisted until the Jews are vanquished and even expelled. Zionism challenged previous historical experience when Jewish minorities enjoyed cultural efflorescence and prosperity as a protected minority as *dhimmis*, perhaps an enviable position when compared with the often-virulent anti-Semitism of Christian Europe.

Confrontation is deeply rooted in Islam which defines the world as a dichotomy between *dar al-Islam* [home of Islam] and *dar al-harb* [territory of war]. Islam did not experience the Enlightenment, so a very limited range of secular thought is part of its public discourse. Whereas Europe spent several hundred years and many wars to separate State from Religion, they remain deeply intertwined in Muslim societies. There is no "wall of separation" in Arab states as Jefferson famously declared for the American experiment. Nevertheless, some nuance has developed along with increasing contact with the West over the last two centuries. This has necessitated compromise to accommodate the classic ideal of a pan-Islamic *umma* to the modern system of discrete nation-states operating within codes of international law.

The evolving attitude towards Jerusalem may well serve as an index of the relationship between theology and anti-Zionist/Israel politics. It is a prominent issue in the attempt to create a pan-Arab, Islamic politics from the 1920s and 1930s to Arafat's rejection of Clinton's proposals regarding the city's disposition at Camp David in July 2000. It also features in the continuing flood of current UN resolutions dismissing the Jewish connection to the city. The discussion of Jerusalem is also central to the dispute over indigeneity—or being historically first.

Alongside the Islamic extreme and uncompromising commitment to *jihad* [Holy War] of those who actively and violently oppose Israel, other theological options such as *houdna* [cease-fire] offer alternative routes to accommodation, even if it is only temporary. Similarly, a tradition of moderate and pragmatic *fatwas* [legal interpretations of Islamic law] allows for relationships with the Jewish state. This subject requires attention since some Muslim states including Jordan, Egypt, several Gulf states, Morocco and probably more by the time the manuscript is published will have acknowledged the existence of the Jewish state and its legitimacy.

Despite the special toxicity of the Arab and Muslim nexus, a measure of accommodation is increasingly evident within Israel itself. While acceptance of Israel as a Jewish state has yet to be fully established, the reality of Zionism's success a century after Balfour and seventy-five years of independence has impacted and begun to tilt the balance in Israel's favor. How far this process continues remains an open question.

Part III

Chapter 9. The final chapter is composed of three sections. The first reviews the secular and religious issues with a view to establishing their connections to the present. The second examines the forms of delegitimating that emerged after independence. There is then a concluding observation.

From the beginning, Zionism understood that it was essential to achieve public recognition of the legitimacy of the plan to reestablish the Jewish national homeland in Palestine. The opening sentence of the Zionist program, endorsed at the Zionist Organization's founding conference in Basle, Switzerland in 1897, forthrightly stated its goal: "Zionism seeks to secure for the Jewish people a publicly recognized, legally secured homeland in Palestine."[19] The debate focused on whether to declare openly this intention. It was in this context that they added a key word to the initial draft: *öffentlich* in German, or "openly," that became "publicly" in the English translation.

The decision to promote the legal acceptance of a Jewish entity in Palestine overtly was unanimous. Those who initially had reservations at this founding moment were concerned about the negative reaction this pronouncement would arouse but ultimately relented. They were correct in their concerns, although it is unlikely any could have foreseen the multitude of forms and the persistence of objections that have since been made. More than seventy-five years after its establishment, campaigns to delegitimate Israel continue both on earlier grounds articulated prior to independence and through new means.

The primary contemporary assault is made through "lawfare"—a new instrument of legal challenge that alleges criminal behavior and is designed to undermine the standing of the state. This tactic is often carried out through NGOs and agencies of the United Nations. At the same time, opponents of a Jewish state continued to draw and disseminate scenarios of why and how the Jewish state may be disestablished, notably through the idea of "a state of all its citizens" or a binational entity. Thus, persistent, complicated, and at times virulent challenges to Israel's legitimacy have continued into the present century along with public appreciation for the achievements of the new Jewish state and its position in the family of nations that Zionism's founders so earnestly sought. At the same time, since 1967 the energetic settlement of lands assigned to Palestinians undermine its standing that has been based since the 1930s on transforming Mandatory Palestine into two states for two peoples. Although Zionism's achievements enjoy relative success and the appreciation and approval of its supporters, its detractors remain adamant and continue to challenge the legitimacy of its realization.

Notes

1. This document will be referred to repeatedly in the course of this book. The main body of the text, dated November 2, 1917, reads: "His Majesty's Government view with favour the establishment in Palestine of a national home for the Jewish people, and will use their best endeavors to facilitate the achievement of this object, it being clearly understood that nothing shall be done which may prejudice the civil and religious rights of existing non-Jewish communities in Palestine or the rights and political status enjoyed by Jews in any other country." https://www.jewishvirtuallibrary.org/text-of-the-balfour-declaration; Standard works include Leonard Stein, *The Balfour Declaration* (New York: Simon and Schuster, 1961) and Jonathan Schneer, *The Balfour Declaration: The Origins of the Arab-Israeli Conflict* (New York: Random House, 2010).
2. Moshe Weinfeld, *The Promise of the Land: The Inheritance of the Land of Canaan by the Israelites* (Berkeley: University of California, 1993), Chap. 8. On fluctuations of borders see Nili Wazana, *All the Boundaries of the Land; The Promised Land in Biblical Thought in Light of the Ancient Near East* (Winona Lake, Indiana: Eisenbrauns, 2013), Chap. 3. See, for example: Gen: 12:7; 13:14–17; 15:7; 48:4. The definition of borders is not germane to this Introduction. Nor is the issue of the conditionality of the Jewish presence that is maintained in, for example, *Leviticus* 25:18 and 26:31–34, *Amos* 5:6–9 and 6:1–7 and *Jeremiah* 7:1–7. Conditionality will become relevant in Chap. 6 when we discuss the debate within Judaism over *when* and *how* it is appropriate for Jews to reassert their claim.

3. An important caveat that must be made here. Aside from the rare but dramatic injunction that the Land should be held exclusively by the Israelites as in the charge given Joshua in crossing the Jordan to conquer Canaan, most biblical and subsequent sources assume that the Hebrews would be living together with other peoples in the Promised Land as, in fact, they did. The issue here is one of preeminence, as it was assumed to have existed in the ancient world and that Zionism has attempted to reassert in the contemporary period. See David Frankel, *The Land of Canaan and the Destiny of Israel; Theologies of Territory in the Hebrew Bible* (Winona Lake, Indiana: Eisenbrauns, 2011). For the view that the alleged extremism based in adherence to biblical injunction towards other inhabitants of Canaan in motivating contemporary Israeli policy see Rachel Havelock, *The Joshua Generation; Israeli Occupation and the Bible* (Princeton: Princeton University Press, 2020). Joshua and those that follow him did not completely fulfill this divine injunction, even as others did not.
4. Robert Bellah, "Civil Religion in America," *Journal of the American Academy of Arts and Sciences*, 96:1(Winter 1967), 1–21.
5. Charles Liebman and Eliezer Don-Yehiya, *Civil Religion in Israel; Traditional Judaism and Political Culture in the Jewish* State (Berkeley: University of California Press, 1983).
6. Peter Berger, *The Many Altars of Modernity: Toward a Paradigm for Religion in a Pluralist Age* (Boston/Berlin: De Gruyter Mouton, 2014). See, too, Ilan Troen, "Multiple Modernities: A View from Jerusalem," *Social Science and Modern Society*, 53:2 (2016), 153–62.
7. Michael Walzer, *The Paradox of Liberation; Secular Revolutions and Religious Counterrevolutions* (New Haven: Yale University Press, 2015).
8. Seymour M. Lipset, *The First New Nation: The United States in Historical and Comparative Perspective* (New York: Basic Books, 1963).
9. "*Resolved by the House of Representatives (the Senate concurring)*, That Congress reaffirms "In God We Trust" as the official motto of the United States and supports and encourages the public display of the national motto in all public buildings, public schools, and other government institutions." *House Concurrent Resolution 13* (112th Congress, 1st Session).
10. http://avalonlaw.yale.edu/17th_century/mayflower.asp
11. John Locke, *Second Treatise of Government*, Chap. 5, "Property," pp. 10–18, first published 1689. http://www.earlymoderntexts.com/assets/pdfs/locke1689a.pdf. On Locke's relation to America see Barbara Arneil, *John Locke and America* (Oxford: Oxford University Press, 1996).
12. Jonathan Winthrop, *Reasons for the Plantation in New England* (1628): see http://winthropsociety.com/doc_reasons.php.
13. John Quincy Adams, *An Oration Delivered at Plymouth, December 22, 1802, at the Anniversary Commemoration of the First Landing of our Ancestors at that Place* (Boston: Russell and Cutler, 1802), https://archive.org/details/orationdelivered00ada.
14. Quoted in R. Douglas Hurt, *The Indian Frontier, 1763-1846* (Albuquerque: University of New Mexico Press, 2002), p. 137.
15. Gideon Shimoni, *The Zionist Ideology* (Hanover, NH: UPNE, 1995), Chap. 8.
16. Marshall formulated his theories in three court cases: the Marshall Trilogy: *Johnson v. McIntosh* (1823), *Cherokee Nation v. Georgia* (1831) and *Worcester v. Georgia* (1832); Eric Kades, "History and Interpretation of the Great Case of

Johnson v. McIntosh" (2001). *Faculty Publications.* 50. https://scholarship.law.wm.edu/facpubs/50. For a critical review of what took place on the ground, see Lindsay G. Robertson, *How the Discovery of America Dispossessed Indigenous Peoples of Their Lands* (Oxford: Oxford University Press, 2005). Robertson is particularly pertinent for demonstrating how greed, corruption and politics shaped the position of Marshall and the contesting claimants. He also observes how Marshall's theories, particularly *discovery*, came to be used by the Indigenous themselves in protecting their rights as in the case of the Mabo in Australia. See, too, Stuart Banner, *How the Indians Lost Their Land: Law and Power on the Frontier* (Cambridge: Harvard University Press, 2005).

17. Peter Russell, *Recognizing Aboriginal Title: The Mabo Case and Indigenous Resistance to English Settler Colonialism* (Toronto: University of Toronto Press, 2005).
18. It is complicated trying to obtain precise data since Arabs may be counted twice, particularly those who reside in East Jerusalem that both the Palestine National Authority (PA or PNA) and Israel claim. My figures derive from two sources: U.S. Department of State, *2020 Report on International Religious Freedom: Israel, West Bank and Gaza.* https://www.state.gov/reports/2020-report-on-international-religious-freedom/israel-west-bank-and-gaza/west-bank-and-gaza/#:~:text=The%20U.S.%20government%20estimates%20the%20total%20Palestinian%20population,Muslims%2C%20with%20small%20Shia%20and%20Ahmadi%20Muslim%20communities; and Sergio Della Pergola. "World Jewish Population, 2020," in Arnold Dashefsky and Ira M. Sheskin, eds., *The American Jewish Year Book, 2020, volume 120* (2020) (Cham, SUI: Springer), Chap. 7.
19. The Executive of the Zionist Organization, *The Jubilee of the First Zionist Congress 1897-1947* (Jerusalem, 1947). There are alternate translations of the original German. The one rendered here is published by the Zionist Organization itself in its official record of the proceedings of the Congress. See Lawrence J Epstein, *The Dream of Zion; The story of the first Zionist Congress* (Lanham, MD: Roman and Littlefield, 2016), pp. 57–94.

Part I
Secular Claims

Chapter 2
Conquest, Treaties and Self-Determination

Introduction

Until after World War I, *conquest* and the *treaties* that followed victory on the battlefield were widely invoked in claiming territory. It was on this basis that mandates were instituted at the 1920 League of Nations conference in San Remo, Italy. In subsequent decades, competing principles, specifically respect for the territorial integrity of existing states and for the right of self-determination, gained standing. Until that change, however, conquest was universally recognized and gave the victorious parties the right to divide the spoils.

The dawning awareness that the Ottoman Empire might be vanquished in the course of the Great War made it possible to imagine a reordering of the Middle East, and the region was stirring with the possibility of change. The significance of this possibility should not be underestimated. It may be remembered that in 1683, perhaps at the zenith of power in relation to Europe, the Ottoman armies besieged Vienna, capital of the Habsburg Empire. But it is not commonly appreciated that for 400 years, or until their defeat in World War I, the Ottomans controlled vast territories in Europe, Asia, and Africa. It was in a process of slow withdrawal and decline that Ottoman borders receded towards the Turkish heartland as Europe rose to power and influence across much of the world.

By the mid-nineteenth century, Turkey was often referred to as the "sick man of Europe" and its vulnerability was exploited by European powers, large and small. Turkish Sultans had been forced to concede rights to Christian nations including Britain, the United States, Belgium, Portugal, Greece, and Brazil. Through a system of "capitulations," the Ottomans granted traders from these states exemptions from Ottoman prosecution, local taxation, military conscription, and intrusion into the homes of foreign nationals and recognized foreign citizens as subject to the courts of their home countries rather than Ottoman institutions. This meant that the local consuls of foreign powers could protect their citizens and their interests. From the fourteenth through the eighteenth centuries, when the Ottoman Empire was a military power, such exemptions were made to entice foreign merchants and encourage economic development. By the end of the nineteenth century, they signaled Ottoman weakness; European states were in the ascendant.[1] But it was not seriously considered that four centuries of Ottoman rule were about to end, any more than the fall and dissolution of the Soviet Union was anticipated.

With the outbreak of World War I in 1914, Europe was poised to claim Ottoman lands through conquest. The right to do so is unabashedly recited and legitimated in a legal history concerning the disposition of Ottoman lands in *A Survey of Palestine; Prepared in December 1945 and January 1946 for the information of the Anglo-American Committee of Inquiry*.[2] The document is important both an official summary of decisions taken until that date and a preface to United Nations resolutions that lead to the partition of Palestine in 1947. The operative principle is that a succession of rulers followed the demise of the Ottoman Empire, beginning with the capitulations and culminating in total military defeat of the Ottomans at the end of World War I when the British captured Palestine, including Jerusalem, and maintained "boots on the ground."

The British conquerors thus became the Ottomans' actual and legitimate successors. In so doing, they sought and received the assent of their American, French, and Italian allies. Their legal right to the conquered territory was further validated by the newly created League of Nations that sponsored a mandate system to govern territories whose sovereignty passed from losers to winners in the Middle East, Africa, and islands in the Pacific. The Americans did not join the League, but in October 1924, signed a special, parallel "Convention between the United Kingdom and the United States of America respecting the Rights of the Governments of the two Countries and their respective nationals in Palestine." Portions of the document's opening paragraphs clearly declare the rights that accrue to conquest:

> Whereas by the Treaty of Peace concluded with the Allied Powers, Turkey renounces all her rights and titles over Palestine; and
>
> Whereas Article 22 of the Covenant of the League of Nations as embodied in the Treaty of Versailles provided that, in the case of certain territories which, as a consequence of the late war, ceased to be under the sovereignty of the States which formerly governed them, mandates should be issued...
>
> Whereas the Principal Allied Powers have agreed to entrust the mandate for Palestine to His Britannic Majesty; ...Whereas the United States of America, by participating in the war against Germany, contributed to her defeat and the defeat of her Allies, and to the renunciation of the rights and titles of her Allies in the territory transferred by them but has not ratified the Covenant of the League of Nations embodied in the Treaty of Versailles ... the Government of the United States and the Government of His Britannic Majesty desire to reach a definite understanding with respect to the rights of the two Governments and their respective nations in Palestine...[3]

This official review of the *rights* to Palestine begins with a recitation of conquest. It focuses on October 1917 when the British prevailed in battles near Beersheva and Gaza and continues through General Allenby's entry into Jerusalem at the head of Allied Forces. Thereafter the country was placed under military administration. In the wider Middle Eastern context, the battle against the Turks ended with an armistice on 30 October 1918. A few months later, in January 1919, "the Supreme Council of the Peace Conference decided that the conquered Arab provinces, including Palestine, were not to be restored to Turkish rule."[4] With the backing of its allies, Britain received Palestine in its division of the spoils.

Nevertheless, arguments arose as to whether the disposition of Palestine conformed to proper international practice. Since in the case of Palestine there were conflicting written commitments to the Zionists and Arabs, opinions differed as to which had priority and legitimacy. The issue was further complicated by the fact that both Jews and Arabs claimed rights based on their role in the military actions of the winning side. Both had fought alongside the British expecting to have a say in the arrangements the victorious British would eventually impose.

Unusual Claimants

The disposition of Ottoman territories in 1920 involved perhaps the most powerful nation in the world at a time when more than one quarter of the world was included in the British Empire, where, it was said, the "sun never sets." When WWI ended, there were no independent Arab states in Ottoman territory nor was there a Jewish state. Yet there were hopes and movement towards achieving them when the British defeated the Turks.

Zionism, of course, was an "organization," not a sovereign political entity. Nevertheless, the World Zionist Organization, formally established in 1897 through the initiative of Theodor Herzl, engaged in international diplomacy. From the 1880s, precursor organizations and individual philanthropists had been programmatically engaged in purchasing land to develop networks of agricultural colonies for Jewish settlement in Palestine. By the first part of the twentieth century, Zionism had established agricultural settlements as well as new urban centers, especially Tel-Aviv and the Jewish quarters of Haifa and Jerusalem, that would serve as a base for a modern economy and as cultural and political centers of a Jewish polity. Various political and philanthropic associations, with main offices located in Europe, bound these settlements together and directed the institutions Zionists created.

In 1897, the World Zionist Organization inaugurated a program of international diplomacy aimed at achieving Ottoman agreement for Jewish rights in the region that came to be defined as Palestine. Herzl initially imagined such a project could be achieved primarily through negotiation with the Turks but recognized the support of western powers would be important to overcome Ottoman resistance. Ultimately, of course, the Zionist program was enabled by the Allied victory over the Ottomans.[5]

At about the same time, Arab nationalism was emerging, initially among secular intellectuals who were often Christians, but also, particularly in the Hejaz, and in various urban settings like Beirut, Damascus, and Jerusalem, among traditional Islamic elites. They began to imagine reconfiguring the weakened Ottoman Empire that was being challenged by the great imperial powers who coveted control of the

Middle East and North Africa. Like the Zionists, these elites endeavored to advance their interests through the good offices of the great imperial powers.[6]

World War I suggested scenarios of what might emerge in a postwar era. The British and French, the most significant world powers with extensive empires, were eager to extend their power and presence in the Middle East well beyond the Ottoman capitulations. Their ambitions in the region are usually dated from 1798 to 1801 when Napoleon Bonaparte's army invaded Egypt, Syria, and what became Palestine. In the course of the nineteenth century, the French and British continued to penetrate the region. They built and controlled the Suez Canal (1854–1869), fought the Crimean War (1853–1856) against Russia together with the Ottomans, and forced enhancement of the "capitulations." With their growing military, commercial, and political power, British and French involvement in the Ottoman Empire increased, and with it came an appetite for more.

The outbreak of World War I made possible even more ambitious interventions. A catastrophic stalemate on the western European front led the British and French to try to secure advances elsewhere. They coordinated their efforts if only to avoid conflicts with one another as they contested for mastery over the region. A relationship that mixed cooperation with competition was formulized in the Sykes-Picot Agreement in 1916, named respectively for the lead British and French negotiators: Sir Mark Sykes and Francois Georges-Picot. Through this pact and subsequent modifications, the British achieved consent for primary influence over the territory presently occupied by Israel, Jordan, and Iraq. The French received responsibility for Syria and Lebanon.[7]

As the Allies and their armies gained control of the region, they became the arbiters of the Middle East. Negotiations over how to dismember the Ottoman Empire into Mandates began with discussions at the Versailles Peace Conference in January 1919. The crucial conference on Palestine took place at San Remo in April 1920. Its terms were subsequently approved by the League of Nations in July 1922 when a specific British Mandate for Palestine was formulated and announced. It explicitly ratified the 1917 Balfour Declaration that assigned Palestine as the "national home" of the Jewish people. It largely satisfied the Zionists but failed to recognize that another people aspired to similar rights in the same territory. Rather, it explicitly granted **non**-*national* rights. That is, the Arabs of Palestine were not referred to as a "people" or a "nation" but merely as "inhabitants" or members of "existing non-Jewish communities" with *civil* and *religious* rights.

The hierarchy of control was clear. The British replaced the Ottomans as masters of the territory. The Jewish population was expected to grow substantially and to enjoy national rights. The Arab inhabitants were offered protection, but with limits to their status. Thus, the San Remo Convention of 1920 declared: "The Mandatory shall have full power of legislation and of administration;" it is "responsible for placing the country under such political and economic conditions as will secure the establishment of the Jewish national home;" and is also responsible "for the safeguarding of the civil and religious rights of all inhabitants of Palestine, irrespective of race and religion."[8]

This formulation, celebrated by Zionists, outraged Arabs as another instance of "perfidious Albion"—the all-too common treachery of the British in their pursuit and control of empire. Elevating the Balfour Declaration over pledges that had been made to them for control over Palestine was an act of betrayal that infected their relations with Great Britain in coming decades. Perceived British duplicity was made public during the Bolshevik revolution in 1917 when Russia's new rulers exposed secret correspondence showing Czarist Russia had been a party to the deliberations of Sykes and Picot who promised, but did not deliver, Turkish territory and influence for Russia.[9]

It appears that duplicitous imperialist powers had made vague promises to the Arabs while pursuing their own interests. Whether or not this interpretation of secret wartime negotiations is accurate, it has sustained generations of historians and polemicists engaged in reconstructing how European powers dealt with Arabs. Even though the Balfour Declaration and the commitment to a Jewish polity was public policy anchored in international law and treaties, its terms too, were open to interpretation and even ultimate reversal. Like the Arabs, Jews soon moved from celebration to frustration and bitter criticism. The British had begun to hedge on its terms as early as 1922. In the face of Arab protests, they greatly diminished the area defined as "Palestine," and subsequently curtailed Jewish land purchases and immigration. By 1939, Britain had withdrawn its commitment to foster a Jewish national homeland. Zionist commentators joined in charging Britain with duplicity.

It is interesting to note, then, that both Zionism and Arab nationalism rode on the unsteady and unreliable coattails of British imperialism. The Arabs' charges of duplicity were even more contentious and difficult to adjudicate since they were based on secret negotiations; they lacked the public acknowledgement of the Balfour Declaration. The British found that equitable distribution of spoils of war was difficult in a region where intense and conflicting nationalisms of Jews and Arabs demanded the rewards of active collaboration with the victors. The concrete rewards of battle and conquest claimed for fighting on the side of the victors proved no less elusive and unreliable than their written and spoken promises.

Beset by these competing demands, Britain ended its role as Mandatory power in February 1947, and transferred its prerogatives as victor in both world wars to the United Nations, the successor to the League of Nations. As the agreed arbiter, the UN would dispose of Palestine. The international community made treaties to formalize battlefield outcomes and assigned sovereignty or control over lands in Asia, Africa, and Oceania, including Palestine.[10]

The Jewish Narrative

During the early, dark periods of World War I when great losses and few gains were made on the front in Western Europe, the British and French sought the support of both Arabs and Jews.

Two successive Jewish fighting units emerged. The Zion Mule Corps was organized as a logistical support group for the British in the Gallipoli campaign. The Jewish Legion was proposed when this corps disbanded as a frontline combat force to fight alongside the British in Egypt and Palestine in 1917. It, too, was disbanded with the end of the war in 1919.[11]

The separate Jewish forces were not large and did not constitute an army composed of brigades and regiments. The Zion Mule Corps, for example, first called the Assyrian Refugee Mule Corps, was organized in March 1914 in Alexandria. The city's Grand Rabbi, Raphael della Pergola, administered the oath of service to the British army to about five hundred volunteers. Prominent among them were Jewish refugees who had been expelled by the Turks from Palestine, and Jewish soldiers who, like Josef Trumpeldor, had served in the Russian army in the Russo-Japanese war. When the Zion Mule Corps disbanded, 120 of its members formed the basic building block of the Jewish Legion that numbered about 5,000 by the end of the war. Volunteers joined from among Jewish immigrants from Eastern Europe to Britain and the United States.

While the actual significance of the support given by Zionists and Arabs has been disputed, both sides nurtured narratives of heroism and their essential contributions to the war against the Ottomans. Zionists lauded the Zion Mule Corps that fought in Gallipoli, a peninsula in European Turkey along the Dardanelles, in 1915, and gave rise to the Jewish Legion that served in Egypt and in Palestine 1917–1919.

At the outbreak of World War I, some Zionist leaders had argued that joining the winning side with a distinctive Jewish fighting force could advance claims to some form of territorial independence since in usual practice, victors were rewarded with territory. Among them were such notable leaders as Vladamir Jabotinsky, Yosef Trumpeldor, and Pinhas Rutenberg who acted to create Jewish fighting units, and David Ben-Gurion and Itzhak Ben-Zvi, the future prime minister and president of Israel respectively. All advocated a separate and distinct Jewish unit, not merely individual Jews serving in the armies of the Allies. The first three insisted from the beginning of the war that such a Jewish force join the Allied cause. Ben-Gurion and Ben-Zvi argued for fighting on the Turkish side until they realized the Allies would likely win. Moshe Sharett (nee Shertok), the future second prime minister, actually enlisted in the Ottoman army in 1916. In any event, the Turks rejected their proposal and expelled them to Egypt, where they encountered the pro-Allies Zionist leadership who were making headway in their contacts with the British. It was only then that they joined the Allied side.

The most prominent recruits were Jabotinsky and Trumpeldor. They publicly and conspicuously agitated for an identifiable Jewish force. They argued that it was insufficient to make a claim based on philosophical or historical arguments. It was essential to advance claims through actual combat that resulted in victory. By joining the fighting in the battles for Megiddo and the Jordan Valley they assumed the mantle of "liberators" of the homeland. This understanding was reflected in their 1917 letter to the Prime Minister, Lloyd George: "We ask for a Jew the privilege the Welshman has—to fight for his country; to fight like a Welshman does—in Regiments of his own, not scattered and nameless" individual soldiers in the larger

British army.[12] They expected that Lloyd George, who was Welsh, and who supported the formation of the Welsh Guards in 1915 would understand their desire for a national identity. At the same time, they understood lobbying was necessary since both the French and especially Arabs were concerned about the disposition of the territory of what came to be the British Mandate for Palestine. Both those who supported the creation of the Jewish Legion and those who opposed it appreciated that an identifiable Jewish fighting force would strengthen Zionist claims to Palestine. In the aftermath of the Balfour Declaration of November 1917, Zionism's supporters claimed that the victory over the Turks at Megiddo and the Jordan Valley contributed to the "liberation" of Palestine, thereby affiliating Zionism with the legitimate goals and methods of other nationalist movements.[13]

Ze'ev Jabotinsky. Ze'ev Jabotinsky, founder of the Jewish Legion and of Revisionist Zionism in British Uniform with a traditional candelabra on cap and lapel of uniform as symbol reflecting unique identity of the unit. Courtesy of the Government Press Office

Soldiers of the Jewish Legion. Soldiers of the Jewish Legion at the Western (Wailing) Wall after the capture of Jerusalem in 1917, providing substance to claim as participants in the liberation of Palestine. Soldier with glasses in middle is likely Jabotinsky. Courtesy of the Government Press Office and also found at https://commons.wikimedia.org/wiki/File:Jewish_legion_hako-tel_1917.jpg

Photo taken by T. E. Lawrence of his soldiers. Bedouin soldiers on camels at the battle for Aqaba in present-day Jordan. Lawrence led Bedouin troops primarily along the Hejaz railway from Arabia through Jordan to Damascus. He did not see combat in Palestine. General Edmund Allenby lead British and allied forces, including the Jewish Legion, in that campaign. See: https://exploret-hearchive.com/lawrence-battle-of-aqaba. No restrictions on use. See: https://archives.marist.edu/LTP/LTP.xml

Lawrence at battle for Aqaba. Lawrence in Bedouin garb at Aqaba during campaign against the Ottomans. See: https://explorethearchive.com/lawrence-battle-of-aqaba. No restrictions on use. See: https://archives.marist.edu/LTP/LTP.xml

This militant branch of the Zionist movement identified with the allied cause despite the Zionist Organization's official neutrality since Jews were fighting on both sides of the conflict. As a result of their neutrality Zionist headquarters was moved from Berlin to neutral Copenhagen instead of establishing formal offices in London. Nevertheless, major Zionist activity was conducted in the British capital, and with the war's end, the official center of international Zionism moved to London. This was appropriate since, with the communist takeover of Russia and the defeat of the Central Powers, the weight of the Zionist movement had already shifted to the English-speaking world where large numbers of European Jews had been resettling for almost half a century.

Whatever the actual impact of this modest fighting force on the course of the war and in Allenby's campaign for the conquest of the Holy Land/Palestine, it has loomed large in Zionist history and lore and, certainly at the time, it enhanced the impact of the Balfour Declaration of November 1917. In fact, it was for this reason that this force was disbanded. The British did not want a distinctively Jewish force engaged in advancing their Mandate in a country with a large Arab population that was hostile to the avowed ends of the Mandate. Nevertheless, in the Zionist narrative, even this short duration assumed significance. Its ranks numbered Jews who would play an enormous role in establishing a Jewish state two decades later. As noted above, they included David Ben-Gurion, Israel's first prime minister and minister of defense and Itzhak Ben-Zvi, second president; Levi Eshkol, future prime minister; Dov Yosef, leading Labor politician; Jacob Epstein, sculptor; Nahum Gutman, author and artist; Gershon Agron, founder of the Jerusalem Post; Berl Katznelson, intellectual and labor leader; Eliyahu Golomb and Yaacov Dori, military commanders; Eleazar Sukenik, archaeologist; and James de Rothschild, philanthropist and British politician.

The notion that conquest confers a right to territory was enshrined in Israel's 1948 Declaration of Independence. The first half of this document lists the justifications accepted in international practice for achieving territory for a national state, specifying claims rooted in historical connections, purchase, working and improving the land, and treaties. It also features rights acquired by force of arms through the role of the Jewish Brigade, a successor to the Jewish Legion of World War I: "In the Second World War, the Jewish community of this country [Palestine] contributed its full share to the struggle of the freedom- and peace-loving nations against the forces of Nazi wickedness and, by the blood of its soldiers and its war effort, gained the right to be reckoned among the peoples who founded the United Nations." In other words, distinctive Jewish forces participated in both World Wars with the explicit intention of serving the creation of a Jewish state.

The Arab Narrative

A distinctive Jewish force participated in the larger effort against the Turks. Its explicit goal was to liberate Palestine. The Arab forces did not concentrate on liberating Palestine, and the Arab side demanded far more than Palestine as their reward. They sought control of the entire Middle East in which Palestine constituted a small portion. However, whether Palestine would be included as part of their reward became the crux of an extensive debate.

Under the leadership of Hussein bin Ali, the Sharif of Mecca and leader of the Hashemites, the objective evolved into a grand union across the Middle East. Out of a base in the Hejaz, a region in the Arabian Peninsula that is now Saudi Arabia, they adopted a pan-Arab vision with members of the Sharif's family designated for thrones in the region. Yet despite the prestige of the Sharif, the Arab alliance was composed of diverse forces and shifting elements rather than a single fighting force directed by one supreme Arab leader and operating in concert with the British. The British, for their part, maintained connection with a competing Saudi clan, with forces lead by regional tribesman that fought within their region rather than in a directed and programmatic campaign across the entire Middle East.

The Hashemite forces played a significant role in securing several key targets in coordination with the British. They helped wrest control of the Hejaz from the Ottomans by disrupting the crucial link of the Hejaz railway that connected Damascus with the holy city of Medina. It was the latter link that set the agenda for the most famous and crucial battles in which Arab forces were engaged. After fighting to clear the Ottomans from their strongholds along the coast of the Hejaz and up to Aqaba and then along the lines of the railway towards Damascus, the Hashemites entered that major city as its conquerors. It was this contribution and triumph in these areas that earned Arabs rights when the British carved up the Middle East. They won related thrones in Iraq and Transjordan. They also ruled briefly in Syria through Faisal, a son of Hussein, and initially in the Hejaz. By 1924–1925, the Hejaz with the holy cities of Mecca and Medina fell into the hands of Saudi rivals. The fate of Palestine was but one element in a far greater frustration.[14]

The lack of a comparable Arab-led campaign for Palestine is significant. The conquest of Palestine was a central British objective achieved by a British force under General Allenby. And the British chose Amin al-Husseini, a member of a non-Hashemite family of Jerusalem-based notables, to lead Palestine's Arabs as Mufti of Jerusalem. Palestine was a vague commitment expressed in the exchange of 10 letters between British officials, primarily Henry McMahon, the British High Commissioner in Egypt, and the Sharif of Mecca between July 1915 and March 1916. This produced a statement of intentions to be fulfilled after the conclusion of a war that broke out four months later in July. The territory in question was not precisely delineated and marked. One letter spoke in terms of "the limits and boundaries proposed by the Sharif of Mecca" except for "portions of Syria" lying to the west of "the districts of Damascus, Homs, Hama and Aleppo." This expressed ambition of the Sharif received no definite commitment in response. Moreover, such language left open room for considerable and apparently unending conflicting interpretations, not least as to whether Palestine was to be included.[15]

By contrast, Jews had developed a Palestinian identity by World War I, with a coherent and extensive network of institutions, common interests and goals, and a military force explicitly assembled to enhance their efforts. Palestine was the consistent focus of the rhetoric of Zionism and of the diplomatic efforts of its institutions. This concentrated focus contributed to persuading the British to commit to fostering a Jewish national home in Palestine in a public manner well before the conclusion of hostilities. After securing the assent of their allies, the British had their commitment published in the press to assure its widest possible dissemination. Nothing comparable took place regarding the secret correspondence with Arab leaders. It took more than two decades for significant portions of the negotiations to be made public by George Antonius who published them in the appendices of his 1938 *The Arab Awakening*.[16]

Arabs parlayed the contribution of its armed forces into control of most of the Middle East, but it was frustrated when it came to Palestine. It used violence successfully to pressure the British to whittle down and ultimately to recede from their earlier public commitments to foster a Jewish national home in Palestine. By 1937 the British endorsed partition for a much-reduced area designated for a Jewish entity and by the mid-1940s it moved towards terminating its responsibility for the Mandate with the expectation that an Arab Palestinian state would emerge. Arab defeats in the 1948 War and in subsequent conflicts did not diminish recourse to military means. The PLO National Charter of 1968 repeatedly endorses the use of force in the "liberation" of territories that it holds belong to the Palestinian people. Article 9 states: "Armed struggle is the only way to liberate Palestine. This it is the overall strategy, not merely a tactical phase." Thus paragraph 19 declares: "The partition of Palestine in 1947 and the establishment of the State of Israel are entirely illegal, regardless of the passage of time, because they were contrary to the will of the Palestinian people and to their natural right in their homeland, and inconsistent with the principles embodied in the Charter of the United Nations, *particularly the right to self-determination.*" [My emphasis]. In effect, Arab nationalism invoked this concept to claim exclusive rights to the land and simultaneously to dismiss the right to self-determination of the Jewish "others."[17]

Competing Legal Principles

Neither the Arabs nor the Jews took exception to the post-World War I settlement. Both accepted the rights accruing to Britain as the legitimate successor to the Ottomans. Even before the war ended both lobbied the British to obtain concessions and recognition of their primacy in claiming rights in the country. There is an historic irony in this initial position. By the end of World War II and the establishment of the United Nations, conquest was being set aside by new rules intended to govern international behavior and ensure that peaceful negotiations replaced the use of force and no longer had the same standing it had a century earlier. The victors were carving up the Ottoman Empire while at the same time rejection of the use of force was being incorporated in the system of international law.

The right to wage war was not entirely rejected; it is widely recognized that some wars are just and others unjust.[18] Rather the legitimacy of conquest was modified and refined. This process began with the founding of the League of Nations that expressed disdain for war in its Covenant. Its creation of the mandate system was apparently a step away from traditional imperialism since mandates were ultimately intended to become self-governing, independent states. In fact, conquering powers, notably the British and French, expected to tie future mandates and the states that evolved from them into their imperial networks, but not as outright colonies. Rather, the victorious allies expected conquered territories to become client states. This strategy was clearly first employed in the British plan to transform Iraq by 1932 from a mandate into an ostensibly independent state and a member of the League of Nations. Conquest was on a course to formal rejection as a recognized right but, in fact, still expected it to bring benefits although they were camouflaged by the system of mandates.[19]

The need to mask traditional imperialist actions and intentions became increasingly necessary from the 1920s as growing anti-war agitation, undoubtedly stimulated by the disastrous consequences of the violence of the First World War I, began to gain considerable traction. More specifically in 1928, the United States, France and Germany signed the Kellog-Briand Pact, known officially as the "General Treaty for Renunciation of War as an Instrument of National Policy." It held that force was not a proper instrument for resolving "disputes or conflicts of whatever nature or of whatever origin they may be, which may arise among them." The U.S. Secretary of State, Henry Stimson extended the treaty by declaring in 1932 the "Stimson Doctrine." While directed initially against the Japanese move into Manchuria, acceptance of the general principle spread. By the establishment of the United Nations in the following decade, the assertion of the traditional right of conquest lost standing. As a leading scholar of the issue has concluded: "The proposition that a state that emerges victorious in war is entitled to claim ownership or jurisdiction of territory of which it has taken possession during a war was a recognized principle of international law until the early years of this [twentieth] century."[20]

The case of the Israel/Palestinian conflict is complicated because of the application of other rights by both of the parties. As we shall see as this volume proceeds, it is rare that rights are uncontested both on their own merits or unchallenged by competing ones that are given greater standing. In this case, the PLO Charter well expresses a competing principle: conquest alone is insufficient to secure the right to a territory; it has greater standing when it also accrues to peoples through the right to *self-determination*.

Contrary Legal Views

Henry Cattan (1906–1992) and Julius Stone (1907–1985) were contemporaries on opposite sides of basic legal issues. These two distinguished jurists wrote extensively on issues relating to the Israeli/Arab conflict before, during, and after the Mandate, including events they witnessed after Israel's establishment. Their writings address the multitude of contrary views of conquest and the legitimacy of resulting treaties. Moreover, particularly in the three decades after the establishment of Israel, neither lived in Israel/Palestine and their writings reflect the international debate of Israel on the legitimacy of establishing the Jewish state.

Henry Cattan eloquently and trenchantly articulated the Arab critique in a series of well-read books outlining the Palestine case after the 1948 War.[21] Born in what is now West Jerusalem and trained in law in Paris and London, he achieved distinction as a barrister practicing in both Jerusalem and Syria during the Mandate and relocated to Paris after the 1948 war. In the crucial period from 1946 to 1948, Cattan served as a delegate of the Arab Higher Committee--the central political organ of the Palestinians during the Mandate--and was a leading voice in presenting the Arab case before UN commissions.[22] Julius Stone was an effective counterpart. Born in Leeds to Jewish immigrants from Lithuania, he was educated in Leeds before taking degrees in law at Oxford and Harvard. During a distinguished academic career, he specialized in jurisprudence and international law and published more than two dozen books on these subjects including several on the Arab-Israeli dispute. He taught in Australia and the United States, particularly at the University of California, and had deep connections with Israeli jurists and the Zionist movement.[23]

Their detailed arguments on the legitimacy of the Balfour Declaration, the Mandate, and the international agreements that supported an independent Jewish state in Palestine elucidate the issues we are considering, and particularly the implications of the "right of self-determination" and for whether "conquest" and resulting assignments of territorial rights have merit.

Henry Cattan

Cattan relegates conquest to a secondary right that is relevant only in special circumstances. In the case of Palestine, it does not supersede the rights of legitimate owners who have the right to take back their lands. He observes that "The rule that conquest does not destroy the title of the legitimate sovereign is not an entirely new concept." He goes on to cite cases where peoples threw off the yoke of victors to reclaim their lands largely in recent European history as well as in Africa where Ethiopia returned to traditional control of the native population with the end of Italian rule. In all such cases, the nation, long resident in the land, retained "residual" sovereignty. As a jurist writing in the second part of the twentieth century, he applied the relatively recent concept that legitimacy of title is based on "the principle of inadmissibility of the acquisition of territory by war."[24]

Cattan relied less on analyzing particulars of the international agreements governing the British Mandate, such as what was written in the letters exchanged by British officials and Arab leaders, than on scrutinizing their legal basis. In Cattan's judgment, a Jewish polity of any sort was illegitimate from the beginning. Instead, the Mandate should have created a manifestly Arab state in Palestine.

Cattan's argument does not cite the Arab role in freeing lands from Ottoman rule nor does he consider rights the British won through conquest. Rather, he asserts that all the lands of the Middle East, not just Palestine, were and had always been "Arab," since time immemorial, including under the suzerainty of the Turks. The land was even Arab before David's conquest of Jerusalem and through all successive conquests. In other words, the land is inalienable from its permanent inhabitants whom he designates as "Arab" through all known history. We will examine this contention in detail in subsequent chapters. Here it is sufficient to note that this foundational legal argument is expressed in purely secular, legal language. Like other Christians committed to Arab nationalism, Cattan does not draw on Islamic theology to claim Palestine and the Middle East irrevocably belong to Moslems. Instead, in this secular view, secular historical rights validate the claims of Palestine's Arabs.

The title of his relatively brief but powerful essay captures the fundamental issue: "To Whom Does Palestine Belong."[25] He shapes the argument in terms of the right of "self-determination," a doctrine that emerged as a principle of international law during World War I. Self-determination was famously espoused at about the same time by both U.S. president Woodrow Wilson and by the leader of the Bolshevik revolution, Vladimir Lenin. In the course of the twentieth century, it became part of the formulaic discourse of the League of Nations and later the United Nations.

Widespread endorsement of this shared principle was nevertheless understood variously by individuals and groups with differing motivations. It was a corollary of what was regarded as benign nationalism as it emerged through the nineteenth century. Although he was surely not an anti-imperialist, Woodrow Wilson's formulation captures the general sentiment: "National aspirations must be respected; people may now be dominated and governed only by their own consent. 'Self-determination' is not a mere phrase; it is an imperative principle of action."[26]

In Cattan's view, the establishment of the United Nations further enshrined the principle of self-determination. As Chapter 1, Article 1, part 2 of the UN Charter declares, the purpose UN is "To develop friendly relations among nations based on respect for the principle of equal rights and self-determination of peoples, and to take other appropriate measures to strengthen universal peace." Similarly, article 15 of the 1948 Universal Declaration of Human Rights of the United Nations states that everyone has the right to a nationality and that no one should be arbitrarily deprived of a nationality or denied the right to change nationality. "Nationality" is a fundamental right of all individuals. In Cattan's view, granting official status to the PLO in 1974 was a move to rectify the 'original sin' of not recognizing the nationality of the Arabs of Palestine and their right to an Arab state of their own.

The "catch" in this recitation of "the history that should have been" is that it recognizes Palestinian nationality but not that of Jews. Establishing both a Jewish and an Arab state in Palestine was unacceptable to Cattan and fellow apologists for the Palestinian cause. They insisted on the absolute and exclusive rights of Palestine's Arabs. The territory was entirely theirs and could not be divided. They denied the Jews are a people with their own historic connection to this land. Jews constitute a faith community, not a national group. The inescapable conclusion of this line of thinking is that incorporating the Balfour Declaration into the fabric of international law was an assault of the right of Palestinian self-determination. It was a zero-sum calculation for Cattan. There can be one land for only one people. A Jewish state in Palestine is, by definition, illegitimate. No conquest or document could alter that principle of international law. It is here that secular argumentation echoes the theological formulations we shall soon examine.

This is a crucial point: The denial of Jewish peoplehood was written into the Palestine National Charter in 1968 and it remains a given today among Palestinians and their apologists. Cattan entertained no alternative view. Elaborating on his concept of "residual" rights, he asserted continuous Arab residence in Palestine since pre-Davidic times. Turkish domination was but one episode in that long history: "Prior to its occupation [by the British] in 1917, Palestine was part of Turkey and the Palestinians, like other Arabs who lived in the Turkish Empire, enjoyed equal rights with the Turks and shared sovereignty with them over all the provinces of the Empire, whether Arab or Turkish,"

The Turkish defeat and their consequent surrender of sovereignty did not affect Arab rights. Cattan argued they should have continued as actual or potential rulers irrespective of the change in Turkish status, and bolstered his theory with reference to international law: "the legal effect of the detachment of Palestine from Turkey and the recognition by Article 22 [of] the Covenant of the League of Nations of the existence of its inhabitants as 'an independent nation' was to make of Palestine a state under the law of nations in which was vested sovereignty over the country." The mandate was temporary by definition and intention. The failure of the League or of Britain to recognize Arab sovereignty did not mean that it was vitiated. Arab sovereignty was everlasting. UN recognition of the PLO belatedly corrected a painful and costly historical error. He lauded the UN for moving in this direction.[27]

A further claim is interwoven with the right of self-determination. It is based on an analysis of actual possession. Cattan calculated Jewish land ownership acquired largely through purchase, from the end of the nineteenth century through the establishment of Israel in 1948. His calculations asserted Jews actually owned but a small proportion of Palestinian land. Depending on the district, it was always under 10 percent and sometimes under 5 percent. Cattan then deducted that number from the total land area of the country or its various sections. He inferred that all the rest—more than ninety percent—belonged to Arabs.[28] This calculation is misleading. It might appear logical for a Moslem who believed that all of Palestine was included in *Dar al Islam*—the Abode of Islam—or the land that belongs to the Moslem nation.

That could not be the basis for a legal claim by a Christian like Cattan except for his uncompromising devotion as an Arab nationalist who viewed Arab Christians and Muslims as sharing in the same national culture that excluded Jews. The record of ownership registered in official documents for Jews and non-Jews alike accounts for a small proportion of the land in Palestine. Much of Palestine consisted of unregistered, state land, owned by the Sultan, later by the Crown and, still later, by the sovereign State of Israel. Unregistered land was endemic in territory that belonged to the Ottoman Empire. It has been calculated that the total area of Greece would have to double if all the disputes over land ownership were adjudicated in favor of the claimants. The Ottomans began to implement cadastral surveys and modern land registration only in mid-nineteenth century and the process was not completed when the Empire was dissolved.[29] As in the United States and other countries, land not privately owned by individuals or corporate groups such as religious orders, is owned by the state. In the U.S. more than two billion acres, or one quarter of all the land, is owned by the federal government. In Palestine whose population in 1900 was but 500,000, much of the largely uncultivated, uninhabited, or underpopulated land belonged to the sovereign. Cattan claimed this territory belonged to the Arab inhabitants of Palestine, and that they had rights—but no actual legal or other title—to the whole. In this analysis, land ownership by non-Arabs is an illusion. Cattan sums it up neatly. The British could not confer sovereignty in favor of Jews "because a donor cannot dispose of what does not belong to him."[30]

Julius Stone

For Julius Stone, as for Cattan, a people's right to self-determination is central, and thus may challenge the right of conquest and the validity of treaties. However, Stone's understanding of the concept directly contradicts Cattan's.

Stone judged that both Arab and Jewish national claims were satisfactorily addressed in the post-World War I era and that both national liberation movements achieved a great deal. Arabs established states on lands more than 100 times greater in size and resources than the area allocated Jews when the mandate was officially inaugurated in 1922. Thereafter, the land assigned for a Jewish homeland was continually diminished by British White Papers and proposals for partition. The proportion of territory allotted to the Zionists was 200 times less than designated Arab lands in 1922 and smaller still by 1937. The 1947 partition plan of the United Nations left a very truncated slice of the area the League of Nations originally assigned as the Jewish homeland in 1920.

The limited size of the territory notwithstanding, Stone appreciated that the international community acknowledged the right of Jews to self-determination. Balfour recognized that Jews are a people and entitled to territory. At the core of Stone's analysis, then, is that following the dissolution of the Ottoman Empire, the international community was correct to award territory to the Jews in recognition of their right as a nation, unequal to the other new states in size, but most crucially equal in legal standing. Like the large Arab mandates that earned status as states worthy of incorporation into the UN, Israel too was recognized as a full member in May 1949. Stone argued that Arab attempts to undo Israel's legitimacy was not only wrong in and of itself but could have dangerous consequences in other parts of the world. Such a move would create a dangerous precedent. It would allow groups of citizens to challenge and undermine the legitimacy of member states. The result would be chaos with violence likely in its wake.[31]

Stone also argued that opposition had mobilized Muslim and Arab forces beyond the borders of Palestine and even the Middle East since the Arabs of Palestine were not a separate and distinctive element within this large whole. He maintained that a distinctly Palestinian Arab identity had yet to emerge when the Mandate was established. They understood themselves as part of a Greater Syria within the Arab nation. There was no evidence that Palestine had a distinctive collective or national identity in the ancient world, from the time of its conquest by Arab forces in the seventh century, and through the twentieth century. Thus, the modern, democratic principle of self-determination was not applicable to the Arab inhabitants of Palestine as a discrete identity.

Stone substantiates his reading of history by citing the succinct official characterization formulated in a report of the UN General Assembly in 1947. It has become doctrine among those critical of Cattan's defense of Palestinian rights:

> The desire of the Arab people of Palestine to safeguard their national existence is a very natural desire. However, Palestinian nationalism, as distinct from Arab nationalism, is itself a relatively new phenomenon which appeared only after the division of the 'Arab rectangle'

by the settlement of the First World War. The National Home policy and the vigorous policy of immigration pursued by the Jewish leadership has sharpened the Arab fear of danger from the intruding Jewish population.

This interpretation had considerable currency before the PLO emerged on the world stage and was awarded observer status at the UN in 1974.[32]

Stone further developed his arguments in legal language and precedents in *Israel and Palestine; Assault on the Law of Nations* (1981) where he reviews a raft of international decisions responding to the applications of various self-identified national groups who invoked the right of self-determination.[33] He questioned the assertion Palestinians were a discrete "nation" at the time when the Ottoman Empire dissolved. As we have just observed, in so doing, he was echoing official international opinion that it was not. He argued not only on historical grounds but in practical legal terms. Whether or not the Palestinians had become a distinctive people at the time of his writing (1981), using an anachronism to undo legitimate decisions of the past would be unjust, illegal, and patently dangerous to world order. He contended that the "Palestinian Arab Nation" emerged only in the 1960s. In legal language this would amount to adoption of a "*post-natus*" position. That is "born afterwards" like a second or younger son. Thus, one should not maintain that "the earlier allocations under the self-determination principle should be somehow revised or even canceled to take account of the later appearance of a new claimant." Doing so, argued Stone, would amount to suspending a legitimate treaty or contract and undermining the principle that "promises must be kept (*pacta sunt servanda*)." While, in fact, circumstances may change, altering or eliminating a treaty can be done only by mutual agreement. Although there may be dissension regarding when this principle may be applied, it is well-understood and widely accepted. The point is that unilateral rejection of what had been agreed is not only questionable but an invitation to international chaos.[34]

Stone argued Israel's legitimacy as a state for the Jewish people was anchored in a series of legitimate international agreements beginning with Balfour. Stone and others reiterated this argument from the 1970s to rebut claims made at the United Nations that by then had become a platform for denouncing the legitimacy of the Jewish state. The attack reached an apogee in November1975 when the UN General Assembly voted 72 to 35 in UNGA 3379 (with 32 abstentions) that "Zionism is a form of racism and racial discrimination." The resolution was revoked by the General Assembly in 1991, but its assumption that Zionists trampled the absolute rights of the local population still underlies attacks on Israel's legitimacy.—a subject further explored in the final chapter. In the zigs and zags of its decisions, the UN has reneged on its commitment to support "the ancient historic connection" of the Jews with Palestine and that Jews were in Palestine "as of right and not on sufferance," referencing Winston Churchill, Secretary of State for the Colonies' famous 1922 dictum.[35] Its wavering has resulted in an ambiguous internal structure. On the one hand, Israel remains a recognized and legitimate state; on the other, the UN Secretariat maintains a Division for Palestine Rights that regularly disseminates the narrative of Israel's illegitimacy beginning with Balfour.

At the same time, segments of the scholarship of the Arab-Israeli conflict and of the public press continue to maintain that granting legitimacy to a Jewish national homeland was a "mistake" of tragically historical proportions.[36] This claim could carry more weight if self-determination were uniformly applied among local populations throughout the remains of the Ottoman Empire. In fact, leading members of the Hashemite family were imported from the Hejaz to rule new mandates. Democratic institutions and practices were lacking nearly everywhere as local "notables" and their families enjoyed extraordinary power.[37] In the extraordinary mosaic of distinctive identities of the Levant and beyond, mandates were created without inquiring into the preferences of local populations and imposing political boundaries that encompassed distinctive and conflicting populations. As we shall discuss later, enormous energies were invested in constructing national identities, although with limited and often temporary success.

The Yishuv was an exception in developing democratic institutions and a coherent identity that were readily carried over into the founding and shaping of a state. Nevertheless, self-determination could have defused the competing claims had Arabs accepted the principle of partition in 1937 or even 1947. Arab demands for recognition of their rights were heard, but self-determination for both communities became a non-starter given Arab insistence on its exclusive applicability to themselves.

As this discussion of conquest has demonstrated, the creation of a system of international law at the end of World War I did not yield clear and undisputed legal principles that could ensure impartial agreement. Conflicting interpretations marshal different sets of facts and there are different views on which rights have priority. Might is no longer assumed to make right, in theory if not always in practice, and *conquest* does not trump all other rights. As a result, international agreements on the rights that accrued to the victors in a conflict are no longer universally accepted. Moreover, the significance and validity of both conquest and treaties have been undermined by deeply conflicting views of self-determination. The right that both sides endorse in the abstract may be difficult to accept when applied to the other. In the case of Palestine, both sides had reason to expect their territorial claims were viewed as legitimate, and both continue to claim priority.

The foregoing helps explain why the category of conquest and its subsequent rejection remain central to Israel's struggle for legitimacy. It has been a commonplace to cast the Arab/Israeli conflict as a consequence of the 1967 war and the fundamental problem as Israel's "occupation" of Arab lands. Critics of this view have challenged that the conflict began two decades earlier and that the *real* issue is "the 1948 file," that is, the fact that Israel was established and recognized as a sovereign Jewish state by the international community. Yet there is ample evidence the dispute begins a quarter century earlier with the creation of the Mandate and the affirmation of the Balfour Declaration as the legal and moral basis for a Jewish state. The challenges to Israel's legitimacy significantly predate the existence of the state.

Arguments in secular language within a framework of what may be considered principles of international law do not guarantee legitimacy. Neither conquest nor the other legal precedents for claiming territory identified by Chief Justice Marshall garner unequivocal support. As with the right to take land by conquest, other means too are subject to change over time and to conflicting interpretations that prioritize some rights over others. Moreover, as I will argue, concurrent theological discourses with principles derived from divine revelation and conflicting beliefs regarding to whom the Lord has assigned territory and to whom it has been denied are inextricably bound up in questions of legitimacy. Belief systems continue to animate the societies and individuals involved and are intertwined with principles of secular international law and custom that aim to be universal. Part II examines claims to rights based in theology how the secular and theological both conflict with each other and complement one another. Their interconnections illuminate the deep roots of the dissonance and the difficulty of resolving questions of legitimacy.

Notes

1. William L. Cleveland, *A History of the Modern Middle East* (Boulder: Westview, 1994), pp. 50–52; "Capitulations," *1911 Encyclopedia Britannica/Capitulations*. https://en.wikisource.org/wiki/1911_Encyclop%C3%A6dia_Britannica/Capitulations.
2. *A Survey of Palestine; Prepared in December 1945 and January 1946 for the information of the Anglo-American Committee of inquiry* (Jerusalem: [Mandatory] Government Printer, 1946), 2 vols.
3. *A Survey of Palestine*, vol. 1, p. 11.
4. *A Survey of Palestine*, vol. 1, p. 2.
5. Isaiah Friedman, *Germany, Turkey, and Zionism 1897-1918* (Oxford: Clarendon Press, 1977).
6. George Antonius, *The Arab Awakening; The Story of the Arab National Movement* (Beirut: Libraire Du Liban, 1969).
7. Isaiah Friedman, *Palestine: A Twice Promised Land? The British, the Arabs and Zionism 1915-1920*, vol. 1(New Brunswick: Transaction, 2000).
8. *San Remo Convention*, https://wwi.lib.byu.edu/index.php/San_Remo_Convention.
9. Antonius, *The Arab Awakening*, chapter 10 and appendices, pp. 413 ff.
10. A comprehensive account covering particularly Britain's entry and exit to arbiter of the Middle East is found in Wm. Roger Louis, *Ends of British Imperialism; The Scramble for Empire, Suez and Decolonization* (London: Tauris, 2006).
11. Martin Watts, *The Jewish Legion and the First World War* (New York: Palgrave Macmillan, 2004).
12. Watts, *The Jewish Legion*, p. 84.
13. Watts, *The Jewish Legion*, pp. 89 and 147 ff.
14. Antonius, *The Arab Awakening*, Chaps. 12, 13.
15. There is a large literature on this topic. Good access into the debate is found in items cited above: Antonius, *The Arab Awakening* and Friedman, *Palestine: A Twice Promised Land?*
16. Antonius, *The Arab Awakening*, appendices.
17. *The Palestinian National Charter: Resolutions of the Palestine National Council July 1-17, 1968*, https://avalon.law.yale.edu/20th_century/plocov.asp.

18. Michael Walzer, *Just and Unjust Wars; A Moral Argument with Historical Illustrations* (New York: Basic Books, 2000).
19. Susan Pedersen, *The Guardians: The League of Nations and the Crisis of Empire* (Oxford: Oxford University Press, 2015).
20. Sharon Klorman, *The Right of Conquest: The Acquisition of Territory by Force in International Law and Practice* (Oxford: Oxford University Press, 1996).
21. Relevant books are Henry Cattan: *Palestine, the Arabs and Israel; The Search for Justice* (New York: Longmans, 1969); *Palestine: The Road to Peace* (Harlow: Longman, 1971); *Palestine and International Law* (London: Longmans, 1973); *The Palestine Question* (London: Croom Helm, 1988).
22. https://en.wikipedia.org/wiki/Henry_Cattan
23. Leonie Star, *Julius Stone: An Intellectual Life* (Oxford: Oxford University Press, 1992); "Julius Stone," *Wikipedia*: https://en.wikipedia.org/wiki/Julius_Stone.
24. Henry Cattan, "The Status of Jerusalem Under International Law and United Nations," *Journal of Palestine Studies*, 10:3 (Spring, 1981) 13.
25. Henry Cattan, *To Whom Does Palestine Belong?* (Beirut: Institute for Palestine Studies, 1969).
26. "*President Wilson's Address to Congress, Analyzing German and Austrian Peace Utterances (Delivered to Congress in Joint Session on February 11, 1918)*": http://www.gwpda.org/1918/wilpeace.html
27. Cattan, "The Status of Jerusalem Under International Law and United Nations," *Journal of Palestine Studies*, 10:3 (Spring, 1981), 3–15.
28. Henry Cattan, *To Whom Does Palestine Belong?* pp. 7–10.
29. Suzanne Daley, "Who Owns This Land? In Greece, Who Knows?," *New York Times*, May 26, 2013. https://www.nytimes.com/2013/05/27/world/europe/greeces-tangled-land-ownership-is-a-hurdle-in-recovery.html.
30. Cattan, *To Whom Does Palestine Belong?* p. 5.
31. Julius Stone, *Israel and Palestine – Assault on the Law of Nations* (Baltimore: Johns Hopkins, 1981).
32. *United Nations: Special Committee on Palestine* (UNSCOP), September 3, 1947, paragraph 166. https://www.jewishvirtuallibrary.org/united-nations-special-committee-on-palestine-unscop. The issue of when a distinctive Palestinian identity began is highly contested. See, for example, The review of Benny Morris in *Israel* Studies 3:1 (Spring, 1998), 266–272 of Rashid Khalidi, *Palestinian Identity: The Construction of Modern National Consciousness* (New York: Columbia University, 1997). Golda Meir drew on the later development of a distinctively Palestinian identity in a famous or notorious denial. See You Tube: https://www.youtube.com/watch?v=19M91iwP994. (particularly beginning minute 7:00). Recent scholarship also deals with the name given to what we know as Palestine, arguing that it becomes prevalent only at the beginning of the twentieth century. See Emanuel Beska, Zachary Foster, "The Origins of the term "Palestinian" ("Filastini") in late Ottoman Palestine, 1898-1914," *Academic Letters*, July 2021.
33. Julius Stone, *Israel and Palestine; Assault on the Law of Nations* (Baltimore: Johns Hopkins University Press, 1981), pp. 18 ff.
34. Stone, *Ibid*.
35. British White Paper of June 1922. https://avalon.law.yale.edu/20th_century/brwh1922.asp

36. The view that the Balfour Declaration was a "mistake" can be found in numerous references around its centenary. Typical is "What we got wrong: The Guardian's worst errors of judgment over 200 years", *The Guardian*, 7 May 2021, https://www.theguardian.com/media/2021/may/07/guardian-200-what-we-got-wrong-the-guardians-worst-errors-of-judgment-over-200-years. In scholarship a prominent recent example is John Quigley, *The Legality of a Jewish State: A Century of Debates over Rights in Palestine* (Cambridge: Cambridge University Press, 2022).
37. On the term "notables" see Albert Hourani, "Ottoman Reform and the Politics of Notables," in *The Modern Middle East*, ed. Albert Hourani, Philip S. Khoury, and Mary C. Wilson (Berkeley: University of California Press, 1993); James L. Gelvin, "The 'Politics of Notables' Forty Years After," *Middle East Studies Association Bulletin*, 40:1 (June 2006), 19–29.

Chapter 3
From Discovery to Rediscovery: The Economic Absorptive Capacity of Palestine

The concept of "discovery" in international law was famously articulated by Chief Justice John Marshall. In a series of cases, notably *Johnson v. McIntosh* (1823), Marshall expounded on the legitimacy of claims made by European powers during the 15th and subsequent centuries as they took possession of foreign lands. Although control could be established by conquest, purchase and treaty, Europeans could also validate claims through discovery.[1] If these territories were not inhabited by fellow Christians and subject to a European monarch, they could be claimed by the European states that "discovered" and colonized them. In effect, the rights of natives were not considered. While discovery may seem less relevant today, and its legal standing challenged because it bypasses the rights of the indigenous,[2] note that "discovery" is still operative in the modern world where explorers expect to lay national claims to hitherto uncharted areas in Antarctica, on the ocean floor, and in space. Moreover, it is still cited in the United States to validate rights to lands that indigenous people inhabit or claim.

Nevertheless, "Discovery" may seem to be an odd category for establishing claims to Palestine when compared to its use in the opening up of the so-called "New World" by Europeans in the aftermath of the voyages of Columbus. What, after all, remained to be revealed beyond those shores of the Eastern Mediterranean where significant civilizations left written records that have informed and inspired mankind? Palestine may be one of the most documented areas of the globe. That extensive record has long been part of the cultural heritage of monotheism and the West. And, it is precisely that record and its interpretation that looms significant for the Arab-Israeli conflict. Explorers and archaeologists, usually supported by their national governments, ventured forth in ever increasing numbers to "*re*-discover" a past they wished to know better, and to reclaim lands for reintegration into the modern world.

© The Author(s), under exclusive license to Springer Nature
Switzerland AG 2024
S. I. Troen, *Israel/Palestine in World Religions*,
https://doi.org/10.1007/978-3-031-50914-8_3

SUNDAY-SCHOOL GRAPES.

"Sunday School Grapes". "Sunday School Grapes" from Mark Twain's 1869 *Innocents Abroad of the New Pilgrims' Progress* (1869). The reference is to the biblical story of the twelve spies sent by Moses to investigate Canaan. (*Numbers* 13:1–33 and *Deuteronomy* 1:22–40). Except for Joshua and Caleb, ten were intimidated by the inhabitants but all reported the richness of the land typified by returning with a branch of a cluster of grapes. In this rendering, the Palestinian landscape is starkly bare, as continually observed, in contrast to the exaggerated size of the fruit. This view is typical of visual and verbal descriptions of the Palestine encountered by tourists and explorers

Jerusalem in the 1870s. Jerusalem in the 1870s from Mount Scopus in the east. The "Old City" at that time was encompassed in its historic walls with minimal population beyond. The sole tree in a relatively underdeveloped landscape reflects that historic reality. Jerusalem now (2023) has well over 950,000 inhabitants with a congested hinterland, most of which developed after 1948 with a further catalyst provided by the aftermath of the 1967 June War. (Photo by Felix Bonfils of Beirut, courtesy of Yad Yitzhak Ben-Zvi Photo Archive)

The desire to rediscover the Holy Land entered a dramatic new phase during the nineteenth century and through the first part of the twentieth as conflict erupted over its resources and capacities. What is pertinent is how exploration was used to establish a legal claim to the country. The debate focused on the extent of Palestine's potential for integration into the modern world and who might be best equipped to accomplish it. This has led to a renewed interest in the exploration of that which was thought to be so well known.

Explorers hoped to find new sources of key raw materials in the chemicals of the Dead Sea and possible oil or metal deposits beneath the surface. There were political advantages to Palestine's being a land bridge between Asia and Africa and at the traditional crossroad between Europe and those venues. A "silk route" had once crossed the Negev on the way to the Red Sea. Palestine/Israel is now strategically located proximate to the Suez Canal. Thus cultural, economic, and political objectives supported a considerable enterprise of "discovery" and "rediscovery" of Ottoman territory that Europe sought to incorporate into its orbit.

Initially it was British, French, German, Italian and American explorers who set out to enhance and to verify the enormously rich textual evidence of the ancient Hebrews and the Near Eastern civilizations amongst whom they lived. They sought to increase understanding of the Bible by illuminating the context out of which it was created. Westerners, whatever the extent of their religious beliefs, were typically educated in the Bible. The notion of "walking in the footsteps" of Biblical figures and events, actually a kind of pilgrimage, was a deeply felt motive for many. As this interest grew, waves of explorers, often under the sponsorship of their governments, ventured from the eastern Mediterranean coast to Persia and across northern Africa from Egypt to Morocco.

Proprietary cultural rights had deep roots. The need to decipher texts stimulated scholarship in the languages of the ancient Middle East and their translation. The architecture of public buildings in Western capitals imitated the columns, arches, and layout of public spaces. Artifacts, like Egyptian obelisks, were removed to European capitals and inspired imitation from Rome and Paris to Washington. All testify to the intimate, historic relationship to the largely Christian West felt to the Middle East and to its effort to discover a retrievable past. This connection was different from the relationship between the West and most other places in the world. There was intense competition to expand knowledge of the heritage from which Western Christian culture had drawn. The important point here is that this exploration significant affected the way positions in the Arab/Israeli conflict were framed as Jews and Arabs sought roots for their identities in ancient civilizations. (An additional perspective on the significance of how alternative interpretations of history impact the contest for Palestine is examined in Chap. 5)[3]

From the first half of the nineteenth century, like a latter-day Columbus, Cortes, Cabot, or Champlain, explorers were motivated by pragmatic and utilitarian interests and spread out across the region. There was much to learn about raw materials required for a rapidly developing industrial economy. Oil was of paramount interest, but other raw materials were also eagerly sought. Exploring the past as a cultural resource had powerful spiritual and cultural values, the search for natural resources similarly occasioned competition. It is worth recalling the occupation of the hero of Herzl's utopian novel and manifesto, *Altneuland* (1902), that energized Zionists and their supporters. David Litvak was a chemical engineer engaged in extracting chemicals from the Dead Sea. At the time, chemical industries were taking the lead in advanced countries like Germany and Great Britain. Exploiting the Dead Sea promised to be a key to national development well before substantial Zionist settlement actually took place.

Not until 1851 was the "Dead Sea," or "Salt Sea" in Hebrew, understood to be below sea level and a possible repository of chemicals that could have great economic and even strategic value. Some twenty years after an American explorer suggested that the Dead Sea was below sea level, the Royal Geographical Society of London established an international competition that determined the Dead Sea was in fact 405 m below sea level. By then, a succession of investigators began to engage in determining an economical method for extracting its chemicals. When a Zionist entrepreneur from Siberia, Moshe Novomeysky, developed such a method in the 1920s, extracting chemicals from the Dead Sea became a Zionist project that obtained a concession from the Mandate. By WWII, Palestine Potash Company had developed into the largest non-petroleum industry in the Middle East, supplying essential chemicals for the manufacture of ammunition and fertilizer and employing about 2500 workers, divided almost evenly between Jews and Arabs.[4]

The discovery engendered excitement, and initiatives hoping for similar prospects were undertaken elsewhere. For example, the territories from Kansas to the Rocky Mountains were still largely unmapped at the time, and until 1848, were designated on maps as the Great American Desert. This lacuna represents a serious void of what Americans knew of their territory nearly half a century after Jefferson dispatched Lewis and Clark on their famous expedition.[5] Stanley met with Livingston only in 1871 in one of the still unexplored parts of Africa, another part of the globe that excited enormous interest. Robert Peary is credited with discovering the north pole in 1909. Roald Amundsen discovered the south pole in 1911. Others, far less celebrated, engaged in the rediscovery of Palestine. Exploration and the expectation of discovery in Palestine were part of the same global phenomenon.

In 1865, the British established the Palestine Exploration Fund (PEF) in London. Despite an avowed denial of religious motives, the tangle between the religious and secular is apparent. The PEF declared: "We are not to be a religious society; we are not about to launch controversy; we are about to apply the rules of science, which are so well understood by us in our branches, to an investigation into the facts concerning the Holy Land." They engaged in archaeology and conducted expeditions that delved into the natural history, geology, anthropology, history, and geography of the country. Explorers drew maps and noted natural resources, and it was soon apparent that their work had military value. It is not accidental that senior military officers like Herbert Kitchener, a Field Marshal with extensive experience in Africa and in World War I, and T. E. Lawrence ("Lawrence of Arabia") who became well-known for his role in the Arab Revolt and the WWI Sinai and Palestine Campaign against the Ottoman Empire, headed or participated in expeditions.

One direct and explicit implication was the frequently misquoted statement by the Earl of Shaftesbury who pronounced in 1875 before the annual meeting of the PEF that "We have there a land teeming with fertility and rich in history, but almost without an inhabitant—a country without a people, and look! scattered over the world, a people without a country." This was one of the earliest usages of a phrase that would become infamous, often misquoted, and ascribed to Zionists—that Palestine was "a land without a people for a people without a land." That is, observers typically ignored or minimized the presence of a sparse population that numbered only 275,000 in 1800, grew to 411,000 in 1860, and was only about 500,000–600,000 in 1900. It was Zionist settlement that stimulated the increase of the area's population to more than 14,000,000 in the twentieth century (ca. 2020). The focus of explorers and outside observers was on the storied ancient Near East and its potential, not the present.[6]

As noted earlier, the gap between the imagined and real Holy Land is recorded by Mark Twain in his 1869 classic, best-selling *Innocents Abroad, or The New Pilgrims' Progress*. In one humorous episode he describes the sorry condition of what passed for grapes in Palestine, a land he found to be arid, desolate, underpopulated, and underdeveloped. He compared those sorry grapes to the luscious "Sunday School grapes" described in the lessons he learned as a child in Hannibal, Missouri, where the Holy Land was described a bountiful and blessed country "flowing with milk and honey" and the book included a woodcut showing the spies Moses sent to explore the land carrying an enormous bunch of grapes on a pole between them. Biblical Sodom, on the other hand, a byword for sinful perversion, would become a twentieth century center for chemical extractions for the world market, as described above, complete with a hotel built in the Bauhaus style and a seaport to accommodate travelers on the air route the British established between England and India.[7]

Not unlike the desert region around the Dead Sea that provided an extreme picture of barrenness, the entire country appeared underdeveloped and unpromising in its largely semi-arid landscape. It is no wonder that nineteenth century Holy Land explorers and tourists compared the present unfavorably with the ancient past. This contrast generated a critical view of Ottoman rule and current Arab residents who were deemed responsible for the decline, opened a debate as to whether in fact nature or climate change was responsible for the sorry state of the country. If the Ottomans and Arabs were responsible, idealistic Zionist settlers might yet invest enough labor to return the land to its former glory. If, on the other hand, a change in climate was to blame, then it could be argued that due to its unsuitable soil and arid climate, Palestine could only accommodate a limited population in the present. This position suggested that a large influx of Jewish immigrants would necessarily compromise the rights of the resident population.

Prejudice and Rights

This open question led back to the stipulation of the Balfour Declaration that a "national home for the Jewish people" could be established if *"nothing shall be done which may prejudice the civil and religious rights of existing non-Jewish communities in Palestine ..."* To answer it, experts were dispatched to evaluate whether Jewish immigration would indeed prejudice the rights of Arabs. Those rights came to be assessed ostensibly through an economic lens rather than a strictly political, religious, and civil one. If Palestine could not support an increase in population, then the immigration of large numbers of Jews would be in breach of the terms of the Balfour Declaration, and purchase of Arab land would also have to be stopped. The debate about the plausibility of a Jewish state in Palestine came to be phrased in terms of Palestine's "economic absorptive capacity."

The Zionist assessment was that the country had great potential. Not only could it grow and prosper without economic injury to the local population, but on the contrary, the Arab residents were expected to benefit from Zionist development and to share in the prosperity. These optimistic forecasts created an enormous demand for evidence. The evidence, in turn, was assessed initially by a succession of British sponsored investigative commissions and later by additional interested parties. Ultimately special commissions organized under League of Nations and United Nations auspices weighed the evidence, decided on a political solution, and attempted to realize it.[8]

Evidence from Experts

As befitting a modern, secular discourse, the international discussion over rights was rooted in "facts" based on a plethora of data that supported or disproved claims derived from philosophical or legal principles. Experienced British civil servants were initially charged with collecting and interpreting the data. Typical of these was Sir John Hope-Simpson who, in 1930, gave his name to an influential report that bears his name: *Palestine: Report on Immigration, Land Settlement and Development* or the "Hope Simpson Report." This effort was a direct consequence of Arab pressure, including extensive riots in 1929, to limit Jewish immigration and land purchases.

Hope-Simpson began his long and distinguished career in the Indian Civil Service in 1897. He returned to England to serve as Private Secretary to the Ministry of Labour in 1917. He served as a Liberal Member of Parliament from 1922 to 1924, and after an election defeat, spent the rest of his career in a variety of posts in England and in Canada and as a British representative to international bodies in Greece, China, the League of Nations, and ultimately the United Nations. A seasoned civil servant with a keen understanding of politics, he nevertheless could not avoid producing a highly controversial report. Its conclusion advocated modifications in British policy, established less than a decade earlier, in order to protect the rights of the long-term residents of Palestine. Despite the wealth of details offered as "facts," his Report generated contradictory evidence and counterarguments to its political conclusions.

The beginning of the Report sets the tone and establishes the basic problem: to locate and define how much of Palestine's land could be cultivated. This was a key issue because it was assumed one could extrapolate from this information the extent of the population the country could support. We soon learn there was insufficient data and also contradictory estimates. The problem persisted through the British Mandate. Indeed, by 1948 when the British departed, they had succeeded in mapping only 20 percent of Palestine's total land area.[9] In addition to the absence of such basic information, fundamental data on soil quality and its potential uses were also neglected and subject to contention. It was impossible to assess conflicting claims about what crops could be grown and where.

As a result, Arabs and others who opposed Jewish immigration and settlement produced consistently minimalist assessments; Zionists and others put forward evidence that the country could sustain a significantly larger population. During the 1930s the minimalists triumphed and effectively checked both land sales and immigration, precisely at a time of growing danger for European Jews. Ultimately the issue was not decided by universally agreed scientific evidence but by political pressure and facts on the battlefield. The Jewish victory in the 1948 War of Independence ended the theoretical dispute on Palestine's capacity to absorb immigrants. Evidence of the country's capacity to sustain a growing population through economic growth that benefited both Jews and Arabs has been provided by what actually transpired. Although we now know the minimalists were wrong, it is still essential for this study to examine the debate over the claims of Jews and Arabs in real time. It would also be appropriate to appreciate how the "scientific" arguments put forward by the contending sides served to sustain views that supported long-held positions, rooted in religious and historical beliefs, that provided legitimacy to their claims.

Debating the Economic Absorptive Capacity of Palestine

A fascinating range of experts engaged in passionate argumentation for both sides. The economic absorptive capacity of Palestine was the most publicly debated issue and experts brought a vast literature of findings before the international commissions created to adjudicate competing claims. The debate was intense and extensive. Indeed, in a 1945 letter to President Truman, Chaim Weizmann claimed that "Palestine, for its size, is probably the most investigated country in the world."[10]

The emergence of this debate was unanticipated. In the eyes of supporters of Zionist settlement, both Jews and non-Jews, the country was underdeveloped and underpopulated. Many therefore welcomed the promulgation of the first immigration ordinance of the British Mandatory authorities on September 1, 1920, that was expected to open Palestine for rapid colonization by Jewish immigrants. This first ordinance was liberal, admitting any Jew who was healthy in body and mind and assured of a livelihood, provided he did not pose any political or criminal threat.[11]

The anticipated influx of Jewish pioneers did not occur for a variety of reasons: there were more attractive destinations; the paths of alternative emigration were well-organized; and Palestine was economically unattractive and lacked the physical comforts found elsewhere. Moreover, concerned lest they could not successfully absorb a mass immigration, Zionist authorities did not attempt to recruit large numbers for immediate *Aliyah* [immigration to Israel]. This gave Arabs who opposed the creation of a Jewish majority in Palestine time to organize and lobby against British policy.[12]

In the face of this growing opposition, over the next two decades the British retreated from an open-door policy through a series of White Papers. It was the first of these, officially presented in June 1922, that introduced "economic absorptive capacity," the concept used to limit Jewish immigration which, as the White Paper stipulated: " … cannot be so great in volume as to exceed whatever may be the economic capacity of the country at the time to absorb new arrivals. It is essential to ensure that the immigrants should not be a burden upon the people of Palestine as a whole, and that they should not deprive any section of the present population of their employment."[13] In effect this echoed the Balfour Declaration's conclusion, and, in so doing, diminished the prospect of unqualified support for the Jewish national homeland.

This declaration meant that Zionists could not merely claim Jewish rights to Palestine in terms of decisions of the international agreements established by the British and the League of Nations. The burden of proof was on Zionism to demonstrate the settlement of Jews in Palestine was economically feasible and would not be detrimental to local Arab inhabitants. Proof relied on the calculations of experts in disciplines as varied as archaeology, economics, sociology, geography, and civil engineering. Some research was conducted independently, and its political implications were transparent to academic, political, and public audiences. Other studies were consciously created or directed with a view to establishing desired results. The debate, carried out at a time of intense opposition and even violence against Zionism at home, growing pressure for refuge due to the rise of European fascism and anti-Semitism, and a world-wide depression that was closing the gates to immigration, was accompanied by intense anxiety, tension, and frustration.

Archaeology and Politics

Archaeological research provided the initial corpus of evidence used to ascertain Palestine's absorptive capacity. Although archeologists became interested in charting and understanding fluctuations in the size of populations long before the Balfour Declaration and quite apart from it, conflicts over immigration policy encouraged interpreting the past to draw conclusions about the future. This exercise was facilitated by Palestine's extraordinarily rich documentation in written materials and physical remains. The historical record was used to generate two conflicting interpretations: one school blamed people, specifically Arabs, for failing to maintain the fertility of the Holy Land; the other argued that climatic change, not the local population, was responsible for the country's poverty and lack of development. A fierce moral-political argument emerged from this "scientific" and historical debate. If people rather than climate were responsible for a decline in Palestine's productivity, if another people—the Jews—could increase Palestine's productivity and claim the land. This principle was well known and appreciated, as previously noted, both in religious and secular sources.

The precursors of modern archaeology arrived in Palestine in mid-nineteenth century to identify places associated with Biblical events. Among the first and most important was Edward Robinson, a teacher of Hebrew at Andover Theological Seminary in Massachusetts, who first came to the Holy Land in 1838. Defining himself as a "biblical geographer," he pioneered the development of biblical topography or the identification of sites mentioned in the Bible. With the establishment of the British-sponsored Palestine Exploration Fund in 1865, Robinson's field of inquiry was substantially expanded. Particularly noteworthy are the early P.E.F.-sponsored maps of Palestine and volumes on topography with placenames that featured biblical sites associated with past Jewish residence, and identification of fauna and flora based on the surveys carried out by Lieutenants Conder and Kitchener (later Lord Kitchener of Khartoum). Together with the work of another soldier-scholar, Lieutenant and later Sir Charles Warren who undertook an extensive study of Jerusalem, these P.E.F. reports constitute an impressive body of data on the ancient history of the Holy Land. Such research continued through the British Mandate. The Mandatory Government's *Statistical Abstract of Palestine for 1944-45* identifies 2048 ancient sites, that are identifiable from the Bible or other ancient sources, or that had long been abandoned or renamed.[14]

New analytical techniques introduced at the end of the nineteenth century by the British archaeologist Sir Flinders Petrie, made it possible to evaluate the physical remains of archaeological sites to establish chronologies. This analytical breakthrough enabled assessments of the relative vitality and size of populations during such periods as the Bronze Age, ancient Hebrew, Hellenistic, Roman-Byzantine and the Moslem. Still missing, however, was a conclusive theory to explain the reasons for fluctuations in prosperity and population size from one period to another.

The conventional wisdom was that the depletion of the soil and disrepair of the country could be blamed on the Arab population which had inhabited the land for centuries and on the Ottoman authorities that neglected it. Lieutenant Conder asserted in his 1876 report to the Palestine Exploration Fund on *The Fertility of Ancient Palestine* that the "curse of the country is bad government and oppression. Justice and security of person and property once established, Palestine would become once more a land of corn, vines and olives, rivaling in fertility and in wealth its ancient condition, as deduced from careful study of such notices as remain to us in the Bible and in the later Jewish writings."[15] At the same time, in *The Land of Promise* (1875), Sir Charles Warren predicted optimistically, "Give Palestine a good government and increase the commercial life of the people, and they may increase tenfold and yet there is room. Its [the land's] productiveness will increase in proportion to labour bestowed on the soil until a population of 15 million may be accommodated there." [16] This perception supported the Zionist view that the land could be made far more bountiful with effective management and modern methods of cultivation.

The most important challenge to this view came from Ellsworth Huntington, a Yale professor of geography and leader of a controversial approach that applied determinism to the study of geography. His work was brought to public attention by *Palestine and its Transformation* (1911) that was widely quoted by Arab proponents of a restrictive interpretation of the economic absorptive capacity. Supported by a fund administered by Yale president Arthur T. Hadley and by the Palestine Exploration Fund, Huntington was interested in "the effect of physical environment upon the distribution of living beings and upon man's mode of life and thought" and wanted to investigate whether man or nature were responsible for the country's decline.[17] Like most visitors and researchers he noted that in the past the land had been far more densely populated, and phrased his question about the reasons for the change in epic historical language:

> Something has clearly changed. Has it been the type of inhabitant? Is the present state of the country worse than that of the past because the idle Arab has displaced the industrious Jew, and the vacillating Turk the strong Roman? Has the substitution of misrule and oppression for a just, firm government caused the physical deterioration of the country? Or has nature herself suffered a change which has brought in its train depopulation, and all the miseries of the present unsettled conditions?[18]

Huntington was convinced it was the climate that had changed. Higher temperatures and less rain caused unfavorable semi-arid and even desert conditions. Lower temperatures and more rain created an environment that could sustain a more substantial agriculture. Thus, when the climate was more favorable during the Roman-Byzantine period, the area's population reached perhaps its greatest extent in its recorded history. It was drought and heat, not the failings of people, that caused the decline of civilizations: "Rain is the missing element ... Irrigation is necessary to insure against famine in bad years, but no more water can be obtained. The supply appears to have decreased permanently."[19]

Two young Zionist leaders, David Ben-Gurion and Yitzhak Ben-Zvi, recognized the political implications of Huntington's analysis and quickly responded with their best-selling book [in Yiddish] on the means for colonizing Palestine, *Eretz Israel in the Past and in the Present* (1918). Exiled from Ottoman Palestine and living in New York, Ben-Gurion and Ben-Zvi spent much of their time at the New York Public Library assiduously reading everything they could find in English, German, French and Hebrew relevant to the country's past and potential.[20] Basing themselves on Conder, whom they describe as "the greatest authority in all that pertains to Eretz Yisrael," they argued that a population of 10 million could live in historic Eretz Yisrael or the Palestine of both sides of the Jordan River.[21] Their two volumes of evidence provided a distinctly Zionist political message. They explicitly acknowledged the Arab presence in contemporary Palestine and argued that the land could be redeemed by industrious Jews. They also suggested the Arabs were in fact the descendants of the Judeans/Jews who had remained loyal to the land while accepting Christianity and Islam.[22]

Their findings were supported after the First World War when American and European archaeologists and scholars of the ancient Near East organized a systematic and institutionalized effort to recreate the social and economic history of the ancient Middle East. Operating through the Rockefeller-funded American Schools of Oriental Research throughout the region, these scholars blended philology, linguistics, critical textual analysis, the study of material culture, and whatever else was available into an instrument of great analytic power. Their expanded objective, in addition to religious and Biblical scholarship, was to write the social and economic history of the region.

Of the accomplished scholars attracted to the study of Palestine, the central figure was William F. Albright of Johns Hopkins University and the American School of Oriental Research in Jerusalem. In a series of popular lectures published in 1931, Albright synthesized a picture of ancient Palestinian society that went beyond validation or illumination of the Bible. He painted a picture of a Palestine in which there were dense populations in some areas as early as the Iron Age. However, together with most scholars, he singled out the Roman-Byzantine period as having a peak of four or more million—three times as many inhabitants as were present in Palestine during the inter-war period and as many as ten times the population in mid-nineteenth century. It appeared that ancient Palestine enjoyed a flourishing agriculture, considerable international trade, large towns throughout the country, even in the Negev desert, and large cities on the coast. His readers understood that the country could prosper if modern technology were placed in the hands of Jews with the knowledge and ambition to use it.[23]

Nelson Glueck, a disciple of Albright and the foremost scholar of Negev archaeology, also unearthed evidence that man, not climate, was responsible for success in settling the country's deserts. Like Ben-Gurion and Ben-Zvi, he explicitly countered Huntington's argument by placing blame for desertification on nomadic Bedouins, Arabs, inferior government, and wars "rather than drastic changes in the weather." Indeed, from his studies on the Negev, Glueck concluded that climate was not the limiting factor: "Never in historical times had radical and permanent changes in climate placed it (the Negev) beyond the pale of settlement."[24]

The findings of Glueck, Albright and others were succinctly summarized at an international conference sponsored by the Research Council of Israel shortly after the establishment of the State. Israel now had to determine for itself at what rate it should take in immigrants, and old concerns persisted. As Adolf Reifenberg, a Hebrew University archaeologist, proclaimed: "The Israel we see today is but the ruin of a once flourishing country... It is human mismanagement, which has brought about a continuing deterioration in the natural conditions." Placing Palestine in an international context, other scholars from Western Europe, the United States and North Africa concurred. In Palestine, as in other desert areas in the world, people rather than climate determined the outcome of what was termed the struggle between the "Desert and the Sown". Organization and social values were the key to development.[25]

During the Mandate, when Zionism was pressing it claims before the international community, except for Huntington, archaeological research unambiguously supported the proposition that Palestine could sustain an increased population including an influx of Jewish immigration. Usually cited at least in introductions to reports by the various international commissions on the Arab-Zionist conflict, this historical evidence lent moral force to the Zionist demand that Palestine could absorb multitudes of Jewish refugees who would work to reclaim the land. However persuasive this view was to experts, it had little impact on British policymakers who bowed to Arab political pressure.[26]

Testimony of Foreign Experts

Experts began coming to Palestine in significant numbers and on an organized basis soon after the Balfour Declaration. It was widely believed in Europe and the United States that the rejuvenation of Palestine was imminent since Jerusalem and the Holy Land were once again in competent hands. In addition to the British who were now charged with superintending the development of the country, the international Zionist network recruited experts from a diversity of fields. Monetary resources were few, the conditions harsh, and the task immense. It was clear that developing Palestine into the Jewish National Homeland required informed and detailed planning. Beginning 1919, experts dedicated to enhancing Palestine's economic absorptive capacity arrived with experience in the dry lands of the American West, the Far East, particularly China, and in the deserts of North Africa, to research and advise.

This diverse group investigated a host of relevant issues. Elmwood Mead (1858–1936), head of the US Bureau of Reclamation, for example, contributed to the 1928 *Report of the Experts*, a study commissioned by American Zionists to support and shape the development of Zionist villages. Urban and regional planners, Patrick Geddes (1854–1932) and Patrick Abercrombie (1879–1957) of Great Britain, contributed to the development of Tel-Aviv, Jerusalem, and Haifa in the expectation that the overwhelmingly rural and agricultural country required urban development. Walter Lowdermilk (1888–1974) of the U. S. Soil Conservation Service with international experience in water and soil issues focused on augmenting the acreage available for agriculture and, based on his experience with the Tennessee Valley Authority, for providing hydroelectric power. The fact that many experts were non-Jews usefully augmented the objective and scientific status of their views and suggestions.[27]

Jean Gottmann, one of the leading geographers of his generation, contributed to the Zionist side of the debate. Although now best known for *Megalopolis* (1961), a study of the urban region of the American northeastern corridor from Boston to Washington, D.C., Gottmann's earliest work centered on Palestine. His doctoral dissertation was a reaction to the British 1930 White Paper based on a negative evaluation of Palestine's economic absorptive capacity that drastically curtailed Jewish immigration. He argued in conferences and published papers that through proper cultivation and irrigation, the arid and neglected areas of Palestine could be made fruitful and a productive home for a large population.[28]

Since Palestine's economic absorptive capacity was at issue, however, it was the economists, among the social science experts, whose views were paramount. The most important and comprehensive study was *Palestine: Problem and Promise, An Economic Study* (1946) produced by a team of American economists—Robert Nathan, Oscar Gass, and Daniel Creamer. Nathan, the chief author, had earned a reputation as one of the bright young men of the New Deal through his work as Director of the National Income Division of the U. S. Department of Commerce and Chairman of the Central Planning Division of the War Production Board. Their work became the standard piece used to persuade international forums in the critical period before the U.N. vote on partition.

The aim of their research, made explicit at the outset of the study, was to fill "the need for an authoritative and objective appraisal of the economic potentialities of Palestine." The study was funded by "the American Palestine Institute, a non-partisan research organization," that raised about $100,000, probably the largest sum theretofore committed to social science research on an issue of public policy. In keeping with their scientific and objective commitments, the organizers announced that as a matter of policy, "the cost of the study was borne by individuals and organizations of varied, even divergent, views with regard to Zionism." They accepted funds from those who were identified on a "range from ardent Zionism through what may be called neutrality to a position of opposition to political Zionism." What bound everyone together was an agreement on "the need for this objective study."[29] *Palestine: Problem and Promise* examined natural resources, agricultural prospects, manufacturing possibilities in a variety of industries, construction requirements particularly in housing, the amount of capital necessary for development, and the possible sources of such funds. In sum, the experts produced a comprehensive analysis of how the country could be developed to absorb more than a million immigrants, particularly refugees from Europe, who might want or need to come during the following decade. As founding-director of one of the most active economic development consulting firms in the post-war decades that surveyed more than fifty countries, Nathan and his colleagues concluded that human resources are even more important than natural ones since people with talent are the key to development. They argued that despite limited natural resources, Palestine could be made productive because it possessed an enormous asset in the talent and dynamism of the Jewish population. This view became an important part of the political arsenal of supporters of a Jewish state as they pleaded their case before the great powers and the United Nations. But although the findings of economists corroborated the view held by archaeologists, urban planners, agricultural development experts and geographers, experts could not persuade British policymakers to change their position.[30]

Institutionalized Zionist Research

Systematic official research on Palestine's economy was initiated in the 1920s with British efforts to collect regular and standardized statistics on society and the economy. They published data in the *Palestine Blue Book* beginning in 1926 and a *Census of Industry* in 1928. They also compiled data as background for official reports and White Papers. However, data collection began earlier, with the opening of an official Zionist office in Palestine in 1907 under the direction of Dr. Arthur Ruppin. Ruppin arrived from Germany to investigate conditions in the country and to superintend development programs. To this task he brought scientific training in sociology, demography and social statistics, law, and business as well as the backing of Germany's wealthiest and most powerful Zionists. After publishing a prize-winning book on the sociology of the Jews through the centuries (1904), he focused increasingly on the problems of resettling Jews in their own land. Soon after arrival in Palestine he undertook the first census of Jerusalem in perhaps two thousand years. Appointed lecturer in sociology at the founding of the newly established Hebrew University in Jerusalem in 1925, throughout his life in Palestine (1907–1943) Ruppin remained one of the central figures conducting research into Palestinian society and economy and formulating and implementing settlement policy.[31]

Prior to the 1930 White Paper and Nazi control in Germany, Ruppin did not press for large-scale immigration. On the contrary, as in his 1919 essay, "The Selection of the Fittest," he argued that Zionist authorities should carefully screen candidates for pioneering and give preference to those who were able and willing to work the land. Here, and elsewhere, he advanced the idea that a gradual approach was required to develop a backward, neglected and resource-poor country.[32] Even in 1933, in the face of the increasing threat from Nazism, Ruppin claimed in an address before the

Zionist Congress in Prague that only some tens of thousands of German Jews could be absorbed. His analysis was based on a "scientific" formula that for every Jew settled on the land, only another two to three could be settled in towns. According to this calculation, the Jewish population of Palestine was necessarily limited since Jews owned a modest amount of land and more was hard to acquire. As one of the key Zionist officials responsible for Jewish settlement in Palestine, Ruppin initially advised that the primary solution to the immediate dangers facing German Jewry was to organize their transit to the United States, Latin America and other countries. He estimated that at most, "Palestine can absorb a considerable population—a quarter, a third, and perhaps even a half—of the 200,000 German Jews who will leave their native land in the next five, eight or ten years." However, even this minimal estimate alarmed Arab critics and British officials and politicians.[33]

Ruppin's estimates were rooted in an expectation shared with many European Jews and Zionists prior to the rise of the Nazis to power in the 1930s. Like Ruppin, they feared that if too many pioneers came only to be disappointed by the harsh climate and primitive conditions, it could be disastrous for Zionism. Although they believed the country could ultimately absorb some millions, they assumed it would take decades to get around restrictions on land purchases, establish an adequate infrastructure, and build a stable economic base. As noted above, even Ben-Gurion and Ben-Zvi predicted Palestine could support a population of ten million only within a century. Initially, the Zionists complied with British insistence on a reduced number of immigrants. They would proceed at a slower pace with the agricultural colonization of Palestine, believing the time would come for more rapid development. They did not anticipate a wholesale Arab attack on the British and League of Nations commitment to make Palestine the Jewish National Home.

Altered and threatening political circumstances also changed Zionist assumptions and attitudes. The violent assaults on European Jews meant the Yishuv had to develop a paradigm for moving quickly beyond agricultural settlement and in the process, push back on Arab demands and the Mandatory's restrictions. In the first instance, this meant asserting that more land could be reclaimed for farming than the Arabs admitted and pressing the British to allow for it. Secondly, it required expanding the industrial sector and building cities.[34] Models for development had to allow for immediate absorption of large numbers of refugees. This led to a shift in the conventional view of Palestine as an agricultural country to exploit its potential as an urban and industrial one. As the critical need to provide refuge intensified during the 1930s, the quest for a new model became acute. An impasse with the British was reached in 1943, at the height of the destruction of European Jewry. As the British and Americans were formulating plans for post-war reconstruction in Europe and elsewhere, the British High Commissioner proclaimed his vision for a postwar Palestine: "Palestine is essentially an agricultural country."[35] The Zionist leadership understood this meant continuing restrictions on Jewish immigration, a permanent Jewish minority, and no chance for an independent Jewish polity.

By Israel's independence, Zionist planners and settlement experts reformulated the optimum model for Promised Land. It would have to be 80 percent urban and but 20 percent rural. The original agricultural ideal and imagery were so entrenched, that it is not commonly appreciated that the goal of a land whose population was 20 percent rural was never reached. The 80 urban/20 rural formula, presented in the new state's Master Plan of 1950, was the distillation of extensive collaborative research.[36] The plan enabled Israel to enact the 1950 Law of Return. The adoption of this liberal and open-ended policy of Jewish immigration and settlement brought the debate over the country's economic absorptive capacity to an end.

By then it was too late for an untold number of potential Jewish immigrants who might have entered the country in the decade prior to the Holocaust and during it. Israel's future could not and must not be limited to rediscovering and recovering "a land of milk and honey" through agriculture. Success in the 1948 War of Independence meant that Jewish immigration was subject to the decisions of Jewish institutions and no longer restricted. Moreover, there was access to additional land and assets that had belonged to the Arab population, those that had departed on their own and those who were expelled. Zionist authorities would build a state beyond the agricultural country imagined by the British, the Arab sector, and traditional, romantic Zionism.

However, during the Mandate, there was a gap between the rights the Arab sector sought to defend and those claimed by the Jewish sector that could not be bridged. Zionist authorities unsuccessfully demanded legal immigration that experts thought possible and justifiable. At the crucial moment in 1939 on the eve of World War II, when immigration could have been significantly expanded, the British issued a White Paper that reneged on its commitments in accepting the League of Nations Mandate for Palestine and their own Balfour Declaration. It announced a limit of 75,000 legal entry permits over the next five years. However, even these were not fully distributed. Open land sales to Jews were also to have ended. The Zionist project appeared to be over. With no legal recourse available and unable to persuade the British to honor the Mandate, the Zionist leadership organized illegal immigration. Between 1939 and 1948, about 110,000 illegally entered the country by breaching a British naval blockade.[37]

During this decade, the British navy blocked scores of ships from landing in Palestine and their passengers were redirected to detention camps primarily in Cyprus or returned to Europe. These actions that Zionist massively publicized—as in the case of the refugee-carrying *Exodus 1947*—mobilized world opinion against the British and contributed to their concluding that they could no longer manage the situation in Palestine. While the British and Arabs saw the demand for immigration as illegal, world public opinion considered it morally necessary.

While "rediscovery" by modern experts was essential in making the Zionist case, there were other demands that also pressed for opening the country to Jewish immigration. This point is captured in a portion of the Sari Nusseibah's (b. 1949–) autobiography, *Once Upon a Country: A Palestinian Life*. A member of the Palestinian elite whose roots reach back to the circle around Muhammad, Nusseibah was a founder of Al-Quds University and its first president, he also famously joined an

Israeli intellectual, Mark Heller of Tel-Aviv University, in support of a two-state solution. In the following passage he imagines a conversation with his mother during the 1930s, when his family and community fought Jewish immigration:

> That night, during a visit with Mother, I posed a question. Just suppose, I began, that in the early years of the century an elderly and learned Jewish gentleman from Europe had come to your father to consult with him on an urgent matter. And suppose this gentleman told Grandfather that a looming human catastrophe of unimaginable proportions was about to befall the Jews of Europe. And suppose this gentleman added that as an Abrahamic cousin with historic ties to Palestine, he would like to prevent the genocide to come by seeking permission for his people to return to the shared homeland, to provide them with safety and refuge. What do you think Grandfather would have said? I asked her.
> Her answer surprised me. I was prepared for a long conversation full of conditions with clauses and caveats, but instead she replied straightaway with a wave of her hand, "What do you think? How could have anyone refused?" It was amazing for me how easily compassion sliced through fifty years of pain.

This retrospective judgement of what should have happened, not only did not take place, but remains rare among Palestinians, so bitter and entrenched has opposition been. Whatever other rights Jews invoked to claim Palestine, whether based on conquest, international treaties, self-determination, and—as we shall explore in the following chapter—those based on the right of labor, purchase and history, all were similarly rejected. The regret found in Nusseibah's dream was never actually expressed in real, historical time. By World War II, the legitimacy of a Jewish National Home appeared to be stymied on legal, political, and practical grounds. The economic absorptive capacity of Palestine was a large, public, and bitterly contested issue. A constricted view persuaded the British to backtrack on their promise; it energized those who believed in the country's potential.

There is now no doubt that the Zionists were correct. There was and remains room for a much larger population at far greater levels of prosperity than naysayers could recognize or perhaps even imagine. Including Jews, Arabs, and others, the population has grown about twenty-times more populous over a century from the 700,000 when Britain wrested control of Palestine.[38] Growth has brought about a totally unanticipated issue. Ecological considerations may require limitations to future development.[39] Israel is now widely termed the "Start-Up Nation" with an extraordinary record of entrepreneurship and scientific innovation. On a global scale, Israel's record is remarkable. From its beginnings—well before the polemics over the country's potential erupted—Zionism and its supporters were future-oriented. For the Arab side, the political view informed unnecessarily limited expectations and possibilities. As we have already seen and will continue to observe, positions on contentious subjects are maintained in tandem with positions on other issues that combine to reinforce perspectives of the opposing sides. This phenomenon becomes all the more significant when each side also holds to distinctive values and beliefs that derive from fundamental cultural/religious differences.

Notes

1. *Roxanne Dunbar-Ortiz, An Indigenous Peoples' History of the United States* (Boston: Beacon Press, 2014), pp. 197–201.
2. UN Economic and Security Council, *Impact on Indigenous Peoples of the International Legal construct known as the Doctrine of Discovery, which has served as the Foundation of the Violation of their Human Rights*, E.C.19/2010/13, 3 February 2010.
3. Followers of Edward Said view the growing intrusion and mastery of the West as a phenomenon in which Western imperial powers lorded it over Oriental society and culture that they sought to control and denigrated. Multiple contrary views have emerged, perhaps notably that of John MacKenzie, who find considerable appreciation for the Orient as well as creative interaction. When applied to the Arab/Israeli dispute, the Saidian perspective casts Zionists as typical external imperialists intent on disregarding if not diminishing local culture. See Edward W. Said, *Culture and Imperialism* (New York: Random House, 1994); John M. MacKenzie, *Orientalism: History, theory and the arts* (Manchester: Manchester University Press, 1995).
4. Ilan Troen, "The Price of Partition, 1948: The Dissolution of the Palestine Potash Company," *Journal of Israeli History*, 15:1 (March 1994), 53–81; Ran Or-Ner, *Tide below sea level; Jews, English, Palestinians, and Jordanians in the Potash Factories* (Tel-Aviv: Riesling, 2022) [Hebrew].
5. For extensive sections on discovery in Daniel Boorstin, *The Americans; The National Experience* (New York: Vintage, 1967); and Daniel Boorstin, *The Discoverers: A History of Man's Search to Know His World and Himself* (New York: Vintage, 1985).
6. Justin McCarthy, *The Population of Palestine: Population History and Statistics of the Late Ottoman Period and the Mandate* (New York: Columbia University Press, 1990); *Jewish Virtual Library,* "Population of Israel/Palestine (1553–Present)," https://www.jewishvirtuallibrary.org/population-of-israel-palestine-1553–present. The question of when Jews, outsiders, and the Palestinians themselves viewed the local Arab population as a distinct nationality or "people" will be treated in Chap. 5 and passim.
7. Troen, "The Price of Partition," *op. cit.*
8. The two most important and referenced were the *Anglo-American Committee of Inquiry* (1946) https://avalon.law.yale.edu/20th_century/angap04.asp; and the *United Nations Special Committee on Palestine* (1947): https://search.archives.un.org/united-nations-special-committee-on-palestine-unscop-1947.
9. Dov Gavish and Ruth Kark, "The cadastral mapping of Palestine, 1858-1928," *The Geographic Journal*, 159:1 (March 1993), 70–80.
10. Chaim Weizmann to Harry S. Truman, Dec. 12, 1945. *Weizmann Papers* (New Brunswick, NJ, 1979), vol. 22, p. 78.
11. Moshe Mossek, *Palestine immigration policy under Sir Herbert Samuel: British, Zionist and Arab attitudes* (London, 1978), p. 7 and pp. 157–161; Yehoshua Ben-Arieh, *The Making of Eretz Israel in the Modern Era; A Historical-Geographical Study,1799-1949* (Berlin: De Gruyter, 2020), Chap. 3.
12. Mossek, 58–60; *British White Paper, Cmd. 1700*, 22-29. Gur Alroey, *An Unpromising Land; Jewish Migration to Palestine in the Early Twentieth Century* (Stanford: Stanford University, 2014).

13. *British White Paper, Cmd. 1700*, pp. 17–21; Royal Institute of International Affairs, *Great Britain and Palestine, 1915-1945* (London, 1946), pp. 60–70.
14. Robert A. Macalister, *A century of excavation in Palestine* (London, 1925); David Amiran, "The pattern of settlement in Palestine," *Israel Exploration Journal*, 3: 2 (1953), p. 68; *Statistical abstract of Palestine, 1944-45*, p. 273.
15. Claude R. Conder, "The fertility of ancient Palestine," *Palestine Exploration Fund Quarterly Statement* (July 1876), 32.
16. Charles Warren, *The land of promise* (London, 1875), pp. 5–6.
17. Ellsworth Huntington, *Palestine and its transformation* (Boston: Houghton Mifflin, 1911), pp. 4–5. The book was also intended to bring a Christian message. Huntington wished to demonstrate how natural environment "prepared the way for the teachings of Christ." Since there was much water for supporting life during the time of the Romans, Huntington argues the population present to receive Christ's teachings was large. Among the proofs was that in 30 A.D., at the time of the Baptism of Christ, "the sea [of Galilee] stood high." Later, in "333 A.D., the Dead Sea stood as low as now. A dry era." The ensuing climatic catastrophe served to disperse the people of Palestine and therefore contributed to the dissemination of Christian teachings. Huntington was also writing in a new scientific tradition that endeavored to study climatic changes and the influence of these changes on history. See Hubert Lamb, *Climate: present, past and future* (London, 1972), pp. xxv–xxvi.
18. Huntington, *Palestine and its transformation*, p. 39.
19. Huntington, *Palestine and its transformation*, pp. 281–2.
20. David Ben-Gurion and Izhak Ben-Zvi, *Eretz Israel in the past and in the present*, (Hebrew) trans. from Yiddish by David Niv (Jerusalem: Yad Ben-Zvi, 1979). 25,000 copies were sold in three years and yielded funds that provided the main support of the American branch of Poalei Zion who supported the writing the book.
21. Ben-Gurion and Ben-Zvi, *Eretz Israel*, p. 223. The formula by which they arrived at this number is interesting, if naive. They investigated how many people were living in various parts of the country at the time and compared this with the numbers indicated by archaeological or biblically based textual evidence. In this way, they demonstrated that in many locations the contemporary population was but one-tenth of the ancient. The conclusion was simple. Since one million people were presently living in the area they examined, then ten million could live there in the future. Ben-Gurion and Ben-Zvi, *Eretz Israel*, pp. 214–222.
22. Ben-Gurion and Ben-Zvi, *Eretz Israel*, p. 227. They also suggested that the Arabs resident in Palestine were descendants of the Hebrews who converted to Christianity and Islam. This surmise foreshadows Palestinians reaching back in history to imagine themselves as Canaanites as will be discussed in Chap. 5.
23. William F. Albright, *The archaeology of Palestine and the Bible* (Cambridge, MA: American Schools of Oriental Research, 1974).
24. Nelson Glueck, *Rivers in the Desert: a history of the Negev* (New York: Norton, 1968), pp. xii and 283. See, too, Michael Evenari, "Twenty-Five Years of Research on Runoff Desert Agriculture in the Middle East," in *Settling the Desert*, ed. Louis Berkofsky, David Faiman and Joseph Gale (New York: Gordon and Breech, 1981), pp. 3–28.

25. Adolf Reifenberg, "The struggle between the "Desert and the Sown,"" in *Desert research: proceedings, international symposium held in Jerusalem, May 7-14, 1952 sponsored by the Research Council of Israel and the United Nations Educational, Scientific, and Cultural Organization* (Jerusalem, 1953): pp. 378–391.
26. Aryeh Issar, "Climatic changes as the critical factor in the settlement and abandonment of the desert frontier in Israel," Sede Boqer, unpublished paper, November 1987; Aryeh Issar and Haim Tsoar, "Who is to blame for the desertification of the Negev, Israel?" S. I. Solomon, M. Beran, W. Hogg, eds., *Proceedings of a conference on the influence of climatic change and climatic variability on the hydrologic regime and water resources: International Association of Hydrological Sciences*, publication no. 168 (Wallingford, Oxfordshire : International Association of Hydrological Sciences, 1987), 577–583.
27. Walter C. Lowdermilk, *Palestine: Land of Promise* (London: Harper, 1944).
28. Jean Gottmann, *Études sur L'état d'Isräel et le Moyen Orient, 1935-1938* (Paris: A. Colin, 1959). His impact on Palestinian geography was such that when the Hebrew University decided to establish a Chair in his discipline soon after the creation of the State, he was invited to be its first incumbent. This and other personal information derive from an interview with Professor Gottmann.
29. Robert Nathan, Oscar Gass, and Daniel Creamer, *Palestine: problem and promise, an economic study* (Washington, 1946), pp. v–vi.
30. Observations are from a personal interview with Mr. Nathan.
31. Arthur Ruppin, *Arthur Ruppin: memoirs, diaries, letters*, ed. Alex Bein (London; Weidenfeld and Nicolson, 1971).
32. Arthur Ruppin, "The Selection of the Fittest," in *Three decades of Palestine* (Jerusalem: Schocken, 1936), pp. 66–80.
33. Ruppin, "Settling German Jews in Palestine," in *Three decades of Palestine*, p. 278.
34. Troen, *Imagining Zion*, Chaps. 6 and 8.
35. David Ben-Gurion, *The reconstruction programme: an address to the Joint Meeting of the Elected Assembly of Palestine and the Zionist General Council, March 24, 1943*, Central Zionist Archives, S25/1943.
36. Aryeh Sharon, *Physical planning in Israel* (Jerusalem: 1951); and Erika Spiegel, *New Towns in Israel*; (urban and regional planning and development (New York: Praeger, 1967) Plan is examined in a concurrent report: Abraham Gruenbaum, *Four year development plan of Israel 1950-1953* (Hebrew) (Tel-Aviv, 1950).
37. "Immigration to Israel: Aliyah Bet (1939–1948)," *Jewish Virtual Library*. See: Aliyah Bet (1939–1948).
38. The data for 2020 is 9.3 million total population of the State of Israel and 4.8 million on the West Bank and Gaza. This total of 14.1 million is derived from two sources: U.S. Department of State, *2020 Report on International Religious Freedom: Israel, West Bank and Gaza*. https://www.state.gov/reports/2020-report-on-international-religious-freedom/israel-west-bank-and-gaza/west-bank-and-gaza/#:~:text=The%20U.S.%20government%20estimates%20the%20total%20Palestinian%20population,Muslims%2C%20with%20small%20Shia%20and%20Ahmadi%20Muslim%20communities; and Israel Central Bureau of Statistics, *Population of Israel on Eve of 2021*, see: https://www.cbs.gov.il/en/mediarelease/Pages/2020/Population-of-Israel-on-the-Eve-of-2021.aspx.

The number of Jews appears to be accurate and uncontested. The number of Arabs is disputed. Yoram Ettinger, a former Israeli ambassador, heads a research group that claims that the number of Arabs in the West Bank and Gaza is exaggerated by about a million. See: https://theettingerreport.com/category/jewish-arab-demographics/

39. Ilan Troen and Carol Troen, "Has Israel Reached he Limits of Growth? The economic and ecological absorptive capacity of Israel/Palestine," *The Journal of the Middle East and Africa*, 8:4 (2017), 309–23; Alon Tal, *The Land is Full; Addressing Overpopulation in Israel* (New Haven: Yale University, 2016).

Chapter 4
Possession and Dispossession Through Labor and Purchase

Introduction

Zionism and its supporters assumed that purchasing land and improving it through labor were unquestionably legitimate long before Arabs complained Zionism was a threat.[1] Although criticism of Zionists granting preference for Jewish workers emerged as Jewish immigration grew, the purchase of land by Jews was a different story altogether. Objections rooted in the religious identity of purchasers were established under Ottoman rule. When the British wrested control, acquisition of land by Zionist entities was understood as a manifest means of establishing a Jewish polity. Initially legal during the Mandate, and without the oblique circumventions and subterfuge that had characterized land purchases during the Ottoman period, objections to Jewish purchase came to be framed in terms of the injury to the Arab rural population. However, the transfer of unworked and un-reclaimed land was hardly the exclusive cause for uprooting or displacing fellahin nor were Jewish land purchases. The reduction of rural populations was a universal phenomenon that Palestine could not escape. Jewish pioneers did replace Arab peasants in settled and cultivated areas although the extent and causes, as will be suggested here, have been exaggerated and often concealed.

Arab opposition to the sale of land to Jews was well organized and widely supported. It generated increasing pressure on the British to limit Jewish immigration and land purchases. Within but two decades, through the 1939 White Paper, the British rescinded the promises made to Jews. The British chose the Arab side even as there remained support for Zionism to take root and grow in the country. Both sides had powerful adherents. The inability to resolve the contest between them gave rise to the idea of partition, first through a British commission in 1937 and subsequently in a United Nations decision a decade later. This contest of "rights" could not be resolved as a purely legal matter. Political pressures from both sides,

© The Author(s), under exclusive license to Springer Nature Switzerland AG 2024
S. I. Troen, *Israel/Palestine in World Religions*,
https://doi.org/10.1007/978-3-031-50914-8_4

the impact of realities both inside Palestine and Europe, and the eruption of violence that resulted in war ultimately determined the course of this bitter contest.

Labor

In the introduction, we outlined how, beginning with the Puritan invocation of Biblical verses that commanded mastering land and transforming it into a fertile garden, the virtue of labor was secularized. Enlightenment thought and Natural Law were cited to legitimate settlement from the early landings of English settlers on the Atlantic coast to the expansion of Americans to the Pacific through the nineteenth century. The revolutionary and post-revolutionary generations invoked the Jeffersonian ideal of the yeoman farmer. Through investment of labor, Americans took control of the continent, clearing forests and preparing the land for cultivation. White settler farmers took possession, curtailing the rights of the native Americans and confining them to lands reserved for them. The resulting possession and dispossession were sanctioned in John Locke's *Second Treatise on Government* that delineated hierarchies of ownership. The least title is held by one who does not invest labor such as a nut-gatherer. A shepherd invests more labor and thereby acquires greater rights. The farmer earns the strongest title due to the greatest exertion. Americans legislated this principle and established 1,500,000 homesteads of at least 160 acres. These lands were acquired with the minimal fee of registration but without purchase from the government. American pioneers had to work the land to actually achieve title. Similar legislation was enacted in lands associated with the British in Canada, Australia, and New Zealand.

Working the land was also a basic tenet of Zionism that granted the Jewish people title to Palestine. Zionism celebrated and even sanctified *avodah* [labor or work] in an emerging civil religion where it was a core value. A major Zionist youth movement called itself simply *Habonim*—"the builders." In the 1920s the infrastructure of the Yishuv was built in large measure by Labor Brigades [*geduday avodah*], young people who had recently immigrated from Europe who worked the land, paved the roads, and otherwise "built" the country. Labor, under a variety of names and alliances, was the major political movement that dominated Zionist politics before and after the state was established. Labor was celebrated in ideology, literature, song, poetry, and art. The iconic image of Zionist pioneering—the *halutz* and *halutza*, young men and women, tanned and muscular, carrying their tools against a transformed countryside with an appropriate slogan celebrating them and their exertions, was emblazoned on posters. Their ethos was captured in a popular song from the earliest days of Zionist pioneering: *we have come to the land to build it and be rebuilt by it* [*anu banu artzah livnot u'lehibanot bah*] and celebrated in "*Avodah*,"["work"] a 1935 landmark film documentary depicting the labors of Jewish pioneers.[2] Indeed, a paean to labor was suggested as an appropriate candidate for Israel's national anthem, instead of *Hatikvah* [the Hope]. Composed in 1894 by the young Hayim Nahman Bialik (1873–1934) who became Zionism's national poet, it bore the title "The People's Blessing" [*Birkhat Ha'am*] or *Techezaknah*—from the first word of the poem]:[3]

> Strong be your hands, O our brethren, who cherish
> The soil of our homeland, wherever you be;
> Never be downcast, but, lest your folk perish,
> Toil on exultant your people to free ...
> Scorn not small deeds, but, scoffers despising,
> Rescue your people with hoe and with plough,
> Till God's voice from the hills gives the signal for rising:
> The time for redemption has come; it is now.

Reverence for labor was widespread among Zionists and in Western thought. Aspiring to live on and cultivate land, Americans wrested control over a fertile, underused, and significantly unpopulated continent, and as other former Europeans had done elsewhere, took over desirable lands far from home. In contrast, Jews did not emigrate to a vast, fertile territory. They returned to an underdeveloped, semi-arid region that generations had prayed to regain, determined to "make the desert bloom" through their own labor. In traditional religious language, their task was to "redeem" the land [*ge'ulat ha aretz*]. They were neither subjects nor representatives of European empires. Their sole support was from voluntary organizations of fellow Jews or, in some cases, their own limited capital. Moreover, unlike European colonists elsewhere, they were obliged to address the rights of those already resident in the land. This obligation is explicit in the Balfour Declaration and the documents subsequent to it. Jews were not granted land. They did not use force to obtain it. Land had to be purchased and prepared for a national project. This required draining swamps, clearing rocks, digging wells, and installing irrigation. Everywhere it required introducing farming techniques different from the methods employed by local peasant agriculture. Zionist pioneers aimed at more than subsistence. It was a daunting task.

Restrictions on immigration and purchasing land that had been established by the Ottomans were expected to end under British rule. They did not. The British acceded to the demand of Palestine's Arab peasants to limit the intrusion of Jewish outsiders whom they viewed as threatening their communities and their right to continue working the land and maintaining their culture as they had always done. While British and other European colonizers typically disregarded such rights where they settled elsewhere, the British took care to ensure that Palestine would be different.

British concern for balancing the conflicting rights of Jewish settlers and Arab residents thereby became the frame for Jewish settlement. Jews might immigrate to the country and settle so long as, in the language of the Balfour Declaration, "nothing shall be done which may prejudice the civil and religious rights of existing non-Jewish communities in Palestine." Whether that could be done and how it was accomplished became the subject of a vast literature central to the Jewish-Arab conflict over Palestine.[4]

Sanctification of Labor

The celebration, and actually *sanctification*, of labor was deeply embedded in the Zionist movement, and not just limited to the various streams of "Labor" Zionism. It was an essential part of the search for "normalcy." All branches of Zionism wanted to change the civil status of Jews and to achieve the promised equality of citizenship in post-Enlightenment nineteenth century Europe. Many argued that Jews themselves had to change to become equal partners in a democratizing and nationalistic Europe after centuries of confinement to a ghetto. Jews had been barred from engaging in productive work, especially working the land, and confined to providing intermediary services related to commerce such as selling cattle, processing food products, and the like. The search for "normalcy" came to be expressed as "inverting the pyramid." That is, it was deemed necessary to establish a working class that included a significant number of farmers. That process was naturally extended to Palestine by those Jews who believed the return to the homeland was essential and an expression of their own national commitment.

This idea was powerfully promoted by the Russian-born Ber Borochov (1881–1917) who forged a blend of socialism with Jewish nationalism and participated with like-minded Zionist leaders in establishing *Poale Zion* [Workers of Zion]. For Borochov, devotion to Jewish nationalism was fundamental and he urged solidarity among Jewish workers. This entailed a strong proletarian base to radically replace the predominance of allegedly non-productive classes at the top that was said to characterize Jewish society. While that base was intended to be both agricultural and urban, in the Russia of 1900 where but ten percent of the Jews engaged in agriculture, it meant creating a Jewish peasant class.[5]

Borochov supported mobilizing the masses of European Jews for settlement in Palestine and advocated Jewish and Arab cooperation in an alliance between the two working classes, a concept of working-class solidarity borrowed from European socialist thought. However, in Palestine as in Europe, national loyalties persisted as socialists fought against other socialists in the trenches during World War I. Attempts to forge alliances between Jewish and Arab workers rarely succeeded even in new industrial enterprises such as the railroads and oil refineries. While the dream of class solidarity proved chimerical, the commitment to change Jewish occupational and class structure remained vital.[6]

Aaron David Gordon (1856–1922) was probably the most important individual who articulated and exemplified the ideal of labor. He maintained that the question of labor ultimately determines to whom the land "belongs," or who legitimately possesses it. Born into a family related to Baron Horace Guenzburg, one of the richest Jews in Russia, Gordon managed one of the Baron's estates through 1903. Middle-aged, white collar, and married with two almost grown children, he then emigrated to Palestine to become a simple worker. He was acting on a philosophy that he would soon share with a wide and appreciative readership.

A secularist, but religiously educated and deeply imbued with a mystical religiosity, he came to advocate what is known as the "religion of labor." A mystic, he romanticized the life of a peasant and life in nature as the essential path for Jews who would emigrate to Palestine. Emigration, too, was an essential part of his beliefs. A person or a people required connection with soil. A nation needed to be rooted in its own land. This basic idea involved not only inverting the pyramid but insisting that it be done in the land from which the nation had sprung. He therefore left the comfort of middle-class life in Russia for that of a simple farmer in Degania, Palestine's first collective farm.

His perspective bears close reading for it encapsulates a view shared across the broad spectrum of Zionist thought and action:[7]

> The Jewish people have been completely cut off from nature and imprisoned within city walls these two thousand years. We have become accustomed to every form of life, except to a life of labor—of labor done at our own behest and for its own sake. It will require the greatest effort of will for such a people to become normal again. We lack the principal ingredient for national life. We lack the habit of labor—not labor performed out of external compulsion, but labor to which one is attached in a natural and organic way. This kind of labor binds a people to its soil and to its national culture, which in turn is an outgrowth of the people's soil and the people's labor.

The ideology he espoused was acted on by thousands of pioneers and valued even by those who went to Palestine's cities to join its growing bourgeoisie. It was also the principled base on which one of the most contentious issues in the Yishuv was debated: should Jewish landowners hire cheaper Arab labor or employ only Jews. For Gordon, the choice was obvious:

> Let me put it more bluntly: In Palestine we must do with our own hands all the things that make up the sum total of life. We must ourselves do all the work, from the least strenuous, cleanest and most sophisticated, to the dirtiest and most difficult. In our own way, we must feel what a worker feels and think what a worker thinks—then, and only then, shall we have a culture of our own, for then we shall have a life of our own.

Blending a commitment to work within a commitment to collective, national ends was widespread. This choice was also pragmatic. Gordon's search for work led him from place to place and he endured great hardship. He did not live to enjoy an idealized life of a peasant on one parcel of land on which he and generations of his folk would work and construct the ideal society. But he embodied a search for individual and collective rootedness that was at the heart of the Zionist enterprise.[8]

The challenge of creating a Jewish working class was taken up even before the Zionist movement was formally established. When the Alliance Israelite Universelle set out to educate the Jews of Northern Africa and the Middle East beginning in the 1860s, its agenda included not only literacy in French culture but vocational schooling—skills for Jews who would work the land of Palestine. Thus, in 1870, it founded Mikve Israel, the pioneer agricultural training institution outside Jaffa for underprivileged Jewish youths living in the four holy cities of Jerusalem, Hebron, Safed and Tiberias. That effort trained some of the earliest pioneers of the agricultural colonies established in the 1880s and 1890s. By then, the Baron Rothschild, patron of many early settlements, had begun to send his experts from estates in France and North Africa to introduce Jewish farmers to advanced European methods. Even this paradigmatic capitalist considered farming to be ennobling. In so doing he achieved two purposes: he returned Jews to the land, and he lifted up their level from subsistence and the backward methods of local peasants. This became the pattern for philanthropists and Zionist organizations that exported European trained experts and brought Palestinian youth to Europe or the United States to learn the latest agricultural methods. This process of programmed education and scientific investigation lead to increasingly sophisticated knowledge of what might best be grown in the country. The result, ultimately, is that Israel became a highly sophisticated and successful center of agricultural research and training that not only transformed the local countryside but greatly contributed to agriculture in semi-arid regions worldwide.[9]

Necessity demanded no less. Creating a landed people required ingenuity, perseverance, and substantial financial investment. The challenge was not only environmental and human, but political. There was never enough land to satisfy the numbers of potential pioneers. The stark choice was either to find some way to productively employ Jews on available land or witness their departure to other venues.[10]

When land acquisition was not entirely blocked, it was significantly hindered by Palestine's Ottoman rulers. It therefore became essential to establish the minimal allotment necessary for supporting a family. At the end of the nineteenth century, the Baron Rothschild's experts thought in terms of 400 dunams (100 acres) per family, but that objective was gradually reduced to 100 dunams (25 acres) by the 1920s and in some models, that assumed women would help operate the farm thereby saving labor costs, even to 40 dunams (10 acres). The reduced allotments of land necessarily changed farming from field crops such as grains to dairy, poultry, vegetables, and fruits. The result was a variation of truck farming or market gardening where growers brought their produce to local markets to feed a growing urban population. Zionism did not lead to large estates cultivating bulk crops for sale in distant markets. Only citrus exports expanded as both Jews and Arabs developed and promoted the well-known brand "Jaffa" orange.[11]

Through this process, Jewish agriculture became increasingly distinct from traditional Arab farming in practices, implements, choice of items for cultivation and introduction of modern methods. In one respect there was similarity. Both Jews and Arabs lived in villages rather than homesteads or other individualistic forms of economic and social organization. For Arabs, villages often had a particular traditional religious, ethnic, tribal, or family cast; for Jews they were a practical way to encounter and master the land as well as communities of shared origins and ideological or religious orientation. Whether the few individual landowners or the large number of pioneers who preferred a form of communal ownership in a moshav or kibbutz, they entered into cooperative ventures if only to purchase equipment and other necessities and to sell their produce. This led to country-wide institutions that grouped together villages with similar characteristics that, in turn, sponsored and supported the establishment of new villages. Unlike America beyond the Appalachians where the land is marked with geometric grids enclosing individual farms, sometimes of significant size—the isolated "little house on the prairie"—an aerial view of Palestine reveals an irregular pattern of clusters of villages with distinctive sociological and ethnic characteristics.[12]

Villages made it possible for Zionist agencies to settle the maximum number of Jews on a minimal amount of land available for purchase and to nurture them to economic independence in the shortest period possible. When widespread Arab attacks erupted in 1929, defense became the priority. From that time on, purchases of land and limited resources were concentrated in areas that could be defended. This conscious policy produced the "N" of settlement that began in the upper Galilee to the Sea of Galilee, extended westward across the Jezreel Valley to the Mediterranean in the Haifa region, and then southward down the Mediterranean coast. Hundreds of moshavim and kibbutzim were planted within this "N" in the nearly two decades leading to independence in 1948. It also produced the settled territory out of which the Jewish state could be authorized and created.[13]

"Constrast of Jewish and Arab and Arab agriculture and technology. Arab farmers using traditional methods while Jewish agriculture made increasing use of machinery, especially tractors rather than human labor or animals, as well as modern scientific innovations."
Reproduced through the courtesy of the Yad Izhak Ben Zvi Photo Archive

Introduction of tractors. Photo of Jewish farmers using tractors as well as animals during an early stage of transition to modern methods in the Jezreel Valley, 1920. Courtesy of the KKL Archives, Jerusalem

Sanctification of Labor

Introduction of electricity. Hydroelectric dam built over the Jordan River in 1930 as part of a national Zionist initiative to modernize Palestine through electrification and irrigation. There was no generation of electricity in Palestine until after World War I and the British Mandate. This project was imagined and directed by Pinhas Rutenberg (1879–1942), Zionist leader and a founder of the Jewish Legion in WWI. Courtesy of the Central Zionist Archives

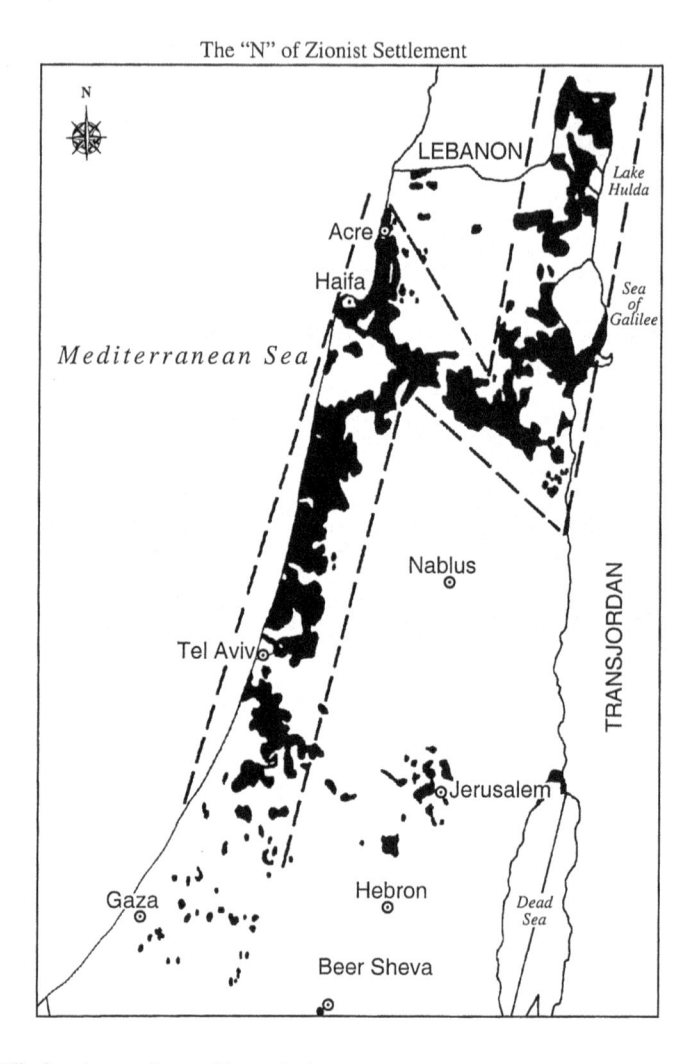

Map of "N" of settlement (created by author)

Arab protest that began with the countrywide violence of 1929 escalated in response to the actual and potential success of this strategic plan. The British responded with the White Papers of 1930—The Hope-Simpson Report and the Passfield White Paper—and as violence erupted even more dramatically during the "disturbances" of 1936–1939, produced the White Paper of 1939. They collected data to test the fundamental issues of how much land Jews might purchase and how many could settle in the country without impinging on the Arab population. This last White Paper concluded there would be no partition. This tragic context was not merely an abstract legal question.[14] Jewish immigration was limited to 25,000 annually and not to exceed a final total of 75,000 in the five years until 1944, among the most catastrophic years in Jewish history. By way of comparison, a total of 130,000 Jews entered Palestine from 1933 to 1936, with 62,000 in the peak year of 1935.[15]

The legal position established by the British was clear. However dire their need, the number of Jews allowed to enter the country was contingent on Arab objections to their presence and a calculation designed to ensure Jews would be a permanent minority in a modest sized, even small country. Leading British leaders, such as Lloyd George, Winston Churchill, and other supporters of the Balfour Declaration, claimed the real issue was fulfilling that commitment or betraying it. Clearly, the territory then designated as Palestine—from the Jordan River to the Mediterranean—sustains a far larger population of Jews and Arabs, and at far greater levels of prosperity, than the static, agricultural economy insistently imagined by the drafters of the White Papers. There was a total population of approximately 500,000 Arabs and Jews in 1900; nearly 2,000,000 when the British left Palestine in 1948; and more than 14,000,000 in 2020.

Disputes over abstract legal principles were not primarily resolved by legal arguments or adherence to formal commitments. By 1939, with World War II looming, the financial and military costs of governing a fractious country beset with competing nationalisms were becoming apparent to Britain. Moreover, Britain did not want to compromise its standing with the Arab world, so it acceded to the Arab position. Convinced their cause was both urgent and just, Zionists persisted. Ben-Gurion, the leader of the Yishuv, expressed this position succinctly in September 1939 with the outbreak of war: "We shall fight the War as if there was no White Paper, and the White Paper, as if there was no War."[16] The Yishuv consequently mounted a massive effort in "illegal" immigration during and after the war, and largely through collusion with Arab landowners, managed to circumvent restrictions on land acquisition so that the Jewish population and the extent of settlement continued to grow. At the same time, British support gave the Arabs of Palestine and beyond a sense of entitlement and justification for control over all of Palestine.

Background to Land Ownership in Palestine

To assess the contest over how much land was actually available and how it might be acquired, it is essential to examine how title to land in Palestine was established during the Mandate, at a time when there was no Arab state and no Jewish state.

The roots of the land law system established by the Ottomans and then modified or developed by the British through their Orders-in-Council, 1922–1940, went back to the Muslim conquest of Palestine between 636 and 640 C.E. Absolute ownership of the land was vested in the sovereign since it was won in a *jihad*, or holy war. It was therefore free from the tenurial rights of a feudal overlord as was widespread in Europe at that period.[17]

Under the Ottomans, there were several classes of land rights. M*ulk* and *miri* were the most widespread categories of ownership. *Mulk* was privately owned and could be considered "allodial" with title vested in individuals. The owners of *mulk* land had absolute and unfettered freedom in its use and disposition. It is important to note that there was little *mulk* land in Palestine, and it was found typically only in cities or in garden areas.

Miri, on the other hand, designates a conditional *usufruct* tenure of land held by grant of the state. That is, usufruct (*usus* or "use" and *fructus* or "fruit") is a legal right accorded to a person or party that confers *temporary* rights to its use to derive income or benefit from someone else's property. On this type of land, the state still benefits from regulations governing its use. *Miri* also benefited the state since it could be transferred to another individual if registered with fees paid for it. The state therefore owned and controlled the overwhelming amount of the land through the widespread presence of *miri*. These were never purchased outright. They were leased with various fees, typically taxes or tithes, associated with their use.

The state also had ultimate responsibility for other forms of land ownership. *Waqf* was land assigned to religious foundations whose revenues were directed to ecclesiastical institutions. Finally, and especially significant for Palestine, there was *mewat*, "dead" or underdeveloped land, that was also under state ownership. It encompassed relatively large proportions of what was included in the borders of Mandatory Palestine.

In effect, the Ottoman state and its British successor were invested as the most significant owners and disposers of land in Palestine. This would result in the British, as holders to the keys of control, becoming the target of both Jewish and Arab nationalist pressures. It was a position so difficult to manage that they were ultimately forced to surrender it.

The main source of tension over ownership and transfer of land in Palestine, however, was inherited from the Ottomans. When the British undertook responsibility for Palestine, they encountered a bureaucratic nightmare. The Ottomans had promised in mid-nineteenth century to establish order to claims of ownership with an exact survey of land titles and their registration, but that intention was ineffectively carried out and very far from completion. Little land was measured and registered, and many records had been lost. While the British made some progress, they, too, never provided a completed registry of ownership.[18]

Title to land in Palestine inevitably became a morass of conflicting claims. This was not unique in the lands carved out of the Ottoman empire, but such disorder contributed to the incendiary quality of the conflict in Palestine. What can be ascertained with relative certitude is that between the opening of the land registry under the British in 1920 and 1945, Jews purchased and registered 938,365 dunams [4 dunams = 1 acre]. They also owned through purchase 650,000 dunams during the late Ottoman period for a total of about 1,588,000 dunams.[19] In addition, they leased land from individual Arab owners and the Mandate. Had there been no opposition to Jewish settlement and had not the British removed entire sections from the possibility of purchase under Arab pressure, Zionist authorities would have purchased much more from willing Arab sellers and purchased or leased additional land from the Mandate itself. Thus, the politics of opposition undoubtedly suppressed the extent of land available for Jewish settlement. Nevertheless, the extent and location of Jewish acquisitions was significant enough that both the Peel Commission and the United Nations were able to draw maps for both an Arab state and a Jewish one together with an area around and stretching from Jerusalem towards the Mediterranean that was designated for international control.

By the time of British withdrawal in May 1948, Jews owned about 1,621,000 dunams with leases of another 181,000 dunams of state land, amounting to 11.4 percent of non-desert area north of the sparsely inhabited Negev. Sixty-six percent of Jewish land was in the northern valleys and the "fertile accessible coastal plain." In 1945 they owned 23 percent of the coastal plain, 30 percent in the northern valleys, and four percent of the hill country. Though this was a moderate amount of territory compared to the entire mandated area, that is, the land that became part of Israel's 1949 armistice lines, it was far less than the five million dunams the Zionists had expected to purchase in 1925. A lack of funds impeded Jews from aggressively buying more land before and after the establishment of the Mandate. By the time more funds became available, Arab opposition created immense obstacles. Nevertheless, the land Zionists succeeded in acquiring was crucial in enabling the creation of a Jewish national home for it was on these acquisitions that settlements were located and developed.

The modest percentages of land registered to Jewish ownership create the impression of the massive superiority of Arab holdings. This illusion, often employed in polemics, implies that the remaining land was "Arab." That is a distortion. As indicated above, it was the state—Ottoman and then British—that had title to most of the land in Palestine and it had the right to dispose of untitled and unregistered land. Thus, the percentages owned by Jews was significant to enable partition into Jewish and Arab entities. Identification of "Arab" is discussed in the chapter on Islam, along with the concept of the *Abode of Islam*.

A visual sense for the extent of the land that was not under cultivation is provided in the pages of several books of photographs. Palestine was extensively photographed from the air from WWI and subsequently by both the Germans and the British. The initial reason was obviously military. This base together with aerial photographs taken later by both Zionist and Palestinian advocates are striking and revealing. In two compendiums by Walid Khalidi, the pioneering Palestinian historian, hundreds of communities are captured with the "before-the-Nakba" or catastrophe of the 1948 War and the "after." His work shows villages, often destroyed and transformed into a Jewish settlement or town, and importantly also their extent and surroundings. B. Z. Kedar demonstrates, from an Israeli perspective, what the country looked like during WWI and, at the same points repeatedly until 1991, for a different purpose. His "before" is to demonstrate what the state has achieved. Both show very large areas of underdeveloped land, a record of how the country appeared to visitors during the Mandate. While Khalidi registers the destruction of what had been and Kedar celebrates what was yet to come, both illuminate the very considerable extent of untilled vacant lands available for Palestine's future development.[20]

Jewish Land Purchases

From the end of the nineteenth century to 1917, Jews managed to raise enough funds to purchase 420,000 dunams despite Ottoman restrictions. Agents for Jewish philanthropists and Zionist associations were successful in encouraging Arab owners to sell because of a dramatic increase in land prices.[21] During the Mandate, Arab landowners, inside and outside Palestine, continued to profit from the Zionist program. External sellers included very wealthy Arab residents in Lebanon, notably the Christian Sursock family of Beirut, but also prominent Muslim Palestinian families, including leadership who publicly advocated against sale to Jews and privately sold lands for the highest prices they could obtain. Indeed, even before World War I, reports in the Palestinian press directed critical public attention to this phenomenon.[22] Surprisingly, these transfers to Zionist hands included waqf lands that were to benefit Muslim religious establishments. Among sellers during the Mandate were members of the al-Husseini, al-Hajj, and al-Nashabibi families who included members of the Arab Executive. Other sellers were holders of public office such as mayors of Jerusalem, Tiberias, Gaza, Jaffa, as well as representatives of emerging Palestinian and trans-Arab organizations that lobbied against purchases by Jews.[23] So it is noteworthy that this deviation from public policy by large Arab landowners made Jewish settlement possible. The sale by small, individual landowners is less glaring and related to private needs and circumstances.[24] Given that unlike Europeans who settled in lands beyond their home countries, Jews did not have a colonial power supporting acquisition of land, the Zionist project could not have succeeded without the complicity of the local population. Nor was there a country on whom the settlers could depend as when the United States purchased much of what became western portions of the United States and Alaska. In Palestine, purchase was critical for realizing Zionist aspirations. It was at this critical and vulnerable point that the Arabs placed as much pressure as they could to stop Zionist settlement, even as some privately continued to sell land to Jews.

Dispossession

The purchase of land by Jews necessarily displaced some Arab farmers. However, attention to the fuller context, indicates that there were other factors at play and that purchase by Jews was not necessarily decisive in the transformation of the Palestinian countryside. Fellahin society was disintegrating before and without reference to Jewish settlement. It is an illusion to imagine stability existed or was possible in rural Palestine and that barring the arrival of Jewish pioneers, the rural Arab population would have continued to grow and prosper. Palestine was subject to similar processes that were impacting and uprooting farmers elsewhere. Traditional farming methods, particularly on relatively small parcels in a semi-arid country, was not a recipe for successful land tenure. Whether voluntarily or by force of circumstances, fellahin were leaving the land to find work, particularly in new urban centers. Specific problems stemmed from changes within the Ottoman Empire. Moreover, Jewish settlements brought benefits to many of those who remained.[25]

Farmers had been leaving their farms since the onset of the industrial and agricultural revolutions in many parts of the world. A useful measure of the general prosperity of a society is the proportion of the population that remains tied to agriculture. In the most successful countries, a decreasing proportion of the citizenry is engaged in farming and ever-increasing numbers are employed in diverse occupations. Moreover, in order to successfully introduce modern methods such as irrigation and machinery, farms must have far greater areas than that used for subsistence agriculture. Palestine's population was stagnant at a mere 250,000 in 1800, and it had increased to only 500,000 by century's end under conditions of persistent and rampant poverty. The population began to grow in the nineteenth century due to enhanced security, new farming methods introduced by Europeans—German Templars and Jews—and by the creation of alternatives to agriculture. Jews played an important role in these developments, as reflected in building what soon became the country's largest and wealthiest city, Tel Aviv-Jaffa, and in developing Haifa into a significant commercial and industrial hub.[26]

Security was crucial. Numerous observers deplored the limited and ineffective Ottoman control over the countryside. Large landowners did not provide protection from marauding Bedouins who pillaged and exacted tribute from the fellahin. In *The Land of Israel: A Journal of Travels in Palestine*, published in London, in 1865 by the Society for Promoting Christian Knowledge, H. B. Tristram described the damage inflicted by marauding Bedouins who "can muster 1000 cavalry and always join their brethren when a raid or war is on the move. They have obtained their present possessions gradually and, in great measure, by driving out the fellahin, destroying their villages and reducing their rich corn-fields to pasturage."[27]

Outside observers regularly described the wretched living conditions along the coastal plain, as in this description from 1913 that the Peel Commission included in its 1937 report:

> The road leading from Gaza to the north was only a summer track suitable for transport by camels and carts... in the rainy season it was impassable... no orange groves, orchards, or vineyards were to be seen until one reached Yabna village. Trees generally were a rare sight in these villages...Not a single village in all this area was water used for irrigation... Houses were all of mud. No windows were anywhere to be seen... Every house was divided in two parts—one part slightly elevated above the other. The family lived in the elevated part while in the lower part the cattle were housed. The cattle were small and poor. So were the chickens...The ploughs used were of wood. European ploughs were not known in the whole area... Fields were never manured... Every second year the fields were measured by stick and rope and distributed among the cultivators. Division of land always led to strife and bloodshed. The yields were very poor... The sanitary conditions in the village were horrible. Schools did not exist... The rate of infant mortality was very high. There was no medical service in any of the villages distant from a Jewish settlement... [28]

To varying degrees these conditions characterized life in the Galilee, the Beisan and Jezreel valleys, and down the coast. The Negev was not surveyed. It lacked areas of regular cultivation, towns or cities, and appeared to have remained unchanged over centuries. As noted above, Palestine's total population in the ancient world was far larger than at the end of the Ottoman period. A primary cause was centuries without a sovereign interested and able to protect and develop large areas of what would eventually constitute modern Palestine. Basic steps to organize and register title to land did not even begin until mid-nineteenth century, and then primarily as a means to facilitate tax collection and to allay blood feuds between villages, landowners, and cultivators.

Only towards the end of the nineteenth century did the Ottomans begin to develop transportation, including railroad lines, and to encourage development of largely vacant areas.[29] While significant improvements were undertaken during the Mandate by the British and Zionist settlement organizations, the massive transformation of the country began with the establishment of Israel. There was no comparable Arab authority or organization committed to developing the country and its economy. As a result, one scholar has observed, Palestine of the Mandate had a "dual economy." The Jewish sector far outpaced the Arab. The Yishuv came to enjoy a substantially higher standard of living and institutions that provided health, educational, and social services.[30]

The exports of the citrus industry (the noted Jaffa orange), perhaps the most profitable and extensive agricultural activity, did not prove an adequate exception despite the potential benefits that greater cooperation could have provided. Both the Jewish and Arab in the citrus sector enjoyed prosperity but on parallel tracks.[31] But most fellahin continued to live in relatively poor conditions. Indeed, some scholars maintain that these conditions explain the failure of a much larger Arab population to overcome the Jewish minority in the 1948 War that resulted in independence for Jews and the *Nakba* [catastrophe] for Arabs.[32] The *Nakba* was not simply a result of the Arab armies' failure to coordinate their campaigns or by collusion between Abdullah, the Jordanian king, and Zionist leaders. It was also attributable to the disintegration of Palestinian rural society that had began well before the arrival of Zionist pioneers.[33]

Oppressive tax and land tenure systems benefited large landowners and mostly urban merchants and moneylenders. The peasantry was often obliged to sell leases to their land to members of this economic elite, who, in turn, rented it back to fellahin to raise capital. In other words, many fellahim were legally dispossessed, even if some maintained access to land. Tenancy arrangements resulted in their precarious status as debtors. Substantial portions of their crops were required to pay these debts, but at least they could retain connection to land.

The dire situation of Palestinian Arabs at the height of the conflict between Jewish and Arab claims is attested to by statistics from a variety of reports. In 1936, 85 percent of the fellahin were illiterate. They were not using modern methods or power-driven machinery. A majority were in unproductive indebtedness to moneylenders who were often also the landowners. The standard rates were up to 30 percent in interest per year or even 50 percent for three months. As many as 40 percent lived on land owned collectively by village members that was, by custom, redistributed every few years. By tradition, they often farmed a collection of separate patches. The result of the above factors was a disincentive to invest in new methods such as irrigation and modern methods of agriculture. Probably another 25 percent were tenant farmers who paid a third of their income to absentee landlords in a semi-feudal relationship. Even those who were not in debt barely made a living on property composed of disconnected segments.[34]

In addition to being disadvantaged by Turkish reforms and the feudal underpinnings of Palestinian rural society, Islamic inheritance law compounded the challenges facing the peasant population. Since the law required land to be equally divided among the sons, the plots of land were continually smaller. The inevitable outcome was that many men became agricultural wage earners or left the land entirely. This was the prevailing situation when wealthy landowners sold land to Jews at inflated prices. Discontent and dissolution were widespread before and without relation to Jewish land purchases. Expressions of frustration were directed at landlords, merchants, the British, and not only Zionists. Yet even small numbers gave substance to critics of Jewish settlement.

Attempts to Alleviate Dispossession

To ameliorate this situation the Mandatory enacted legislation against usury, reduced taxes on grain production, and encouraged borrowing from government-approved banks. The British also built roads and promoted agricultural credit societies and diversification in produce to enhance income. But even before the Mandate was officially endorsed by the League of Nations, British authorities legislated provisions intended to alleviate the lot of fellahin threatened with removal. In 1920 and 1921, they enacted ordinances to regulate removal of agricultural tenants from land sold by their landlord. The Governor of a district (later the Director of Lands) was required to disallow transfer of agricultural land unless the tenant retained enough to maintain himself and his family.[35]

This did not work as intended since few tenants applied for such intervention. Rather, they buckled under the pressure of Arab landlords to whom they were in debt and accepted a measure of compensation. The Report termed this practice "unscrupulous pressure" by those to whom fellahin stood in a quasi-feudal relationship. At the same time, Zionists generally followed a policy of not purchasing land unless all tenants had been removed by the seller before the sale. The law meant to secure land so the fellahin could at least subsist was evaded by Arab landowners.[36]

The British persisted in efforts to improve and repair the inadequacies of the initial ordinances. The 1929 Protection of Cultivators Ordinance provided compensation for improvements made by tenants and for the disruption caused by removal. In 1933, under this scheme, 664 Arab families received compensation, but most claims were dismissed. In legislative terms, such a comprehensive Cultivators (Protection) Ordinance should have solved or seriously alleviated the problem. However, landlords still found means of evading the intention of the Ordinance by offering leases for less than the one-year minimum that entitled tenants to claim a relationship to the land they farmed. Leases of nine or ten months became the norm, long enough to cultivate and harvest a winter and a summer crop but not long enough to earn protection under the law.

The effort to tighten legislation in favor of tenants was criticized by Zionist authorities as a means to obstruct purchases of land by Jews: "It affords too great an opportunity for bogus claims and puts a premium on trespassing with the result that endless delays and great expense are incurred in resisting and buying off these claims before a clear title and undisputed possession of land can be obtained." British authorities acknowledged the validity of this complaint since, in the words of the State Domain Committee, current regulations were "a serious obstacle to the reasoned development of the country" in that it placed in the hands of tenants and trespassers a weapon with which they were able to victimize the landlords.[37]

The British failed to devise a scheme that satisfied the needs and rights of both landlords and tenants. Potential Jewish buyers wanted unencumbered land. The desire and need of Jews to acquire land undoubtedly contributed to the distress of the Arab farmers but it was just one of many tensions and accusations that characterized disputes over land tenancy and transfer.

Another failed effort to solve this problem was to resettle displaced Arab cultivators. Beginning in 1931, the British proposed to offer alternative lands, including those under their domain. The Arab Executive declined to participate in such a commission. The British persisted on their own and established a register of displaced farmers. Of the 3271 applications for resettlement in 1936, eighty percent were disallowed.[38]

The Jewish National Fund was also willing to engage in land transfers with the government to facilitate creating new lands on which Arab farmers might settle. They hoped that by inducing peasants to vacate lands they might create blocks for Jewish settlement. Such schemes were occasionally realized. In some areas, such as near Safed, Arab tenants were granted loans from the Mandate and, after a suitable period of working the land and building homes, received title. In other areas, such as Wadi el Hawarith near Tulkarm, resettled tenants refused to pay even nominal rents. The problem was complex, and solutions hampered by the need for cooperation by all the concerned parties.[39]

Arab and Jewish Land

Running throughout this painful and difficult history of claims and counterclaims is the view held by Jews and Arabs that land is embedded in national identity. It belongs to one group or another. That understanding, shared by a portion of the international community represented by the British, underlies the 1937 proposals for partition into a Jewish and an Arab state. That idea held for the following decade through the 1947 UN partition plan and through the present. What characterizes all partition proposals is a concern for the places holy to Christianity. Palestine was not only imagined a land for two states for two peoples. Rather, the country was to be divided into three parts. The additional section is an international area with holy sites sacred to Christians centered around Jerusalem. Since Christians lacked significant numbers on the ground, internationalization was the practical scheme to ensure Christian interests would be maintained apart from Muslim or Jewish control.

Religious identity was crucial in viewing the same territory and obtaining rights to it. Even the right to enter Palestine during the Ottoman period was based on connection to religious communities. For example, significant numbers of Circassians, a Muslim people from the northwest Caucasus region were dislocated by wars with Christian Russia and moved into the Middle East during the late Ottoman period. They could immigrate, settle, and purchase land. On the other hand, Christian Europeans and Jews were subject to disabilities or prohibitions. This helps explain why attempts by Jews to settle in Palestine encountered official as well as passionate and powerful popular opposition. There may well have been frictions but not of the same intensity nor framed by national, religious, or ethnic conflict.

The point is that the religious/national identity of those purchasing land and those investing their labor was crucial. Tensions would certainly have been generated even within the same population by transferring lands and dispossessing those who had been working it. Disintegration of the rural population engaged in traditional and relatively unproductive agriculture would certainly have continued. The right of a buyer to purchase and to work the land is a secondary issue whatever the consequences for tenants. The incendiary question concerns the religious identities of the landowner, the purchaser, and the farmer.

As noted above, identity was a fundamental issue under the Ottomans. They limited immigration and access to land to curtail the erosion of their authority by European states and European immigration. Jews were especially vulnerable to these restrictions because both they needed land and because, unlike Christian Europeans, did not automatically enjoy protection of Christian states and churches. When faced with difficulties, they turned to the consuls of the states in which they were citizens, and that included the American consuls. Muslims who were also moving to the Holy Land from Egypt or other Ottoman territories beyond Palestine and even from across the Mediterranean from the Balkans, faced no discrimination. As the Ottoman Empire drew to a close, the British declaration they would foster a Jewish national homeland in Palestine raised an alarm over especially Jewish immigration and land purchases.

In other words, what could have been an internationally sanctioned right to purchase land and invest labor was undermined by national and religious identity. Like much else in the Ottoman Empire, individual identity was subordinated to group identity. In fact, this was and remains the common experience in much of the world. I explore this in the next chapter on the uses of history to claim land as well as in Part II that examines claims based in theology. It appears that at least in Palestine, and perhaps throughout the Middle East, historical rights of groups, a subject omitted from Chief Justice Marshall's categories of rights, supersedes the rights discussed in this and in preceding chapters. Of all the secular rights examined in this first section, identity forged in history appears to have primacy.

Notes

1. Alan Dowty, "'A Question That Outweighs All Others'; Yitzhak Epstein and Zionist Recognition of the Arab Issue," *Israel Studies*, 6:1 (Spring, 2001), 34–54; Alan Dowty, "Much Ado about Little; Ahad Ha'am's 'Truth from Eretz Yisrael,' Zionism, and the Arabs," *Israel Studies*, 5:2 (Fall, 2000), 154–181.
2. Ofer Ashkenazi, "The Symphony of a Great Heimat: Zionism as a Cure for Weimar Crisis in Lerski's *Avodah*," in Jay Geller and Leslie Morris, *Three-Way Street; Jews, Germans, and Transnational* (Ann Arbor: University of Michigan Press, 2016), pp. 91–11.
3. https://jewishfilm.org/Catalogue/films/avodah.htm; https://opensiddur.org/prayers/civic-calendar/state-of-israel/yom-haatsmaut/the-peoples-blessing-by-hayyim-nahman-bialik-1894/
4. Moshe Mossek, *Palestine immigration policy under Sir Herbert Samuel: British, Zionist and Arab attitudes* (London: Frank Cass, 1978).
5. Arthur Hertzberg, "Ber Borochov," *The Zionist Idea; A Historical Analysis and Reader* (Philadelphia: Jewish Publication Society, 1997), pp. 353–74; Gideon Shimoni, *The Zionist Ideology* (Hanover, NH: University Press of New England, 1995), pp. 179–88.
6. A critical analysis of the priority of nationalism over class solidarity among Zionists in Palestine is Zeev Sternhell, *The Founding Myths of Israel: Nationalism, Socialism, and the Making of the Jewish State* (Princeton: Princeton University Press, 1999).
7. Aaron David Gordon, "People and Labor (1911)," in Hertzberg, *The Zionist Idea*, pp. 372–74.
8. For the challenges confronting labor through the biography of an ideological leader see Anita Shapira, *Berl: The Biography of a Socialist Zionist, Berl Katznerlson, 1887-1944* (Cambridge: Cambridge University Press, 1984).
9. S. Ilan Troen, *Imagining Zion; Dreams, Designs, and Realities in a Century of Jewish Settlement* (New Haven: Yale University Press, 2003), Chaps. 2 and 3.
10. For the entries and exists of potential pioneers see Gur Alroey, *An Unpromising Land*, op. cit.
11. Troen, *ibid*; Nahum Karlinsky, *California Dreaming: Ideology, Society and Technology in the Citrus Industry of Palestine, 1890-1939* (Albany: SUNY, 2005).
12. Troen, *Imagining Zion*, Chap. 1.
13. Troen, *Imagining Zion*, p. 71.
14. Arieh Kochavi, "The struggle against Jewish immigration to Palestine," *Middle Eastern Studies*, 34:3 (July 1998), 146–167.
15. *Arab and Jewish immigration to Palestine from 1920-1945, prepared by the British Mandate to the United Nations*, https://www.palestineremembered.com/Acre/Books/Story835.html.
16. David Ben-Gurion, "Minutes, Mapai Central Committee," 12 September 1939, *Ben-Gurion Archives* (Sde Boker) [Hebrew].
17. A useful summary and explanation of types of land, their uses, and government regulations can be found in *Anglo-American Committee of Inquiry, A Survey of Palestine prepared in December 1945 to January 1946* (Palestine: Government Printer, 1946), vol. 1, pp. 225–308. An essential summary and overview are A. Granott, *The Land System in Palestine; History and Structure* (London: Eyre and Spottiswood, 1952); A useful overview of the issues raised in this section by

an authoritative source that references official documents of the period, see Esco Foundation for Palestine, "Problems of the Arab Cultivator," *Palestine; A Study of Jewish, Arab, and British Policies* (New Haven: Yale University Press, 1947), pp. 704–722.
18. Dov Gavish and Ruth Kark, "The cadastral mapping of Palestine, 1858-1928," *op. cit.*
19. Kenneth Stein, *Land Question in Palestine, 1917-1939* (Chapel Hill, N.C.: University of North Carolina Press, 1984), pp. 173–211 and appendices.
20. Walid Khalidi, *Before Their Diaspora: A Photographic History of the Palestinians, 1876-1948* (Washington, D.C. : Institute for Palestine Studies, 1991); and W. Khalidi, *All That Remains: The Palestinian Villages Occupied and Depopulated by Israel in 1948* (Washington, D.C. : Institute for Palestine Studies, 1992); the opposite perspective using aerial photos is B. Z. Kedar, The Changing Land between the Jordan and the Sea: Aerial photographs from 1917 to the Present (Jerusalem and Tel Aviv: Yad Ben-Zvi and Israel Ministry of Defense, 1999).
21. K. Stein, *Ibid.*
22. Emanuel Beska, *From Ambivalence to Hostility: The Arabic Newspaper Filastin and Zionism, 1911–1914* (Bratislava: Slovak Academic Press, 2016), pp. 75–94.
23. Arieh L. Avneri, *The Claim of Dispossession: Jewish Land Settlement and the Arabs* (New Brunswick, New Jersey: Transaction Books, 2006), 219–234; Stein, *Land Question in Palestine, 1917-1939*, pp. 228–238; Yehoshua Porath, *From Riots to Rebellion: The Palestinian-Arab National Movement*, 1929-1939 (London, 1977), vol. II, pp. 80–84.
24. Ruth Kark, "Consequences of the Ottoman Land Law: Agrarian and Privatization Processes in Palestine, 1858–1918," in Raghubir Chand, et. al, ed. *Societies, Social Inequalities and Marginalization, Marginal Regions in the 21st Century* (Cham, Switzerland: Springer: 2017), pp. 101–120. By the beginning of the Mandate, 144 large landholders held 3,130,000 Ottoman dunums of land in Palestine, whereas 16,910 peasant families cultivated 785,000 duunums. A. Scholch. "European Penetration and the Economic Development of Palestine, 1856–82," in R. Owen, ed., *Studies in the Economic and Social History of Palestine in the Nineteenth and Twentieth Century* (Carbondale, IL: Southern Illinois Press, 1982), p. 24.
25. Issa Khalaf, "The effect of socioeconomic change on Arab societal collapse in Mandate Palestine," *International Journal of Middle East Studies*, 29:1 (Feb. 1997), 93–112; Arieh L. Avneri, *The Claim of Dispossession: Jewish Land Settlement and the Arabs* (New Brunswick, New Jersey: Transaction Books, 2006), pp. 219–234; Stein, *Land Question in Palestine*, 228–238; Granott, *The Land System in Palestine*, p. 87.
26. Troen, *Imagining Zion*, Chaps. 5, 6. For a critical view of the reorganization of the Palestinian landscape in a comparative perspective see Gary Fields, *Enclosure; Palestinian Landscapes in a Historical Mirror* (Berkeley: University of California Press, 2017).
27. H. B. Tristam, *The Land of Israel: A Journal of Travels in Palestine* (London: Society for Promoting Christian Knowledge, 1865) p. 488, quoted in Moshe Aumann, *Land Ownership in Israel* (Jerusalem: Israel Academic Committee on the Middle East, 1970), p. 118.
28. *Report of the Royal Commission* (Peel Commission) chapter 9, para 43, pp. 233–234.

29. As an example of Ottoman initiated development see Ruth Kark and Seth Frantzman, "Bedouin, Abdül Hamid Ii, British Land Settlement, and Zionism: The Baysan Valley and Sub-district 1831–1948," *Israel Studies*, 15:2 (Summer 2010), 49–79.
30. Jacob Metzer, *The divided economy of Mandatory Palestine* (Cambridge: Cambridge University Press 1998), pp. 55–58. Other useful studies closer to the period include David Horowitz, *Economic trends of Jewish development* (Jerusalem: Jewish Agency, 1947), can be found in the Central Zionist Archives: CZA S25/5934, 1937.
31. Karlinsky, *California Dreaming*.
32. Issa Khalaf, "The effect of socioeconomic change on Arab societal collapse in Mandate Palestine," *International Journal of Middle East Studies*, 29:1 (Feb. 1997), pp. 93–112.
33. Khalaf, "The effect of socioeconomic change on Arab societal collapse," 93–94.
34. J. C. Hurewitz, *The Struggle for Palestine* (New York: Norton, 1950), pp. 32–33.
35. Ibid.
36. *A Survey of Palestine, op. cit.*, p. 288.
37. *A Survey of Palestine, op. cit.*, p. 292–293.
38. *A Survey of Palestine, op. cit.*, p. 296.
39. The story of the dispossession of the tenants of Wadi Hawarith has drawn much attention. A detailed and sympathetic study is Raya Adler, "The Tenants of Wadi Hawarith: Another View of the Land Question in Palestine," *International Journal of Middle East Studies*, 20:2 (May, 1988), 197–220.

Chapter 5
History as Legitimacy

Claims Derived from History

Historical narratives are interwoven in all categories of secular claims to territory. Nevertheless, "history" merits separate attention since it has emerged in recent decades as singularly important, contentious, and even sensational. Appeals to secular history began to become significant after the Enlightenment through the nineteenth century. Before then and to the present it is theology that has often connected peoples to territory both through interpretations of the past and expectations for the future. The function of theology in supporting legitimacy is treated in later chapters. This chapter examines how territorial rights are legitimated without reference to the presumed role of God in the past and to divine intentions.[1]

History emerges as increasingly integral to nationalism through the nineteenth century by describing where the group originated, how it acted over time, and expectations for its future role in human affairs. "Manifest Destiny," for example, was invoked in America during the first half of the nineteenth century to justify supplanting natives with white settlers across the continent. It spoke to the future role of the American people though without reference to the past. In the case of the conflict over Palestine, history is commonly used by the contending parties to legitimate control over land by invoking past experience and achievements.

Since territory is rarely inhabited exclusively by a single group for long periods, territories are crowded with as many self-serving historical justifications as there are groups living in them. These may be expressed in the genesis of a national literature in novels, stories, poetry, and folklore as well as in flags, symbols, anthems and more. In the case of Zionism, the flag of the State of Israel as well as its national anthem were introduced and became widely accepted at the end of the nineteenth century. The flag was modeled on the *tallit* or prayer shawl with its blue stripes on white background emerged by the 1890s as the banner of the Zionist movement together with the six-pointed star or shield of David that itself became popular in

© The Author(s), under exclusive license to Springer Nature Switzerland AG 2024
S. I. Troen, *Israel/Palestine in World Religions*,
https://doi.org/10.1007/978-3-031-50914-8_5

mid-nineteenth century to signify Jewish national identity. By the 1890s, Zionist organizations were parading the prototype of the Israeli flag in settlements in Palestine, American cities, and it was featured in 1904 together with a display of the flags of other nations at the World's Fair in St. Louis.[2] Israel's national anthem dates from the same period. Both were closely associated with the newly emerging Jewish national movement and its claim to Palestine. The final stanza of *Hatikvah* or "the hope" declares:

As long as in the heart within,	Our hope is not yet lost,
The Jewish soul yearns,	The hope that is two-thousand years old,
And toward the eastern edges, onward,	To be a free nation in our land,
An eye gazes toward Zion.	The Land of Zion, Jerusalem.[3]

During this period much contemporary patriotic music was written to reflect distinctive national characteristics through folk materials and events as in the compositions of Bartok (Hungary), Sibelius (Finland), Smetna (Czech Republic), Copland (United States); "classical" forms that were shared widely across Europe were deemed universal and free of nationalist meanings.

Historical references in multiple cultural forms defined and declared national identities and distinctive national aspirations that were conveyed and nurtured in politics. In the case of Zionism, they proclaimed a public assertion before the international community that modern Jews constitute a "people" and merited a "homeland." The League of Nations played a key role in ratifying and corroborating the Zionist narrative concerning the Jewish past in Palestine. The League went further. Referencing the Balfour Declaration, it promised to support the return Jews to their homeland in Palestine as active members of the family of nations.

The Significance of Being "First"

History is used to legitimate both Jewish and Palestinian nationalism and is written into their foundational documents. Both the Israeli Declaration of Independence (1948) and the Palestinian National Charter (1968) make extensive use of history. The Israeli narrative begins with the ancient world and continues into the present, while the Palestinian focuses on more recent events. As suggested later in this chapter, a more recent effort to place the origin of present-day Palestinians in the ancient world is a new phenomenon that follows from the spread of a contemporary legal definition of "indigeneity" from around the 1960s.

Jews had an enormous advantage in deploying historical arguments since widespread acquaintance with the Bible established them as significant historical actors for nearly two millennia, from the period of Abraham (ca. 1700 BCE) through the destruction of First Temple (586 BCE). Thereafter, through well after the Romans conquered Jerusalem and destroyed the Temple in 70 C.E., a host of writings in Hebrew, Greek and multiple other sources testify to their role in the country's history and beyond. So do a plethora of physical remains identifiable with the Hebrews. Their presence in the Holy Land for such a long period is extraordinarily well documented and generally accepted as valid.[4] So is the continuity of their role in history through an exile that brought them to many lands where the association with their homeland was accepted as part of their identity. This record is detailed in the opening paragraphs of the Israeli Declaration:

> *The land of Israel was the birthplace of the Jewish people. Here their spiritual, religious and national identity was formed. Here they achieved independence and created a culture of national and universal significance. Here they wrote and gave the Bible to the world.*
>
> *Exiled from Palestine, the Jewish people remained faithful to it in all the countries of their dispersion, never ceasing to pray and hope for their return and the restoration of their national freedom.*
>
> *Impelled by this historic association, Jews strove throughout the centuries to go back to the land of their fathers and regain their statehood. In recent decades they returned in masses...*

This widely accepted appreciation of Jewish history poses challenges claims of Palestinian rights. The Palestinian National Charter opens with an assertion that has no definite beginning: "*Palestine is the homeland of the Arab Palestinian people; it is an indivisible part of the Arab homeland, and the Palestinian people are an integral part of the Arab nation.*" The many paragraphs that follow recite recent history, beginning with the charge that the Balfour Declaration of 1917 has undermined their historic if indeterminate connection with Palestine. Nevertheless, in the face of losses in wars with Israel, the Charter insists that "*The Palestinian Arab people possess the legal right to their homeland and have the right to determine their destiny after achieving the liberation of their country in accordance with their wishes and entirely of their own accord and will.*" Moreover, whatever the length of the connection, "*The Palestinian identity is a genuine, essential, and inherent characteristic; it is transmitted from parents to children.*"

The Charter's assertion of Palestinian legal rights as historic entails a sweeping denial of the historic legitimacy of Jewish claims. There are repeated repudiations of Balfour, the Mandate, partition and all other international decisions and actions in support of the Jewish claim. The Charter explicitly rejects that Jews constitute a nation with a valid historic claim to the Holy Land in Article 20: "*Claims of historical or religious ties of Jews with Palestine are incompatible with the facts of history and the true conception of what constitutes statehood. Judaism, being a religion, is not an independent nationality. Nor do Jews constitute a single nation with an identity of its own; they are citizens of the states to which they belong.*" Instead of being a legitimate nation with a history and rights, Article 22 maintains that "*Zionism is a political movement organically associated with international imperialism and antagonistic to all action for liberation and to progressive movements in the world. It is racist and fanatic in its nature, aggressive, expansionist, and colonial in its aims, and fascist in its methods ...*"[5]

Ancestors are central to competing historic claims of being the earliest presence in the ancient land. Palestinians infer their ancient history from documents and physical remains of civilizations that have long since disappeared. To be "first" they trace their origin to the ancient Canaanites who, according to the Bible, preceded the Hebrews as occupants and rulers of what became Palestine. A strident subset of historical claims about the arrival of Bedouins to the Negev takes us back only six centuries at most. However near or distant, historical narratives have become intimately intertwined with the polemics of the contemporary conflict.

While ancient texts and monuments record a prominent Jewish presence in the ancient world, the connection between that people and modern Jews is vigorously denied. Some Palestinian analyses claim that European Jews are actually descendants of the Khazars, a Turkic people who dominated a large region around the Caspian Sea between Eastern Europe and southwestern Asia and converted to Judaism more than a millennium ago. It is claimed that, with the end of that empire, their descendants spread westward into the lands of Europe. This narrative is said to prove that contemporary Jews are merely a religious group. They are unrelated to the Hebrews, a people who may have once lived in Canaan with, at best, a passing significance.[6] This fanciful narrative is invoked as evidence that recent Jewish immigrants are merely Europeans. In the age of European expansion, they ventured across the globe and usurped the lands of natives. As such they are the most recent participants in a colonialist enterprise, not an authentic people returning to a homeland. A related but distinctive charge declares the very idea of a Jewish people is an "invention" of some European Jews in the nineteenth century.[7]

The intentional impact of such inventions is to mask the fact that the Arab/Israeli conflict is actually between two competing native, national movements. The creation of the State of Israel is but another example of European settler-colonialism and, *ipso facto*, illegitimate. We will reexamine the charge that Zionism is a colonial-settler movement at the end of this chapter. Suffice to observe here that this contention is leveled against Jewish claims stemming from purchase, investment of labor and immigration. The fundamental criticism is that the Zionists have intruded on the region. As strangers their presence is illegitimate and their settlement project is inherently flawed, no matter how it was carried out.[8]

Defining "Indigeneity"

The injection of "indigeneity" into the Arab/Israeli conflict is recent. It conflates a critique of Zionism with a contemporary legal concept conceived to protect the rights of authentic indigenous peoples such as the First Nations in Canada and the Aborigines in Australia. It was rarely applied in a modern legal sense to the Arabs of Palestine and the Arab/Israeli conflict. "Indigenous" was used by Arab spokesmen following the Balfour Declaration and the decision of the League of Nations to establish the British Mandate in association with the right to "self-determination" of a majority population that claimed the presence of ancestors prior to immigration of Zionist pioneers. It is not surprising that they viewed the growing immigration of European Jews as a form of European imperialism and colonialism. As noted earlier, the Ottomans were wary of Europeans and particularly of Jews who wished to settle. "Indigenous" was used to designate settled populations throughout the post-Ottoman Middle East. Arabs in Palestine were not exceptional to demanding the right to self-determination and many imagined themselves as part of a future enlarged Syrian Arab state.[9]

The contemporary use of "indigenous" comprises a wide international definition designed to protect vulnerable populations unknown to Europeans prior to the discoveries of Columbus in regions far from the Arab Middle East. It was first applied to the Arab-Israeli conflict during the 1990s to advocate Bedouin claims in disputes over land ownership in Israel's Negev. It has since gained currency to assert historic claims across the internal divisions within Arab society in Israel. This use features in the opening sentence of the *Future Vision of the Palestinian Arabs in Israel* (2007), a document prepared by a large cross-section of the Palestinian Arab leadership in Israel. It declares "*We are the Palestinian Arabs in Israel, the indigenous peoples, the residents of the States of Israel, and an integral part of the Palestinian People and the Arab and Muslim and human Nation.*" The use of the plural in "States" and "*peoples*" is intentional and reflects the contention that "Palestinian" is a category that embraces diverse subgroups that constitute the contemporary non-Jewish population. The definite article *the* implies Palestinian Arabs are the sole acknowledged long-resident population with rights over the land. By implication, Jews are not part of this ancient history; they are but recent foreign interlopers.[10]

All uses of "indigenous" are obviously based in historical interpretation. In ordinary usage "indigenous" applies not only to people but to plants and animals. The Latin root means "native" or "born in a country" and indicates that something exists naturally in a particular place. It is readily interchangeable with "native" in reference to humans, fauna, or flora; "alien" and "foreign" are antonyms. Although the term first appeared in the mid-seventeenth century and enjoys minor but continual use until the mid-twentieth century, "indigenous" acquired present-day legal and political use during the 1960s. The International Labor Organization applied the term to support the rights of disadvantaged and vulnerable tribes in Central and South America, descendants of the native inhabitants exploited by European colonization.[11] Protecting indigenous communities included safeguarding their cultures and languages as well as rights to their lands, natural resources, and environment.

Over the following decades, the movement became part of the agenda of the UN and NGOs,[12] and culminated in the United Nations Declaration on the Rights of Indigenous Peoples in 2007.[13] Its application has been incomplete and contentious. The UN "declaration" is not legally binding. It is not a "treaty" due to internal dissension and disagreements on who is "indigenous" and which rights should be protected.

The movement spread from Central and South America to include the First Peoples of Canada and Native Americans. Canada and the United States initially delayed signing and ultimately registered reservations. Both argued that sovereignty resides in the modern state and is not shared with indigenous groups. The same assertion was adopted in other parts of the world, notably Australia, New Zealand, and other lands where "aboriginals"—an alternative term for "indigenous"—demanded the right to their territory and their own culture. Similarly, European and

African states resist applying the term since that has such obvious potential for internal political disruption as in Spain, Belgium and the former Yugoslavia where "indigenous" groups contend with the national government for control of territory.

Advocates for Negev Bedouin rights adopted the "indigenous" argument despite or perhaps because of its fuzziness, into the discourse of the Israel-Arab dispute.[14] As I noted, the *Future Vision Documents* uses the term to designate Arab citizens of Israel, and its focus on "affiliation, identity and citizenship of the Palestinian Arab in Israel" and it uses "indigeneity" to mark a dichotomy between Jews and Arabs. While some Jewish citizens were considered "native" under the Ottomans, unlike native Arabs, their rights were curtailed.

The international community that supported the creation of a Jewish polity typically viewed Jews as native to Palestine. Through the Balfour Declaration (1917), the British Mandate for Palestine (1922), and the UN decision to partition Palestine into a Jewish and an Arab state (1947), affirmed the legitimacy of an independent Jewish polity in Palestine. Modern Jews, too, saw themselves and were viewed as continuous with an ancient people and with the right to re-establish themselves in their Promised Land. The Mandate explicitly gives recognition *"to the historical connection of the Jewish people with Palestine and to the grounds for reconstituting their national home in that country."*[15] The *"re"* means "again." Jews were entitled to *re-turn, re-build, re-store, re-establish* and *re-constitute* themselves in their historic homeland. Moreover, Jews were a "people" and entitled to the rights other peoples enjoyed. This was part of a broad international consensus.

When the Ottomans captured Constantinople (1453) and Jerusalem (1517) as part of a campaign to gain control of the entire Middle East and beyond, the Jews were there. Ottoman territories comprehended a multitude of ancient populations of different religions and ethnicities. Within this mosaic of identities, in accordance with established Islamic practice that dates from the spread of Islam in the seventh century, Christians and Jews were relegated to the status of *dhimmis*. That is, they were legally protected by the authorities but were required to pay a special tax due to their inferior status. Jews could attain prominence and own land in the Ottoman Empire. Although they were legally separate and inferior, they belonged. Indigeneity was not at issue.

Jews similarly assumed they belonged. No one questioned their deep roots in the Middle East. Some contemporary scholars have come to identify them as "Arab-Jews." While some had roots in the Middle East extending back more than two millennia, others were relatively "recent" arrivals as émigrés from the Spanish Inquisition inaugurated in 1492. It was imagined these Oriental Jews might serve as a bridge between the newly arrived Zionist pioneers from Europe and their Arab neighbors. Such efforts ultimately failed. The local Arab population felt threatened by the influx of a possibly emergent majority of Jewish *dhimmis*. When tensions rose and then erupted in the 1920s, the long-resident, local communities of largely Sephardi Jews identified with the new arrivals.[16]

The distinction between long-settled Jews and new arrivals is made explicit in the clauses of the Palestinian Liberation Organization's 1964 Charter and repeated in subsequent iterations of official statements. Articles 5–7 state that *"The Palestinian personality is a permanent and genuine characteristic that does not disappear. It is transferred from fathers to sons.*" Palestinians are "*Arab citizens who were living normally in Palestine up to 1947 ... whether in Palestine or outside.*" Moreover, "*Jews of Palestinian origin are considered Palestinians if they are willing to live peacefully and loyally in Palestine.*"[17] Article 6 in the Charter's 1968 version clarified that: "*The Jews who had normally resided in Palestine until the beginning of the Zionist invasion will be considered Palestinians.*"[18] In other words, according to the Charter, some Jews could be considered natives or indigenous, but not those who hailed from Europe. They were tainted by the anti-imperialistic charge that defines them, *a priori,* as intruders, alien to Palestine.

More to the point, categorization of all Jews by the Charter is not merely time-bound by area of residence. Neither European nor Palestine-born Jews are regarded as members of a distinctive people. They are not a nation but merely members of a confessional faith, as are Christians. Both are *dhimmis*, without inherent rights of governance and sovereignty. Thus, length of residence in Palestine is irrelevant to the possibility of viewing Jews as having equal rights. Even when indigenous, they are *not* a *people*.

This view is in stark contrast to how the international community related to Jews as an authentic historical people who may or may not hold to a distinctive faith. International recognition for the legitimacy of a Jewish polity in Palestine was grounded in this understanding in the period when national rights of peoples—not as members of a faith community — were given primacy, as in Wilson's 14 Points and in the concept of a League of *Nations*.

The refusal to recognize Jews as a people remains a crucial element in the discourse that delegitimizes Zionism, a discourse that draws not only on both newly formulated secular arguments but also on traditional theology. Defining the Arabs of Palestine as the sole *indigenous people* in that territory has far-reaching implications. Unsubstantiated assertions that the Palestinians are *the* indigenous people implicitly brands Jews as invaders and the Jewish state as a colonial-settler society with an imperialistic mission.

Ironically, the move to strip Jews of nationality was abetted by some nineteenth century assimilationist Western European Jews, chiefly French and Germans "of the Mosaic Faith," who identified themselves as citizens of newly formed European states. As demonstrated by Jonathan Gribetz's analysis of publications of the PLO research center in Beirut, Palestinians adopted this position in the 1960s from the profoundly anti-Zionist American Council for Judaism (founded in 1942).[19] While many Jews did not define themselves as Zionists, they viewed themselves as a people. From the earliest sacred sources, they are described as a "chosen" people [*'am segulah*], bound together by an eternal covenant with the Lord. Palestinian nationalism nevertheless chose to define Jews as a faith community, like Christians, and denies they are a people.[20] This entrenched idiosyncratic view is embodied in Palestinian rejectionism. It willfully ignores how Jews understood themselves over millennia and even how the Nazis and their accomplices determined to eradicate the entire Jewish *people*, and not mere individuals with a particular religious identity. A final bitter irony is that Europeans often characterized Jews as "Orientals," swarthy alien others who did not belong in their midst.[21] In sum, the secondary or inferior status assigned to Jews in the Middle East is an old story. The attempt by the League of Nations to alter the status of Jews was met with opposition, both political and physical, that relentlessly challenged revolutionary but temporary changes and eroding them until they were entirely erased by the implications of the 1939 White Paper.[22]

Secular History

However fuzzy its definition, indigeneity is a historical category and can be examined in both religious and secular frames. For Jews, Christians, and Muslims, the land between the Jordan and the Mediterranean is not just a place. It is the Promised Land and the Holy Land or *Eretz HaKodesh*, *Terra Sancta*, and *Al-Arḍ Al-Muqaddasah*. Views of Israel/Palestine and its peoples are inevitably filtered by sacred texts and beliefs. Beginning with the Hebrew Bible, monotheistic theologies include historical narratives of God's promises in assigning this land. These theological narratives are the core subject of Part II of this book. Here, I focus on non-theological or secular views.

Secular historical discourse that identifies indigenous ancestors is fundamental to national movements claiming contested territory. In the case of Israel/Palestine, the exceptionally rich layers of textual evidence and physical remains that testify to the antiquity of its civilizations tempted contemporaries to conceive of a bridge connecting the recent with the distant past. That process began with the rise of nationalism among various populations towards the end of the Ottoman Empire and in its immediate aftermath. It burst forth again following the 1967 Six-Day War with the catastrophic defeat of Nasser. That event contributed to cultivation of local identities and the demise of pan-Arabism's vision of a unified Arab nation spanning the Middle East and extending through North Africa.

Local identities were also nurtured earlier, the two World Wars. Kemal Ataturk, the leader of the secular Turkey, who emerged from the demise of the Islamic Ottoman Empire advanced a claim of Turkey's Hittite origins.[23] At around the same time, particularly in the 1920s, Mesopotamian antiquity was reclaimed by nationalists in Iraq. Egyptians, notably the Coptic Christian minority, reached back beyond Islam to connect with the Pharaonic period. Lebanese Maronite Christians adopted the Phoenicians as their ancestors. By the end of the 1930s even a coterie of Jews imagined themselves as the Hebrew branch of a Canaanite people.[24]

After Nasser's colossal defeat in the 1967 Six-Day War, additional distinctive historical identities appeared. The Hashemites claimed descent from Ishmael, the son of Abraham and from Fatima, the daughter of the Prophet Muhammad, and from other leaders of early Islam who lived in the Hejaz, or present-day Saudi Arabia. Associated for more than a millennium with leading families of the Hejaz, they needed to establish a local identity when the British transplanted a branch to rule (Trans)Jordan. They did this by asserting a connection with the Nabateans, the best-known and most successful inhabitants of the area who ruled the region from the second to fourth century B.C. through the Roman conquest and into the second century C.E. This narrative was widely disseminated in post-1967 currency that pictured King Hussein of Jordan, the traditional defender of Islam's holy places, flanked by the Al-Aqsa Mosque on one side and Petra, the famed Nabatean city cut from red sandstone near Aqaba and Eilat, on the other.[25]

The Arabs of Palestine, too, identified themselves as indigenous by adopting the Canaanites and particularly one of the main subgroups: the Jebusites of Jerusalem. This stratagem of adopting the ancients, as noted above, was first implemented in the post WWI period but more recently in the example of the Hashemites of Jordan in the aftermath of the 1967 War. However, Palestinians have the most difficult challenge of any group in the region given the general acceptance of the long Jewish connection to the same land and a lack of textual or material evidence attesting to a connection with Canaanite ancestors. Nevertheless, the need to supplant Jewish historical claims with their own as the sole indigenous people of modern Palestine required this device.

Modern Palestinians and Antiquity

Since the end of the 1960s, some official, historical Palestinian narratives have expunged the ancient Hebrew presence. They thereby incidentally, but implicitly, undermined the Christian connection to the Holy Land since Christian sacred texts declare that Jesus is a scion of the House of David. As a result, most Christians accept the reality of a Jewish people at least until the arrival of Jesus and the Roman conquest. That is when the role of Jews as a people in history is diminished or eliminated. This gave rise to a significant theme in Christianity, termed replacement theology or supersessionism. This topic is extensively explored in Chap. 6. We focus here on the assertion that the Jebusites are progenitors of Palestine's Arabs. Ironically, Jebusites are known largely through the Bible and Jewish liturgy where they are mentioned multiple times in the daily prayer service. Their memory has been preserved by Jewish texts and practice. No such prominence exists within Arab or Muslim traditions.

Until the end of the 1960s, the myth of Jebusite origins was marginal in Palestinian national thought. But after Nasser's defeat in the 1967 War and the consequent disillusionment with Pan-Arabism, it became significant in the search for local identities. Moreover, the unanticipated debacle culminated with Jews in control of the Temple Mount or *Haram esh-Sharif* and the Al Aqsa Compound for the first time in two millennia, and this stimulated Palestinian historical revisionism. Their dismay was amplified by both real and symbolic threats. Extreme Jewish groups threatened to take exclusive control of the Temple Mount and destroy Moslem sacred sites.[26] Moreover, in 1996 a large celebration of the putative 3000-year history of Jerusalem since King David's conquest was held against the advice of Israeli scholars who argued the event was a politically inspired fabrication and an unwise challenge to Arab sensibilities.[27] This public assertion of Jewish claims provoked a counter-myth: Jerusalem was a Canaanite city that absorbed successive waves of conquerors. Members of UNESCO echo this claim when they declare the Jews have no substantial connection to Jerusalem and that Jerusalem is a Canaanite/Palestinian city.[28]

An early website of Al-Quds University, a Palestinian institution established in Jerusalem, formulated the claim: the real founders of Jerusalem are Canaanite Jebusites who were successively conquered, but repeatedly absorbed invaders. Among the list of conquerors are numerous ancient peoples including Egyptians, Hittites, Philistines, Assyrians, Babylonians, and Persians. No Hebrews are mentioned, we are told, because there is "no trace at all of a person called 'King David.'" The website supports this removal of Jews from history by referencing "minimalist" Biblical scholars. Moreover, it aggregates decontextualized questions raised by other biblical scholars to make it appear the entire Biblical narrative regarding the Hebrews is unsubstantiated. They ignore the fact that even these scholars support the essential historicity of the Biblical text as a whole.[29]

This anti-Israel approach that denies or minimizes the significance of the Jewish presence is endemic in the Danish "minimalist" school of biblical criticism. The "Danish School"—as it is also called — originated in Copenhagen around 1970 and spread to England, centering in Sheffield, and has flared out from there. The common thread is that the Old Testament is an intricate and complex deception invented by Hebrew scribes some two and a half millennia ago during the period of Persian and Hellenistic influence over Judea. Out of scattered echoes of a distant past, this ancient and manipulative clerical establishment created foundation myths and historic narratives to lend credence to their theology and serve their immediate political purposes. This required fabricating details and exalting the Davidic line and its connection to Jerusalem. In sum, the Bible, from the patriarchs to the Exodus and through the Davidic dynasty, is a deceptive and calculated ruse.[30] The number of scholars engaged in Danish minimalism is relatively small and their impact on Biblical scholarship has been marginal, but their claims have reached a wide audience in popular and scholarly journals and have been enthusiastically endorsed by Palestinian supporters in the Arab/Israeli dispute.[31]

The use of history to support claims for legitimacy has been complicated by the politicization of biblical scholarship. The problem is illustrated by the work of Keith Whitlam, a recognized leader of the minimalist approach. Significantly, his claim for scholarly authority derives from textual analysis explicitly inspired by Edward Said, the author of *Orientalism* (1978) and a member of the Palestine National Council, the Palestine Liberation Organization's formal governing apparatus. Employing Said's terminology, Whitlam dismisses mainstream biblical scholarship as mere "Orientalist discourse" that has conspired to "erase" the Palestinians from history. He asserts "Biblical studies has formed part of the complex arrangement of scholarly, economic, and military power by which Palestinians have been denied a contemporary presence or history." To use a favorite phrase, there is a conspiracy to "silence" Palestinian history.[32]

The Palestinian theologian, Naim Ateek, offers yet another form of erasure. Acknowledging the reality of Jews as historical actors through the prism of the

Bible, he removes them from a role in post-Biblical history through a version "Liberation Theology" (a topic to which we return in Chap. 7 on Christianity in a discussion of supersessionism). Ateek views the Church as the New Israel, replacing and thus erasing the role Jews had previously played in a Covenant with the Lord. Referencing *I Peter* 2:5, he asserts that Palestinian Christian Arabs are "living stones," the direct descendants of those who inhabited Palestine and accepted Jesus. They are the foundation stones for a Christian renewal in the Holy Land.[33] The only evidence Ateek supplies to support his claim of this historical continuity is his name: *ateek* in Arabic (as in Hebrew) means "ancient". He appropriates the story of the Israelites' Exodus from Egypt, that has long been central to Judaism and Jewish collective identity, for repurposing in characterizing modern Palestinian identity. For Ateek, the Exodus story presages the return of Palestinian exiles from 1948 to their Promised Land. This narrative has been propagated abroad through Sabeel, the organization Ateek and fellow clerics founded. They participated in producing *Zionism Unsettled: A Congregational Study Guide* (2014),[34] intended for use in Presbyterian and many other church education programs, and the *Kairos Palestine Document* (2009) that is described as "A moment of truth, a word of faith, hope and love from the heart of Palestinian suffering." These narratives decry the post-1967 "occupation" as a "sin against God," and exhort "the international community to stand by the Palestinian people who have faced oppression, displacement, suffering and clear apartheid for more than *six* decades." [author's emphasis] Both documents weave theological and secular arguments into their critique of contemporary Israel. The time frame of this claim indicates a core issue. It is not the post-1967 occupation alone that is so troubling. It is the establishment of a Jewish state in 1948.[35]

"Indigenous" Bedouins

The legitimacy of Israel's land holdings has been repeatedly challenged by some Negev Bedouin who have been particularly vocal in pressing their claims before Israeli courts and in the public square.[36] To assess their claims, it is crucial to contextualize them. Many Bedouins did not arrive in Palestine until the nineteenth century, along with the Circassians from the Caucasus, Arabs and Jews from across the Ottoman Empire, and Europeans including German Templars, Jewish religious pilgrims, and the first Zionist pioneers. Significant development in the littoral lands of the Eastern Mediterranean in the nineteenth century attracted population from the vast Ottoman hinterland to Alexandria in Egypt, Jaffa in Palestine, Beirut in Lebanon, and around the coast to Smyrna (Izmir) in Turkey. The conquest of Palestine by the Albanian-born Egyptian ruler, Mehmet Ali, in the 1830s significantly opened the area for immigration and modest growth. This influx contributed to the growth of the Palestine's population in the nineteenth century.

Palestine was an ancient and contested nexus of trade routes, not a remote or isolated territory with an indigenous population only recently "discovered" by European explorers. There is ample written testimony and physical articles providing evidence for its vibrancy as well as relative dormancy over extended periods. Palestine, including the Negev, must surely be one of the best-known territories—*terra cognita*—on the globe. In this part of the Middle East, there are records attesting to identifiable peoples, including Jews, as resident for thousands of years. However, unlike the indigenous people of the Americas, including the First Peoples of Canada, and the Aboriginals of Australia, there is no evidence that the Negev Bedouin are the original inhabitants. The most extravagant Bedouin estimates in support of claims to indigeneity report continual residence for six centuries and more as descendants of nomadic tribes from the Arabian Peninsula. Even this claim of relatively recent residence has been successfully challenged by serious scholars in their writings and in testimony before Israeli courts.[37]

No independent Bedouin narratives or written texts record their origins and subsequent history. Studies of tribal names over the centuries indicate that many forebears of present-day Bedouins arrived in the Negev relatively recently and primarily from Egypt.[38] The claim that they are indigenous, since time immemorial, is unfounded. A nomadic people, diverse Bedouin groups ranged over extensive areas in the Middle East, including the Sinai and Negev. They did not establish permanent sites of residence, as did the Nabateans who established and maintained an impressive complex of cities over many centuries in the ancient world, particularly in present-day Israel and Jordan. Not until the end of the nineteenth century did some Negev Bedouin begin to transition to agriculture and permanence although without marking the land with significant urban concentrations or agricultural settlements. On the contrary, from mid-nineteenth century under the Ottomans, then under the British Mandate, and finally after the establishment of Israel in 1948, the Bedouins have resisted and ignored calls to register lands. As a result, there is no documentation attesting to continuing presence and land ownership, much less indigeneity.

The ongoing political and legal battle over property rights features regularly in the pages of scholarly journals and books, a politicized public square, and contests in court. Unsupported legal claims are typically rejected by Israeli courts. Words and language play a role here too. Depending on their views scholars and polemicists may refer to unregistered Bedouin settlements as "illegal" as opposed to "unrecognized," the term used by Bedouins and their supporters to highlight disregard by a hostile state.[39]

Mere self-definition as indigenous is not sufficient and even the best recent scholarship does not make a convincing case that the Bedouin meet the criteria for indigeneity. The methods by which nomads assert rights to territory are distinct from the way modern states define and register rights to land. Hearsay and alleged family memories including imprecise landmarks of territory may be highly significant in terms of a group's collective memory but inadequate for adjudicating actual rights to territory. The perplexing insistence that the Bedouin have inherent rights to land because they are indigenous seems to serve a rhetorical and strategic purpose in applying the colonial-settler paradigm to delegitimate Zionist settlement.

Other significant distinctions are relevant here. Indigenous peoples elsewhere make claims in the name of collective, tribal rights. Claims by Negev Bedouins often advance private interests. Most Bedouins do not contest Israel's designation of land ownership and have accepted settlements with the government. Moreover, despite clashes over issues like honor killings and polygamy, Arabic and Islam will unquestionably remain dominant throughout the region and are permanently and officially recognized by law.

Moreover, many Bedouins, in Israel and beyond, are already making the complex transition to modern life. For the increasingly few Bedouin who prefer to live apart and autonomously, this remains possible but with significant cost in terms of the services enjoyed by citizens integrated in Israeli life. Even a semi-nomadic life is not easily accommodated within the relatively small and compact state. Whatever their individual preferences, the dominant motif in Bedouin society and politics is an expressed desire for enhanced access to the benefits of Israeli society.

We have argued that there is a polemical advantage to assigning sole indigeneity to Bedouins and other Palestinian Arabs. This widespread stratagem Zionists are intruders and a colonial-settler society. It is this term that has infected much academic as well as public discourse. We now turn to an additional discussion of the appropriateness of that central challenge to Israel's legitimacy.

Further Misapplication of the Colonial-Settler Paradigm

The regnant, if not hegemonic, argument by sociologists, historical geographers, and political scientists to delegitimate Israel is that Zionists established a "colonial-settler" society. While an earlier generation of social scientists supported and even celebrated Jewish settlement in Palestine in the extensive discussions over the country's economic absorptive capacity. It is now argued that the Zionist project is illegitimate. Jewish settlement is condemned for its negative and destructive consequences that may require dismantling the Jewish state. This view is, in large measure, a product of applying a radically different historical paradigm.

An influential proponent of this alternative is found in Gershon Shafir's *Land, labor, and the origins of the Israeli-Palestinian conflict, 1882-1914*.[40] Shafir follows on charges first levelled by Maxine Rodinson around the 1967 Six-Day War. Rodinson, a political radical and a Jewish convert to Islam, argued that Zionism constitutes a colonial-settler movement from its beginnings.[41] The idea of Israel as a foreign implant maintained by imperialistic western powers has long been rife in leftist circles. A typical example is Galina Nikitina's *The State of Israel; a Historical, Economic, and Political Study*, published in Moscow in 1973, but based on an earlier Russian study. Nikitina describes Zionism as a form of "bourgeois nationalism" carried out by a foreign implant with no actual connection to Jews of the ancient world. This frame has been widely disseminated in popular works that adopt this analysis.

More recently, Shlomo Sand's international best-seller *The Invention of the Jewish People* (2009) provided a framework and language to receptive audiences already critical of Zionism.[42] Sand charges that Zionism falsely conjures the myth of a recent "return" of an ancient people to their homeland. The ancient Jews disappeared through assimilation; claims of Jewish peoplehood are an invention of nineteenth century Central European intellectuals who imitated the period's folk nationalism by retrospectively imagining a golden age that spawned a people that successfully traversed the centuries intact.[43] Sand relies on the work of critics who claimed that contemporary Jews descended from the Turkic Khazars and other converts. He shares, with some nineteenth and early twentieth century Reform Jews, the view of Jews as merely a faith community devoted to a particular religion rather than a people. The fact that this notion has become eccentric and contrary to the beliefs of an overwhelming majority of Jews in the past and present is discussed in Chap. 6, on Judaism. Nevertheless, the existence of this ideological context outside of the Middle East is important. Palestinian challenges to Zionism did not have to rely on criticism they formulated on their own. It was readily available abroad and receptive to their objections to Israel's legitimacy.

Comparison is a crucial and valuable method for gaining insight into all manner of phenomena. It is a very human activity and fundamental to building categories for the analysis of the world we live in. It is entirely proper to identify and categorize types of settler societies in the 400 years of colonialism that began with Columbus. It is similarly appropriate to ask whether such colonial models apply to Zionism in whole or in part. However, using a comparative framework based solely on European colonialism to interrogate Zionism faults it by definition. To use a phrase: one cannot be a little pregnant. Either one is or is not. Thus, comparing Jews to the Portuguese, Spanish, Dutch, French, and the English places them in an exclusively European historical framework. Zionist settlement may be more or less benign in this exercise, but it remains colonialist. This frame does not consider that Jews were "returning" home rather than serving in an imperialist mission. This is but one anomaly in a historical experience of millennia that itself is anomalous.

It is puzzling that a universal reference for investigating the colonial-settler model is the seminal work of D. K. Fieldhouse, a British scholar whose writings have continued to influence generations of researchers after the appearance in 1966 of *The colonial empires: a comparative survey from the eighteenth century.*[44] Written during heyday of de-colonization and on the eve of one of the great flashpoints of the Arab/Israeli conflict, the 1967 Six-Day War, Fieldhouse's comprehensive work contains no mention of Zionism. Except for a passing reference to the Balfour Declaration of 1917, Jews and Zionists are totally absent from his work. They play no role in this far-reaching account of European colonial expansion.

It is useful to speculate why Fieldhouse, a common and basic source for scholars who hold to the colonial-settler paradigm, did not apply "colonial-settler" to Jewish settlement that had already been in progress for more than 80 years when he published his interpretation. A likely explanation is that Jews do not fit the rubric he established for the Dutch, British, French, Spaniards, Portuguese, Germans, and Italians. During the first 40 years of Jewish settlement that took place in the Ottoman Empire, they were not part of the process of imperial expansion in search for power and markets. Zionism was not a consequence of industrialization and financial interests. Indeed, as numerous scholars have noted, Jewish settlement was so unprofitable that it was judged to be economically irrational.[45] In sum, scholars and polemicists have wrenched out of context an exactingly developed colonial-settler analysis to describe a distinctive and different historical experience.

Zionism did not establish plantations or other large units of capitalistic agriculture. It created small truck farms and modest-sized collective colonies. These were more homogeneous communities with the shared ideology that emphasized working the land in the name of the Jewish people. They had nothing in common with the large plantations managed by European settlers operating with a significant force of native labor or of smaller holdings farmed by individuals for their own profit. Small landholders or collective communities had little need for large-scale use of native labor. Ideologically and practically, Jews worked the land themselves. Moreover, Fieldhouse explicitly denies the applicability of "apartheid" to the Zionist experience.[46] Instead, he found much to endow Zionism with a positive exceptionalism: "There can be no doubt that the Zionist case for a Jewish home, and possibly state, somewhere or other, though not necessarily in Palestine, had stronger moral and physical justification than that of most other modern colonizing movements."[47]

It is ironic that the Zionists' to working the land themselves is being used to delegitimate the Zionist enterprise in its entirety. The economic and cultural separation between Jews and Arabs is attributed solely to an anti-Arab Zionist ideology and praxis and have contributed to indicting Israel as an "apartheid state." In fact, Muslims had for centuries insisted on separate and unequal status for Jewish *dhimmis*, tolerated second-class members of society and a distinct and separate community. Indeed, in a 2008 work, Fieldhouse posits that if the Ottoman Empire had not joined the losing side of World War I, and if it had continued its long-established form of officially institutionalized segregation based on religious identity, separation between Jews and Muslims would have continued rather than espousing a Western civic culture aspiring to a state of all its citizens. As Fieldhouse argues: "A reasonable prediction was that the Jews would continue to constitute a millet, along with the many other religious minorities of the Ottoman empire, clinging to their distinctive religious customs and perhaps preserving the peculiar collectivism of their new rural settlements, but in no sense forming a 'nation', still less a state, as Herzl had projected."[48]

Separation between Jews and Muslims was the norm throughout the Arab Muslim world. It had been imposed by the Moslem Turks and their predecessors from the rise of Islam in the seventh century. It is preposterous to imagine that a handful of Jews living in remote agricultural colonies under Turkish rule could overturn such deeply engrained and accepted practices by establishing an egalitarian and integrated civil society that is aspired but not fully actualized even in the United States. Yet, that has become an operative paradigm and critique.

The misuse of the label "settler society" distorts in another crucial way. British "settler societies" were intended as "replicas" and "true reproductions of European society,"[49] and "The French imperial mission was to mold their colonies into replicas of France and eventually to incorporate them into the metropolis."[50] On the other hand, Zionist settlements were at once distinct from Europe and different from Arab society. In fact, strict binary categorization wherein Jewish pioneers were either European or a distinctive new creation misleads rather than illuminates and defines.

European and American technology, political ideas and other aspects of modern culture were transplanted to Palestine, as they were to other parts of the world by colonizers or by local peoples on their own. Zionist society was consciously and programmatically cast into a unique mold dedicated to creating the "new Jew" as Arieh Saposnik exactingly explains in *Becoming Hebrew: The Creation of a Jewish Culture in Ottoman Palestine.* By the end of the 1930s the term "*sabra*" was introduced to describe the youth produced as this process proceeded. It was beset by the inevitable tensions of competing impulses to preserve elements of the known and traditional and simultaneously to embrace innovation in adapting to the ancient/new homeland. In sum, there was neither utter imitation in the process of transplantation nor abrupt and decisive separation and rejection. This tension was at the core of the idea of "reconstitution" referenced in the Mandate.[51]

Misconstruing Zionists as colonizers represents them as occupiers in a land where they do not belong. In what must be an extreme anomaly in the history of colonialism, Zionism's critics view Palestine as occupied by two imperial powers—the British and the Jews. In light of the multitudes of Jews who desperately sought entry into Palestine prior to independence, this characterization of Jewish power appears as a cruel joke.

The post-colonial analysis rejects or ignores the perspective in which earlier generations of humanists and social scientists worked. (See Chap. 3) During the pre-state period when the "economic absorptive capacity" of Palestine was central to the agenda of public and scholarly discourse, Jewish settlement was measured internally and longitudinally, with reference to the country's long history and the Jewish association with it. Making the desert bloom was an achievement to be admired, not condemned. Yet a misappropriated comparative framework constructs the Jewish presence in Eretz Israel horizontally, exclusively within a frame bookmarked by the onset of European colonialism and by its demise.

The fusion of insights of post-colonial studies with various combinations of liberation theology, minimalist scholarship, and the findings—or their absence—of revisionist archaeology is not surprising. It is also instructive that scholars whose early academic work locates Zionist settlement solely within the settler-society model often go on to question whether Israel ought to continue to exist as a Jewish state. Their central question is whether a Jewish state can also be democratic. The answer is uniformly negative since, by definition, no settler society can be democratic. Accordingly, the original sin of colonialism has inevitable consequences that only the most radical procedure can excise. This charge and its radical solutions have no disciplinary boundaries.

The challenges to Jewish national rights and territorial claims are unlikely to be a passing fashion. They have proliferated in learned monographs and journal articles and seek to supplant an earlier scholarship that had different points of origins and arrived at contrary conclusions. What seems clear is that the past century has witnessed a paradigm shift in the scholarship concerned with Palestine and the public discourse it spawns. In all the models employed to explicate the Arab/Israeli conflict, historical evidence—or its absence—are crucial. So, too, are the societies in the ancient and modern worlds to which Palestine and Israel are to be compared.

Conclusion

Appeals to history produce diverse narratives and interpretations that that may support distinct and contending political agendas. The histories, ancient and contemporary, of the country and its populations are so abundant that unanimity and agreement are unlikely. Multiple histories contest the legitimacy of the Jewish state. Every legal principle that once legitimated Zionism has elicited challenges: conquest, self-determination, discovery, treaties, labor, purchase, and history. A Jewish entity, even one so small as that originally proposed in a partitioned Palestine, was rejected. This suggests that challenges to Israel's legitimacy cannot be understood as stemming solely from secular principles discussed in preceding chapters. In what follows I argue these exist in parallel to primary challenges embedded in theological discourses about Jews and Jewish sovereignty in the land once termed "Judea," and God's promises that remain part of the cultural legacy that is the inheritance of the modern world.

Notes

1. Chaim Gans, "Historical Rights; The Evaluation of Nationalist Claims to Sovereignty," *Political Theory*, 29:1 (February 2001), 58–79; Tamar Meisels, "'Historical Rights' to Land," *Territorial Rights* (Dordrecht: Springer, 2009, 2nd edition), pp. 31–51. The praxis of this connection is also treated in previous chapters and in what follows. I would add to the discussion an interesting volume exploring the issue of nationality and land rights together with a pertinent essay. See Stanley L. Engerman, "Jewish Land—Israel Lands: Ethno-nationality and land regime in Zionism and in Israel, 1897–1967," in Stanley L. Engerman and Jacob Metzer, eds., *Land Rights, Ethno-Nationality, and Sovereignty in History* (London: Routledge, 2004), pp. 87–110.
2. Jonathan Sarna, *American Jews and the Flags of Israel* (Waltham, MA: Brandeis University, 2016).
3. The words of Hatikvah have evolved since first sung at the end of the nineteenth century, we use here the latest "official" version. See: Ilan Ben-Zion, "How an unwieldly romantic poem and a Romanian folk song combined to produce 'Hatikvah'," *The Times of Israel*, 6 April 2013: https://www.timesofisrael.com/how-an-unwieldy-romantic-poem-and-a-romanian-folk-song-combined-to-produce-hatikva/
4. There is a significant debate over the beginnings of the Jewish or Hebrew people but not the reality of their presence in the country. See: Israel Finkelstein and Neil Silberman, *Archaeology's New Vision of Ancient Israel and the Origin of Its Sacred Texts* (New York: Simon and Schuster, 2002).
5. *The Palestinian National Charter: Resolutions of the Palestine National Council July 1–17, 1968*, https://avalon.law.yale.edu/20th_century/plocov.asp
6. Shaul Stampfer, "Did the Khazars Convert to Judaism," *Jewish Social Studies* 19.3 (2013): 1–72. For a significant source of the charge that European Jews

are descended from the Khazars see Arthur Koestler, *The Thirteenth Tribe: The Khazar Empire and Its Heritage* (New York: Random House, 1976).
7. Shlomo Sand, *The Invention of the Jewish People* (London: Verso, 2009); for a pertinent response see Anita Shapira, "Review Essay: The Jewish-people deniers," *The Journal of Israeli History*, 28:1 (March 2009), 63–72
8. Maxime Rodinson, *Israel: A Colonial Settler State* (New York: Monad Press, 1973); Gershon Shafir, *Land, Labor and the Origins of the Israeli-Palestinian Conflict 1882-1914* (New York: Cambridge University Press, 1996).
9. Rashid Khalidi, *Palestinian Identity: The Construction of Modern National Consciousness* (New York: Columbia University, 1997); Yehoshua Porath, *The Emergence of the Palestinian-Arab National Movement, 1918–1929* (London: Cass, 1974).
10. National Committee for the Heads of the Arab Local Authorities in Israel, *The Future Vision of the Palestinian Arabs in Israel* (Nazareth: National Committee for the Heads of the Arab Local Authorities in Israel, 2006).
11. https://www.google.com/search?q=indigenous+meaning&ie=utf-8&oe=utf-8&client=firefox-b; Erika Sarivaara, Kaarina Maatta, and Satu Uusiautti, "Who is Indigenous? Definitions of Indigeneity," *European Scientific Journal*, 9.10 (2014).
12. UN/WGIP (Working Group for Indigenous Populations), "Official Definitions of Indigeneity," https://johansandbergmcguinne.wordpress.com/official-definitions-of-indigeneity/; website of the UN Office of the High Commissioner for Human Rights for resolutions, reports and other essential items, http://www.ohchr.org/EN/Issues/IPeoples/Pages/WGIP.aspx
13. https://www.un.org/development/desa/indigenouspeoples/declaration-on-the-rights-of-indigenous-peoples.html
14. Ismael Abu Saad, "The Education of Israel' s Negev Bedouin: Background and Prospects," *Israel Studies* 2.2 (1997): 21–39; Ilan Troen and Carol Troen, "Indigeneity," *Israel* Studies, 24:1 (Summer 2019), 17–32; Havatzelet Yahel, Ruth Kark, and Seth J. Frantzman, "Are the Negev Bedouin an Indigenous People?," *Middle East Quarterly* (2012): 3–14; Seth J. Frantzman, Havatzelet Yahel, and Ruth Kark, "Contested Indigeneity: The Development of an Indigenous Discourse on the Bedouin of the Negev, Israel," *Israel Studies* 17.1 (2012): 78–104, especially 87–8.
15. "The Palestine Mandate," 1922, http://avalon.law.yale.edu/20th_century/palmanda.asp
16. There is an emerging literature on Sephardi Jews beginning at the end of the Ottoman period and their relationship to their Arab neighbors and the developing Zionist movement. See, especially, Jonathan Marc Gribetz, *Defining Neighbors: Religion, Race, and the Early Zionist-Arab Encounter* (Princeton, NJ: Princeton University Press, 2014); Abigail Jacobson and Moshe Naor, *Oriental Neighbors: Middle Eastern Jews and Arabs in Mandatory Palestine* (Waltham, MA: Brandeis University Press, 2016).
17. "PLO Charter," 1964, http://www.palwatch.org/main.aspx?fi=640&doc_id=8210
18. *The Palestinian National Charter*, 1968, http://www.mfa.gov.il/mfa/foreign-policy/peace/guide/pages/the%20palestinian%20national%20charter.aspx
19. Jonathan M. Gribetz, "The PLO's Rabbi: Palestinian Nationalism and Reform Judaism," *Jewish Quarterly Review* (2017), 90–112.

20. Article 20 of "The Palestinian National Charter: Resolutions of the Palestine National Council July 1–17, 1968," states: "The Balfour Declaration, the Mandate for Palestine, and everything that has been based upon them, are deemed null and void. Claims of historical or religious ties of Jews with Palestine are incompatible with the facts of history and the true conception of what constitutes statehood. Judaism, being a religion, is not an independent nationality. Nor do Jews constitute a single nation with an identity of its own; they are citizens of the states to which they belong." See: http://avalon.law.yale.edu/20th_century/plocov.asp
21. Ivan Davidson Kalmar and Derek Penslar, eds., *Orientalism and the Jews* (Hanover, NH: UPNE, 2005).
22. Orde Kittrie, *Law as a Weapon of War* (Oxford: Oxford, 2016).
23. Can Erimtan, "Hittites, Ottomans and Turks: Ağaoğlu Ahmed Bey and the Kemalist Construction of Turkish Nationhood in Anatolia," *Anatolian Studies* 58 (2008), 141–71. The Hittite claim was stamped by 1922 on the remains of the Ottoman Empire with the establishment of the Kemalist state of modern Turkey. See Umut Uzer, *An Intellectual History of Turkish Nationalism* (Salt Lake City: University of Utah, 2016).
24. Franck Salameh, *Charles Corm; An Intellectual Biography of a Twentieth Century Lebanese "Young Phoenician"* (Lanham, MD: Lexington Books, 2015); Asher Kaufman, *Reviving Phoenicia: The Search for Identity in Lebanon* (London: Tauris, 2004).
25. See http://www.kinghussein.gov.jo/his_nabateans.html; Fakhry Malkawi, Michele Piccirillo, and Hasan ibn ʻAlī Saqqāf, *The Holy Sites of Jordan* (Amman, 1996), 13; Salam Al-Mahadin, "An Economy of Legitimating Discourses: The Invention of the Bedouin and Petra as National Signifiers in Jordan," *Critical Arts* 21 (2007), 86–105.
26. Motti Inbari, *Jewish Fundamentalism and the Temple Mount; Who Will Build the Third Temple?* (Albany: SUNY Press, 2009).
27. Basic work on the topic of Jerusalem is Yitzhak Reiter, *Jerusalem and its Role in Islamic Solidarity* (New York: Palgrave Macmillan 2008), and *Contested Holy Places in Israel-Palestine: Sharing and Conflict Resolution* (London and New York: Routledge 2017).
28. https://www.haaretz.com/israel-news/full-text-of-unesco-s-resolution-on-jerusalem-1.5450617; Dore Gold, 7 May 2017, in how UNESCO has been distorting history and deceiving the international community: "Abbas, UNESCO, and the test of diplomacy," http://jcpa.org/video/abbas-unesco-test-diplomacy/
29. See the former website of "Al-Quds University Jerusalem, the Old City An Introduction," www.alquds.edu/gen_info/index.php? This site has been removed. Write the author at troen@brandeis.edu for a copy.
30. Leading works of this school include Thomas L. Thompson, *Early History of the Israelite people from the written and archaeological sources* (Leiden, 1992) and Philip Davies, *In search of ancient Israel* (Sheffield, 1992). A perceptive review and criticism of this scholarship is found in Marc Brettler, "The Copenhagen School: The historiographical issues," *Association for Jewish Studies Review*, 27(2003), 1–21. Minimalism need not lead to erasure of David or of much standard biblical history. Rather, it can lead to an affirmation of this past but with a modest appreciation of the presence of the ancient Hebrews. For an alternative minimalist view see Neil Asher Silberman and Israel Finkelstein, *The Bible*

Unearthed: Archaeology's New Vision of Ancient Israel and the Origins of Its Sacred Texts (New York: Touchstone, 2002).
31. For a discussion of their role in the public polemics of the politics of the Arab-Israeli conflict see Jacob Lassner and S. Ilan Troen, *Jews and Muslims in the Arab World; Haunted by Pasts Real and Imagined* (Lanham: Rowman and Littlefield, 207), pp. 230–242.
32. Keith Whitlam, *The Invention of ancient Israel; the silencing of Palestinian history* (London: Routledge, 1996), pp. 3–4 and 225.
33. Naim Ateek, *Justice and Only Justice: A Palestinian Theology of Liberation* (Maryknoll, NY: Orbis Books, 1989).
34. http://new.israelpalestinemissionnetwork.org/component/content/article/70/256-zionism-unsettled
35. World Council of Churches, *Kairos Palestine Document; A moment of truth: A word of faith, hope and love from the heart of Palestinian suffering*. See: https://www.oikoumene.org/resources/documents/kairos-palestine-document
36. The differences between the Bedouin case and conventional ones elsewhere are described in great detail in a recent and passionately argued pro-Bedouin study: Alexandre Kedar, Ahmad Amara, and Oren Yiftachel, *Emptied Lands; A Legal Geography of Bedouin Rights in the Negev* (Stanford, 2018). For a counterview see Ilan Troen and Carol Troen, "Indigeneity," op. cit.; Frantzman, Yahel, and Kark, "Contested Indigeneity," 78–104; Yahel, Kark, and Frantzman, "Fabricating Palestinian History," 3–14. Israeli courts rejected the Bedouin perspective in a key case. See *Jerusalem Post*, "Court rejects 6 Bedouin Negev Land Lawsuits," 19 March 2012, https://www.jpost.com/National-News/Court-rejects-6-Beduin-Negev-land-lawsuits
37. Toviyah Ashkenazi, *The Bedouin in the Land of Israel* (Jerusalem, 1957), 30; Joseph Ben-David, *The Bedouin in Israel—Social and Land Aspects* (Jerusalem, 2004), 36, 57–9, 424—81 [both in Hebrew]; Reuven Aharoni, *The Pasha's Bedouin* (London: Routledge, 2007), 30–1. The most extravagant claim presented even extends to the fifth century B.C.E. See Abu Saad, "Education as a Tool of Expulsion from the Unrecognized Villages," *Adallah's Newsletter*. vol. 8, Dec. 2004 at https://www.academia.edu/7615959/Education_as_a_Tool_of_Expulsion_from_the_Unrecognized_Villages1?email_work_card=view-paper
38. Gideon Kressel and |Reuven Aharoni, *Egyptian Emigres in the Levant in the 19th and 20th Centuries* (Jerusalem: Jerusalem Center for Public Affairs, 2013). Tracking nomadic movements over time is very difficult everywhere. See, for example, John R. Bowen, "Should We Have a Universal Concept of 'Indigenous Peoples' Rights?" *Anthropology Today*, 16:4 (2000), 12–16. Nevertheless, claims of Bedouin indigeneity in the Israel-Palestine context are made without inhibition.
39. Kedar, Amara, Yiftachel, *Emptied Lands,* op. cit.
40. Gershon Shafir, *Land, labor, and the origins of the Israeli-Palestinian conflict, 1882–1914* (Berkeley: University of California, 1989)
41. Rodinson, Maxime. "Israel, fait colonial?" *Les Temps Moderne*, 1967. Republished in English as *Israel: A Colonial Settler-State?* (New York, Monad Press, 1973).
42. Shlomo Sand, *The Invention of the Jewish People*, op. cit; and Shlomo Sand, *The Invention of the Land of Israel; From Holy Land to Homeland* (London: Verso, 2012).

43. op cit.
44. Dennis K. Fieldhouse, *The colonial empires: a comparative survey from the eighteenth century* (London, 1966).
45. Baruch Kimmerling, *Zionism and territory: the socio-territorial dimensions of Zionist politics* (Berkeley: University of California, 1983); Simon Schama, *Two Rothschilds and the land of Israel* (New York, 1978); and Ran Aaronsohn, "Settlement in Eretz Israel—a colonialist enterprise? "critical" scholarship and historical geography," *Israel Studies*, 1:2 (Fall, 1996), 214–229.
46. D. K. Fieldhouse, *Western Imperialism in the Middle East 1914–1958* (Oxford: Oxford University Press, 2008), p. 175.
47. Fieldhouse, *Western Imperialism*, p. 117.
48. He faults criticism of communal separation and inequalities in contemporary Israel as the inevitable product of exclusionary processes that had begun around World War I. As Fieldhouse frames this distortion: "It is only teleology that makes it possible to reach this conclusion." Fieldhouse, *Western Imperialism*, pp. 126–27.
49. Fieldhouse, *Western Imperialism*, p. 239 and p. 250.
50. Fieldhouse, *Western Imperialism*, p. 318.
51. *Becoming Hebrew: The Creation of a Jewish Culture in Ottoman Palestine* (Oxford: Oxford University Press, 2008); Tamar Katriel, *Talking Straight: Dugri Speech in Israeli Sabra Culture* (Cambridge, UK: Cambridge University Press, 1986).

Part II
Theological Claims

Chapter 6
Judaism's Claims: A Multiplicity of Interpretations

Introduction

The Jewish claim to the Promised Land varies regarding borders but is definite in principle. The triad of God, People and Land is established in the many iterations beginning in *Genesis* from Abraham and his descendants through Moses, the judges and kings,. For example: *Deuteronomy* 1:8—"See, I have given you this land. Go in and take possession of the land the LORD swore he would give to your fathers—to Abraham, Isaac, and Jacob—and to their descendants after them." The promises to land are covenantal but also conditional.

Jews have viewed these covenants as a justification for their presence in the land as well as an explanation for their exile. A traditional belief, expressed after the destruction of the first Temple in 586 B.C.E., resulted from failure to fulfill covenantal obligations, not God's weakness. Unlike other ancient peoples who disappeared together with their gods, Jews accepted that the destruction of the First and Second Temples were due to their own failings. They held to the belief that God's promise of their connection with the Promised Land would one day again be fulfilled.

This faith in an everlasting and a mutual Covenant with God has been repeated for three millennia in prayers and in the rituals of the life-cycle. When a newborn boy is circumcised on the eighth day after birth, his father declares; "Blessed are You, Lord our God, King of the universe Who has sanctified us with His commandments and commanded us to enter him into the Covenant of Abraham our father." This affirmation bespeaks an unbroken connection with the Jewish people and the land God promised Abraham.

Divine authority in assigning land is expressed in both direct statements and in rules governing conduct regarding land use. The idea of the Jubilee as instituted in *Leviticus* (25:23) requires that the land lie fallow every fiftieth year: "But the land must not be sold beyond reclaim, for the land is Mine; you are but strangers resident with me." Ownership itself is described in the Hebrew as *achuzato* [אחוזתו] that can

© The Author(s), under exclusive license to Springer Nature
Switzerland AG 2024
S. I. Troen, *Israel/Palestine in World Religions*,
https://doi.org/10.1007/978-3-031-50914-8_6

be translated as "His holding." Man has *tenure* over land and may cultivate it for forty-nine years but in its fiftieth it returns to the Lord and may be reapportioned after the Jubilee. Human *tenure* is temporary. The distinction between *ownership* and *tenure* is still maintained in the secular Jewish state. Those who possess lands in fact acquire a lease that may be sold or purchased, but the lease itself may be renegotiated after 50 years.

Islam was also influenced by the ideas of divine ownership. Conquest is a religious act for Muslims, so that land ownership became endowed with qualities of holiness and tradition. Conquered land came under the absolute sovereignty and control of the caliph, God's representative on earth. The state or ruler could parcel it out or lease it in exchange for tax payments or for various services rendered to the government. As observed in Chap. 4 on categories of ownership under Muslim rule, Divine ownership, through His earthly agents, remains a powerful idea in monotheistic theology and in the Holy Land.

Drawing on religious tradition, secular Zionists transformed it in the context of modern nationalism and antisemitism. It seemed obvious that the time had come for Jews to return to the land as they had been promised. Israel's secular Declaration of Independence, in which God is never directly referenced, nevertheless summons up the traditional eternal bonds between God, Israel and the land. Reiterated in many variants in sacred or rabbinical texts, the expectation of return was a fundamental article of national belief:

> *I will maintain My covenant between Me and you, and your offspring to come, as an everlasting covenant throughout the ages, to be God to you and your offspring to come. I assign the land in which you sojourn to you and to your offspring to come, all the land of Canaan, as an everlasting holding. (Genesis 17:7,8)*

In Israel's secular Declaration of Independence, the second paragraph recounts how faithfully Jews have maintained this basic principle:

> *After being forcibly exiled from their land, the people remained faithful to it throughout their Dispersion and never ceased to pray and hope for their return to it and for the restoration in it of their political freedom.*

Many religious Jews and many Christians, particularly Evangelical Protestants, believe Jewish presence will be "restored" when God chooses—to use the nineteenth century Protestant term. Suggestions by the British a century ago that Jews should accept lands in Africa or elsewhere as a temporary asylum were formally rejected by the great majority of Zionists despite rampant European anti-Semitism and the desperate need for refuge. Throughout centuries of wandering in the many lands of the Diaspora and however long they resided in them, *Eretz Israel* remained the only valid historic and future homeland to Jews yearned to return. The fact that this conviction was unquestioned by Jews and by much of the world community is evident from the succession of resolutions passed by the League of Nations and the United Nations in the aftermath of the First and Second World Wars that credited the connection of Jews to Palestine.

The debate that ensued among religious Jews about the right to develop a modern state in Palestine was not about whether Jews would be reestablished in the Promised

Land but over *when* and *how* their return would be accomplished. These two issues make for a critical divide that is the concern of this chapter. I begin with the secular call for human effort and initiative pitted against the theological reliance on the Messiah.[1]

Ultraorthodoxy: Waiting for the Messiah

Belief in the coming of the Messiah is reiterated daily in the prayer of Orthodox and ultraorthodox Jews beginning with the *Yigdal*—"Magnify [O Living God]"—that declares the thirteen principles of faith at the beginning of the *Shacharit* or morning service. It states: "By the End of Days He will send our Messiah—to redeem those longing for His final salvation." [יִשְׁלַח לְקֵץ יָמִין מְשִׁיחֵנוּ - לִפְדּוֹת מְחַכֵּי קֵץ] Redemption is promised. However, there is wide latitude in interpreting *when* that time may come. Ultraorthodoxy holds that moment has not arrived and that Jews may not hasten its arrival. They will be apprised of the moment when God chooses. This means that Zionism either misjudged the present or worse, is intervening in the Divine plan. In either case, this arrogance is a form of blasphemy. There are two well-known exponents of this extreme view.

Perhaps the most important is the ultraorthodox community known as the Satmar Hasidim. Founded in a city in Hungary of that name (now in Romania) at the beginning of the twentieth century, the Satmar reestablished themselves largely after being devastated by the Holocaust. Although most live in New York, a significant community also exists in Israel. Their total number worldwide may be around 75,000; their position and voice resonate far beyond.[2] The Satmar's fundamental position is anti-modernist and rooted in a rejection of the Enlightenment. They maintain the distinctive garb of their European communities and preserve Yiddish as their language of internal communication. They also reject integration into the modern state and distance themselves from participation in society. In Israel, they reject governmental funding for schools and the state curriculum that includes modern subjects such as the sciences, languages, and general history. They refuse service in the army which is normally compulsory. Moreover, they eschew other ultraorthodox groups such as *Chabad* and *Agudat Israel* who have found ways to accommodate to life in a modern state without compromising their theological principles. Their contempt for those who have made what they view as compromises rivals their hostility towards Zionism. Indeed, the Satmar blame the Holocaust on the Zionist heresy of attempting to ingather the exiles and establish a Jewish polity in the Holy Land as "forcing of the end," or trying to bring about the Messianic age prior to God's intention.

This extreme position is based on an interpretation of a verse that appears three times in the *Song of Songs* (2:7, 3:5 and 8:4): "I adjure you [...] that ye awaken not, nor stir up love until it please." That is, Jews should remain in exile until "it please" God to redeem them. They must neither immigrate to the Holy Land nor rebel against the nations in which they reside that will hopefully continue to provide sanctuary until the arrival of the Messiah. Exile is preferable to changing what has been the divinely ordained fate of Jews in centuries past. Those who reside in Israel are enjoined to live separately from Zionists. In effect, they maintain the attributes of exile even when living in the Holy Land.

The *Neturei Karta*, numbering perhaps up to five thousand, are even more extreme and who live primarily in Jerusalem.[3] Their origin is more recent than the Satmar's splinter from ultraorthodoxy. Organized in Jerusalem at the end of the 1930s by Rabbi Amram Blau, they took their name from the Aramaic for "guardians of the city,"—the scholars and scribes who preserve Judaism in its truest form. Those who compromise with the secular Zionist state and any form of modernity betray Judaism and threaten to destroy it. Even more extreme in their rejection of Zionism than the Satmar, this small group gained considerable notoriety by embracing active enemies of Zionism, notably the PLO and Iran. The embrace has been reciprocated, and *Neturei Karta* have participated in anti-Israel conferences and demonstrations including those in which the Israeli flag is burned amidst calls for the end of the State of Israel.

For *Neturei Karta*, the Holy Land has only religious, not political meaning. Blau proclaimed in 1947, when the establishment a Jewish state was under public discussion, that "our Holy Torah teaches that we should take no interest in the political realm while in exile, until the coming of the Messiah, may he come speedily and in our own day, and there is nothing in this position to antagonize our Arab neighbors. We have no interest in living in our Holy Land except to imbibe its holiness and to fulfill the commandments which can only be fulfilled here." They expected that by taking such a public position they would not antagonize Arabs and would keep their community safe.[4]

Engaged Ultraorthodoxy

Such extremism is exceptional. Ultraorthodoxy's most significant component, Agudat Israel [Union of Israel], rejects the state's educational systems and avoids participation in other essential areas of citizenship including army service. However, there is also significant accommodation: they vote, engage in politics, and accept government financial support. Despite considerable variation among such ultraorthodox groups, all consider themselves *Haredi*. This Hebrew term means "trembling" and is derived from the verse in *Isaiah* 66:5: "Hear the word of the LORD, ye that tremble at His word … Your brethren that hate you, that cast you out for My name's sake, have said: 'Let the LORD be glorified, that we may gaze upon your joy', but they [the skeptics] shall be ashamed."

Agudat Israel is the name both of a leading Israeli political party and a worldwide movement of ultraorthodox communities. It originated among the most traditional of the Orthodox Jews who opposed the *Haskalah*—the movement that embraced aspects of the Enlightenment. Opposition to change and adherence to strict observance are hallmarks. The resulting insularity inhibits building bridges to other religious Jews similarly devoted to strict observance, but it has allowed for selective openness to engagement in the world in which they live. That did not extend to formal participation in the Zionist movement. World *Agudat Israel* was founded in 1912 when it split from the "*Mizrahi*" movement of other orthodox Jews who committed themselves to Zionism in 1902 and called themselves *Mizrahi*, from the Hebrew *Mercaz* and *Ruchani* that translates as "spiritual center."

Small communities of Agudat Israel did move to Palestine during the Mandate, drawn to living in the Holy Land for its sacredness rather than its potential as a modern Jewish polity and refuge. Their numbers swelled after the destruction of European Jewry in World War II but most preferred to continue to live in exile in those countries willing to take in survivors, particularly in the United States. Representatives of those settled in Palestine sent out recruiters to the Displaced Persons camps in Europe to urge survivors to come to Palestine, arguing that the Holy Land did not endanger true believers. Recruiters contended that the hardships they had endured in the European inferno had so hardened them that they were "spiritually immune" and would surely contribute to effecting change in the religious climate of the secular Yishuv.[5]

Ironically, *Haredim* who settled in Israel prospered under the protection of the secular Zionist state and have become an effective player in Zionist politics as their community grew. In Israel, *Agudat Israel* have provided the essential leverage to form majority coalition governments since the 1980s and have leveraged political influence for the benefit of their communities. Indeed, thanks to the protection and support of the Zionist state, there are now more yeshivas in Israel with more students than in pre-war Poland. In the period between 1944–1964 their number increased from 35 to 83 with a student population that grew from 2553 to 12,434.[6] By 2016 the number had grown to more than 80,000 students and it continues to increase.[7]

Integration into Israeli life has been gradual and is likely to remain partial. Although total rejection of the state more than seventy-five years after its creation is unrealistic, *Agudat Israel* continue to wait patiently for the coming of the Messiah. Living in Israel does not mean support for Zionism's attempt to intervene in historical processes. Nevertheless, they try to enforce Jewish observance by using the state they spurned to legislate prohibiting public transportation and commercial activity on the Sabbath, support for inspection and adherence to dietary laws (*kashruth*) and, in general, pressuring the state to advance all Jewish society to *halakhic* purity. Their demands for state budgets for welfare, housing, education, health and other services rises in relation to their growth in numbers and political power. This has led to increasing tensions between the non-Zionist *Haredi* minority and the secular Zionist majority.

This religious/secular divide is not what was expected when the *Agudat Israel* movement was founded at the beginning of the twentieth century. Change has not been linear but we can identify a general trend. At the time of the struggle for independence, ultraorthodox men participated in the struggle. Leading rabbis signed the Declaration of Independence, and young men integrated into the work force. They even established a few religious kibbutzim. By the end of the second decade of independence, there was a retreat from such engagement. At present, there are some indications that the pendulum is making halting movements to reverse. There is a renewed search for a more activist and integrated approach to living in the Jewish state with involvement in vocational training and even small initiatives aimed at integrating into special army units.

Poalei Agudat Israel (PAI) or *Agudat Israel Workers* were a singular element of the *haredi* community that engaged with Zionism more intimately. They began as a labor union in the Polish city of Lodz in 1922, long before a network of generous philanthropists supported young men engaged in fulltime study of Torah. In Europe, ultraorthodox Jews worked for a living, and since secular socialist organizations did not meet their needs, they organized a union of their own. Like other such workers associations, they engaged in politics. Those who emigrated to Palestine before and after the war naturally joined the Histadrut—the General Federation of Labor. Though largely associated with socialist Labor, it was an appealing rubric because it supported the rights of workers and provided health services. Thus, on the crucial divisive issue of how to relate to the 1937 Peel Commission's recommendation that Palestine be partitioned into a Jewish and an Arab state, they aligned with Ben-Gurion's Labor party to support partition. Compromise on the wholeness of the Holy Land for pragmatic reasons became a hallmark of the PAI. They were involved over the next four decades in nearly all Labor-led coalitions or until Labor itself was voted out of its dominant leadership role in 1977.[8]

Religious Zionism

Orthodox Jews have been a significant part of the Zionist movement from its beginnings. Whether in alignment with Labor Zionism or the Zionist Right, they have engaged with joining religion with Zionism. From mid-nineteenth century, a movement developed among observant orthodox Jews who held both to a belief in the Messiah and the centrality of Torah study even as they supported the settlement of Palestine. In the lore of Zionist history, there were two outstanding rabbinical leaders who disseminated this formula. They were the rabbis Yehudah Alkalai (1798–1878) and Zvi Hirsch Kalischer (1795–1874). Both were theological innovators, deeply rooted in traditional rabbinic thought and discourse, but were also radical innovators, in that they argued for human action as precipitating divine redemption.[9]

Alkalai, a Sephardic rabbi who lived in Bosnia and had studied in his youth in Jerusalem, thought Jews might persuade the Ottomans to sell lands that Jews could settle to form their own society. He assessed that Jews in the Ottoman Empire, as in Europe, were potential objects of anti-Semitism and should align themselves with the growing nationalism spreading in the Balkans and Greece.

Kalischer, a German-born rabbi who served in Poland, held similar views regarding modern national movements. He urged international Jewry to purchase land and prepare youth to farm in Palestine. These necessary steps would contribute to realizing the messianic age. As a consequence, *Mikveh Israel* [Hope of Israel], an agricultural training school near Jaffa was established in 1870 and supported through the largesse of the French-Jewish Alliance Israelite Universelle. Kalischer's and Alkalai's activism precipitated the growing interest of observant Jews in establishing, supporting, and engaging in Jewish agricultural settlement in Palestine. This kind of activism attracted adherents and threatened those who favored ultraorthodoxy.

Eastern European Jews were especially active in the settlement effort. Calling themselves *Hibbat Zion* [Lovers of Zion], they created a network of local societies that raised funds to purchase land for settlement in the Holy Land. They held conferences, published extensively their proposals in pamphlets and in the press and its member local societies financially supported individual settlements in the two decades before Herzl founded the Zionist Organization in 1897. During the First Aliyah (1881–1903), *Hibbat Zion* established villages based on a large measure of cooperation between individual landowners rather than on the socialist programs that emerged in the first decade of the twentieth century and thereafter. Members in these communities characteristically bonded together in covenants with detailed regulations [*takanot*] that universally began with a quotation from the Bible and set out organizational details such as hiring a rabbi and instruction in religion. One compilation in seven volumes includes hundreds of such covenants made throughout Eastern Europe and extended to immigrant societies in the United States. The avowedly secular and socialist phase of Jewish settlement did not begin until the Second Aliyah (1903–1914).[10]

This movement of religious Jews, often with rabbinical leadership, eagerly embraced Herzl's initiative. However, profound differences, Herzl's many secular adherents and other religious Jews led to internal friction within the Zionist Organization that festered and ultimately resulted in schisms within Zionism and between this movement and religious Jews who became *haredim*. It is telling that in Herzl's utopian novel, *Altneuland* (1902), his hero's rival is a rabbi named "*Geyer*," which is German for "vulture." This characterization was resented and rejected by religious who remained committed to Zionism but splintered into their own movement, affiliated but separate from mainstream Zionist institutions. Like Alkalai, Kalischer and *Hibbat Zion*, many religious Zionists supported the Zionist program to create an international organization, raise funds, engage in diplomacy to achieve recognition and support, and to establish Jewish settlements and a polity in Palestine. Nevertheless, their firm opposition to the official Zionist program of secular educational and cultural activity led to a permanent schism in the Zionist Organization. In 1902 religious Zionists organized *Mizrahi*, with a parallel educational stream to serve Religious Zionists that precluded a unified, common school system that most new states established.

Substantial as well as subtle distinctions characterize the approach of Religious Zionists to settling Palestine. First, Religious Zionism distinguished itself from the ultraorthodox *Agudat Israel* by accepting nationalism as a political movement to achieve collective aims. That is, unlike ultraorthodoxy that rejected nationalism in its secular framework, Religious Zionists believed that modern nationalism could be consistent with traditional peoplehood and serve as an instrument for protecting and achieving Jewish interests. Moreover, although they shared the traditional belief that redemption was in divine hands, they rejected the view that Jews were required to remain passive and wait patiently for the Messiah. For all the common ground with ultraorthodoxy in devotion to study of sacred texts, rabbinic writings, and adherence to Jewish law, they objected to self-imposed isolation from the modern world and sought to protect and improve the condition of Jews at a time when the dangers for Jews were already patently evident. In other words, nationalism, emigration to Palestine, and settlement were consistent with Jewish law in a framework that comprehended compromise, paradox, and mystical inspiration. Their efforts produced a coherent and unifying set of principles around which observant Jews could support the Zionist project.[11]

The evolution of this amalgam of modern nationalism with Judaism can be observed in the approaches of Rabbi *Yitzhak Yaakov Reines* (1839–1915) and Rabbi *Avraham Yitzhak Ha-Cohen Kook* (1865–1935).[12] Reines, who is credited with being the founding leader of Mizrahi, distinguished Zionism from messianism. He found no problem with the cooperation of orthodox and secular Jews in support of Zionism since the shared and distinctive values were clearly delineated. While different approaches to education led to a schism, *Mizrahi* continued to cooperate in practical work and pragmatic politics and has been part of most governing coalitions from the Mandate and through the establishment of the state to the present.

Reines's efforts to distinguish mundane Zionism from ultimate redemption, notwithstanding, it was difficult for orthodox Zionists to repress a sense that they were indeed accomplishing God's intentions and that secular Zionists, too, were engaged in realizing the same historical prophecy even if they did not acknowledge it. They demanded that religious symbols and practice, such as observance of the Sabbath and festivals and dietary laws be supported under state auspices.

Kook became the first chief Ashkenazi rabbi in Palestine under the Mandate and was a towering figure among Religious Zionists and in the Yishuv as a whole. Significantly, he never officially joined Mizrahi but he went much farther in effacing the distance between the religious and secular spheres. He endowed secular Zionists with the mantle of carrying out the Divine plan even if they did so unconsciously and unintentionally. Their nonobservance and even heresy was a passing phase in the working out of the messianic process. He expected the process would culminate in their eventual return to religious belief and behavior. Drawing on the example of the generation of backsliding Jews that Ezra encountered on the return from Babylonian exile after 539 B.C.E., Kook observed that they participated in the building of the Second Temple despite rampant ignorance, and responded warmly to the dissemination of oral law by rabbis.[13]

He believed that could happen again. It was a kind of dialectic that conformed to his mystical faith in the realization of the Divine promise. The prayer for the new state that achieved recognition as an official formulation with Israel's establishment expresses Kook's expectation, describing Israel as "the Beginning of our Redemption":

Our Father in Heaven, Rock and Redeemer of Israel, bless the State of Israel, the first manifestation of the approach of our redemption. Shield it with Your lovingkindness, envelop it in Your peace, and bestow Your light and truth upon its leaders, ministers, and advisors, and grace them with Your good counsel. Strengthen the hands of those who defend our holy land, grant them deliverance, and adorn them in a mantle of victory. Ordain peace in the land and grant its inhabitants eternal happiness ... Draw our hearts together to revere and venerate Your name and to observe all the precepts of Your Torah, and send us quickly the Messiah son of David, agent of Your vindication, to redeem those who await Your deliverance.[14]

Although exact authorship of the prayer is a matter of debate, it is an accurate reflection of Rabbi Kook's teachings.[15] Assurance by the Chief Ashkenazi Rabbi that they had a place in such a foreordained plan earned Kook respect and affection among many of Palestine's secular pioneers.

Rabbi Kook lived with paradox and dialectics. However, many Religious Zionists could not reconcile the tensions between their faith and the requirements of pragmatic politics. A similar difficulty also confronted secular Zionists who split over maintaining deeply held ideologies and the need to address real threats confronting European Jewry. In 1937, two years after Kook's death, the Peel Commission's recommendation to partition Palestine resulted in a wrenching rift among Zionism's subdivisions. Accepting partition meant giving up most of the biblically designated Promised Land and agreeing to the internationalization of Jerusalem. Secular pragmatists, led by Labor's Ben-Gurion, opted for this extreme concession arguing it would create a refuge for Jews beset by raging anti-Semitism and could lead to a sovereign state with expanded borders. For Jews who believed that God's promise granted the entire territory, partition meant compromising sacred ideals and territory. Pragmatists opted to settle for the compromise expressed in the Peel Commission's famous phrase: "half a loaf is better than none." *Mizrahi*'s leaders were split on what to do but largely opposed. Some simply did not vote.[16] On this occasion, the pragmatic side of the Zionist movement won with a small majority. Peel's plan was not implemented and a crisis among Religious Zionists and within the secular branches of the Zionist movement was averted. A decade later, in the aftermath of the Shoah, the need for a state was self-evident and *Mizrahi* leaders not only supported the UN 1947 partition plan but also signed on to Israel's Declaration of Independence despite a problematical opening paragraph that ascribed the Bible ("*Book of Books*" in the original) to human inspiration rather than Divine revelation. Even representatives of *Agudat Israel* added their signatures. The unprecedented extermination of six million Jews produced, at least temporarily, a reassessment of shared priorities.

However, the debate over territorial compromise and relinquishing portions of the Promised Land resumed in the aftermath of the 1967 Six-Day War. Israel had won control over all the territory between the Jordan and the Mediterranean, and much more that stretched down into the Sinai and up through the Golan Heights into Syria. Control over Jerusalem and the West Bank generated the greatest excitement. These territories included sites of significant Biblical events in which the Hebrews and their God interacted, as well as several locales whose Jewish populations had been expelled during the 1948 War of Independence—the ancient city of Hebron and the Etzion Bloc, a cluster of agricultural settlements proximate to Jerusalem's southern border. When small but determined groups of religious Jews initiated the resettlement of these venues after the war. They acted on their own and against the government's explicit wishes and caused considerable uproar. Nevertheless, these early West Bank settlers met with general acquiescence because of the symbolic, emotional, and historical resonance of these sites. There was also a sense that the extension of Israeli presence was limited and did not compromise the possibility of a territorial accord with the Arabs.[17]

It was settlement in other areas of the West Bank, or Judea and Samaria as they came to be called by challengers to government policy, and of the Gaza Strip that ignited a serious national debate. Maintaining control of these areas meant a fundamental reordering of claims to the Promised Land that starkly contradicted an international consensus expressed in United Nations Resolution 242 that reaffirmed the commitment of international diplomacy after the 1967 Six-Day War to achieve partition.

It was here that the legacy of the former Chief Rabbi Kook and the actions of the new and younger leadership in Religious Zionist camp collided with both the older leadership and with Labor that still held the reins of power. For Religious Zionism, the internal struggle pitted newly released messianic longings against a tradition of accommodation and pragmatism. This crisis was catalyzed when Rabbi Zvi Yehuda Kook, the son of Rabbi Avraham Kook, announced what came to be viewed as a prophetic vision that stirred the latent and repressed yearnings for acting in accord with an assumed Divine plan to imminently restore Israel's promised patrimony.

In 2007, *Arutz Sheva*, the news network of Religious Zionism, recalled Zvi Kook's sermon to celebrate Israel's forthcoming fortieth Independence Day, shortly before the outbreak of the Six-Day War in 1967. The sermon reflects not only the sensation of the moment when the IDF captured Jerusalem with its sacred Western Wall and Temple Mount but the capture of the West Bank. Rabbi Zvi Kook's "prophecy" began with:

> "When G-d restored the return to Zion, we thought we were dreaming. (Psalms 126). It seems like a dream today, but people tend to forget the unbelievable power of the events of 40 years ago."

From there it echoes the opening sentence of his sermon at *Mercaz Harav*, the yeshiva established by his father that became the spawning ground for the settler leadership in the aftermath of the war: "*Where is our Hebron, where is our Shechem?*" Kook lamented those who would settle for the 1949 armistice lines (Green Line) established after the War of Independence. In quotation after quotation from the Bible, he recalls the Covenant and its promise that the entire Land of Israel would be restored to Jewish hands. The theme throughout is that Jews should recognize they were living in messianic times and welcome the recovery of the Promised Land. He also references the Talmudic formulation that "the times of the Messiah are 40 years." As the messianic epoch is one of many steps, requiring the investment, hopes, prayers, and patience of generations, the listeners should expect to leap forward to a foreordained time.[18]

Extreme elements in Religious Zionism acted on this expectation. Their disregard for the presence and rights of the Arab residents has repelled many Jews in and beyond Israel, including fellow Religious Zionists. Convinced they were not only acting in accord with a Divine plan but embodying its realization they have defied both Israeli law and policy. While relatively mild forms of protest and rebellion against legitimate authority began in the aftermath of the 1967, after the 1973 October or Yom Kippur War followers of Rabbi Zvi Kook, organized as *Gush Emunim* [Bloc of the Faithful], established "outposts." These small settlements usually composed of "caravans" or mobile homes set on hilltops in Judea and Samaria challenged the Israel army charged with removing them. Over the next two decades dramatic escalations involved both terrorist attacks on Jewish settlers and Jewish initiated damage to Palestinian property as well as outright violence including firebombs that resulted in injury and death.[19]

In addition, small groups of fervent, radical believers, anxious to advance the messianic moment, agitated against government policy in Jerusalem at the *Holy Mount/Haram al-Sharif*, at sites sacred to Jews and Muslims. There were plots in the 1980s and 1990s by extremist religious groups—often termed the Jewish Underground—to destroy the Al Aqsa Mosque so that it might be replaced by a third Temple dedicated to reconstituting Jewish rites. Baruch Goldstein, an American-born follower of the ultra-nationalist Rabbi Meir Kahane, killed 29 worshippers and wounded 125 Muslim worshippers at a shrine sacred to Jews and Muslims, the Cave of Patriarchs near Hebron in 1994. Yigal Amir, a right-wing university student, convinced he was obeying the teachings of radical rabbis, assassinated Israeli Prime Minister Yitzhak Rabin in November 1995. Rabin's assassination caused outrage and introspection among Religious Zionists since Amir was a product of Bar Ilan University, the flagship institution of Religious Zionism. The Rabin assassination indicated the difficulty in setting limits to those who believe they are obligated to carry out a divine plan.

Most religious Zionists have tried to check such outrages. They supported banning the extremist Rabbi Meir Kahane as a "racist" and proscribing his political party from the Knesset. Nevertheless, there has been a marked evolution of religious Zionism over the past century. As observed above, a majority had been willing partners to relatively moderate and pragmatic secular Zionism despite an undercurrent that held to more vigorous nationalistic views. In the aftermath of the 1967 War a new generation, acting as a self-appointed vanguard, pushed for a militant and uncompromising policy towards the conquered territories. They successfully challenged the party's traditional leadership and formally shifted the movement further to the right when it joined the Likud government of Menachem Begin in 1977. Since then, Religious Zionism, as well as ultraorthodox parties, have partnered with the nationalist secular Right. Only a small splinter group, the short-lived Meimad party, maintained the historic alliance with Labor.

The foregoing descriptions of ultraorthodoxy and orthodoxy—from haredim to Gush Emunim and beyond—reflect how modern Judaism, as practiced in Israel, has arrived at diverse and contrary interpretations in their approach to Zionism and the Holy Land. Moderation, pragmatism, accommodation, and extremism can be supported by varying interpretations of the same sacred texts. There are yet other variations within Judaism. Perhaps most noteworthy is *Brit Shalom* [Covenant of Peace], a movement that was willing to forego exclusive Jewish sovereignty over the whole of the Promised Land. While established in Palestine during the 1920s largely by Central European immigrants, its principles have also had strong resonance among some Jews in the Diaspora. However, before turning to examine this group, we will present the evolution of views among American Reform Jews who have come to represent the largest religious movement in the largest Jewish community in the Diaspora.

Reform Judaism

Our attention has been exclusively on Orthodox Jewry and largely those who reside in Israel. Yet Zionism, as a creation of diaspora Jewry, encompasses other views espoused by non-Orthodox views. Reform Judaism, a movement that began in Germany in the nineteenth century and spread to the United States, has become the mainstream expression of many American Jews. Although Reform as well as Conservative Judaism have limited expression in Israel, they impacted on how Diaspora Jewry related to Palestine and have influenced international discourse. It is Reform that paradoxically voiced the strongest initial opposition to Zionism but came to provide significant leadership for the Zionist project and support of Israel.

The position of Reform has changed dramatically from the end of the nineteenth century when Herzl created the Zionist Organization. It moved from rejection to support. Change can be traced through the official platforms of the Central Conference of American Rabbis, the major association of American Reform rabbis.[20] Its "Pittsburgh Platform," issued in 1885, is dedicated exclusively to the relationship between Reform Judaism and the settlement of Jews in Palestine. It dramatically departed from traditional interpretations of the Covenant in declaring that Reform Judaism no longer expected Jews to return to the Land of Israel. The 1885 platform proclaimed: "We consider ourselves no longer a nation, but a religious community, and, therefore, expect neither a return to Palestine...nor the restoration of any of the laws concerning the Jewish state." This position was presaged by mid-nineteenth century Reform in Germany which expunged references to any form of "restoration" of the Jewish people in Palestine from the liturgy on the grounds that nationalism and statehood were not compatible with Reform theology.

Aspiring to become accepted as citizens of the states in which they resided, they rejected alternative national loyalties and posited Judaism as a faith with universal ethical aspects, not the national religion of a particular people. The desire to demonstrate faithfulness to Jewry's new home in the United States replaced *Eretz Israel* as the Promised Land and elevated America as the alternative, new Zion. San Francisco's Reform Congregation Sherith Israel exemplified this idea in a new version of the Exodus story. Rather than leaving Egypt for the desert where Jews received the Ten Commandments, its stained-glass windows depicted Moses descending with the two tablets of inscribed stone from the imposing El Capitan Mountain into California's Yosemite Valley, a symbolic representation of Jews arrival in the new Promised Land in America.[21]

By 1937 Reform had reversed its stand on Jewish peoplehood. The "Columbus Platform" declared that "Judaism is the soul of which Israel [the people] is the body." The document reasserts Jewish peoplehood: "We affirm the obligation of all Jewry to aid in its [Palestine's] up-building as a Jewish homeland by endeavoring to make it not only a haven of refuge for the oppressed but also a center of Jewish culture and spiritual life." This exhortation was accompanied by a reaffirmation of Reform Judaism's universal message: "We regard it as our historic task to cooperate with all men in the establishment of the kingdom of God, of universal brotherhood, justice, truth and peace on earth. This is our Messianic goal." In other words, Reform Judaism's universalistic and messianic aspiration now affirmed the traditional, particularistic, and national expectation that had long characterized Judaism. They would coexist.[22]

The same body completed the transformation in its 1976 "Centenary Perspective" stating: "We are bound to...the newly reborn State of Israel by innumerable religious and ethnic ties .... We have both a stake and a responsibility in building the State of Israel, assuring its security and defining its Jewish character." This did not preclude a commitment to the legitimacy of the Diaspora and its communities: "The State of Israel and the Diaspora, in fruitful dialogue, can show how a people transcends nationalism even as it affirms it, thereby setting an example for humanity, which remains largely concerned with dangerously parochial goals." In this declaration, the Reform movement implicitly acknowledged the paradox as it attempted to balance its support for Zionism with opposition to narrow nationalism.[23]

In less than a century, the Reform movement, that aspired to adapt Jews to full participation in post-Emancipation Europe, reasserted Jewish peoplehood and Judaism's traditional, national aspirations and, by mid-twentieth century, no longer disavowed Zionism. Not unlike the Orthodox, it sought simultaneously to support a connection with its ancient heritage and the integration of the Jewish state into the emerging family of democratic, nation-states. Freed of the angst of being charged with dual-loyalties, Reform synagogues displayed both the American and the Israeli flags.

Opposition to these changes decreased but nevertheless persisted. The echoes of rejection reverberated in the American Council for Judaism, an organization founded in 1942 and determined to remain faithful to the anti Zionist Pittsburgh Platform despite their movement's retreat in the 1937 Columbus statement. They rejected support of Zionism as a response to Nazi Germany and sympathized with Arab resistance to Jewish settlement in Palestine. Under the leadership of highly regarded rabbis and of its Executive Director, Elmer Berger, the American Council for Judaism mounted a national campaign with the support of scattered Reform congregations. Its president, Lessing Rosenwald, an heir to the Sears, Roebuck fortune, appeared before the UN commissions on Palestine and argued against a Jewish state in Palestine or anywhere. Instead, he favored a bi-national, Jewish and Arab state. The organization declined after Israel was established but, as we saw in Chap. 5, its position that Jews constitute a faith community rather than a people resonated with the Palestine Liberation Organization, and is referenced among opponents of the Jewish state.

The force of tragic circumstances persuaded many adherents of Reform to acknowledge that modern Jews also needed a homeland and a refuge. One can correlate the rising threats to the Jewish people worldwide with Reform's support of Zionism. The initial upsurge came during World War I and the Russian revolution that brought chaos and violence to Eastern European communities. Support for Zionism grew again in the 1930s when, despite rising anti-Semitism in Europe, potential immigrants were barred from entering the United States. The crisis of World War II and the Holocaust emphasized the urgent need to find a haven for refugees and pointed to Palestine as the most appropriate venue. The dangers of contending nationalisms convinced increasing numbers of Jews that they, too, required to endorse a nation-state for the security of their own people. In the process, Judaism's rich traditions provided the justifications for supporting Israel.

The Return to Zion was never entirely eliminated from Reform. In the early twentieth century, a small splinter group of leading rabbis and academics associated with Hebrew Union College in Cincinnati, the main training institution for the Reform rabbinate, resigned over their movement's rejection of Zionism. Their ranks grew as European anti-Semitism intensified. By the interwar period, the leadership of American Zionism included such respected Reform rabbis as Abba Hillel Silver of Cleveland, Louis Newman and Stephen Wise of New York. Judah Magnes, who also served in New York and lead in pioneering a community-wide organization of the city's diverse elements, famously left for Palestine. There he became founding Chancellor of the Hebrew University of Jerusalem and a dissident Zionist advocating for a bi-national state.[24]

Reform not only affirmed that *Eretz Israel* was central to the life of the Jewish people, but supported the establishment of several kibbutzim, study programs for youth, and a branch of its rabbinic seminary in Jerusalem. Maintaining a vital connection with a Zionist state did not compromise their loyalties as citizens of other countries. They transformed the messianic idea to a vision of spiritual universalism rather than a final moment of divine intervention in the history of the Jewish people and humankind. Yet, the same prophetic vision of justice created space for criticism of the Zionist project. While Reform Judaism came to be among the most active and vocal supporters of the Jewish state, the movement also spawned critics of how Israel managed relationships between its Jewish and Arab citizens. Thus, support for the state's legitimacy also included vigilance regarding its policies.

This shared consensus was tested in the aftermath of the 1967 war. While celebration of the remarkable success of Israel in its own defense was nearly universal, the newly acquired territories became a source of intense friction. It is from the ranks of Reform Judaism, particularly among those who labelled themselves "progressive," that much criticism emerged. The ongoing conflict between Jews and Palestinians, and continuing Israeli control with the threat of formal annexation during the more than half century—at the time of this writing—have rekindled the debate between universalists committed to the vitality of Jewish life in the Diaspora, pragmatists who sought accommodation with the long resident non-Jewish populations of Palestine/Israel, and those committed to Jewish control over the whole of the Land of Israel. The fact that the most ardent advocates of continuing Israeli control come from camps within Orthodoxy, the historic rival and adversary of Reform Judaism exacerbates the conflict. Moreover, the methods used to maintain control, from the formal power of the state to unauthorized violence by extremist West Bank settlers, has pitted a universalist approach to human rights against a parochial nationalism.[25]

The Religious Basis for a Bi-National State

Rabbi Judah Magnes (1877–1948), a leading member of Reform who emigrated to Israel to become the founding chancellor (1925–1938) and president (1938–1948) of the Hebrew University in Jerusalem, died in New York shortly after he testified before the United Nations against the partition of Palestine into separate Jewish and Arab states.[26] Born in Oakland, California, and educated in American institutions, he also studied in Berlin and Heidelberg where he received a doctorate and became a close associate of leading Central European Jewish intellectuals. He was an early supporter of Zionism, serving as secretary of the American Zionist Federation from 1905 to 1908. His commitment was strengthened and refined through a long association with Martin Buber (1878–1965), also an early Zionist associated with Herzl's Zionist Organization. Although Buber lacked formal rabbinical ordination and a traditional pulpit, he was a singularly significant and innovative religious thinker with a huge impact on Jewish thought through writing, lecturing and leadership in institutions of Jewish learning.[27]

Magnes and Buber, together with like-minded associates, identified themselves as fervent Zionists and advocated for the immigration of Jews into Palestine and the transformation of the country through the gamut of working the soil to intellectual endeavor and institution-building. Concerned about the fate of European Jewry, they differed from fellow Zionists by favoring a bi-national Jewish/Arab polity. This bi-national idea led to their partnership in establishing *Brit Shalom* in 1925, and *Ichud* ["union"—of Arabs and Jews] in 1942 as well as other collaborations in the run up to Israel's independence in May 1948. The first—*Brit Shalom*—was a response to the British Mandate's charge to establish only a Jewish national homeland in Palestine. The second—the *Ichud*—was a negative response to the Biltmore Program, the plan Ben-Gurion and American Zionists formulated in 1942 that explicitly declared their intention to create a sovereign Jewish state in Palestine."[28]

The Zionism of Buber and Magnes was rooted in a markedly and radically different interpretation of messianism from that of ultraorthodoxy and Religious Zionism. They did not place their hope for redemption on divine intervention in human affairs or on human efforts to hasten it. They envisioned a modern democratic state, not one governed by Jewish law as codified and interpreted by rabbis. Moreover, they rejected building a new Temple in place of those that had been destroyed. Rather, they prioritized education that would enlighten Jews who came to build the land and who, together with Arabs, would create an exemplary society that would inspire Jews, Arabs, and mankind in general. While they saw Palestine as a refuge for threatened Jewry, they were willing to forego a majority to establish exclusive Jewish hegemony but insisted on a balance of power that would preserve essential Jewish interests. They were wary about potential abuses of power by Jews, and held a generous view of potential reciprocity by Arabs, though they encountered little evidence of it in their attempts at outreach.

Buber, in his philosophical and religious work, strove to enhance appreciation for the practice of human relations as a religious priority. He emphasized "dialogue"—the term closely identified with his distinction between relationships he termed "I-Thou" (two subjects) and "I-It" (subject-object). He hoped that praxis in the case of Palestine would mean overcoming conflict between Jews and Arabs in a shared polity. Although there were many paths that lead him to these concepts, it was the trauma of World War I and in the catastrophe of massive human destruction wrought by competing nationalisms that lead him to urgently press for suppression of ethnic nationalism, even among fellow Zionists.[29]

Nevertheless, like other religious Zionists, he believed in the Covenant that demanded adherence to divinely mandated ethical codes and asserted the Jewish connection to the Promised Land. This was famously expressed in his correspondence with Mahatma Gandhi in 1939 when it was becoming clear that European Jewry was in grave danger. Buber asked for Gandhi's blessing for Zionism. Gandhi refused, arguing that Palestine belonged to the Arabs. Among the many points in Buber's response was the traditional Jewish explanation that land does not "belong" exclusively and irrevocably to any people but to God, and that man's tenure is conditional on behavior. Buber avoided claiming exclusive rights through the covenant but emphasized the role of working land productively and maintaining ethical relationships with others that inhabit it. A well-known passage is worthwhile repeating here:

> ...I believe in the great marriage between man (*adam*—in Hebrew) and earth (*adamah*—in Hebrew). This land recognizes us, for it is fruitful through us: and precisely because it bears fruit from us, it recognizes us. Our settlers do not come here as do the colonists from the Occident to have natives do their work for them; they themselves set their shoulders to the plow and they spend their strength and their blood to make the land fruitful. But it is not only for ourselves that we desire its fertility. The Jewish farmers have begun to teach their Arab brothers, the Arab farmers, to cultivate the land ... together with them we want to cultivate the land—to "serve" it, as the Hebrew has it ... We do not want to dominate them: we want to serve with them ....[30]

This plea did not persuade Gandhi. The largest Muslim population in the world inhabited the Indian subcontinent. Gandhi had pragmatic concerns for a region that, like Palestine, was threatened by violence and bloodshed, and his concern was justified. In January 1948 he was assassinated by an extreme Hindu nationalist who believed Gandhi was too accommodating to Muslims. It is noteworthy that Buber's admiration for a fellow pacifist was shared by Ben-Gurion. The only picture that Ben-Gurion hung on his bedroom wall at his Sde Boker home in Israel's Negev was that of Gandhi who was revered for his philosophy and for his leadership in seeking independence from the British. Whatever the basis for Buber's and Ben-Gurion's admiration, their appeal to Gandhi was a case of unrequited admiration.

Magnes, too, was anti-nationalist and a pacifist. His views were first expressed in reaction to the jingoism that led to the 1898 Spanish-American War and, later, in 1917 with American entered World War I and Magnes was chairman of the pacifist People's Council of America for Democracy and Peace and serving as rabbi of New York's leading Reform synagogue.[31] In Palestine, Buber and Magnes were joined by a small but significant group of largely Central European intellectuals who had also witnessed the disaster of World War I and what they understood to be its lesson for Palestine in abjuring conflict and war.

Some left B'rith Shalom and its binationalism early, as did Hans Kohn, who also left Palestine to become a leading American academic specializing in nationalism. Kohn first heard Buber in Prague in 1909 when he spoke before a Zionist youth society about Palestine as the necessary and optimal venue for Jewish spiritual and cultural rejuvenation. Kohn emigrated to Palestine after World War I but was frustrated by the growing Arab-Jewish rift and the political strategies adopted by Zionist authorities. He left Palestine for the United States in 1934, increasingly agitated in the aftermath of the 1929 riots that represented for him deep frustration with the Zionist movement for not advancing towards Arab-Jewish reproachment.[32] Other members left Palestine prior to or just after independence where they found positions in the American academy, notably in the New School for Social Research, which had become a beacon for liberal and progressive Jews who fled Nazi Germany.

The relatively few who remained after independence continued to have limited influence after the bloody 1948 war. Among the Jewish public, Buber and his ideas were highly admired as idealistic but impractical and romantic. They were ignored by the Arabs of Palestine. As the conflict continued, binationalism remained an unattainable and utopian ideal with little attraction except among critics of Israel's actions which they perceived as relying excessively on the use of power. Some followed a Soviet and leftist line claiming Israel was an illegitimate colonial-settler society and merely a pawn or ally of Western imperialism. For a few, binationalism remained a vital, moral idea inspired by the religiously informed values Buber espoused.[33]

Buber and Magnes and their associates were part of an intellectual elite that had limited influence on the politics of the conflict. However, their presence in the discourse of the conflict has been lasting and requires consideration. The caveat they first placed on the political emphasis of Herzlian Zionism and the political leadership of Israel are a lasting tradition in Zionism. Sacred texts and religious values endure. They caution against the abuse of power and inspire visions of a just society.

Summary Observation

As I have tried to demonstrate, there is no one "Jewish" view that constitutes an agreed expression of *when* or *how* to engage in establishing a sovereign Jewish state. There is broad consensus of the eternal Covenant between God and Abraham. That does not translate into agreement on the nature of the Jewish state and its actions. Nearly all agree on the legitimacy of the venue and the historic reality of the Jewish people. However celebrated or problematic this position may be for Jews; the success of Zionism poses a challenge for Christianity and Islam. According to their historic doctrines, the (possibly) miraculous return of Jews to reclaim and rebuild their ancient homeland should never have happened. It is to this understanding of the two other main streams of monotheism that we now turn.

Notes

1. The influential overview of this topic remains the classic Aviezer Ravitzky, translated by Michael Swirsky and Jonathan Chipman, *Messianism, Zionism, and Jewish Religious Radicalism*, (Chicago: University of Chicago, 1995).
2. David Biale, David Assaf, Benjamin Brown, Uriel Gellman, Samuel Heilman, Moshe Rosman, Gadi Sagiv, and Marcin Wodzinki, *Hasidism; A New History* (Princeton: Princeton U Press, 2018), especially for the Satmar see: pp. 73 ff. and 685–93; Zvi Jonathan Kaplan, "Rabbi Joel Teitelbaum, Zionism, and Hungarian Ultra-Orthodoxy, "*Modern Judaism*, 24: 2 (May 2004), 165–178; for an accessible popular review of who the ultra-Orthodox are and where they come from as well as the tensions between them and secular Israeli society see Noah Efron, *Real Jews; Secular Versus Ultra-Orthodox and the Struggle for Jewish Identity in Israel* (New York: Basic Books, 2003).
3. Kimmy Kaplan, *Amiram Blau; The World of Neturei Karta's Leader* (Jerusalem: Yad Ben-Zvi and Ben-Gurion U of the Negev, 2017) [Hebrew]
4. Quoted in Moshe Halbertal, "Exile and the Kingdom," *The New Republic* (March 15, 1998).
5. Michal Shaul, *Holocaust Memory in Ultraothodox Society in Israel* (Bloomington, Indiana University, 2020), pp. 122–124.
6. Shaul, *Holocaust Memory in Ultraothodox Society*, Appendix A, pp. 293–298.
7. "Yeshiva funding hits all-time high, as number of full-time seminary students rockets," *The Times of Israel*, 6 March 2016. https://www.timesofisrael.com/yeshiva-funding-hits-all-time-high-with-new-government-boost/
8. Elliott Horowitz, "Religious Labor," *Tablet*, May 23, 2013, https://www.tabletmag.com/sections/israel-middle-east/articles/religious-labor; https://en.wikipedia.org/wiki/Poalei_Agudat_Yisrael
9. Arthur Hertzberg, "Rabbi Yehudah Alkalai," *The Zionist Idea: A Historical Analysis and* Reader (Philadelphia: Jewish Publication Society,1997), pp. 102–108; Jody Myers, *Seeking Zion: Modernity and Messianic Activism in the Writings of Tsevi Hirsch Kalischer* (Oxford: Littman Library of Jewish Civilization, 2003).

10. *Documents on the history of Hibbat-Zion and the settlement of Eretz Israel* (Hebrew), comp. and ed. Alter Droyanov and Shulamit Laskov, 7 vols. (Tel-Aviv, 1982–1993); S. Ilan Troen, *Imagining Zion; dreams, designs, and realities in a Century of Jewish Settlement* (New Haven: Yale, 2003), Chap. 1.
11. Gideon Shimoni, "National-Religious Zionism," *The Zionist* Ideology (Hanover, NH: University Press of New England, 1995), pp. 127–65.
12. Yehudah Mirsky, *Rav Kook; Mystic in a time of revolutions* (New Haven: Yale University Press, 2014).
13. Quoted from Kook, *Igrot ha-ra'aya* vol I, p. 348 from Gideon Shimony, *The Zionist Ideology* (Hanover, NH: Brandeis University Press, 1995), pp. 148–9.
14. "Jewish Prayers: Prayer for the State of Israel," *Jewish Virtual Library*. See: https://www.jewishvirtuallibrary.org/prayer-for-the-state-of-israel
15. Yoel Rappel, *Prayer for the Peace of the State* [ha-Tefilah li-shelom ha-medinah] (Modiin: Kinnereth Zmorah Bitan, 2018) [Hebrew]. Rabbi Kook's successor, Rabbi Yitzhak Herzog (1888–1959), continued this tradition and added shortly after independence a new prayer to the those recited daily by observant Jews, asking God to bless the State of Israel as "the Beginning of our Redemption" (*reyshit tz'michat ge'ulateynu*). Joseph Tabory, "The Piety of Politics: Jewish Prayers for the State of Israel," in *Liturgy in the Life of the Synagogue: Studies in the History of Jewish Prayer*, eds Ruth Langer and Steven Fine (Winona Lake, IN: Eisenbrauns, 20 05), pp. 225–46.
16. Itzhak Galnoor, *The Partition of Palestine: Decision Crossroads in the Zionist Movement (Albany: SUNY, 1994)*.
17. This topic generates over the years a large and ever-expanding literature. See, for example, Gershom Gorenberg, *The Accidental Empire; Israel and the Birth of the Settlements, 1967–1977* (New York: Henry Holt, 2006); Ian Lustick, *For the Land and the Lord: Jewish Fundamentalism in* Israel (New York: Council on Foreign Relations, 1988); Michael Feige, *Settling in the Hearts: Jewish Fundamentalism in the Occupied* Territories (Detroit: Wayne State, 2008); Sarah Hirschhorn. *City on a Hilltop: American Jews and the Israeli Settler Movement* (Cambridge, MA: Harvard, 2017).
18. Yossi Baumol, "The Days of Jerusalem and Hebron; The power of events of 40 years ago," *Arutz Sheva*; Eliezer Don-Yehiya, "Messianism and politics; the ideological transformation of religious Zionism," *Israel Studies*, 19:2 (2014), 239–263.
19. Motti Inbari, *Jewish fundamentalism and the Temple Mount: who will build the Third Temple?* (Abany: SUNY, 2009) and *Messianic religious Zionism confronts Israeli territorial compromises* (New York: Cambridge, 2012); Ehud Sprinzak, *Brother against brother: violence and extremism in Israeli politics from Altalena to the Rabin assassination* (New York: Free Press, 1999).
20. Central Conference of American Rabbis, "Reform Judaism and Zionism: A Centenary Platform," (Miami, FL: June 24, 1997). https://www.ccarnet.org/rabbinic-voice/platforms/article-reform-judaism-zionism-centenary-platform/
21. Jonathan Sarna, *American Judaism; A History* (New Haven: Yale University Press, 2019, 2nd ed.), pp. 202–203. For a classic review of the change in Reform see Naomi Wiener Cohen, "The Reaction of Reform Judaism in America to Political Zionism (1897–1922)," *Publications of the American Jewish Historical Society*, 40:4 (June 1951), 361–394; Mel Urofsky, "American Jews and Israel: The First Decade and Its Implications for Today," S. Ilan Troen and Noah

Lucas, eds., *Israel; The First Decade of Independence* (Albany: SUNY, 1995), pp. 733–50.
22. Reform Judaism, *The Columbus Platform (1937)*, https://www.jewishvirtuallibrary.org/the-columbus-platform-1937
23. Reform Judaism, *A Centenary Perspective; Adopted at San Francisco, 1976*, https://www.sacred-texts.com/jud/100.htm
24. Arthur Goren, ed., *Dissenter in Zion: From the Writings of Judah L. Magnes* (Cambridge, MA: Harvard University Press, 1982; Norman Bentwich, For *Zion's Sake. A Biography of Judah L. Magnes. First Chancellor and First President of the Hebrew University of Jerusalem* (Philadelphia: Jewish Publication Society of America, Philadelphia,1954). David Barak-Gorodetzky, *Judah Magnes: The Prophetic Politics of a Religious Binationalist (Philadelphia: Jewish Publication Society, 2021)*.
25. The literature on extremism is large. It may include Reuven Firestone, *Holy War in Judaism; the Fall and Rise of a Controversial Idea* (Oxford: Oxford University Press, 2012), particularly Part IV; Motti Inbari, *Jewish Fundamentalists and the Temple Mount* (Albany: State University of New York, 2009); and Ehud Sprinzak, *Brother Against Brother: Violence and Extremism in Israeli Politics from Altalena to the Rabin Assassination* (New York: Free Press, 1999).
26. Arthur Goren, ed., *Dissenter in Zion*; Norman Bentwich, *For Zion's Sake. A Biography of Judah L. Magnes. First Chancellor and First President of the Hebrew University of Jerusalem* (Philadelphia: Jewish Publication Society of America, 1954).
27. Paul Mendes-Flohr, *Martin Buber: A Life of Faith and Dissent* (New Haven: Yale University Press, 2019); Paul Mendes-Flohr, ed., *A land of two peoples: Martin Buber on Jews and Arabs* (Chicago: University of Chicago Press, 2005).
28. Susan Lee Hattis, *The Bi-National Idea in Palestine During Mandatory Times* (Haifa: Shikmona, 1970).
29. Paul R. Mendes-Flohr, *A Land of Two Peoples*, pp. 82–81.
30. Martin Buber, "From an open letter to Mahatma Gandhi (1939)," in Arthur Hertzberg, *The Zionist Idea; A historical analysis and reader* (Philadelphia: Jewish Publication Society, 1997), pp. 463–65.
31. Goren, *Dissenter in Zion*.
32. Hans Kohn, "Zionism is Not Judaism," in Paul R. Mendes-Flohr, ed. with commentary, *A Land of Two Peoples; Martin Buber on Jews and Arabs* (New York: Oxford University Press, 1983), pp. 95–100; Hans Kohn, *Der Araberfrage [The Arab Question]*, translated by Wilma A. Iggers, in *The Jews of Bohemia and Moravia: A Historical Reader* (Detroit: Wayne State University Press, 1992), pp. 239–242. Noam Pianko, *Zionism and the Roads Not Taken; Rawidowicz, Kaplan, Kohn* (Bloomington: Indiana University Press, 2010), Chap. 5.
33. George Mosse, "Can Nationalism be saved? About Zionism, rightful and unjust nationalism," *Israel Studies*, 2:1 (March 1997), 156–73.

Chapter 7
Christianity's Claims: A Kaleidoscope of Theologies

Introduction

The return of Jews to Palestine presented Christianity with a complicated challenge. It raised theological issues that had appeared settled and dormant for centuries. Diverse and conflicting responses are unsurprising from a stream of monotheism long characterized by schisms related to authority, structures, beliefs, and practices that resulted in a variety of established churches and a multitude of "denominations." Thus this chapter delineates several broad categories of response to the Zionist project. Some draw on positions formulated about seventeen centuries ago; others originate in beliefs articulated only in the last two centuries; still others are a product of twentieth century reckonings over the relationships between Christians and Jews, especially in the aftermath of the Holocaust. In addition to perspectives espoused by Christians living primarily in Europe and North America, I examine the more recent responses of Christians living in Palestine/Israel. It is they who directly encounter Jews who returned to establish a presence in the Holy Land and now have sovereignty over it.

The fundamental question that impacts the relationship between Christianity and Judaism and bears directly on the Jewish state is whether God still "speaks" to the Jews. In other words, how are Christians to understand the Covenants between God and the Jewish people, beginning with Abraham and throughout the "Old" Testament? Did the coming of Jesus abrogate those Covenants, or do they remain in force? Do the Jews still have a role in history, and if so, what is it? Do they still have a connection to the Promised Land and what may it be? The answers either confirm or deny the validity of the prophetic vision of the "ingathering of the exiles" to the Promised Land and to the establishment of a Jewish state.

The longest-held view is that the prophetic message to the Jews has lapsed. There is a "New" Testament as well as a New Israel and a Church that has replaced the Jews as an entity with a special relationship to the Lord. The theological

© The Author(s), under exclusive license to Springer Nature Switzerland AG 2024
S. I. Troen, *Israel/Palestine in World Religions*,
https://doi.org/10.1007/978-3-031-50914-8_7

significance is that with the coming of Jesus, Christianity "replaced" Judaism. *Replacement* theology, or *supersessionism,* are the terms that designate this belief. Modifying and even challenging this dominant perspective is a relatively recent and far from complete development.

Some Christians have accepted the continuing validity of the Jewish people and their ongoing Covenant with the God of Abraham. In this view, there can be multiple Covenants, initially with Jews and later with Christians. In other words, Jews still have a role in history as foreordained in Biblical texts, and a Jewish state is a possibility that can even be supported. However, for much of two millennia Christianity overwhelmingly embraced supersessionism. The negative impact of this theological position on the relations between Christians and Jews in Christian lands cannot be overstated.

In the early centuries, before Emperor Constantine embraced Christianity in 312 A.D and established it as the official religion of the Roman Empire in 380 C.E., Judaism enjoyed preferential treatment while there was widespread prejudice against Christianity. The Church fathers differed on how to regard Judaism that continued to prosper alongside the growth of Christianity. Substantial Jewish communities flourished in Palestine even after the emperor Hadrian crushed the Bar Kochba rebellion in 132–136 C.E. It was Hadrian who changed the name of Judea to *Syria Palaestina*, signaling his intention to erase both the actuality and memory of a Jewish presence in Jerusalem and in the country. Nevertheless, even after the Byzantine Empire instituted its new policy, Jews continued to reside and thrive in Palestine, primarily in the Galilee. Constantine's decision to become a Christian, however, inaugurated a far more significant shift that was accompanied by the dissemination of an authorized theology.

Introduction

"Pope Francis in Jerusalem, 2014". Pope Francis laying a wreath in Yad Vashem's Hall of Remembrance at site of eternal flame memorial in May, 2014. Onlooking, left to right, are Chief Rabbi of Israel Meir Lau, Prime Minister Benjamin Netanyahu, President Shimon Peres, Chairman of the Yad Vashem Directorate Avner Shalev. Courtesy of the Government Press Office

The emerging position is usually associated with St. Augustine (354–430 A.D.), a theologian and ecclesiastical official from North Africa who announced that the Jews' role in history had ended. St. Augustine asserted that the Lord's Covenant with Abraham and his descendants had been fulfilled. Jews were henceforth passive and condemned to suffer for their role in the crucifixion of Jesus and for rejecting Him as Savior. Augustine's teachings led to the imposition of varying degrees of legal, economic, and social disabilities on Jews. The dissemination of this negative and hostile view also had more dire consequences. Programmatic massacres inspired by the zeal of the Crusades, such as the infamous massacre of the Jews of York in 1190, and forced conversions, as during the Inquisition, were interspersed with pogroms and other sporadic violence against Jewish communities. Systematic and institutionalized bias of the Church towards Jews persisted for centuries. Contemporary Christians have charged that Church-inspired anti-Semitism contributed to the Holocaust. As we shall see, the latter perception resulted in soul-searching and a reconsideration of supersessionism including support for the Jewish state.[1]

Substantial change only began during the Enlightenment with a decline in ecclesiastical influence and the emergence of a new politics. Initially, Jews might be permitted to join the host society provided they converted. The possibility that Jews could be citizens without converting only gradually took hold through the nineteenth century. It was Napoleon who publicly entertained new relationships between French society and the Jews. His 1798 campaign to conquer Egypt and Syria began to challenge and erode the power and authority of the Ottoman/Muslim rulers through the capitulations (see Chap. 2). Their defeat during World War I led to the dismemberment of their empire. Thus, it was not until the end of the nineteenth century that pressure brought by France and other Western powers, including the United States, enabled Jews not only to imagine but to actually inaugurate resettlement in Palestine. In effect, the civil status and political possibilities for Jews slowly but steadily improved in a Europe that was still largely Christian, but in which Christianity played a less formal and powerful role than it had previously.

Catholicism

An oft-cited account of the January 1904 meeting of Theodor Herzl, head of the World Zionist Organization, with Pope Pius X, illustrates the power and prevalence of supersessionism into the twentieth century. An unequivocal response to Herzl's importuning to support the Zionist movement, Pope Pius X explained[2]:

> We cannot give approval to this movement. We cannot prevent the Jews from going to Jerusalem—but we could never sanction it. The earth of Jerusalem, if it was not always holy, has been made holy by the life of Jesus Christ. I as head of the Church cannot possibly say otherwise. The Jews have not recognized our Lord; we therefore cannot recognize the Jewish people.

The Pope went on to declare that if somehow the Jews did settle in Palestine *en masse*, the Church would make sure there would be churches and priests there to baptize them. His imperviousness to the ongoing Jewish connection to the Holy Land was revealed when he asked Herzl why "it must be Jerusalem." It should be noted that Catholicism had long coveted an enhanced presence in Palestine, particularly Jerusalem, given the preeminence of Eastern Christian Churches since the Byzantine period. By the beginning of the twentieth century, both Catholics and Eastern Churches as well as some Protestant denominations had made significant inroads in Ottoman territory through a growing infrastructure of churches, monasteries, convents, schools, hospitals, hospices, and other facilities for pilgrims.

The uncompromising attitude of the Vatican was maintained, and it refused to recognize the Jewish state's legitimacy until well after the establishment of Israel. Resistance to the very notion of a Jewish state was poignantly illustrated when Pope Paul VI made a pilgrimage to the Holy Land in 1964. When the Pope crossed the Jordan River to Israel for an 11-hour visit, Israel's President Zalman Shazar greeted him. The Pope never uttered the name "Israel" in his remarks thanking the President. Rather, he thanked "the authorities" and studiously avoided mentioning the word "Jews." On the other hand, he used the occasion to praise his mentor, Pope Pius XII, and defended his silence over the fate of Jews during the Holocaust. By contrast, in 2000 Pope John Paul II came to Israel for a five-day pilgrimage that took him to

Jerusalem, Bethlehem, Nazareth, and sacred venues in the Galilee associated with the birth of Christianity. In the interim between these papal pilgrimages, a transformation took place in Catholicism in its relation to Jews. The Vatican had moved from viewing Israel as a kind of non-state, and its Jewish citizens as a non-people.[3]

Diplomatic relations were formalized in 1994 and the Vatican formally recognized the State of Israel as an entity in the world community of nations, although it still not recognize Israel as a "Jewish" state. Achieving this change was both revolutionary and complicated, and it did not comprehend all elements of a large and diverse church. Not all cardinals exhibited understanding and friendship; different orders within the Church voiced different attitudes towards Israel. Since the 1960s, for example, the Brothers and Sisters of Zion have been committed to improving Christian-Jewish relations; the Dominican Marcel Dubois, motivated by a desire to come close to Jews in their land, founded Bet Isaiah in West Jerusalem and served as a faculty member at the Hebrew University of Jerusalem. These initiatives contrast with the École Biblique, a Dominican scholarly institution in East Jerusalem, that was far less interested in and sympathetic to Israeli society. Lay Catholics, too, have publicly expressed and acted on the new attitude acknowledging the ongoing role of Jews in history. Moreover, Israel could not have come into being in 1948 without the favorable votes of numerous Catholic states in Europe and Latin America. It is important to note, however, that support was actually for a tripartite division of the Holy Land composed of Jewish and Arab states in addition to an internationalized Jerusalem under UN control that contains key Christian holy sites and over which they anticipated substantial influence.[4]

The official break from supersessionism did not take place until the first half of the 1960s with the pronouncements of the Second Vatican Council, a church commission established by Pope John XXIII and continued by Paul VI, to adjust Catholic theology and politics to the contemporary world. In particular, the *Nostra Aetate* [In our time] Declaration on the Relation of the Church with Non-Christian Religions represented the theological turning point and the advent of a new era of recognition and reconciliation. The Declaration was attacked by ultraconservative Catholic sectors and by Arab delegates, resulting in a minimization of its centrality and a less auspicious final version than the original draft. Nevertheless, *Nostra Aetate* was a landmark statement and remains the most important document regarding Catholic relations with the Jewish people since St. Augustine. Subsequent formulations, the *Guides* (1974) and the *Notes* (1985), have supplemented its positive teachings.[5]

Nostra Aetate disputed the teaching that the Jews were responsible for the death of Jesus Christ. It stated that some Jews called for His death but the Jewish people of that time and in all subsequent generations cannot be held guilty then or through the present, and should not be viewed as rejected or accursed by God. The Declaration thereby repudiated the basis for Christian anti-Semitism from its beginnings and embraced the revolutionary idea that the Old Testament Covenants between God and the Jewish people could be considered to remain in effect and relevant. Finally, it urged Christians to recognize the Jewish sources of Christianity.[6]

A key element in change was how Christian society, including Catholics, confronted the Holocaust and its horrors. Such introspection began in the 1930s among some Catholic and Protestant theologians who, alarmed by Nazi Germany's threatening policies, openly linked anti-Semitism to supersessionism. This insight proliferated as knowledge of the Holocaust spread during and after World War II along with dawning recognition that anti-Semitism and its consequences were not solely the product of secular racist and nationalistic ideologies but rooted in traditional Christian denigration of Jews.

The career and writings of John T. Pawlikowski (1940–), a priest who matured after World War II, illustrate this development. Pawlikowski is one of a number of leading Catholic scholars devoted to fostering Christian-Jewish dialogue and examining the role of supersessionist theology in enabling the Holocaust. Engaged in this effort for 40 years, Pawlikowski summarized a long list of incomplete and unsatisfying attempts to advance reconciliation. He expressed concern about "systematic theologians in particular who … have not addressed the profound implication of *Nostra Aetate*." He concludes that "the church… bears considerable responsibility for the suffering and death that this theology imposed on the Jewish community in Christian-dominated societies."[7] In searching for a path through the supersessionist impasse, Pawlikowski explores how to adapt the long regnant position of a "new covenant" that inaugurated the "new" Christian Church and suggests the idea of two valid covenants, one Christian and the other Jewish. This idea had already gained traction among contemporary Protestant theologians. He expresses sympathy for why Jews seek recognition as authentic actors in history. The door had been opened by *Nostra Aetate*, and many in the laity walked through it, although full acceptance by the Vatican and many theologians remains to be realized.

The landmark symbol of a new approach was the Vatican's recognition of the State of Israel in 1993 under the leadership of John Paul I. This diplomatic event was revolutionary and getting there was not easy. When Israel proclaimed its independence on May 14,1948, the Vatican responded in an article in *L'Osservatore Romano*. "Modern Zionism is not the true heir of Biblical Israel," declared the Vatican organ, "Christianity [is] the true Israel." The Vatican characterized the Jewish state as a purely secular political phenomenon, devoid of any religious significance. This allowed diplomatic recognition without the associated theological challenge, but it summarily dismissed the spiritual basis of the Zionist movement and the continuity of Jewish peoplehood.[8]

The Vatican's cautious and hesitant approach has been manifested in a series of pronouncements by significant theologians. Ecumenical statements often express increasingly explicit recognition for the reemergence of Jews into history. For example, in 2002, leading Protestant and Catholic theologians published *A Sacred Obligation,* a document formulated by moderates who sought accommodation with Jews and, at the same time, appreciated the Arab position. Among its salient clauses is a direct denial of supersessionism in the declaration that God's Covenant with the Jewish people endures forever. Other significant statements include[9]:

- Judaism is considered to be a living modern faith enriched by centuries of development;
- Ancient rivalries must not define Christian-Jewish relations today, particularly Christian worship that teaches contempt for Judaism and thereby dishonors God;
- The Land of Israel is significant for the life of the Jewish people.

These statements are in the rubric of what Pawlikowski terms a theology of "belonging." It affirms that the Holy Land is sacred to Christians, Jews, and Muslims and recognizes Palestinian Arabs—Muslim and Christian— and Israeli Jews belong as legitimate inhabitants of the Land.

Its balanced posture on the Arab/Israeli conflict notwithstanding, *A Sacred Obligation* is consistent with the reluctance of the Roman Catholic Church to acknowledge the legitimacy of the State of Israel as a *Jewish* state. It merely affirms the *presence* of Jews. It does not interject the Church on any side in the Arab-Jewish conflict. The caution of this balanced posture may be necessary in order to protect the diminishing Christian minority, not only in Israel, but throughout the Muslim Middle East. In other words, theological reform is, not surprisingly, constrained by pragmatic political concerns. This is a reminder that evolving historical circumstances may bring about changes in theology as well as revisions in doctrine.[10]

Protestant Alternatives

While Catholics have allegiance to one central Church, Protestants belong to hundreds of distinctive "denominations" with diverse theologies. Nevertheless, there are several large Protestant groupings that have addressed Israel's legitimacy and role in history. Conservative Evangelicals have become the most adamant and powerful supporters of the Jewish state despite a long tradition of supersessionist hostility. Liberal Protestants provided important support even before the establishment of Israel, although there are adherents who hold a more tentative and critical view. Finally, since these discussions are focused on Christianity outside Israel, this chapter concludes with the voices of Middle East Christians, within or proximate to Israel. They have recently come to influence the relationship between Western Christianity and the Jewish state. In expressing the views of those most directly impacted by Israel, their largely critical views have complicated a relationship that was undergoing a positive transformation.

Evangelicalism

At one end of the Christian spectrum are Evangelicals, particularly those who believe in dispensationalism. Dispensationalism defines discrete periods of historical progression, as revealed in the Bible, that constitute stages in God's self-revelation and His plan for salvation. According to dispensationalism, mankind is approaching the seventh and last period in the progression of history when the Millennial Kingdom of Christ will be established for a thousand years (*Revelation* 20:1–10). In the current troubled and tumultuous pre-millennial period, Jews are expected to return in large numbers to their Promised Land and successfully engage with enemies before a battle which precedes the End-Time. Adherents of this belief are termed pre-millennialists.[11] In addition, Evangelicals are part of a worldwide trans-Protestant movement with a central belief in the conversion experience—"born again"—that leads to salvation. It also privileges the literal meaning of the Bible—both the Old and the New Testament—as an authentic source for the word of God. Evangelicals initially enjoyed a strong presence in the English-speaking world, but the movement has taken hold elsewhere, especially in Latin America, parts of the Far East, and Africa. It is estimated that one-fourth of the U.S. population is affiliated with Evangelical denominations and that there are perhaps half a billion believers worldwide.

The impact of Evangelicals on Zionism cannot be overstated. Most of the members of the British Cabinet at the time of the Balfour Declaration were Evangelicals. More recently, significant members of the leadership of the Trump administration were Evangelicals. This is surely part of the explanation for the extraordinary support for the U.S. policy regarding Israel including blocking anti-Israel resolutions in the UN, the long-delayed move of the U.S. embassy from Tel-Aviv to Jerusalem, and providing for Israel's defense needs.[12]

In holding to the validity of the Abrahamic Covenant, Evangelicals support the ingathering of Jews into the Holy Land and welcome Zionism. Whereas supersessionism, maintains Jews are passive, destined to suffer in exile, and denied any further role in history, Evangelicalism assigns Jews an active and central role in world affairs: to (re)establish a Jewish polity in the Land of Israel and to confront the forces of the Anti-Christ at Armageddon [Megiddo in Northern Israel]. In the language of nineteenth century English and American evangelicals, the "restoration" of the Jews to the Promised Land will mark progress towards the conclusion of the historical drama when Jews surrender their faith and accept Jesus. Those who do not will endure a terrible fate. This denouement is inevitable since only those who believe in Jesus as Savior will enjoy salvation and eternal life. In other words, the ingathering of the exiles into the Promised Land is a historical necessity, but Evangelicalism, like supersessionism, envisions that the Jewish people will ultimately come to an end however much Israel may at present merit support. In this sense, supersessionism is not abolished, but only temporarily suspended. Many Evangelicals also support missions to convert Jews, even as they endorse the Zionist program.

As Evangelicalism emerged among British, American, and German Protestants in the nineteenth century, so did a growing sympathy for encouraging beleaguered Jews to return to Palestine. Herzl encountered individuals who professed to "pre-millennialism" and was helped by German Evangelicals to arrange meetings with the Protestant rulers of Germany. As already noted, English Evangelicals comprised the majority of the British Cabinet that adopted the Balfour Declaration. Moreover, American Evangelicals were active in persuading President Wilson to endorse it. During the Mandate, they supported the Zionist position in the Arab-Jewish conflict in the interest of advancing the Divine plan. While End-Time prophecy seemed to uphold the legitimacy of the Zionist cause, there was not yet a vigorous, public, mass movement on behalf of Zionism. That changed modestly after 1948 but developed into massive and enthusiastic support after the 1967 War as Evangelical Christianity grew dynamically around the world.

Some political scientists attribute the U.S. pro-Israeli policy to a powerful Jewish lobby, but this analysis neglects the significant support of leading Protestant clergy and large numbers of laity.[13] In the early years after independence, such commanding figures as Billy Graham, perhaps the most popular Protestant figure of that time, rallied Americans to support the Israeli cause. The breadth and depth of support among Protestants increased dramatically after the June 1967 War when Israel seemed about to be destroyed but unexpectedly—or miraculously — came to control all the historic Land of Israel. Like Religious Zionists, Evangelicals saw this as a transcendent event and fulfillment of prophecy.[14]

The recent ceremony celebrating the transfer of the American embassy from Tel Aviv to Jerusalem, bracketed with benedictions from a pair of Christian Evangelical leaders, illustrates this phenomenon. It opened with a prayer from Robert Jeffress, Senior Pastor of the 14,000-member First Baptist Church in Dallas. It concluded with one from Pastor John Hagee, the founder of the 22,000-member Cornerstone Church of San Antonio and a televangelist who also founded CUFI (Christians United for Israel), the largest pro-Israel charitable organization in the United States, with over 10 million members. Its mission statement clearly states the agenda:

> As the largest pro-Israel grassroots organization in the United States, Christians United for Israel is also the only Christian organization devoted to transforming millions of pro-Israel Christians into an educated, empowered, and effective force for Israel. As we grow in size and influence, CUFI strives to act as a defensive shield against anti-Israel lies, boycotts, bad theology, and political threats that seek to delegitimize Israel's existence and weaken the close relationship between Israel and the United States.[15]

CUFI and pro-Israel Evangelicals base their support on biblical passages like the oft-cited *Genesis* 12:3: "He who blesses Israel will be blessed and he who curses Israel will be cursed."

Mainline Liberal Protestantism

Not all support for Zionism within Protestantism referenced the imminent arrival of the messiah or millennial events as foretold in Scripture. Rather, Christian beliefs and practices challenged contemporary immorality and injustice through personal and political action. A positive attitude toward Jews is also marked by a resistance to missionary work. Proponents of these views, as in Evangelicalism, benefited from interactions between British and American religious leaders. They may be classified as "liberal" Protestants with affiliations to "mainline" churches. This position is epitomized in the work of James Parkes (1896–1981), an Anglican clergyman, theologian, and activist, and Reinhold Niebuhr (1892–1971), an American activist and Reformed theologian who taught at Union Theological Seminary in New York.[16]

James Parkes: An Anglican Theologian

Parkes may be the most significant British theologian who, at mid-twentieth century, opened a path to reconsidering the Jews and their place in history. During a decade beginning in the early 1920s after serving in World War I, studying theology at Oxford, and taking orders in the Anglican Church, Parkes wrote twenty-three books and hundreds of articles. He also spent much time in Europe and was alarmed by rising antisemitism. His first significant publication on the subject was an outgrowth of work in graduate school: *The Jew and His Neighbour* (1929). The rise of Naziism and outrages towards Jews further crystallized his thought. He sympathized with the Zionist project and blamed supersessionism for contributing to antisemitism and, ultimately, for the Holocaust. He came to hold the notion of a "double covenant," one for Jews and another for Christians. A mature formulation of his ideas is found in *The Conflict of the Church and the Synagogue* (1934).[17]

Parkes fought antisemitism from within Christianity in the 1930s and mobilized fellow Christians during World War II to create the Council of Christians and Jews to foster religious tolerance. Among his works are a well-regarded history of the Jews from the ancient world to the modern period. A key point in Parkes' theology is succinctly expressed in an anti-supersessionist declaration: "I see Judaism and Christianity as equals." This exceptional and novel view led him to reject Christian missionary work among Jews and to conclude that both Christianity and Judaism could learn from each other. That view earned him the title of a "Christian Zionist" but without the messianic connotations found in contemporary usage.[18]

Parkes's views also earned him considerable criticism, including among fellow Anglicans who were unwilling to dispense with supersessionism or to forego traditional missionary work among Jews. After the 1948 War, they faulted him for insensitivity to Palestine's Arab refugees. However, the files of his correspondence are also replete with letters of appreciation from fellow Protestants and Jews as well as public figures who applaud his theological positions, his open approval of Zionism, and his condemnation of the outrage perpetrated against Jews.[19]

His pro-Zionism did not preclude concern for Palestinian Arabs. From the end of the 1930s and especially in the aftermath of the 1948 war when a large population of Palestine's Arabs became refugees, he advocated the possibility of return for at least some, recognition of their rights and the dignity of equal citizenship. This position is often overlooked since many of his writings challenge those who adamantly reject the legitimacy of a Jewish homeland. The absolute priority for Parkes was a state for the Jews given the mass assault on their very existence, and his stand was well-known and appreciated on both sides of the Atlantic.

Niebuhr: An American Theologian

Reinhold Niebuhr did not address the issue of Jews in Palestine in terms of covenant and divine promise or as the trajectory of a religious saga. His language and terms of reference are largely secular, but within a Christian frame devoted to the pursuit of justice and an acceptance of human imperfection and susceptibility to immorality. Referring to himself as a "Christian realist," he draws on the language of democracy, idealism, realism, and other philosophical and political discourses to express religious urgency. His writings recall the social gospel message of end of nineteenth and early twentieth century America when Protestant clergy addressed social and political issues through the lens of Christian morality and justice. In a similar fashion, his views on the legitimacy of establishing a Jewish state were rooted in his ethical views rather than in a theological position fixed on covenant.[20]

Niebuhr initially wrote for religious journals such as the mainline Protestant *Christianity and Crisis* and the *Christian Century*, where along with other religious leaders he joined in the analysis of contemporary events. Like Parkes, he was not a practicing clergyman, except at the beginning of his career. He was a scholar with a professorship at Union Theological Seminary, a bastion of liberal Protestantism associated with Columbia University. His pro-Zionism did not stem from the expectation that a Jewish state was part of God's plan in the pre-millennial age.[21]

As a Christian, Niebuhr accepted the idea of original sin as a fundamental truth. Yet in his view, it described the human condition, not the romantic Enlightenment concept of innocence and the possibility of perfection. Appreciation for Niebuhr's theology was widely held. Niebuhr was arguably the most influential Christian theologian of his day in America, and his view resonated among wide swaths of the American public. In March 1948, a few months after the November 1947 United Nations vote on partition and prior to the declaration of the Jewish state in May, he was on the cover of the twenty-fifth anniversary issue of *Time*. The inside essay by Whitaker Chambers, a former communist sympathizer who became a crusader against communism, was entitled "Mankind is living in a Lenten age"—a phrase drawn from Niebuhr's writings. The reference is to the period when Jesus went into the wilderness, before returning to undertake His public ministry. That is, society harbors many corruptions and requires reform. For Niebuhr and those like him, that meant confronting contemporary scourges like Naziism, and doing justice, including to the Jews.[22]

Niebuhr's advocacy was in stark contrast to the disparagement of Arnold Toynbee, the anti-Zionist, Christian supersessionist historian, who famously characterized Jews as mere fossils, condemned to remain passive and suffering observers of history. The historian Arthur Schlesinger, Jr., a close friend and colleague in political action through the Americans for Democratic Action, highlighted Niebuhr's critique of supersessionism in an obituary, also observing that "Niebuhr brilliantly applied the tragic insights of Augustine and Calvin to moral and political issues." Schlesinger continued by describing what he labeled a "Niebuhr doctrine" that he characterized as follows: "In its essence it accepted God and contended that man knows Him chiefly through Christ, or what Mr. Niebuhr called 'the Christ event'. The doctrine, in its evolved form, suggested that man's condition was inherently sinful, and that his original, and largely ineradicable sin is his pride, or egotism ... The tragedy of man is that he can conceive self-perfection but cannot achieve it." [23]

With this understanding, Niebuhr acknowledged partition would not provide absolute justice. Imperfection was part of the human condition. But he prioritized enabling the Jews to continue their long history in their homeland, a modern state recognized by the nations of the world, and free to express themselves without fear of prejudice. His theology led him to recognize and appreciate the validity of the relationship between Jews and Palestine. Jews were an ancient people with a vital presence in the modern world whom Niebuhr viewed as victims of prejudice and patent wrongdoing by Christians throughout history and particularly in the present. With this conviction, Niebuhr became an advocate for their return to the homeland designated in Scripture as the best practical solution to their current distress. This view came to resonate among large portions of the American public. It signaled a change from regnant attitudes In the years following World War I when anti-Semitism was rampant both in Europe and in the United States. Quotas on admittance to college, residential and professional exclusion, and negative characterizations of Jews were commonplace among fellow Christians. His rejection of such negative and hostile views brought him to appreciate Zionism even before the Holocaust and apparently mirrored what was taking place in the public at large.

Like Parkes, Niebuhr did not give the Jews a *carte blanche*. In the unfolding of communal violence in Palestine up to and during the 1948 war, he voiced criticism of Zionism and upheld some claims of Palestine's Arabs. Here, too, his position differed from most Evangelical Christians. But while he acknowledged injuries done the Palestinian Arabs in an imperfect world, Niebuhr privileged the claims of Jews who, in his view, had far fewer options and urgent need. In 1943, he even advanced the idea that one way to solve the Jewish-Arab impasse in Palestine was to transfer the country's Arabs to Iraq.[24] In presenting his pro-Zionist position in testimony before the Anglo-American Committee in 1946, he argued that Jews had no land to call their own but had a natural and historical affinity for and a right to return to Palestine. Moreover, he contended that compromise in the direction of a bi-national solution would inhibit the Jews' ability to absorb immigrants and develop their own unique culture. Finally, he observed that only in a state where they were an assured majority, would Jews not be called on to explain their virtues and vices. This was the only just solution in a dangerous and imperfect world.[25]

This argument was not rooted in Evangelical Christianity nor did it make explicit reference to multiple covenants. Rather, it drew from a very broad range of ideas encompassed in a Christian perspective, and it was appreciated as such by leading academics and opinion-makers from the post-World War II period through the present. From Truman's Secretary of State, Dean Acheson, through presidents Jimmy Carter and Barack Obama, Niebuhr's ideas have been recognized and celebrated. Lyndon B. Johnson awarded him the Presidential Medal of Freedom, and he received honorary doctorates from the Hebrew University of Jerusalem and other institutions. Support for Israel as a Middle Eastern democracy was part of a large global view that became widespread in the West. His warnings of the dangers of Naziism and fascism were followed by criticism of the Soviet Union and communism during the Cold War. His positions on Israel and the Cold War aroused criticism from the political left that faulted the American-led West, including Israel, for aggression, political and economic imperialism, and colonialism.[26]

In 2014, the Presbyterian Church issued a dramatic repudiation of Niebuhr in secular terms in *Zionism Unsettled: A Congregational Study Guide*, a text proposed for religious instruction. Representing a paradigm shift, the guide to understanding Zionism culminates in a scathing critique of Niebuhr. Much of this document argues that Israel is a classic colonial-settler society and as such, illegitimate. But the text leads up to a major section that uses the arguments and language of anti-imperialism and anti-colonialism developed and disseminated by the Left at least since the anti-war movement of the Vietnam War period. This part of the study guide indicts Niebuhr for his role in shaping American foreign policy and, in particular, the Israel--U.S. alliance maligned along with American Cold War policy. This highly controversial curriculum was introduced and then officially withdrawn. Nevertheless, the changes inherent in its language and teachings have been proliferated and absorbed, and they continue to resonate throughout mainline Protestantism.

What accounts for the fact that this former hero is now cast as a villain? When the Jewish-Arab conflict occasioned controversy within mainline Protestantism in mid-twentieth century, Niebuhr was applauded for championing the Zionist cause. Niebuhr's reputation and position are now challenged and seriously eroded by Palestinian Christian voices that speak from within the area of conflict. Tensions and conflict are now regularly manifest within Liberal Protestantism when Church Assemblies debate whether to side with boycotts and divestment (BDS) in protest of Israel. Typically meshed with secular arguments, this critique of current Israeli policies entails a rejection of the right of Jews to a sovereign state.

Interim Observation

At the time of this writing, we are at the diamond jubilee—or seventy-five years—after the United Nations adopted Resolution 181 that paved the way for the partition of Palestine. It is commonly assumed that the UN voted for "two states for two peoples." That is incorrect. As noted above, 181 divided Palestine into three parts, the third consisting of the internationalization of Jerusalem, a proposal that was intended to appease Christians, particularly Catholics. Vatican opposition to Zionism was adamantly expressed, as we have seen, in the 1904 interview between Pope Pius X and Herzl. When it appeared that control over Palestine by Christian Britain would no longer hold, the Vatican came to prefer an Arab state, where it believed its influence would still be considerable. When this option no longer proved feasible, given American and Soviet support for a Jewish state, it came to favor internationalization of Jerusalem with its many sacred sites. This default position was readily shared by Christians of all denominations who testified before UNSCOP (United

Nations Special Commission on Palestine) that any plan for Palestine must take into account an obligation to protect their interests. Thus, Catholics, Evangelicals, Liberal Protestants, and a host of churches came to support the UNSCOP recommendation on a tripartite partitioning Palestine. Without Christian unanimity for 181, support for a Jewish state would not have achieved the two-thirds majority required for implementation: every Arab and all states with a large Muslim population voted unanimously against, and were one vote short of blocking the resolution. When Jerusalem was divided during the 1948 war between only Jews and Arabs, several states with large Catholic populations expressed regret over their vote. Nevertheless, the partition plan that authorized the establishment of a Jewish state had become a fact. This exceptional moment of Christian unanimity, based on diverse reasons for momentary support by some churches and denominations, would not last.[27]

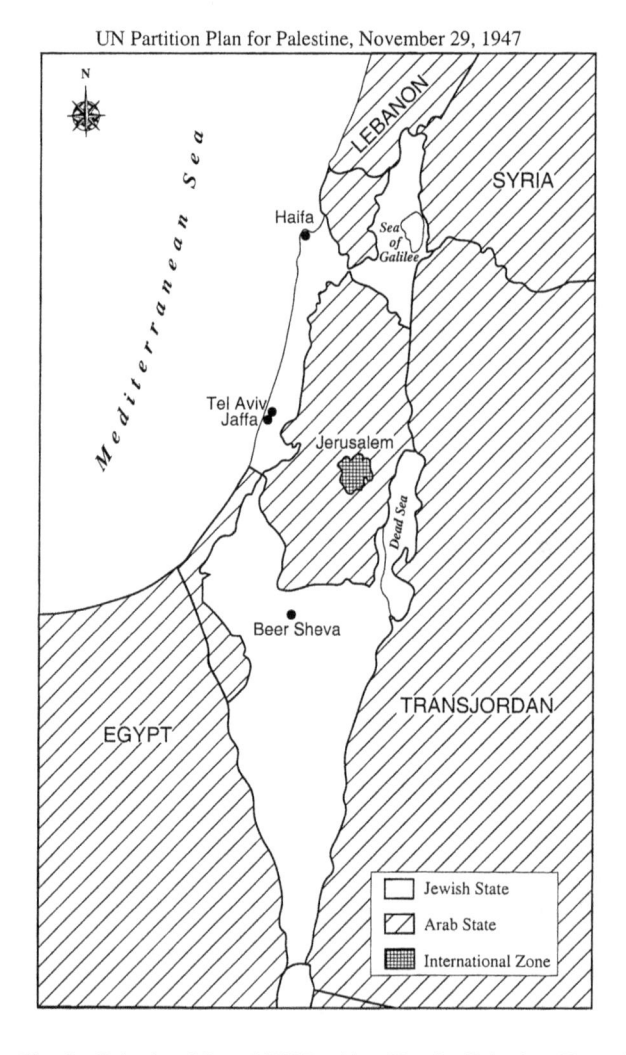

1947 Partition Plan for Palestine. Map of UN Partition Plan for Palestine, November 29, 1947, based on United Nations General Assembly Resolution 181 (created by author)

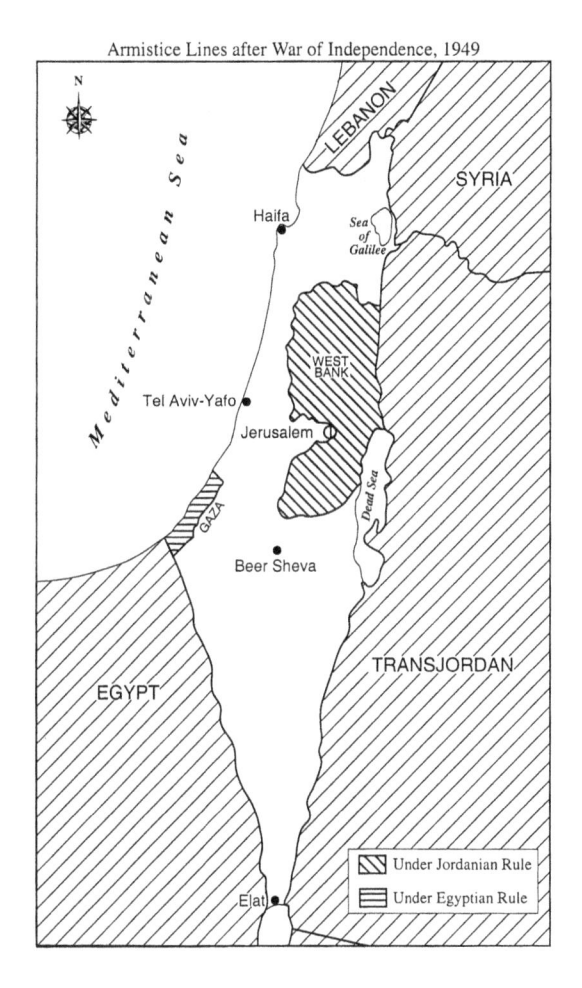

Post 1948 War Armistice Lines

Palestine's Christians

Palestinian Liberation Theology

The historical narrative on which *Zionism Unsettled* is based depicts Jewish settlement in Palestine as a disruptive force in the Middle East as a whole. It claims Palestinian Arabs are the country's authentic natives. With an uninterrupted connection going back millennia, at least to the time of Jesus and even beyond, they are passive, innocent, indigenous population confronted by brutal Zionist intruders. Such a view is an outgrowth and development of the ideas of Naim Ateek (b. 1937), a Palestinian Anglican theologian and former Canon of St. George's Cathedral in

Jerusalem, who applied Liberation Theology to the Arab/Israeli conflict in his widely read *Justice, and Only Justice; A Palestinian Theology of Liberation* (1989). We have briefly encountered Ateek in our discussion of indigeneity (Chap. 5). Here we expand on the religious and political significance of his arguments in connection with Palestinian Liberation Theology.

Ateek's claims are supported by other Palestinian and regional Christians who collaborated to produce the *Kairos Palestine Document* in 2009, a document that has been described as an echo of Ateek's *Justice, and Only Justice*. This theological-political statement announces itself as "A moment of truth, a word of faith, hope and love from the heart of Palestinian suffering." It decries Israel's post-1967 "occupation" as a "sin against God" and exhorts "the international community to stand by the Palestinian people who have faced oppression, displacement, suffering and clear apartheid for more than six decades." The reference to "*six* decades" implies that Israel's sins predate the 1967 Six-Day War and Israel's expansion into the West Bank. *Zionism Unsettled* not only references Israel's establishment in 1948 but objects to all Jewish settlement in Palestine, going back to the end of the nineteenth century. For Ateek, Israel is the illegitimate product of an oppressive colonial political movement. There is no place for the Jews in this narrative, whether by divine promise, cultural continuity, historical exigency, or the right to self-determination.[28]

The Presbyterian study guide, *Zionism Unsettled,* cites academic authorities who are established anti-Zionist scholars, among them Jews whose contributions are apparently meant to endow this narrative with authenticity. However, the whole is inspired by Sabeel Ecumenical Liberation Theology Center, the Jerusalem-based institution established by Ateek in 1989.[29] The narrative evokes the religiously rooted maxim of "speaking truth to power" as if there were an obvious binary where the powerless command the entire truth and the powerful have none. Moreover, in examining this kaleidoscope of Christian theological responses to Israel, it is noteworthy that both the Presbyterian *Study Guide* and Ateek's *Justice, and Only Justice* explicitly espouse supersessionism. They deny the Abrahamic covenant's validity, the continuing relationship between God and the Jewish people, and the Jews' connection to the Holy Land. Thus, the radical and relatively sudden shift from Niebuhr's Christian realism to Ateek's liberation theology suggests that post-war support for Israel in some mainline Protestant churches and their rejection of supersessionism may not be enduring.[30]

It is significant that Liberation Theology was initially developed in the 1960s by Latin American theologians and that it entails Marxism's struggle against colonialism, conflating theology with history and politics. In Ateek's work, supersessionism justifies Palestinian demands for Christian support. [31] Jesus's message supersedes the Abrahamic covenant. He speaks in universal language with no special promises to the Jews. In a purportedly universal argument that mixes a theological with a secular supersessionist analysis, Ateek affirms the historical judgement of the deeply Christian historian, Arnold Toynbee, that the Jewish people have exited history as actors.[32]

Ateek completes the erasure of the Jews through their "replacement" by Palestinians. Thus, in his hands, Exodus is a Palestinian narrative. It tells the story of Palestinians who are seeking historical justice and wish to return to their Promised Land from the venues of their dispersion and dispossession. Like Antonius, who opposed the 1937 Peel partition plan, and Edward Said, who opposed Arafat's recognition of Israel through the Oslo Accords, Ateek equates full justice with the dissolution of the Jewish state. However, in deferring to pragmatism, he proposes a temporary federation between a Jewish and a Palestinian Arab state—a federation he anticipates will dissolve when the Jews leave the country.

Ateek's *Zionism Unsettled* weaves together secular anti-Zionist polemics and theological tropes that can be traced back to *adversus Judaeos* [against the Jews or Judeans] that has been used extensively since the Fourth Century A.D. One scholar likens these tropes to "old wine in new bottles," depicting Jews as invaders who inevitably disrupt a peaceful region, create inequalities, and establish a society based on apartheid.[33] The same argument is at the core of the optimistic declaration of *Kairos Document* that if "there were no occupation, there would be no resistance, no fear, and no insecurity ... Therefore, we call on the Israelis to end the occupation. Then they will see a new world in which there is no fear, no threat, but rather security, justice, and peace." As in *Zionism Unsettled*, the charge is that the trouble started with the first Jewish settlements.[34]

In 2010, a year after the publication of the *Kairos Document*, Palestinian Christian clerics from the Bethlehem Bible College, an Evangelical institution, produced *Christ at the Checkpoint*. They also create public events that dramatize the suffering of Palestinians under Israeli occupation and are designed to mobilize protest on their behalf. In all these instances, the same bill of complaints is presented through a Christian theological prism. The compatibility of these charges with traditional theological positions has recently been made explicit by a leading Palestinian clergyman, Mitri Raheb, a Lutheran from Bethlehem. In an essay entitled "Palestine: Time for a Paradigm Shift," Raheb advocates that Christian theology incorporate the widespread secular critique of colonial-settlerism. He therefore includes Zionism in a section entitled: "The *Theo*politics of Settler Colonialism: The Case of Israel" [my emphasis]. Raheb's explicit association of Zionism and Israel with colonial-settlerism had already been widely disseminated across Western Christian churches in the writings and advocacy of his colleague, Naim Ateek. Raheb's invented term "theopolitics" patently indicates how closely theological and secular political discourses may be intertwined.[35]

There is yet another Christian approach to the Jewish state from within Palestine/Israel and associated with Palestinian Liberation Theology. Elias Chacour, a Melkite Catholic Archbishop, is intimately familiar with the pain and suffering experienced by Christian Arabs caught in the turmoil of Israel/Palestine. A member of a family long rooted in a Christian village in the Galilee, Chacour speaks with eloquent authority. His expression of the plight of those who view themselves as indigenous and uprooted due to Israel's creation is personal, poignant, and deep. The sense of injustice must be taken at face value even when, at times, the logic of Chacour's historic/theological formulations is difficult to fathom. His identity as an Arab is fundamental and he claims with absolute certainty that his personal roots long precede the Covenants between Abraham and the Lord, not merely the first Christians. He declares Abraham was an outsider who came from a foreign land into Canaan where Chacour's forefathers had lived since time immemorial. On this basis he unequivocally identifies himself as a direct descendant of the first adherents of Christianity from the time Jesus lived in the Galilee. Indeed, it is the messages of Jesus of the Beatitudes that were spoken in the Galilee where he serves as a priest that motivate and inform him. Chacour's voice of resolute faith, suffering, and endurance as a "living stone" is all the more compelling because he simultaneously expresses deep sympathy for modern Jews who have endured their own suffering and who have established their state in his homeland, thereby displacing him and his people.[36]

Chacour's writings and personal efforts draw sympathetic attention since he urges reconciliation with those who have caused great injury and continue to inflict injustice. The titles of his books reflect this call: *Blood Brothers; the dramatic story of a Palestinian Christian working for peace in Israel* and *We Belong to the Land; The story of a Palestinian Israeli who lives for peace and reconciliation*. Unlike fellow Palestinian Liberation theologians, he accepts the reality of the Jewish state and seeks an accommodation based on empathy for the suffering of Jews. Thus, even though he also holds to supersessionism, the issue of the legitimacy of a Jewish state is defused. The Christian Arab experience in Palestine/Israel can and does result in substantial differentiation.[37]

Critics of Liberation Theology can be found among pro-Israel Christians abroad, notably Christian Zionists, who offer yet another perspective and political program.[38] This movement within Evangelicalism identifies the critique of Israel as a form of supersessionism. Charges like that of colonial-settlerism are merely a veil: denying Jews are authentic descendants of the people to whom God promised the land simultaneously denies the legitimacy of the Jewish state. Alongside considerable sympathy for the plight of Palestinians, there is also an insistence on Jewish priority based on Scriptures.

A Christian Zionist rejoinder also points to the violence visited by Arabs on Jews, the corruption of Palestinian politics, and Arab unwillingness to appreciate and acknowledge the Jews' investment in labor and purchase to reestablish themselves in the Promised Land. Criticism includes charging the Qur'an with antisemitism. Thus, Christian Zionists from abroad question the motives and legitimacy of Israel's Palestinian Christian critics. In addition, they are concerned that castigating Israel and Jewish behavior might alienate potential converts to Christianity and subvert efforts at peace and reconciliation.

Moreover, critics of Liberation Theology fault their co-religionists in Israel/Palestine for reducing their analysis of "the situation" to a single word: "occupation." Instead, they emphasize a complex historical narrative: Arab armies were poised to overrun and hoped to destroy the country; the Arab League's Khartoum declaration of 1967 responded to Israeli peace overtures with the three "NOs": "No negotiations. No recognition. No Peace"; multiple Israeli peace proposals that included withdrawal from nearly all the West Bank were rejected by Palestinian leadership; acts of terror that caused thousands of Israeli casualties were encouraged and celebrated; thousands of missiles were fired at civilian targets inside Israel following Israel's withdrawal from Gaza; and Palestinian religious, civic, and political leaders have repeatedly declared they reject peaceful coexistence with Israel on any terms.

This critique notwithstanding, Palestinian Liberation Theology has been widely appreciated and its impact may be explained as part of a larger phenomenon—the "indigenization" of Middle Eastern Christianity and the demand that a Christian position must necessarily include Palestinian voices. It is also part of a larger protest by local Arabic-speaking Christians, long resident in the Middle East, who object to control and authority of non-Arab ecclesiastical institutions based in Athens, Moscow, Western Europe and America. One indication is their demand that the liturgy in the churches be conducted in Arabic rather than Greek or Latin. Another is their insistence on appointing local clerics to positions of leadership and an expressed unwillingness to submit to clerics imported from abroad to head local churches. This movement for local control among Middle Eastern Christians was also reflected in reservations about *Nostra Aetate* and its call to reevaluate traditional Catholic doctrine and for reconciliation with Jews.

Concluding Reflection

Despite the significant impact of some exponents of Palestinian Liberation Theology, other Middle Eastern Christians have sought a measure of accommodation with the Jewish state. Eastern Churches, with roots from the early centuries of Christianity, have extensive holdings in land, church buildings, convents, hospices, and the like that have served the local population and pilgrims for centuries. This amounts to sizeable and valuable properties in the cities or holy sites in Jerusalem, Jaffa, Haifa, Nazareth, and around the Sea of Galilee. The Greek-Orthodox church is the largest property owner in Jerusalem and among its valuable holdings in many of the city's neighborhoods is the site of Israel's Knesset and other national government buildings. By and large these properties are held for income but there has also been significant revenue from sales, sometimes accomplished by clandestine methods. Maintaining good relations requires circumspection and sensitivity on the part of both the churches and the Israeli government.[39]

As a result, explicit challenges to Israel's legitimacy may be necessarily muted or moderated. Outside of Israel, this cultivated cooperation does not always hold. Where Arab governments are hostile to Israel, local churches may follow suit. The case of Archbishop George Hakim, head of the Greek-Catholic church in Israel between 1948 and 1967, is classic. Hakim advocated integration into Israeli society and institutions. He urged members of his community to join the Histadrut, the Israeli workers union, and the Histadrut responded by establishing clinics in Arab towns and villages. Hakim also came to embody the possibility of Christian Arab/ Israeli Jewish cooperation, appearing in public and official settings in traditional ceremonial robes. Nevertheless, after he was elected Metropolitan, or head of Melkite Catholic Church for Middle East, Hakim moved to Damascus and his public message changed. Once in Syria, his statements reflected the government's hostility to Israel. Indeed, when Bishop Hilarion Capucci, head of the Greek-Catholic Church in East Jerusalem and the West Bank, was caught smuggling arms from Lebanon to Israel, Hakim came to his defense. Such behavior may also reflect reasonable caution in response to vulnerability in a region where Christians have been on the defensive, particularly with the rise of radical Islamic nationalism, and have endured massive population losses.

There is but one state in the Middle East where the Christian population has actually increased. That is Israel. While Christian Arabs have left this embattled area in large numbers for safety and opportunities elsewhere, other Christians are replacing them. These include literally tens of thousands of Provoslav Russian Orthodox who, since the 1980s, have accompanied Jewish family members through the Law of Return and whose children even serve in the Israeli army. Numerous foreign workers from Romania, the Philippines, and East Africa are resident for short or long periods. Thus, many churches and communities are not directly party to the Arab-Jewish conflict. There are now churches that conduct their services in Hebrew since Greek and Arabic are far more distant to them than Hebrew, which is the language of everyday experience. Thus, for the first time in nearly two millennia, portions of the church liturgy in the Holy Land are recited in the original Hebrew. The relation of this growing non-Arab Christian population to Israel and Jewish/Christian relations has yet to be measured.

There is another complicating factor for Israel's Christians. From the end of the nineteenth century, Christian intellectuals played an important role in developing the concept of Arab nationalism and a shared Arab identity comprising both Christians and Muslims. However, the recent rise of radical Islamic movements that have targeted Christians throughout the Middle East has raised reservations about the possibility of creating a lasting, shared community of identity and interests.[40] Yet even when tensions and outright conflict developed between Christians and Muslims in Lebanon, the Christian Maronite community remained identified with the Arab world, and as such, did not undertake a public and enduring alliance with the Jewish state. Although some may disagree on the significance and relative contribution of Christian and Muslim intellectuals to Arab nationalism, there is no doubt that Christian input was substantial and created a precedent for the alliance that developed over ensuing decades. Christians supported Arab nationalism, criticized Zionism, as exemplified by Antonius, or like George Habash, founder of the left-wing Popular Front for the Liberation of Palestine, advocated and carried out terrorist acts, and Edward Said who advanced critical theses in the academy.

Finally, there is a recent example of a contrary development when a local Christian community distanced itself from pan-Arab nationalism in favor of an alliance with Israel. After a formal request and considerable lobbying, Israeli authorities granted the Israeli Christian Aramaic Association official recognition in 2014 as the "Christian Aramaic Nationality." This modest-sized group of descendants of early Christians who lived in the Middle East prior to the Muslim conquest and who have maintained Aramaic, the *lingua franca* of much of the region at the time of Jesus, pushed back at the pressure to remain separate from Israel within an Arab identity. They openly urge their youth to undertake national service or enlist in the Israel Defense Forces. This dramatic change from the 1950s, when Christians refused to join the IDF,[41] may be a consequence of witnessing the radical reduction of historic Christian communities, most of which predate Islam, and the rise of radical Islamic movements that target both dissident Muslims and Christians, defined as infidels, despite the protections that *dhimmi* status should have offered. The increasing violence against Christian communities throughout the Middle East has alarmed Christians and resulted in a massive exodus of families seeking safety in other parts of the world—from Europe to the Americas and Australia. For those who decide to remain, there are stark choices. Accommodating to a Jewish state that appears to offer security is one option, at odds with the tenets of received theology and politics regnant in the public square.

These selected sketches of the relationship of Christianity to the establishment of a Jewish state reveal, as in the twisting of a kaleidoscope, new and evolving perspectives. Return of the Jews to the Holy Land has been viewed differently by those in direct contact with this new and unanticipated circumstance and among those who have observed it from afar. The result is multiple perspectives and unparalleled complexity in a faith tradition historically beset by schisms.

All can convey their views both in the public square and in internal church or denominational institutions, so that Christians have multiple theological approaches and a variety of secular discourses to choose from in regard to the Jewish state. As the survey in this chapter demonstrates, there is no one Christian perspective. The combination of theology and secular approaches enables multiple and conflicting possibilities.

The diversity observed in Judaism and Christianity is not similarly characteristic of Islam. The range of difference among Muslims is narrower and recent, although perhaps of growing significance. It is to the third stream of monotheistic faiths that we now turn.

Notes

1. The most significant work on Christian as well as Islamic antisemitism is David Nirenberg, *Anti-Judaism, The History of a Way of Thinking* (New York: Norton, 2013). See, too, James Carroll, *Constantine's Sword; The Church and the Jews* (New York: Houghton Mifflin, 2001). For more recent scholarship on the relationship between Western Christianity and the Jews, although not specifically Zionism, see Magda Teter, *Christian Supremacy; Reckoning with the Roots of Antisemitism and Racism* (Princeton: Princeton University Press, 2023). Far more pertinent to Christian attitudes towards Zionism and Israel is also the recent, comprehensive Cary Nelson and Michael C. Gizzi, *Peace and Faith; Christian Churches and the Israeli-Palestinian Conflict*, eds. (Philadelphia and Boston: Academic Studies Press, 2021).

2. *The Complete Diaries of Theodor Herzl*, ed. by Raphael Patai (New York: Herzl Press, 1960), 4:1.
3. A useful article on the complications of the agreements between the Vatican and the Palestine Authority is Leonard Hammer, "The Vatican Joins the Israeli-Palestinian Conflict," *Middle East Quarterly*, 24:4 (Fall, 2017).
4. Uri Bialer. *Cross on the Star of David: The Christian World in Israel's Foreign Policy, 1948–1967* (Bloomington: Indiana University Press. 2005). Raymond Cohen, "Israel and the Holy See Negotiate: A Case Study in Diplomacy across Religions," *The Hague Journal of* Diplomacy, 5 (2010) 213–234.
5. *NOSTRA AETATE: Declaration on the Relation of the Church to Non-Christian Religions Proclaimed by His Holiness Pope Paul VI on October 28, 1965*: https://www.vatican.va/archive/hist_councils/ii_vatican_council/documents/vat-ii_decl_19651028_nostra-aetate_en.html
6. Pim Valkenberg and Anthony Cirelli, ed., *Nostra Aetate* (Washington, D.C.: Catholic University of America Press, 2016), Part IV, pp. 161–213. *JSTOR*, https://doi.org/10.2307/j.ctt1g69zbs
7. John T. Pawlikowski, *Restating the Catholic Church's Relationship with the Jewish People: The challenge of super-sessionary Theology* (Lewiston, New York: Edwin Mellen Press, 2013), p. 11.
8. Paolo Zanini, "Angelo Roncalli *Nuncio* to Paris and the Establishment of the State of Israel," *Israel Studies*, 22:3 (Fall 2017), 102–124; Giulio Meotti, *The Vatican Against Israel; J'Accuse* (Canada: Mantua Books, 2013); Adriano E. Ciani, *A Study of Cold War Roman Catholic Transnationalism* (Ph. Thesis, University of Western Ontario, 2011), See https://ir.lib.uwo.ca/etd/348/
9. "A Statement by the Christian Scholars Group on Christian-Jewish Relations, September 1, 2002: *A Sacred Obligation*. See, too, Philip Cunningham, "Toward A Catholic Theology of the Centrality of the Land of Israel for Jewish Covenental Life," in Philip Cunningham, Ruth Langer, and Jesper Svartvik, *Enabling Dialogue About the Land* (New York: Paulist Press, 2020), pp. 303–334.
10. John T. Pawlikowski, "Toward a Theology of Belonging: A Catholic Christian Perspective," in Philip Cunningham, Ruth Langer, and Jesper Svartvik, *Enabling Dialogue About the Land* (New York: Paulist Press, 2020), pp. 262–281.
11. A widely read popular statement of this belief is found in the best-seller Hal Lindsey, *The Late Great Planet Earth* (Grand Rapids, MI: Zondervan, 1970).
12. The topic is subject of an excellent, growing literature. See Caitlin Carenen, *The Fervent Embrace: Liberal Protestants, Evangelicals, and Israel* (New York: NYU Press, 2012); Yaakov Ariel, *An Unusual Relationship: Evangelical Christians and Jews* (New York: NYU Press, 2013); Jason M. Olson, *America's Road to Jerusalem* Lanham, MD: Lexington, 2018); Daniel Hummel, *Covenant Brothers Evangelicals, Jews and U.S. Israeli Relations* (Philadelphia: University of Pennsylvania, 2019).
13. John J. Mearsheimer and Stephen M. Walt, *The Israel Lobby and U.S. Foreign Policy* (New York: Farrar Strauss Giroux, 2007).
14. On a popular level, the most impactful book has been Hal Lindsey, *The Late Great Planet Earth*. On the growing affiliation of Billy Graham towards a Jewish state see Amy Weiss, "Billy Graham Receives the Ten Commandments: American Jewish Interfaith Relations in the Age of Evangelicalism," *American Jewish History*, 103:1 (January 2019), 1–24.

15. *Christians United for Israel*, https://cufi.org/
16. Other theologians could have been included in this discussion, such as Karl Barth, a German associated with Swiss Calvinism. Barth was known initially for objecting to the submission of the church to the Nazi state and for his views on Jews, Judaism, and Israel that impacted fellow theologians and philosophers. The number of post-Holocaust theologians and philosophers offers many pertinent choices. However, this chapter focuses on representative individuals who were particularly prominent in movements that influenced politics in their respective countries. On Barth see Mark R. Lindsay, *Barth, Israel, and Jesus: Karl Barth's Theology of Israel* (London: Routledge, 2007), Chaps. 2, 4, and 5. There is also available a very succinct review of the fundamental Christian understanding of the place of evil and sin in human character and experience that underlay Barth as well a significant modern thinkers especially Fyodor Dostoevsky and Sören Kierkegaard. This comprehensive view is crucial in understanding the fundamental Christian theological framework out of which Niebuhr viewed his world. See Whittaker Chambers, "Religion: Faith for a Lenten Age," *Time*, March 8, 1948. This is the inside essay of the twenty-fifth anniversary issue on which Niebuhr is featured on the cover. See footnotes 16 and 22 for further context.
17. For an extensive biography see Chaim Chertok, *He Also Spoke as a Jew; The Life of the Reverend James Parkes* (London: Valentine Mitchell, 2006). His vast writings and correspondence are readily accessed at Southampton's University's Parkes Jewish Library and the Parkes Institute for the Study of Jewish/Christian Relations. The correspondence is a treasure trove for interactions between Parkes and similarly inclined Christian and Jewish religious leaders on both sides of the Atlantic. See, too, Alice Eckardt, "Founding Father of Jewish-Christian Relations: The Rev. James Parkes (1896–1981), *Studies in Christian-Jewish Relations*, 3:1 (2008), https://www.researchgate.net/publication/28799696_Founding_Father_of_Jewish-Christian_Relations_The_Rev_James_Parkes_1896-1981
18. See Parkes Archives, University of Southampton, File MS 60 16/615 concerning correspondence with John Pawlikowski references an article by Parkes in the *Journal of Ecumenical Studies*. Fall 1969, 790–794. See, too, James Parkes, *A History of Palestine from 135 A.D. to Modern Times* (London: Victor Gollancz, 1949).
19. Correspondence with Rt. Rev. Geoffrey Allen, Lord Bishop of Egypt in October and November 1950, who returned to England to become a leading Anglican figure, concerning Parkes's alleged lack of sympathy for Palestinians. In the same file there is correspondence with Leo Amery, an ardent pro Zionist public figure, with fulsome appreciation for Parkes and his work on behalf of Zionism. File MS 60 7/21/2.
20. Carys Moseley, "Reinhold Niebuhr's Approach to the State of Israel: The Ethical Promise and Theological Limits of Christian Realism," *Studies in Jewish-Christian Relations*, 4:1 (2009), 1–19.
21. The conduit between Reinhold Niebuhr and James Parkes was usually Ursula Niebuhr, Reinhold's British-born wife. She grew up in Southampton, studied at Oxford and took her doctorate at Columbia. Their shared views were enhanced by similarities in origins and paths taken. Parkes Archives, File MS 60/30/1.

22. Reinhold Niebuhr was the subject of a featured story and on cover of *Time* Magazine, March 8, 1948: http://content.time.com/time/covers/0,16641, 19480308,00.html
23. Arthur Schlesinger, Jr., "Forgetting Reinhold Niebuhr," *The New York Times*, September 18, 2005," and *New York Times*, June 22, 1992. There is also an extended and generous appreciation of Niebuhr, not yet translated, by Eliahu Elath [Epstein], former Israeli ambassador to the United States and to Great Britain, detailing his service and relationship to Zionism: Eliahu Elath, *Through the Mist of Time* (Jerusalem: Yad Ben-Zvi, 1989), pp. 122–138 [Hebrew] See, too, Franklin H. Littel, "Reinhold Niebuhr and the Jewish People," *Holocaust and Genocide Studies*, 6:1(1991) 46–61, typescript found in Niebuhr Papers, Box 14, Folder 15.
24. Rafael Medoff, "Communication: A further note on the "unconventional Zionism" of Reinhold Niebuhr," *Studies in Zionism*, 12:1 (1999), 85–88.
25. Reinhold Niebuhr, "Jews After the War", *Nation*, Feb. 21, 1942, 214–216 and Feb. 28, 1942, 253–255.
26. Typical of his views regarding Israel in the context of Cold War politics is Reinhold Niebuhr, "Our Stake in the State of Israel," *The New Republic*, Feb. 3, 1957. http://www.newrepublic.com//book/review/our-stake-in-the-state-israel
27. Peter Hahn, "Alignment by Coincidence: Israel, the United States, and the Partition of Jerusalem, 1949–1953." *The International History Review*, 21:3 (Sep., 1999), 665–689.
28. Presbyterian Church (USA), *Zionism Unsettled: a congregational study guide ([United States]:* Israel/Palestine Mission Network of the Presbyterian Church (U.S.A), 2014).
29. Dexter Van Zile, "Updating the Ancient Infrastructure of Christian Contempt: Sabeel," *Jewish Political Studies Review*, 23:1 (2011): https://jcpa.org/article/updating-the-ancient-infrastructure-of-christian-contempt-sabeel/
30. Moseley argues that the absence of a theological basis to Niebuhr's views that have made his pro-Zionism vulnerable to contemporary critics. Moseley, "Reinhold Niebuhr's Approach to the State of Israel" *Ibid*.
31. See: Naim Ateek, *Justice, and only Justice, a Palestinian Theology of Liberation* (Maryknoll, NY: Orbis 1989); and *A Palestinian Christian Cry for Reconciliation* (Maryknoll, NY: Orbis 2008), followed by *A Palestinian Theology of Liberation;* the Bible, justice, and the Palestine-Israel conflict (Maryknoll, NY: Orbis, 2017).
32. Ateek, *Justice and only Justice*, pp. 165–66. On Ateek's appropriation of the Exodus story for Palestinian nationalism see M. Raveh, "Universalism and Nationalism in Palestinian Christian Thought: Naim Ateek's Theology and the Paradigm of the Exodus.," *Journal of Ecumenical Studies* 56:3 (2021), 438–455. https://www.muse.jhu.edu/article/802417
33. Adam Gregerman, "Old Wine in New Bottles, Liberation Theology and the Israeli-Palestinian Conflict," *Journal of Ecumenical Studies*, 41:3–4, (Summer–Fall 2004), 313–40.
34. See: https://kairospalestine.ps/index.php/about-kairos/kairos-palestine-document
35. Mitri Raheeb, (2021). "Palestine: Time for a Paradigm Shift," *Academia Letters*, Article 1848, 2021. https://doi.org/10.20935/AL1848. See, too, for an analysis of the relationship between Raheb and Ateek and their distinctiveness in Samuel J. Kuruvilla, "Contextual Theological Praxis as Resistance: Palestinian

Christian Peace-building in the Occupied West Bank" in *Mary's Well Occasional Papers*, 3:1, January (Nazareth, Israel: Nazareth Evangelical Theological Seminary 2014).

36. See discussion on the use of "living stones" in "Modern Palestinians and Antiquity" in Chap. 5.
37. Elias Chacour, *Blood Brothers; the dramatic story of a Palestinian Christian working for peace in Israel* (Grand Rapids, Mich: Chosen Books, 1984); Elias Chacour, *We Belong to the Land; The story of a Palestinian Israeli who lives for peace and reconciliation* (Notre Dame, Indiana: University of Notre Dame Press, 2003).
38. Significant ripostes to Palestinian Liberation Theology and critics within mainline churches are found in a recent collection: Gary R. McDermott, ed., *The New Christian Zionism; Fresh Perspectives on Israel and the Land* (Downers Grove: IL: InterVarsity Press, 2016). See, too, Paul Charles Merkley, *Christian Attitudes towards the State of Israel* (Montreal: McGill-Queen's University Press, 2001), pp. 161–94
39. Una McGahern, *Palestinian Christians in Israel; State Attitude towards Non-Muslims in a Jewish State* (London: Routledge, 2011), esp. Chap. 6: 'Conflict in Nazareth."
40. For reports on the Christian plight in the Middle East and from Islam elsewhere see Charles Sennott, *The Body and the Blood: The Holy Land at the Turn of a New Millennium: A Reporter's Journey (New York: Public Affairs, 2001); There* are many more recent published accounts: *The New American*, "Christian Exodus from Middle East Continues," James Heiser, October 29, 2010; Robin Write, "War, Terrorism, and the Christian Exodus from the Middle East," *The New Yorker,* April 14, 2017; See "The Christian Exodus from the Middle East," *Prophecy News Watch,* May 30, 2017: https://www.prophecynewswatch.com/article.cfm?recent_news_id=1271
41. Franck Salameh, "Christians of the Holy Land, Disintegration and Ideological Necrophilia," in Jon Eibner, *The Future of Religious Minorities in the Middle East* (Lanham, Md: Lexington, 2018), pp. 211–34; Rimah Farah, "The Rise of a Christian Aramaic Nationality in Modern Israel," *Israel Studies*, 26:2 (Summer 2021), 1–28; Randall S. Geller, *Minorities in the Israeli Military, 1948-58* (Lanham, MD: Lexington, 2017), pp. 123–136.

Chapter 8
Islam: Encountering a Contemporary Challenge

Introduction

Islam's encounter with the Jewish state has been the most intense and actively hostile. The Muslim Middle East has mounted armies to wage war, sponsored terror attacks by Islam-inspired "martyrs" ["*shuhada*" in Arabic], supported maneuvers in international organizations to undermine Israel's legitimacy, and preached from the pulpits of mosques to stir up the faithful against the Jewish state. Islam is divided into major and minor schisms, with Sunni as opposed to Shi'a the most pronounced, but it has been far more unified in its opposition to Zionism than Christianity. Not having undergone a reformation, renaissance, and Enlightenment, nor having confronted secularization to the extent that has taken place in the West, Islam's rejection of Israel is traditional and consistent with its historical experience as the dominant religion and culture in the region for the past fifteen centuries. The emergence of a Jewish polity in its midst is thus construed as a challenge to Islam's hegemony and basic beliefs. Moreover, since Israel is identified as a product of the "West," the antagonism towards it is enmeshed in the resentment and hostility towards Europe and America, and the civilizational challenge Christianity has posed for Islam.

An official account of the conflict between Jews and Arabs over Palestine was commissioned in 1977 and only completed in 1988 under the aegis of the United Nations Secretariat through its Division for Palestinian Rights. This document is remarkable not merely for what it contains but for what it leaves out. Published in four parts and comprising nearly three hundred pages, it begins with the Balfour Declaration of 1917 and takes the history of the Arab rejection of Zionism up to 1988. Presumably, a more up-to-date version would supplement material on the recent past but is unlikely to extend the background prior to Balfour. In terms that have become prevalent in scholarship, it is a totally secular analysis of the origins and evolution of the conflict. Remarkable for an account of competition for control

© The Author(s), under exclusive license to Springer Nature Switzerland AG 2024
S. I. Troen, *Israel/Palestine in World Religions*,
https://doi.org/10.1007/978-3-031-50914-8_8

of the Holy Land, there are no Jews, Muslims or Christians expressing views or acting based on their faith.

Rather, this official history focuses entirely on the secular arguments examined in the first five chapters of this book. It repeatedly invokes the Palestinian right to self-determination, the negative consequences of Jewish immigration and settlement, outbreaks of violence between the two communities, historical claims that point to the exclusive indigeneity of Palestinian Arabs, and Jewish responsibility for violence. Islam is mentioned only in the context of the Islamic Conference [now termed the Organization of Islamic Cooperation] that identifies itself as "the voice of the Islamic world" and works to protect Muslim holy sites and to "safeguard and protect the interests of the Muslim world in the spirit of promoting international peace and harmony."[1] Intra-Muslim discourse that impacts on the role of Islam and Muslims in the conflict is otherwise totally absent. Islam is nowhere to be found, even as the voices and roles of Judaism and Christianity are absent. Curiously, Ben-Gurion as a Zionist leader is occasionally quoted, while the Grand Mufti, Muhammad Amin al-Husayni of Jerusalem who played a crucial and vociferous role in the struggle against Jewish settlement during the Mandate, is rarely cited. In a notable exception, he is termed a Palestinian patriot, for calling the faithful for a general strike in 1936. He is not referred to as a religious leader which, by definition, he was in his role as Mufti of Jerusalem.[2]

Religion is likewise typically ignored in a host of standard texts on the Arab/Jewish and Israeli/Palestinian conflict. As with the UN historical account, documents produced by official bodies and statements by numerous individuals are cited and analyzed, but these are notably secular, as if the territory under dispute were devoid of religious significance and competition. This avoidance distorts the analysis of the conflict. To understand Islam's unmistakable hostility to Jewish sovereignty we must begin, not in 1917, but in the seventh century with the rise of Islam and its subsequent relationship to Judaism and Jews. The prevalent secular narrative that casts Jews as European interlopers, and foreign to the Middle East and the Arab world blatantly ignores the extensive connections between Arabs and Jews who lived in Palestine and the Middle East since before the rise of Islam. That erasure obscures the realities and possibilities of Israel's quest for legitimacy.[3]

The Significance of Religion in the Arab State and Politics

Islamic states are by intent theocracies, governed by the "rule of God." God is the supreme sovereign, the source of political authority. The body politic and the sovereign power within it are ordained by God to promote His faith and to maintain and extend His law. God's involvement in human affairs has a benign intent that will be realized when the community of believers submits to the Divine message. Indeed, *Islam* itself means "submission" to faith in God. Moreover, the polity or community over which the sovereign rules is termed the *umma*. Ideally, this is a single universal Islamic community embracing all the lands in which Muslim rule is established and where Islamic law prevails. It may be diverse ethnically and dispersed geographically but is constituted by a common belief held by a world community of believers to advance their values and interests. This principle has been carried into the present in parts of the world where Muslims form a majority in the states in which they reside. That certainly obtains for the modern Middle East where the concept of the *umma* has often found expression by groups intent on creating a single pan-Islamic polity over the entire region.[4]

In classic Islamic thought the world is divided into three parts. The first is where a majority is organized into a polity where Islamic law has primacy. This is termed *dar al-islam* or the "abode of Islam." There is then the portion of the world in lands adjoining *dar al-islam* which are called upon to adopt Islam or face the threat of conflict. That region is termed *dar al-harb* or the "abode of war." There is yet a third non-Islamic territory where an armistice exists with Islamic society. This has been termed *dar al-sulh* or *dar al-hudna* that refer to a "territory of treaty."[5] The historical reality is that since the seventh century, Palestine has been part of *dar al-islam*, except for the interruption of Christian Crusades. Thus, the establishment of a sovereign Jewish state is an unprecedented and powerful challenge to the *umma*, not only for the Arab Middle East but for Muslim societies elsewhere.

The means for rectifying such unacceptable situations is *jihad* or "striving" or "struggling." While this term can also refer to a personal struggle for self-improvement, it is also commonly understood to mean "war" or using force against non-believers. While in the Qur'an *jihad* has two meanings: internal struggle for improvement and external struggle against the non-believer, its contemporary use by fundamentalist Islamic groups designates using force to impose Islamic order within the Muslim world and beyond. In other words, Islam has a vocabulary that can be and has been mobilized for conflict, although this use is not necessary nor inevitable.

An appreciation for the potentially incendiary role of religion was common wisdom from early in the Arab/Jewish conflict. Clearly political problems arose between the competing Jewish and Arab nationalisms, but the fundamental issues are rooted in culture. The Peel Commission recognized this incompatibility in its report: "They [Jew and Arab] differ in religion and in language. Their cultural and social life, their ways of thought and conduct, are as incompatible as their national aspirations. These last are the greatest bar to peace."[6]

Secular discourse usefully exposes the conflicting claims to the territory called Palestine. But competing claims to the *Holy Land* are a different matter altogether. Islam had been dominant in Palestine since 636/7 when the Caliph Umar accepted the surrender of Jerusalem from the Patriarch Sophronius, venerated as a saint by both the Eastern Orthodox and Roman Catholic Churches. The only serious interruption to Muslim control occurred sporadically during the Crusades of the eleventh and twelfth centuries. The Ottoman Turks rule of four centuries, from their conquest of Palestine in 1516 and of the Middle East, ended during World War I. Muslim presence and influence continued through the mandate system that replaced the Ottomans with Islamic states, except for Lebanon in which a precarious balance was forged between Muslims and Christians. Even in this transitory period, members of the Hashemite aristocracy were installed Iraq and Transjordan as Muslim heads of government. Their prestige and power derived not from a democratic mandate but from a pedigree that harked back to a connection with the Prophet Mohammad and their historic function as protectors of holy sites.

There were only two exceptions. Lebanon was established in the 1920s based on power-sharing between Maronite Christians and Islamic factions. However, protagonists claimed a shared Arab identity, so this arrangement held uneasily for about half a century when the initial Christian majority was challenged by a new Muslim majority. Palestine posed a far greater challenge. Jews were not viewed as Arabs and refused to being permanently relegated to a minority. As the influential Lebanese Christian intellectual, George Antonius, critically observed in *The Arab Awakening* (1938), "Arab" is a term that includes only Muslims and Christians. It manifestly excludes Jews. Arab nationalism, so defined, could not accede to the mandate for a Jewish national home in Palestine.

An even more restrictive definition of "Arab" was simultaneously developing that ascribed "Arab" to Muslims. While Antonius contributed to the pan-Arab idea in secular terms that included Christians, Muhibb al-Din al-Khatib (1886–1969), a Syrian intellectual and publisher, working in Saudi Arabia, reflected a significant movement that, beginning in the 1920's, invested Arabness with Islam. Termed the "Semitic Wave Theory," he described a series of waves of Semitic peoples who migrated from the Arabian Peninsula into the fertile crescent and came to dominate it with the emergence of Islam in the seventh century A.D. This historical account contributed to a pan-Arab vision of the history of the Middle East that incorporated various ancient peoples from the Pharaonic period and the Phoenicians through the Muslim conquests. At the end of the Ottoman Empire and the Caliphate (1922) the opportunity and perhaps even the need for new forms of identity were translated into nationalist political ideologies, whether pan-Arab or local. The announcement of the Balfour Declaration that Jews were to be granted a national homeland into this emerging *Arab* landscape injected a foreign element into a region of competing nationalisms with claims on the past and disrupted relationships between them and their territorial ambitions.[7]

Throughout this region, religion was an essential, if not dominant, attribute in the construction of identities and societies. Affiliation with a religious community was central to the legal, political and social construction of Palestine under Islamic rule. The Ottomans supported communal segregation through a system of millets. Although new entities were added during the nineteenth century, the fundamental division based on communities of Christians and Jews was maintained. Both were assigned the status of *dhimmis* [protected persons] under foundational Islamic law established at the beginnings of Islam. This category was initially applied to "people of the covenant" or "people of the book" out of the respect Islam held for the Abrahamic religions that Islam superseded but did not totally replace. In contrast to non-believers and pagans who were expected to convert to Islam, *dhimmis* were entitled to practice their faith though penalties applied such as a special tax [*jizyah*], restrictions on dress, and limited access to public office, service in the military, and occupations. Christians and Jews had separate court systems and were judged according to their own religious law. Their community officials, too, derived their status and power from the same divisions assigned by the Islamic state. The legacy of social divisions through millets is maintained throughout the Middle East, including Israel, where state law grants recognition to communities on select personal issues based on religion and empowers its officials.[8]

Competition between Jews and Christians in currying favor with the dominant Muslims was a natural consequence of this system. Both *dhimmi* communities contended for primacy in influence and advantage in commerce and other fields in which they were concentrated. Occasionally, during the nineteenth century, Jews enjoyed a more favorable position if only because the Ottomans held suspect the connections between local Christians and European Christian powers. Significant change accompanied Zionist settlement. Concern that the Jews might enhance their position within Palestine to the point of becoming preeminent may have contributed to a shift in the balance, with Christians joining with Muslims in constructing a shared notion of Arab nationalism. If Christian Arab nationalists were alarmed by the potential of a Jewish polity, the offense to Muslim nationalists was even more intense. The increase in Jewish immigration and land purchases from the 1880s led the Ottomans to place prohibitions on both.[9]

The point is that religious affiliation is the key indicator of how individuals and groups were perceived and could act in the Arab world from the Muslim conquest through the present. This model of a unitary Islamic *umma* extending across the region persists, even if the *umma* is divided into national states. In Islam, faith and state are indivisible and there is no effort to separate the mosque from the state.

The distinction between church and state did not exist in the West when the United States adopted the novel and unprecedented model that earned it the designation of the "first new nation" at the end of the eighteenth century.[10] The declared separation of an official faith from government has since become the hallmark of many contemporary states. While crosses remain nearly ubiquitous in the flags of democratic European states from Scandinavia to the United Kingdom and to Greece, the cultural and political significance of Christianity in shaping national identity has been reduced. Significantly, the French flag—the tricolor—composed of three colors signifies the reduced public role of Christianity in French identity. The American stars and stripes employ the use of the same colors—red, white, and blue — rather than religious symbols. Many modern, democratic states explicitly root themselves in secular identities, without association to a favored religion, while citizens enjoy equal rights.

Middle Eastern states, including the Jewish one, do not know such pronounced symbolic separation. The supreme authority in Islamic states over the centuries has been the caliphate that was only dissolved in 1922 by the secular Young Turks in a revolution that attempted to redefine Turkey as a secular republic. Successor Arab states of the Ottoman Empire have maintained Islam as the state religion. This is designated in constitutions across a wide area in twenty-six states from the Middle East and from North Africa to the northern portion of the Indian subcontinent: Afghanistan, Algeria, Bangladesh, Bahrain, Brunei, Comoros, Djibouti, Egypt, Iran, Iraq, Jordan, Kuwait, Libya, Maldives, Malaysia, Mauritania, Morocco, Oman, Pakistan, Palestine, Qatar, Saudi Arabia, Somalia, Tunisia, United Arab Emirates, and Yemen. Most of their flags display combinations of the colors of Islam: black, white, red and green. Some use explicit Islamic signifiers as the star and crescent or the inscription of the Islamic creed, as does Saudi Arabia with the *shahada*: "There is no god but Allah; Muhammad is the Messenger of the Allah." The flags developed by the Palestine Liberation Organization since the 1960s all display the Islamic color scheme of black, white, red, and green in varying geometric shapes. These common symbols reflect the primacy of a shared civilization in which Islam is the core expression.

Israel's blue and white striped flag is reminiscent of the Jewish prayer shawl, the *tallith*, and in which the six-pointed star of David is centered, stands apart and separate. The lone Jewish state still does not have normal diplomatic ties with most of the Islamic states, although relations with a small but slowly growing number is a recent phenomenon. None of even these maintain totally normal relations with Israel. Islam plays a critical role in this persistent and defining rejection or inhibiting normal relations. I begin this inquiry into the basis of Islam's charge that the Jewish state is illegitimate by describing how Jews are presented in the Qur'an.

Jews in the Qur'an

The Qur'an refers to Jews as the "Children of Israel" (*banu isra'il*), but there are other terms such a simply "Jews," [*al-yahud*] "the people of Abraham," "the people of Moses," and "people of the book." The Qur'an has some positive descriptions of Jews, particularly in the period of Mecca, but most portrayals are negative. On the positive side, Jews are identified with "the people of the Book [Kitab]," however the reference is limited to revealed truth according to Islam, rather than the entire Biblical account. This elevated Jews above pagans and entitled them to a protected status within Islamic communities and carried some negative consequences.

Many of the negative characterizations also apply to Christians and to members of other faiths that preceded the arrival of Muhammad and his messages. This is not unusual for sacred books. The Qur'an, like the Hebrew Bible and the Christian New Testament, is replete with criticism of those who oppose its authority and the community it represents. This is the nature of revealed monotheistic religions. The story of Abraham in the Old Testament and the texts that follow emphasize the greatness of his God, while the falseness of others is maintained. The same applies to canonized texts in successor variants of monotheism which, by definition, convey authorized revelations of the one, true deity. Moreover, the very nature of canonization is to institutionalize revelation and mark its completion or carefully monitor potential additions. The three monotheistic religions do not welcome, let alone endorse, alternative revelations with the limited and recent exception of some Catholic and Protestant versions of multiple covenants. New "truths" usually challenge accepted verities. In this sense, "supersessionism" or "replacement theology" are inherent in the exclusivity of monotheistic faiths. It is therefore not exceptional that the Qur'an contains polemics against Jews and Judaism, and that instances where Jews challenged the Prophet's authority would become subjects of scorn and invite retribution.

For example, the Qur'an characterizes Jews as a rebellious people as, in fact, does the Bible in multiple instances. They not only rejected Muhammad's legitimacy as the Prophet, but also rebelled against other prophets, mentioned in their own biblical texts, whose stature was unquestioned. (Sura [chapter or section of the Qur'an] 2:87, 92; 3:52, 112, 183; 5:70). Similarly, Jews often failed to fulfill the commandments given in the Torah that they ostensibly respect and accept. They are therefore accursed by God for the lack of belief and refusal to accept divine instructions. Thus, God is angry with them (Sura 3:112). The Qur'an even claims that they followed the words of the Satan in the time of Solomon (Sura 2:102). For these and similar acts of rebellion, they are punished in various ways, including exile from their land (Sura 59:2–4).

A well-known and paradigmatic episode relates the consequences for a rebellious and dishonest Jewish tribe near Medina who did not accept Muhammad in 626 and were vanquished and banished by the Prophet: (Sura 59: 2–4)

> It was He who drove those People of the Book who broke faith … God came up upon them from where they least expected and put panic into their hearts: their homes were destroyed by the own hands, and the hands of the believers … If God had not decreed exile for them, He would have tormented them [even more severely] in this world. In the Hereafter they will have the torment of the Fire because they set themselves against God and His Messenger [Muhammad]: God is stern in punishment towards anyone who sets himself against Him.

In similar vein, they are depicted as disobeying the Lord as they worship the golden calf. (Sura 2:93). The text continues to characterize them as ungrateful unbelievers who cannot be trusted to keep a covenant. (Sura 2:100) It goes on to observe that due to their outrageous and disrespectful behavior and their distorting the true word of the Lord, they will lose any share in the Hereafter (Sura:102). Perfidy inevitably earns them curses from God. (Sura 2:88; 4:51–52).[11]

In what has become a trope that is still repeated more than fourteen centuries later, clerics and polemicists inflame true believers by derogating Jews as "the descendants of apes and pigs." The characterization is widespread and can be heard in mosques, demonstrations in Palestinian areas and wherever it is in the interest of the speaker to whip up the passions of a crowd against Israel. The source for this epithet is also in the Qur'an. Its origins, like the Biblical story of Lot's wife turning into a pillar of salt for defying the instruction of not looking back to Sodom, indicates a punishment by transformation into some other form. This fate for disobedience may be visited on both Jews and others, including Christians. However, the most prevalent contemporary use is in reference to Jews and Israelis. The following three Suras tell of Allah transforming Jews into apes and/or pigs are regularly quoted in diatribes against Jews:

> Sura 2:65: "And you had already known about those who transgressed among you concerning the Sabbath, and We said to them, 'Be apes, despised.'"
> Sura 7:166: "So when they were insolent about that which they had been forbidden, We said to them, 'Be apes, despised.'"
> Sura 5:60: "Say, 'Shall I tell you who deserves a worse punishment from Allah? Those (i.e., the Jews) whom Allah distanced from himself, was angry with, and condemned as apes and pigs…'".[12]

Treatment of Jews in Islamic Societies

Dhimmi status provided real protection and a large measure of security during much of the long course of living under Islamic rule. Change to active hostility and rejection is recent and can be correlated with the challenge Jewish immigration and settlement towards the end of the Ottoman period.

The treatment of Jews under Islam prior to this period has been a much-studied subject. In the nineteenth century European Jews took the lead in this inquiry. They were fascinated by the interactions and borrowings between the two faiths. Indeed, a tradition of extraordinary scholarly inquiry among Jews developed particularly from the mid-nineteenth century beginning with Abraham Geiger (1810–1874), a German Jewish scholar with rabbinical training, who advanced the study of the Qur'an and its relationship to Jewish sources. Ignaz Goldziher (1850–1921), a Hungarian Jewish scholar with deep knowledge of Judaism and Islam, is credited with being one of the founders modern Islamic Studies. He became involved with what became known as "Oriental Studies," when this term enjoyed a deeply respectful and admiring attitude that is far from the pejorative shading Edward Said invested in it. Their work inevitably compared the fate and condition of Jews who remained in the Middle East and North Africa with those who had migrated to Christian Europe. By and large, they viewed the Jewish experience under Islam as positive, if only in comparison with the virulent form of antisemitic racism and the outbreaks of violence it engendered in blood libels and pogroms in Europe.[13]

Such scholars recognized the anti-Jewish tropes found in the Qur'an but studied and appreciated Islam as a whole. They did not consider such texts as representative of Islam in its realization. They claimed the experience of Jews within Muslim society as beneficent when opposed to the overwhelming negative experience prevalent in Christian Europe that culminated in the Shoah. Rather, as the historian Bernard Lewis has observed, the sporadic anti-Jewish outbursts should be contextualized in that they were few in extent and severity and, unlike the European experience, Islamic hostility was also directed at other protected non-believers including Christians and Zoroastrians. One crucial distinction between Islam and Christianity is that, unlike Christianity, Islam did not charge Jews with deicide and assign them with the consequences for such an act. Rejection of the Prophet received a less harsh retribution that the accusation for killing Christ.

The dramatic turn against Jews is a modern phenomenon that followed on Zionist settlement that resulted not only in wars against a Jewish state but in uncommon hostility and even violence against long-established Jewish communities throughout the Middle East and North Africa whose existence long pre-date not only the rise of Islam but also of Christianity. Those well-rooted communities are now largely gone through immigration to Israel and the Jewish Diaspora. Scholarship explains this event as a consequence of two phenomena. The first is the increased exposure to the noxious, antisemitism of Christian Europe within the formerly distant and relatively closed world of the Ottoman Empire. The links in this transfer were originally Middle Eastern Christians with their close ties to brethren in Europe.

In this manner, for example, the Damascus Affair, a notorious blood libel that began in 1840 when a Catholic monk was found missing, illustrates the connection and its consequences. Jews were accused of his murder and of using his blood for ritual purposes; the Jewish community of Damascus was consequently attacked, and its synagogue pillaged.[14]

Antisemitic tropes continued to penetrate through Arab Christians while Muslims remained relatively detached. Christians in Lebanon and Egypt had greater contacts with Europe so that it was the Maronites in Lebanon, Copts in Egypt and other similarly connected Christians located elsewhere who served as conduits. This infestation grew significantly through the Dreyfus trial whose echoes reverberated into the Middle East. The very birth of Arab nationalism is embroiled in this process: Naguib Azouri's (1870–1916) 1905 *Le Reveil De La Nation Arabe* is the work of a Christian Arab and is saturated with antisemitic imagery adopted from the European Christian world.[15] However, probably the most outrageous and consequential transfer was the importation of the *Protocols of the Elders of Zion*, the notorious anti-Jewish tract originally forged in Russia that became a standard of European anti-Semitism. It came to be published and widely distributed in Arabic translation.

This growing incursion of antisemitic literature and ideas culminated in the massive export of Nazi propaganda beginning in the 1920s and increasingly through the 1930s. The growing collaboration of anti-British and anti-Jewish leaders included the Mufti of Jerusalem who was issued an arrest warrant in 1937 for his role in inciting the Arab rebellion of 1936–1939. The Mufti escaped the British, first going to Iraq to advise the pro-Nazi, pan-Arabist regime and then to Berlin on the eve of the Farhud [pogrom] of 1941 where he remained until the end of World War II. During this period, he enlisted twenty thousand fellow Muslims in the Balkans in a special SS unit that participated in actions against Jews. The residue of this collaboration persists. Even today recognition of the Holocaust in education and public discourse is problematic in Palestine and the region, notably in Ayatollah-led Iran.[16]

Mobilizing the Islamic Past

Khaybar

European anti-Semitism supplemented what was developing from within Islam's own negative traditions. These became the central resource in the reevaluation of the Jewish presence in the Abode of Islam. This is exemplified in the present-day notoriety given to events in 638 C.E. at Khaybar, an outpost oasis proximate to Medina where the forces lead by Mohammad defeated local Jewish tribes, confiscated their wealth, killed a large number and ultimately expelled the remainder. These events took place after these tribes rejected the Prophet, broke an agreement, and tried to defeat and kill him. This victory cleared the way for Muhammad's movement to conquer Medina, to secure the Arabian Peninsula and, through his successors, expand Islam to distant lands in Asia, Africa and Europe.

This incident was an early confrontation between Muhammad's followers and Jews. It took place in an oasis of present-day Saudi Arabia, where Jewish tribes were engaged in growing dates and servicing caravans, and it continues to color the relations between the Prophet's followers towards Jews. Muslims frequently reference it in describing what they perceive as the hostility, perfidy, and arrogance of contemporary Jews. They view the Zionist enterprise as temporary and certain to succumb to the fate of Jews at Khaybar nearly fifteen hundred years ago. This yet another instance of how the past, the present and expectations of the future are interwoven in Arab culture.

MEMRI (Middle East Memory Research Institute), a research organization that monitors press and media throughout the Arab world, provides a convenient measure for the ubiquity of references to that event in contemporary Arab discourse. It records hundreds of references to Khaybar annually in newspaper reports, sermons at mosques, and media programs.[17] Oral references are often accompanied by the chant: "Khaybar, Khaybar, oh Jews, the army of Muhammad will return" [*Khaybar Khaybar yā Yahūd, jaysh Muḥammad sawfa ya'ūd*]. This chant was heard by Israeli commandos as they encountered the flotilla, led by the ship, Mavi Marmara, that left Turkey to break the Israeli siege of Gaza in May 2010. It continues to be chanted in anti-Israel demonstrations like those organized along the Israel and Gaza border in the Hamas-Israel conflict.[18]

Invoking Khaybar appears regularly on Egyptian television and is rebroadcasted throughout the Middle East during the holy month of Ramadan that is dedicated to fasting, prayer, reflection and community. In 2013, a show entitled "Khaybar" was announced with the promise that it "focuses on the social, economic, and religious lives of the Jews, including their politics, their plots, and the way they managed and controlled the [Arab] tribes." The show also portrays "the [Jews'] hostility and hatred towards others, along with their treacherous nature, their repeated betrayals, and their despicable racism."[19] Such use of Khaybar is indicative of more general attitude thought appropriate for a period of religious contemplation and celebration. In 2017, an American Jewish woman was featured using her guiles to enlist an Egyptian diplomat to damage Egyptian national security. In 2019, viewers were treated to Jews in control of the world. In 2020, the channel presented a 30-episode show called *El Nehaye* [The End] that tells of a future war to liberate Jerusalem, the destruction of Israel and the dispersion of its Jews to their countries of origin.[20] Thus, more than four decades after the historic 1979 peace treaty between Egypt and Israel, no armed conflict erupted between them; but, nearly 1500 years later traditional tropes project Islam's rejection of the Jews and celebrate the violent attack Muhammad's followers carried out against them.

Jews as Crusaders

The ultimate triumph of Islam is an article faith. In this context, arrangements for peace and accommodation are a transitory stage in the expectation of ultimate victory. Thus, it is possible to initiate a *hudna* or a treaty that is explicitly temporary and may be legitimately broken when it is advantageous to do so. Indeed, this was the case with the treaty between Muhammad and the Jewish tribes of Khaybar prior to their defeat and annihilation. Similarly, temporary accommodation before ultimate victory characterizes the history of Islam's confrontation with the Crusaders. After nearly two centuries of temporary setbacks and repeated incursions by European Christians, Islamic fortitude and persistence was rewarded with triumph. In July 1187, Muslim forces under Saladin (Salah ad-Din) crushed a Crusader army at the Battle of Hattin in lower Galilee. The battle was a turning point that led to renewed Muslim dominance in Palestine. They recaptured Jerusalem and other Crusader strongholds. While a subsequent crusade was mounted with some success, the prior Crusader loss so weakened the effort to conquer the Holy Land that final defeat by Islamic forces soon followed. Islam's victory over Christianity came to be viewed as a heroic if, at times, painful event that exemplified the capacity of Muslims to defend the Abode of Islam from the assault of outsiders. It remains a standard metaphor for faith in the inevitable defeat of the infidel outsiders, most recently is invoked to describe the doomed Zionist attempt to establish a Jewish state in Palestine.

There is irony in casting Jews as contemporary Crusaders. In the two centuries of battles between Christian crusaders and Muslim defenders, Jews were largely onlookers and victims. The Crusaders not only eliminated a Jewish presence in Jerusalem but destroyed Jewish communities on their way to the Holy Land. Nevertheless, the rhetorical and ideological requirement of the Arab/Israeli conflict has transformed modern Jews into latter-day Christian Crusaders.[21]

Contemporary references to Arabs repulsing Jewish/Crusaders abound. A brigade of the PLO army was called Hattin (site of Saladin's crushing victory); before the outbreak of the 1967 Six Day War, Egyptian President Gamal Abdel Nasser was compared to Saladin. The Egyptian press proclaimed that, like Saladin, Nasser would liberate Jerusalem in the spirit of Muslim unity and for the sake of Islam. Section 15 of the Hamas Charter praises Saladin and describes the 1973 Yom Kippur War as Arab victory like Saladin's; the civil war in Lebanon, that began in 1975, was called the "Tenth Crusade," in which Lebanon's Maronite Christians were compared to the Franks; and in the 1990 Gulf War, Saddam Hussein proclaimed: "Salah ad-Din now loudly cries Allah Akbar (God is Great)!"[22]

Yasser Arafat, the leader of PLO, was also often likened to Saladin for his relentless efforts to remove Zionists and reclaim the Holy Land. A favorite trope in his speeches was the claim: "We shall return to Jerusalem and Al-Aqsa, entered by Salah ad-Din." This claim was dramatically reflected in the description of Amos Oz, the renowned Israeli novelist, who reported on Arafat's return in 2000 from the failed Camp David summit: "The whole Gaza Strip is covered with flags and slogans proclaiming the Palestinian Saladin. 'Welcome home, Saladin of our era!' is written on the walls." Oz then reflects: "In silence, astounded, I watch, and I can't help reminding myself that the original Saladin promised the Arab people that he would not make pacts with the infidels: he would massacre them and throw them in the ocean. I see Mr. Arafat dressed in his grey-green combat uniform. It's an Arafat clothed like Che Guevara and treated like Saladin: my heart breaks ... ".[23]

Jerusalem

Embedded within the Crusader story, and central to it from the perspective of Islam, is the loss of Jerusalem or Al-Quds [Holy City]. Arafat famously addressed this topic in May 1994 in the aftermath of Oslo Accord I (1993) and prior to the Oslo Accord II (1995) while on a visit to Johannesburg. While speaking in a mosque, an often-used venue for anti-Israel sermons, he presented what one scholar has termed: "Arafat's Islamic Message:"[24]

> Our main battle is Jerusalem ... I have to speak frankly, I can't do it alone without the support of the Islamic nation. I can't do it alone. No, you have to come and to fight and to start the Jihad to liberate Jerusalem, your first shrine... What they are saying is that [Jerusalem] is their capital. No, it is not their capital. It is our capital. It is the first shrine of the Islam and the Moslems... . This agreement [Oslo Accords I], I am not considering it more than the agreement which had been signed between our prophet Mohammed and Quraysh, and you remember the Caliph Omar had refused this agreement and [considered] it a despicable truce ... . But Mohammed had accepted it and we are accepting now this peace offer. But to continue our way to Jerusalem, to the first shrine together and not alone.

Arafat is referring to the *hudna*/temporary "peace" agreement with the Quraysh, an Arab tribe that controlled Mecca and allowed Muhammad to pray inside the city during this truce. Two years later, when Mohammed grew stronger, he abrogated the agreement, slaughtered the tribe of *Quraysh* and conquered Mecca. Thus, the rhetoric and historical references by Arafat, who was often viewed as not ostensibly religious, resonated with and referenced foundational Islamic beliefs and narratives.

Arafat was within both the local Palestinian and larger Islamic tradition in making Jerusalem the focus of religious aspirations, polemics, and politics. In this, he followed the lead of Hajj Amin al-Husseini, the Grand Mufti of Jerusalem and the paramount Palestinian religious and political leader during the Mandate. It was the Mufti who set the course of Arab nationalist politics with the onset of the British Mandate. There was also a personal connection between the two. Arafat was a member of the al-Husseini family and a distant cousin of the Mufti and began his political activism in Mandatory Gaza as a member of the Muslim Brotherhood and within the circle of the Mufti's activities. This connection marks the vital connection between politics and religion. By the 1960s, Arafat became leader of FATAH, the organization that brought the Palestinian national movement to international prominence. The movement's name reflects the blending of secular with religious terms: *ḥarakat al-taḥrīr al-waṭanī al-Filasṭīnī*, meaning the "Palestinian National

Liberation Movement." From this was crafted the reverse acronym—"FATAH." In religious discourse it signifies the Islamic expansion that led to the breach of the treaty with the Quraysh, and subsequently to the conquest of Mecca, the crucial event in Islamic history that Arafat advertised as the precedent for signing the Oslo Accords.[25]

The focus on Jerusalem in the emerging conflict between Jewish and Arab nationalism was first cultivated by the Mufti who demonstrated how Palestinian interests could be advanced under the umbrella of Arab unity and the mantle of Islamic solidarity.[26] Economic and political disputes with Palestine's Jewish community were carried on together with protecting the interests of Islam. The 1929 countrywide riots that many consider to be the "year zero" of the Arab-Jewish conflict over Palestine ostensibly began over Muslim objections to alleged violations by Jews over the *status quo* on arrangements for prayer at the Western or Wailing Wall at the Temple Mount/Al-Haram Al-Sharif.[27] This local struggle between worshippers over a relatively minor matter quickly escalated into a campaign to involve the Muslim world beyond Palestine. In other words, it was recast as a struggle of Muslims worldwide against the infidels—European Jewish invaders—like the Christian Crusaders of old. Given the significance of religion in Arab political culture, the Wailing Wall episode necessarily became enmeshed in the emerging Arab-Jewish conflict.

The Mufti of Jerusalem made the connection with Islam central to the conflict. The title of his office may have indicated only local authority but his position as president of the Supreme Muslim Council (1922–1937) indicated a wider sphere of influence. Using his role in Jerusalem to solicit support from Muslims outside Palestine, he obtained donations during the 1920s from regional Arab Muslim rulers as well as from India, the largest Muslim community in the world, for the restoration of Al-Aqsa and, importantly, for the Dome of the Rock that he had plated in gold.[28] Inventing a particularly innovative technique for stimulating support, he initiated an international meeting of the Islamic Congress in Jerusalem in 1931. This forum decided to establish an institution to be known as "Al-Aqsa University." Although it was not established, it did reflect an attempt to compete with the Hebrew University of Jerusalem that formally opened in 1925. He was more successful in promoting a sacred burial ground proximate to the Al-Aqsa Mosque that was intended to enhance the status of this site as the third holiest in Islam. The first internment featured that of Muhammad Ali, the revered leader of Indian Muslims.[29]

This contributed to the success of the incipient Palestinian national movement's attempt to place the grievances of Palestine's Arabs over Jerusalem and Palestine on the international agenda. The Mufti's initiatives complemented and strengthened the secular dimension of the Palestinian national struggle. Defense of the faith was likely a far more effective mobilizing force against the Jewish National Home rather than abstract nationalist slogans about self-determination, the perfidy of the British, appeals to international law or historical rights. Defense of a sacred site provided a concrete symbol and goal that was readily and widely adopted by Muslim masses.

Inserting Jerusalem into the heart of the conflict has remained through the present a central tactic of Islamic anti-Israel politics and the effort to delegitimate Israel before the international community. This strategy began when the League of Nations was called on to investigate the violence that accompanied the 1929 controversy over the Western Wall. Claims of alleged dangers to Al-Aqsa and the Al-Haram Al-Sharif have continued unabated in international forums and are included in the annual agendas of the United Nations General Assembly and its various committees, particularly UNESCO. In recent decades charges include the kind of revisionism witnessed in the secular historical narratives in which contemporary Palestinians claim to be descendants of the Canaanites, while the connection of the biblical Hebrews to modern Jews is denied, as is their significance in the city's history. Such claims even contradict what the Mufti's Supreme Muslim Council itself published in 1929 with the onset of the riots. It declared that the Temple Mount's "identity with the site of Solomon's Temple is beyond dispute… this is the spot, according to the universal belief, on which David built an altar unto the Lord and offered burnt offerings and peace offerings (*2 Samuel* 24:25)." Since that time, the Islamic position on the historic Jewish connection to Jerusalem has morphed into an unrelenting opposition to the legitimacy of a Jewish state and to Israel's deepening hold on the city.[30]

Temple Mount in Jerusalem. Aerial view of Temple Mount in Old City of Jerusalem with Al-Aqsa dominating, July 2008. The Western Wall Plaza, the site of Jewish worship, is marked with an "X." Courtesy of the Israel Government Press Office. Yoram Benita photographer

Radical Islam

"Radical" political Islam has swept across the Middle East causing disorder and mayhem throughout the states carved out of the Ottoman empire as well as in proximate ones in Asia and Africa. A common thread in the spread and growth of these movements is an energetic religious fundamentalism critical of modern secular culture in its many forms and imbued with calls to return to primary religious values that are thought to have characterized Islamic society during the peak of its power in the Middle Ages. In the calls for purification there are many targets from the West, in general, to corrupting foreign elements within their midst including adherents of alternative Muslim beliefs, Christians, secular nationalists and, of course, Jews. Zionism, which is seen as a totally foreign implant earns special contempt for its successful encroachment into the Abode of Islam and its characterization as a Western cultural implant carrying out a colonial mission.[31]

This radical, fundamentalist, religious movement has insinuated itself into the Arab-Israeli conflict in an immediate and active way through violent confrontation by the Palestinian Hamas, the Hezbollah in Lebanon, the Ayatollahs in Iran, and extremist groups elsewhere, both Sunni and Shi'a. The targets of Radical Islam are usually the local regime as well as external enemies in the West, notably the United States. Israel, too, considered foreign to *dar al-Islam*, has become a key target, both rhetorical and actual, whether through violence directed inside Israel or abroad to Israeli and Jewish persons and institutions.

The most immediate and active threat to Israel is from Hamas, an offshoot of the Muslim Brotherhood that was established in Egypt in the late 1920s. It has control of Gaza and is engaged in constant, low-level warfare since 2007. Despite the unfavorable balance of forces against it, Hamas persists in firing explosive and incendiary devices from Gaza across the border into Israel and supporting terrorist acts including suicide bombings. Hamas is labelled a terrorist organization by the United States, the European Union, Japan, and numerous other countries. In 1999, it was expelled from Jordan despite earlier intimate and friendly connections. Having won an election in competition with the PLO in Gaza in 2006, it promptly worked to suppress it in a drive for exclusive control over Gaza and the West Bank. Unlike the PLO that has officially recognized and has ongoing relationships with Israel, Hamas totally rejects the Jewish state and is dedicated to Israel's destruction. As such it follows the most extreme and uncompromising of the many possibilities of Islamic theology and tradition.

The name, Hamas, derives from the Arabic for the "Islamic Resistance Movement." This stream in Islamic thought lives in tension with existing Islamic regimes or is an outcast within them. It inevitably follows that it would not tolerate independence for those who are considered foreign to the Muslim homeland. Organized in 1988 after the outbreak of the first Intifada under the spiritual guidance of Sheik Ahmed Yassin (1937–2004), its declared intention is to liberate Palestine through armed struggle and supplant it with an Islamic state.[32] Its military branch is called Izz ad-Din al-Qassam Brigades in memory of a Syrian preacher who had led *mujahadeen* (those who engage in *jihad*) in Libya and Syria before falling in the Arab uprising in Palestine during the 1936–1939. Hamas has named in his honor the short-range "Qassam" rockets they manufacture. Al-Qassam is revered as a heroic leader who contended that the British and the Jews had to be confronted by waging a militant struggle rather than through political accommodation.[33]

The Hamas version of Islam is set out in detail in its 1988 Charter, termed the Covenant of the Islamic Resistance Movement.[34] This blatantly antisemitic declaration describes an insidious world-wide, Jewish movement charged with the malicious manipulation of events in the tradition of the *Protocols of the Elders of Zion*.[35] Article 22 describes Jews as all powerful:

> ... using their wealth, they [have] unleashed revolutions all over the globe... they are behind the French Revolutions and the Communist Revolution... through their financial resources they have been able to control the imperialist nations ... They were behind the First World War, whereby they destroyed the Islamic Caliphate ... and they are behind the Second World War ... they established the United Nations and the Security Council ... in order to dominate the world ...

The aim of this irredentist movement is to destroy Israel. Its Charter abjures secular rights. Each of its thirty-six articles is cast purely in religious terms with appropriate reference to the Qur'an and other sacred texts. The superiority of Islam and the obligation to obliterate Israel are declared in the opening paragraph and maintained throughout. The Covenant's opening paragraph establishes the objective:

> In The Name of The Most Merciful Allah ... Ye are the best nation that hath been raised up unto mankind: ye command that which is just, and ye forbid that which is unjust, and ye believe in Allah. And if they [the Jews] who have received the scriptures had believed, it had surely been the better for them: there are believers among them, but the greater part of them are transgressors ... This they suffer, because they disbelieved the signs of Allah, and slew the prophets unjustly; this, because they were rebellious, and transgressed. (Al-Imran—verses 109–111).
>
> Israel will exist and will continue to exist until Islam will obliterate it, just as it obliterated others before it (The Martyr, Imam Hassan al-Banna, of blessed memory).
>
> The Islamic world is on fire. Each of us should pour some water, no matter how little, to extinguish whatever one can without waiting for the others. (Sheikh Amjad al-Zahawi, of blessed memory).

By contrast, the PLO's secular Charter does not reference Allah or quote sacred texts. Nevertheless, Hamas views the PLO as a possible partner in achieving its ultimate purpose but also sees itself as superior and necessarily the permanent force for realizing the ultimate goal: an Islamic polity in all of Palestine. In practice, Hamas has occasionally indicated it would accept a *hudna* or temporary truce, but it does so within the traditional framework that such an arrangement is temporary and can be broken when circumstances are favorable.

Finally, the Hamas Charter makes a claim, unprecedented in Islam, that all of Palestine is a *waqf* [an inalienable religious endowment for Islam, granted by God in perpetuity]. This overarching concept is not limited to the sanctity of the Haram al-Sharif and similar sites where particular events took place or holy individuals are interred. It lays claim to all of Palestine based on the decision of Caliph Umar,

Palestine's conqueror, not to divide the country among his conquering solders, as was customary, but to establish the whole as a *waqf* belonging to the entire Muslim nation for all time. While attractive and persuasive to the adherents of Hamas, this interpretation, born out of a contemporary political agenda contradicts Islamic practice in Palestine and elsewhere.[36]

Accommodation with Israel: An Alternative Islamic Path

Over the last four decades an alternative tradition of more moderate and pragmatic approaches to Israel has emerged in Islamic thought and practice. Since the peace agreement in 1979 between President Anwar Sadat of Egypt and Prime Minister Begin of Israel, some Islamic states have found ways to recognize Israel and establish formal, public relations with it. In the Oslo Accords of 1993 and 1995, Israel and the PLO agreed to steps that would result in mutual recognition and peace. In 1994 Jordan established formal relations with Israel. Of great significance, and an indication of how change may be possible, Crown Prince Abdullah of Saudi Arabia announced the Arab Peace Initiative (API) at the Beirut Arab League Summit in March 2002 as a proposal for the Arab world to fully recognize the State of Israel. In exchange of the Arab states guaranteeing Israel normal diplomatic relations and security, the API called for Israel to withdraw its territorial control to the June 4, 1967 lines allowing the establishment of a Palestinian state with East Jerusalem as its capital and to come to "a just and agreed solution over the issue of Palestinian refugees." Considering the existential crises Israel had faced during its wars against the Arab states throughout the twentieth century, the API was a novel step towards recognition of Israel's legitimacy. Moreover, the API was initially endorsed by the 22 member states of the Arab League where it was presented. More countries adopted the API when it was endorsed by the 57 member states of the Organization of Islamic Cooperation.[37]

Anwar Sadat in Jerusalem, 1977. President Anwar Sadat at the Israeli Knesset in Jerusalem, Nov. 20, 1977. From left to right, Prime Minister Menachem Begin, President Sadat, and Knesset Chairman Yitzhak Shamir. Courtesy of the Israel Government Press Office

In August 2020, under the sponsorship of the United States, the United Arab Emirates, and Bahrain signed agreements, termed the Abraham Accords, of recognition and normalization. Morocco soon followed. At the time of this writing, it appears that more Arab countries may also join. There has been movement with these and other Islamic states in areas of trade, tourism and even in security matters. Indeed, it appears that concerns over security was a foundational element, and it became more prominent as the Gulf Arab states viewed the threat from Iran growing more urgent and with Morocco eager for American recognition for Moroccan sovereignty over Western Sahara.[38] These relationships, official and unofficial, are expanding at a significant rate. Moreover, Jewish communities are being officially reestablished within Muslim countries and attempts are being made to moderate negative views of Jews and of Israel. This is progressing in the light of day with the blessing of some Islamic clerics. In effect, there are two distinct and opposing developments taking place. On the one hand, an apparently extreme and violent hostility to a Jewish state exists even as, on the other, there are signs of moderation and accommodation.

These changes indicate flexibility and latitude that can exist in Islam. There are alternatives to Hamas and radical, extremist political Islam. The instrument allowing and stimulating change is by *fatwas* or legal opinions on points of Islamic law that muftis are empowered to issue. In effect, the path chosen by the Mufti of Jerusalem during the Mandate has been significantly altered by other clerics. New readings of Islam's rich sacred written literature and select precedents offer opportunities for change and moderation. Thus, *jihad* is no longer the sole, necessary, and legitimate response to the establishment of a Jewish state. Similarly, *hudna* is no longer universally invoked as a temporary expedient to delay inevitable conflict. Moderation, pragmatism and alternate interpretation of texts and the Muslim past can lead to recognition of Israel and peace. This route is surely contentious as evidenced by the assassination of Sadat in October 1981 by members of the Egyptian Islamic Jihad, an affiliate of Al-Qaeda that is banned as a terrorist group by the United Nations, the United States, the United Kingdom, and other states.[39]

Even as the centuries-old doctrine of supersessionism evolved among some Christians into an acceptance of multiple covenants or has been altered and even disavowed, so too have what extremists understand to be Islam's original principles undergone reformulation and refinement. This development can perhaps be at least partially understood as part of a large process wherein Muslim states necessarily find that in entering an international system of modern states the historic Muslim division of the world into different "Abodes" is no longer possible or desirable. Otherwise, it is difficult to explain how the rulers of Egypt, Morocco and other states could enter into a peace agreement with Israel that recognize the Jewish state as legitimate or how others signed on to the Arab Peace Initiative or the Abrahamic Accords. An examination of the history and possibilities of *fatwa* lead to an appreciation of how such change can be theologically justified.

Scholars have charted change in Islamic doctrines over the centuries. At its inception in the seventh century, Islam divided the world into the abodes of Islam and of war. When expansion was halted through the fifteenth century, Muslims were beset by internal division and conflict. Then, with the establishment of the Ottoman Empire at the beginning of the fourteenth century through the end of the seventeenth century, expansion renewed, notably into Europe, but ended with the defeat near Vienna in 1683. Thereafter, recourse to *jihad* lapsed into a "dormant" period in which treaties with non-Muslim states became necessary and normative. After the Ottomans reached the zenith of their power in the eighteenth century, slow retrenchment ensued through the nineteenth century when a weakened Ottoman Empire was forced to limit its engaging in war, whatever historical and theoretical principles found in early Islam. During this period, Christian European powers not only began to expand into *dar al-Islam*, thereby contracting Ottoman borders but forced them to surrender a measure of internal control through the capitulations over non-Muslim inhabitants who previously had been subject solely to Ottoman control. Official recognition was given not only to states but to Christian religious orders, particularly the Franciscans who were accorded primacy in all having to do with Christian holy sites. These steps went far beyond the ten-year *hudna* of the past. They led to a new set of relations with the non-Muslim world. The dissolution of the Ottoman Empire and its fragmentation into states in the twentieth century, along with the need to integrate into an international political system largely suppressed *jihad* as an expression of state policy. However, *non-state* Islamic groups still espouse and act on this religious principle that makes war mandatory against non-believers.[40]

A secular approach to foreign affairs necessarily developed when Muslim states became involved in world affairs, and formally accepted peaceful co-existence. For example, Islamic states are now parties to international non-aggression treaties that are based on the territorial integrity of existing states. Muslim jurists participate in international legal forums that operate under universal norms of legal thinking and behavior rather than *sharia* [Islamic law]. In sum, a Manichean perspective that regards the world as divided into opposing "abodes" is necessarily tempered or even abandoned. This new order is not universally applauded. Islamic extremist groups protest such departures and acceptance of a new world order. There have been reservations by mainstream or conservative Muslims to the 1948 Universal Declaration of Human Rights on the basis that universalism is an externally imposed regime that does not respect cultural distinctiveness. That is why this pathbreaking international document lacks the force of a "treaty" but remains only a "declaration." Nevertheless, there is movement away from systems of law that are solely subservient to religion.[41]

These departures are anchored in new interpretations of Islamic law as originally formulated in the seventh century. In this process, some clerics hold "peace" to a higher Islamic value than *jihad*. Moreover, *jihad* may be justified only for wars of defense. The obligation to disseminate Islam remains, but it may be accomplished by means other than war and forced conversion. Moreover, the benefits of peace may pragmatically outweigh those that might be obtained by waging war. All these considerations entered into learned justifications of Sadat's visit to Jerusalem and authorized the signing of a peace treaty with Israel.

The historian Yitzhak Reiter's review of the history of fatwas issued by the clerical authorities of Al-Azhar University in Cairo, a leading center of theological authority in Islam worldwide, reveals how Sadat's peace initiative was authorized. In an earlier stage in the Arab-Israeli conflict, there was universal condemnation of the UN 1947 decision to partition Palestine. The Al-Azhar sages insisted that Muslims are obligated "to save Palestine and protect the al-Aqsa Mosque."[42] They similarly supported blockading the Straits of Tiran, an action that preceded the 1956 Suez-Sinai War. Military actions against Israel continued to be justified until the aftermath of the 1973 October War which, from an Egyptian view, restored their national honor. Thereafter, a debate has ensued on the appropriate Islamic course.

Clerics who argued against a treaty with Israel faulted Egypt for breaking Islamic solidarity with other Arab states in confronting Israel. They claimed that the agreement was contrary to "the benefit of Muslims." The Al-Azhar authorities countered that Israel had turned towards peace and this required reciprocity according to the Qur'an. They claimed that negotiations are sanctioned because they are conducted through a position of the strength achieved by Egyptian success in the 1973 October War. Support for Sadat's initiative was based on verses in the Qur'an and on an interpretation of events surrounding the Prophet in making treaties. Nevertheless, the Muslim Brotherhood in Egypt and their allies throughout the Arab world publicly denounced Sadat and the treaty with Israel.

In November 1979, the chief mufti of Egypt, Jad al-Haqq, rejected criticism of Sadat in a *fatwa*. It opens with a remarkable statement:

Islam was and remains a religion of security and safety, peace and tranquility, serenity, amity and brotherhood, not a religion of war or conflict or hatred; [it] did not use the sword to dominate and control. Rather, its wars were a means to ensure the doctrine. The noble Qur'an ordered believers to refrain from fighting if it is not necessary, as written therein, "So, if they hold aloof from you and wage not war against you and offer you peace, Allah alloweth you no way against them." Allah also said, "And if they incline to peace, incline thou also to it and trust in Allah."[43]

The Mufti also stated:

> The Hudaybiyya treaty brought a great benefit to Islam and the Muslims. Allah even sent down from the Al-Rath sura [Qur'an 48:1], which defines the agreement as a victory... this ultimately led to the spread of Islam. Even the Prophet's companions had opposed the agreement until they realized its benefits and obeyed the directive of God and his messenger. In our agreement with Israel, we also hope to restore our land and dignity and that under the auspices of peace, we will restore holy and precious Jerusalem to all Muslims.[44]

The Mufti does not deny the use of war to achieve Islamic ends but points out that it is preferable to use peaceful means. The *fatwa* focused on whether peaceful means were beneficial for that purpose. In this case, Muslim lands and believers were returned to Egypt by Israel's relinquishing control over the Sinai and the Muslim position in Jerusalem was strengthened. Moreover, as a precedent, he pointed to the armistice arrangements reached through the negotiations at Rhodes in the aftermath of the 1948 war. They could now be reinterpreted as recognizing Israel as a legitimate entity that is no longer part of *dar al-Islam*. This reading and precedent enabled Arab Muslim leaders from the Oslo Accords through the present to reference such *fatwa*s as a basis for new policies. In all these instances, the *fatwa* upholds the authority of Islamic law in the making of policy.[45]

In sum, new political circumstances could produce different, even contrary declarations. Modern Islamic nation-states deviate from the early doctrine of a single *umma* led by one ruler and necessarily have diplomatic relations with non-Muslim states. Moreover, the fact that many Muslims now reside in non-Muslim states also contributes to the reality that Muslims in many parts of the world necessarily recognize the legitimacy of non-Muslim states. Contemporary law and practice can lead to the emergence of Islamic law more accommodating to non-Muslim states.[46]

Whatever choice is made, Arab rulers seek the sanction of theology in determining policy regarding relations with Israel. Although the future is not yet discernible, the present trend may offer opportunities. The growing acceptance of the legitimacy of Israel within the Arab Muslim world and beyond suggests as much. Whether this is the direction of the future and, if so, how rapidly and widely that may happen is far from certain. Traditional law, attitudes and policy maintain enormous power as does Radical Islam whether through radical states like Iran or non-state actors like Hezbollah, Hamas, and Isis. The Arab Muslim world is rent with schisms and instability that hinder achieving a permanent and all-encompassing change. The internal challenges to regimes, like Jordan and Egypt, that have granted legitimacy to Israel and the absence of completely normal relations indicate caution in assessing how extensive or permanent change may be. The hostility and violence with which

Radical Islam engages established Muslim regimes, let alone with a Jewish one, is further reason for prudence in assessing if and when acceptance can be achieved.

Finally, change may be taking place within Israel's Muslim community. As we noted in Chap. 7 on Christianity, the small community of Aramaic-speaking Christians have recently come to accommodate to a Jewish state even to the point of encouraging its young to join the Israeli army. That is surely too radical a prospect for one of the most powerful movements of Israel's Muslims—the Northern Branch of the Islamic Movement in Israel. With deep roots in the Moslem Brotherhood, the fight against Zionism during the Mandate, and with ongoing connections with Hamas, its position on involvement with the Jewish state entered on a path to change in the 1990s after the Oslo Accords when it became involved in Israeli politics. This change did not include accepting Israel as a fulfillment of a legitimate Jewish aspiration but an acknowledgement of the reality of its existence and an interest in enjoying its benefits within Israel's claim to being a democratic and egalitarian state. This is a remarkable transformation for a movement that had espoused violence as a legitimate instrument in terminating the Jewish state and that had previously been disallowed from participation in national politics.

The justification for this move was expressed in a remarkable speech, spoken in Hebrew for broadcast on all major Israeli channels in the aftermath of the 2021 elections by Mansour Abbas, the movement's leader in April 2021: "I carry a prayer of hope, and the search for coexistence based on mutual respect and genuine equality," he said. "What we have in common is greater than what divides us." He then quotes from the Quran instructing humanity to recall that all were created from one man and one woman, and are obligated to recognize our common humanity. He then continued with an extraordinary declaration:

> I, Mansour Abbas, a man of the Islamic Movement, am a proud Arab and Muslim, a citizen of the state of Israel, who heads the leading, biggest political movement in Arab society, courageously champion a vision of peace, mutual security, partnership and tolerance between the peoples ... I reach out a hand in my name and that of my colleagues and on behalf of the public that voted for me —to create an opportunity for coexistence in this holy land, blessed by three religions and home to two peoples. The time has come for us to listen to each other, to respect each other's narrative, to respect the other ... We have an opportunity to initiate a change and create a civil society greater than its components ... This is the time to find the common ground, to create a different reality for all the citizens of the state.[47]

With ambassadors from Arab Islamic states presenting credentials in Jerusalem and significant normalization between Israel and its neighbors, the Northern Branch has moved to active participation in Israel's politics and government. This falls far short of accepting the legitimacy of Israel as a Jewish state. It is a pragmatic recognition of realities that have emerged a century after Balfour and seventy-plus years after Zionism's evident success. Whether this is but an intermediate or the last step towards accommodation will be revealed in the future. If not in how and why Israel's Islamic Movement arrived at this decision, it does bear resemblance in outcome to those elements in the Christian world that have come to recognize Israel's reality even while not willing to do so as a legitimate expression of Jewish history and the aspirations of its Jewish citizens. Nevertheless, it suggests that in Islam, as among other monotheistic creeds, theologies are mutable or multiple, and that it depends on the believer to choose among the rich possibilities of the faith.

Notes

1. https://en.wikipedia.org/wiki/Organisation_of_Islamic_Cooperation
2. Division for Palestinian Rights (DPR), *The Origins and Evolution of the Palestine Problem: 1917-1988* (United Nations Secretariat: 1989), Part I: https://unispal.un.org/DPA/DPR/unispal.nsf/0/AEAC80E740C78 2E4852561150071FDB0; Part II: https://unispal.un.org/DPA/DPR/unispal.nsf/1ce874ab1832a53e852570bb006dfaf6/57c45a3dd0d4 6b09802564740045cc0a?OpenDocument
3. Jacob Lassner and S. Ilan Troen, *Jews and Muslims in the Arab World: Haunted by Pasts Real and Imagined* (Lanham, MD: Rowman and Littlefield, 2007), Part I.
4. Bernard Lewis, *The Political Language of Islam* (Chicago: U of Chicago Press, 1988), pp. 24 and ff.
5. Lewis, *The Political Language of Islam*, Chap. 4.
6. Quoted in *The Origins and Evolution of the Palestine Problem: 1917-1988*, op. cit., p.23.
7. Nimrod Hurvitz, "Muhibb ad-Din al-Khatib's Semitic Wave Theory and Pan-Arabism," *Middle East Studies*, 29:1 (2006), 118–34; Amal N. Ghazar, "Power, Arabism and Islam in the Writings of Muhib al-Din al-Khatib in *al-Fath*," *Past Imperfect*, vol. 6 (1997), 133–150.
8. Braude, Benjamin, "Foundation Myths of the Millet System," in Braude, Benjamin; Bernard Lewis, eds., *Christians and Jews in the Ottoman Empire* (New York: Holmes and Meier, 1982) pp. 69–90; Bruce Masters, *Christians and Jews in the Ottoman Arab World: The Roots of Sectarianism* (Cambridge: Cambridge University Press. 2001), pp. 61–2; Bruce Masters, "Millet," in Gábor Ágoston, Bruce Masters, eds., *Encyclopedia of the Ottoman Empire* (2009), pp. 383–4.
9. Moshe Ma'oz, "Changing Relations between Jews, Muslims and Christians during the Nineteenth Century with Special Reference to Ottoman Syria and Palestine," in Avigdor Levy, ed., *Jews, Turks, Ottomans; A Shared History, Fifteenth Through the Twentieth Century* (Syracuse: Syracuse University Press, 2002), 108–118; See, too: İlker Aytürk, "Anti-Judaism, Anti-Semitism and Anti-Zionism—Ottoman Empire and the Turkish Republic" in *Encyclopedia of Jews in the Islamic World*, pp. 224–227, https://mail.google.com/mail/u/0/#inbox/FMfcgzGkXcxxLkkVDWpzQkpRrqsVtCJK
10. The classic articulation of this idea is in Louis Hartz, *The Liberal Tradition in America* (New York: Harcourt, Brace, 1955).
11. Reuven Firestone, "Is the Qur'an 'Antisemitic'?," G. H. van Kooten and J. van Ruiten, eds., (Leiden: Brill, 2019), 443–63; Reuven Firestone, "Discourses between Muslims, Jews, Christians and Greeks," Chapter 13, pp. 443 ff.
12. The version of the Qur'an translation usually employed is that of M. A. S. Abdel Haleem, *The Qur'an* (Oxford: Oxford University Press, 2004). Similar sources for contemporary use can be found in *Palestine Media Watch*. See, for example, https://palwatch.org/page/18579. Similarly, numerous current usages can be found through MEMRI [Middle East Media Research Institute]. See: https://www.memri.org/
13. Jacob Lassner, *Jews, Christians, and the Abode of Islam; Modern Scholarship, Medieval Realities* (Chicago: U of Chicago Press, 2012), esp. Chap. 1.
14. Jonathan Frankel, "'Ritual Murder' in the Modern Era: The Damascus Affair of 1840," *Jewish Social Studies*, New Series, 3:2 (Winter, 1977), 1–16.

15. Neville Mandel. *The Arabs and Zionism before World War* (Berkeley: University of California Press, 1976).
16. Bernard Lewis, *Semites and Anti-Semites; An Inquiry into Conflict and Prejudice* (London: Weidenfeld and Nicolson, 1986); Matthias Kuntzel, "Islamic Antisemitism: Characteristics, Origins, and Current Effects," *Israel Journal of Foreign Affairs* (July 29, 2020), 229–240; Jeffrey Herf, *Nazi Propaganda for the Arab World* (New Haven: Yale, 2010).
17. https://www.memri.org
18. https://www.memri.org/tv/memri-flotilla-coverage-al-jazeera-tv-report-freedom-flotilla-its-departure-gaza-activists-board. See, too: https://mfa.gov.il/MFA/ForeignPolicy/Issues/Pages/Gaza_flotilla_violence_premeditated_1-Jun-2010.aspx
19. https://www.memri.org/reports/image-jew-ramadan-tv-show-khaybar-%E2%80%93-treacherous-hateful-other-scheming-and-corrupt
20. Ariel Ben Solomon, "Ramadan series 'Khaybar' is a battle cry against Jews; Special holiday show deals with relations between Jews and Arabs in the seventh century," *Jerusalem Post*, July 11, 2013. See: https://www.jpost.com/Middle-East/Ramadan-Series-Khaybar-re-enforces-anti-Semitic-stereotypes-319568; Abigail Esman, "Jew Hatred Soars as Manas-Israel Fighting Rages," *The Investigative Project on Terrorism*, May 20, 2021. See: https://www.investigativeproject.org/8859/jew-hatred-soars-as-hamas-israel-fighting-rages
21. David Ohana, "Are Israelis the New Crusaders?" *Palestine-Israel Journal*, 13:3 (2005). See: https://pij.org/articles/865
22. David Ohana, "The Cross, the Crescent and the Star of David: The Zionist-Crusader Analogy in the Israeli Discourse", *Iyunim Bitkumat Israel* 11 (2002), pp. 486–526 [Hebrew]; David Ohana, *The Origins of Israeli Mythology; Neither Canaanites nor Crusaders* (Cambridge, UK: Cambridge University Press, 2012).
23. Quoted in Ohana, "Are Israelis the New Crusaders?" See: Amos Oz, "The Specter of Saladin," *The New York Times*, July 28, 2000.
24. Raphael Israeli, "From Oslo to Bethlehem: Arafat's Islamic Message," *Journal of Church and State*, 43:3 (summer 2001), 423–445. Excerpts from the sermon/speech at the Johannesburg mosque can be found at IRIS (Information Regarding Israel's Security), https://iris.org.il/arafats-johannesburg-speech/. See, too: Yitzhak Reiter, *War, Peace and International Relations in Islam; Muslim Scholars on Peace Accords with Israel* (Brighton: Sussex Academic Press, 2011) and Yitzhak Reiter, *Jerusalem and Its Role in Islamic Solidarity* (New York: Palgrave Macmillan, 2008), pp. 114–115.
25. https://en.wikipedia.org/wiki/Fatah#cite_note-15
26. ESCO Foundation for Palestine, "The Moslem and Arab Attitudes towards the Jews," in *Palestine; A Study of Jewish, Arab, and British Policies* (New Haven: Yale University Press, 1947), vol. 1, pp. 516–593; Yehoshua Porath, *The Palestinian Arab National Movement, 1929–1939; From Riots to Rebellion* (London: Cass, 1977), vol. 2, pp. 201 ff. A still useful and succinct introduction to the religious bias of Arab politics in Palestine is J. C. Hurevitz, *The Struggle for Palestine* (New York: Norton, 1950), pp. 50 ff. More recent is Esther Webman, "Rethinking the Role of Religion in Arab Antisemitic discourses," *Religions*,10:7 (2019), 415. https://doi.org/10.3390/rel10070415
27. Alan Dowty, *Arabs and Jews in Ottoman Palestine; two worlds collide* (Bloomington: Indiana University Press, 2019), suggests that the beginnings

are to be found as early as the first Aliyah before the end of the nineteenth century. Other scholars consider the 1929 riots at the Western or Wailing Wall as the beginning. Avraham Sela, "The 'Wailing Wall' Riots (1929) as a watershed in the Palestine Conflict," *The Muslim World*, 84:1–2 (January–April, 1994), 60–94; Hillel Cohen, *Year Zero of the Arab-Israeli Conflict 1929* (Waltham: Brandeis University Press, 2015); Yehoshua Porath, *The Palestinian Arab National Movement, 1929–1939: From Riots to* Rebellion (London: Cass, 1977), pp. 201 ff.
28. Porath, pp. 194 ff.
29. Maoz Azaryahu and Yitzhak Reiter, "The Geopolitics of Interment: An Inquiry into the Burial of Muhammad Ali in Jerusalem, 1931," *Israel Studies*, 20:1 (Spring 2015), 31–56.
30. The Supreme Muslim Council, *Brief Guide to the al-Haram al-Sharif* Jerusalem (Jerusalem: Supreme Muslim Council, 1929), p. 4, quoted in Yitzhak Reiter, *Jerusalem and Its Role in Islamic Solidarity* (New York: Palgrave Macmillan, 2008), p. 45; Gardiner Harris and Steven Erlanger, "U.S. will withdraw from UNESCO, citing its 'Anti-Israel Bias,'" *New York Times*, October 12, 1917. See: https://www.nytimes.com/2017/10/12/us/politics/trump-unesco-withdrawal.html
31. For a much-appreciated analysis of this phenomenon see Emmanuel Sivan, *Radical Islam: Medieval Theology and Modern Politics* (New Haven: Yale, 1990, enlarged edition); For a similar emphasis on the impact of the medieval past on the present see Lassner and Troen, *Jews and Muslims in the Arab World: Haunted by Pasts Real and Imagined*, op. cit.
32. *Robinson, Glenn E. (2004).* "Hamas as a Social Movement," in Quintan Wiktorowicz, (ed.). *Islamic Activism: A Social Movement Theory Approach* (Bloomington: Indiana University Press, 2003), pp. 112–139; Gabriel Weimann, *Terror on the Internet: The New Arena, the New Challenges* (Washington, D.C.: US Institute of Peace Press, 2006), p. 82.
33. Musa Budeiri, "The Palestinians; Tensions Between Nationalist and Religious Identities," in James Jankowski and Israel Gershoni, eds., *Rethinking Nationalism in the Arab Middle East* (New York: Columbia University Press, 1997), pp. 191–206.
34. *Hamas Covenant 1988: The Covenant of the Islamic Resistance Movement"*. The Avalon Project: Documents in Law, History and Diplomacy. Yale Law School. 18 August 1988. Retrieved 15 February 2009. An updated Charter was produced in 2017 but it essentially continues with the same logic of the requirement to eliminate Israel. See: "The Doctrine of Hamas," October 20, 2023, https://www.wilsoncenter.org/article/doctrine-hamas
35. Musa K. Buderi, "The Nationalist Dimension of Islamic Movements in Palestinian Politics," *Journal of Palestine Studies*,24:3 (Spring 1995), 89–95.
36. Yitzhak Reiter, "All of Palestine is a Holy Muslim Waqf land": a myth and its roots, in Ron Shaham, ed., *Law, Custom, and Statute in the Muslim World; Studies in honor of Aharon Layish* (Leiden: Brill: 2007), Chap. 9, pp. 173–197.
37. https://centerpeace.org/explore/arab-peace-initiative/
38. U.S. Department of State, Bureau of Near Eastern Affairs, The *Abraham Accords,* https://www.state.gov/the-abraham-accords/. For a useful analysis of the context see Dennis Ross, *The Abraham Accords and the Changing Shape of the Middle East* (Washington: The Washington Institute for Near East Policy,

June 21, 2022), https://www.washingtoninstitute.org/policy-analysis/abraham-accords-and-changing-shape-middle-east

39. This discussion on the use and evolution of fatwas relies significantly on Yitzhak Reiter, *War, Peace & International Relations in Islam; Muslim Scholars on Peace Accords with Israel* (Brighton, UK: Sussex Academic Press, 2011)
40. For an extended discussion of the evolution of new relationships, including the making of treaties, see Majid Khadduri, *War and Peace in the Law of Islam* (Baltimore: The Johns Hopkins University Press, 1955).
41. Khadduri, *War and Peace in the Law of Islam*, pp. 268–296. Important to note that there are "Islamic Reservations" to human rights treaties in the sense of cultural relativism as opposed to adherence to universalism. Thus, even when Islamic states engage in the international legal system, they do so with reservations deriving from maintaining unique legal and cultural traditions found in Muslim societies and sharia. See: Ahamd Ali Sawad, "'Islamic Reservations' to Human Rights Treaties and Universality of Human Rights within the Cultural Relativists Paradigm," *The Journal of Human Rights of Mofid University*, Semi-Annual, 12:2 (Fall 2017 - Winter 2018), pp.101–154. See: https://www.academia.edu/37865899/Islamic_Reservations_to_Human_Rights_Treaties_and_Universality_of_Human_Rights_within_the_Cultural_Relativists_Paradigm
42. Yitzhak Reiter, *War, Peace and International Relations in Islam: Muslim Scholars on Peace Accords with Israel* (Brighton: Sussex Academic Press, 2011), pp. 79–87.
43. Reiter, *War, Peace and International Relations in Islam*, pp. 101–2.
44. Reiter, *War, Peace and International Relations in Islam*, pp. 99–100.
45. Reiter, *War, Peace and International Relations in Islam*, pp. 116–19.
46. James P. Piscatori, *Islam in a World of Nation-States* (Cambridge: Cambridge University Press, 1986).
47. *Times of Israel*, 1 April 2021. See: https://www.timesofisrael.com/raam-leader-abbas-calls-for-arab-jewish-coexistence-based-on-respect-equality/?utm_source=The+Daily+Edition&utm_campaign=daily-edition-2021-04-02&utm_medium=email and Patrick Kinglsey, "As Secular Peace Effort Stutters in Israel, Religious Mediators Hope to Step In," *New York Times*, July 4, 2021, https://www.nytimes.com/2021/07/04/world/Israel-peace-islamists-raam-party.html?searchResultPosition=1

Part III
Concluding Reflections

Chapter 9
Concluding Reflections

From Zionism's beginning, the legitimacy of establishing the Jewish national homeland in Palestine was understood to be challenging and provocative. The opening sentence of the program endorsed at the Zionist Organization's founding conference in Basle, Switzerland in 1897 forthrightly stated its goal: "Zionism seeks to secure for the Jewish people a publicly recognized, legally secured homeland in Palestine." The delegates deliberated whether to state this goal publicly. They were aware that there were reporters present and were concerned about the effect of stating their intentions. Some thought that steady and persistent practical work in organizing settlement and building an organization would achieve the desired result without making manifest the ultimate objective. Most argued that Zionism needed a forthright approach to address the issue of legitimacy. There was a sense of mistrust and reluctance to rely on the goodwill of a patron no matter how enlightened and sympathetic. It was in this context that the majority added a key German word to the initial draft: *öffentlich* or "openly" that became "publicly" in the English translation. They finally decided unanimously to promote overtly the establishment of a Jewish entity in Palestine.[1]

This approach had already been advocated in a foundational document of Zionism, Leon Pinsker's 1882 essay, *Auto-Emancipation: An Appeal to His People by a Russian Jew*. In its concluding section, Pinsker emphasized the need for an independent Jewish polity "secured by treaties and international law." Only on such a basis could there be "mutual respect" between the Jewish polity and those of other peoples.[2] In the language of Leo Motzkin, a Russian Zionist leader, who spoke at the Basle Congress in defense of the formulation: "When *Auto-Emancipation* appeared 15 years ago the idea was for the first time openly expressed that the Jews desired a "legally secured" homeland and could only hope for it by public activity in this sense." Fifteen years later, after a debate on the exact language, the principle of seeking international legal recognition for Zionism was upheld and became the opening statement of Zionist aspirations. All members of the Basle Program's

© The Author(s), under exclusive license to Springer Nature
Switzerland AG 2024
S. I. Troen, *Israel/Palestine in World Religions*,
https://doi.org/10.1007/978-3-031-50914-8_9

drafting committee and many Congress delegates had legal training, as did Herzl, and they used their skills and training in precisely formulating that objective.

Leaders of the Zionist Organization and supporters pursued public recognition vigorously. In the relatively few years before his untimely death in 1904 at age 44, Herzl conducted intense diplomacy. He attempted to reach the German Kaiser, who was thought to have influence in Turkish affairs, and then the Ottoman Sultan, British leaders, Russian officials, the Pope, and the King of Italy, among others. In the course of this effort, he came up with the idea of a Charter that would legally and publicly empower Jewish settlement in Palestine. The belief in the justice of their cause and a perception of the practical value of international standing led them to invest enormous energies in achieving such a goal.

With Herzl's passing, this objective was relentlessly sought by his successors. Lobbying produced the 1917 Balfour Declaration that endorsed the idea of a "national home for the Jewish people," a concept given international standing by the League of Nations in 1922. In subsequent years, these persistent efforts lead to affirmation of a Jewish state by the United Nations in 1947. Yet the sought-after legitimacy has never been completely achieved.

The Balfour Declaration and its incorporation into the British Mandate for Palestine elicited the beginnings of serious and sustained opposition. Arab leaders voiced reservations in international forums and diplomatic exchanges. The first Arab riots took place in 1920 and 1921; an Arab boycott of Jewish businesses was then organized, and alarm spread in the Arab world. Opposition also developed among Jews, notably among the ultra-Orthodox who insisted the messianic ideal could not be realized by human initiative. Secular Jews were concerned that the hope they placed in the promise of Emancipation might be jeopardized; the majority sought to enhance their situation and resolve problems in the expectation that they would remain in the Diaspora as citizens of the states in which they resided. At the same time, most Christian churches held to established theological positions that maintained that the role of Jews in history had long since been superseded, vitiating Jewish claims to the Holy Land.

Zionism enjoyed some sympathy but little actual support among Jews during crucial early decades. Significant support grew during the dislocations and pogroms around World War I and especially World War II. When the movement began, wider formal acceptance of Zionism was a matter of hope for the future.

The Balfour Declaration and the British Mandate, together with external events that encouraged Jewish settlement in Palestine, placed the Zionist quest on the international agenda and engendered extensive public controversy. I systematically examined the legal principles on which this conflict was fought in the first part of this book. It was in the "court" of public discourse that debates were the means for securing rights to territory: conquest, treaties, self-determination, rediscovery and the country's economic absorptive capacity, acquisition through labor and purchase, and the use of history. Whether singly or in combination, these were the terms around which Jewish claims were made and countered. I review them here briefly and comment on the extent to which they still have viability or significance, and if they have been transformed and acquired new meaning.

Section A. Persistent Categories, Modified Applications

Conquest

In the history of the Holy Land a series of conquerors replaced one another. The British may have had the shortest reign of all. While they utterly defeated the Ottomans, whose control had lasted for more than four centuries, the British dominated the country for merely three decades. They entered Jerusalem in December 1917 and left Palestine in May 1948, though their control began to unravel earlier. Their Mandate for Palestine was to have been limited, lasting only until they could nurture a modern state with a decidedly Jewish character. By the end of the Mandate's second decade, they had altered expectations and policy, and prepared to rule over a country with an Arab majority. Thus, the Zionists' initial jubilation at the promulgation of the Balfour Declaration and the British Mandate was short-lived. The British were unable to balance claims of the contending sides and ultimately lacked the resources and stamina to do so.[3] It is likely that no outsider could have accomplished that feat. A major legacy was partition—the famous "two-state solution"—a still unrealized goal. As British influence waned in Palestine—as it was to do elsewhere in their vast empire—the United States replaced them to some extent, but not as a conqueror with direct claims to the country.

Both Jews and Arabs initially rode on the coattails of British conquest, claiming the right to the spoils of a successful military campaign against the Ottomans, but neither could dislodge the other for control over the entire country. Together, they succeeded in frustrating an international plan for a tripartite division of Palestine wherein the external powers expected to exert control over a condominium centered on Jerusalem. With the country divided between the Jews of Palestine and the Hashemites of Jordan, rather than the local Palestinian Arabs, both sides pressed their claims and gained a measure of international legitimacy and membership in the United Nations. But neither could quash the growing aspirations of the Arabs of Palestine whose quest for recognition and legitimacy was finally acknowledged only in the 1970s.

Israel's 1967 conquest of other areas, notably the West Bank, the Golan Heights, and Gaza did not result in legitimizing Israeli control over them. Whatever the arguments in support of settlements in these areas, there is broad agreement globally that these settlements are illegitimate according to international law. Victory, even in a war that may be defensive and justifiable, no longer can provide the spoils the international community accorded the British and French after World War I. That message has been made even clearer with the Russian invasion of Ukraine in 2022 when significant sections of the international community have responded with boycotts, sanctions, and the provision of armaments for Ukrainian resistance. Although the entry of Israeli forces into Arab territories in the Golan Heights, the West Bank, Gaza, and the Sinai in 1967 was a consequence of a defensive war, holding on to those territories has, in some cases been temporary, and problematical internationally in the rest. Even within Israel there was significant internal opposition from the immediate aftermath of the conflict. Israel's claims for legitimacy have had to be made on other terms for the post-1967 territories and there are still those who dispute the existence of a Jewish state within the 1948 armistice lines. There is no longer ready acceptance of the results of the battlefield, no matter how justified the combat.[4]

Rediscovery and the Economic Absorptive Capacity of Palestine

Zionism adopted a maximalist approach to the development of Palestine with the promise that it could benefit both peoples. The Arab argument was minimalist and based on a view of an agricultural economy based in a semi-arid land, a significant portion of which is still actual desert. Although the minimal view has been proven wrong, it had a powerful impact in limiting Jewish immigration and land purchases.[5] Zionists' belief in the possibilities for development have been borne out. That same area, a century later supports a population of more than 14 million- or twenty-times Palestine's combined Arab and Jewish population but a century ago. The portion directly under the control of Israel enjoys prospects of world-class levels of prosperity and continues to make major contributions to the arts, sciences, and human welfare.

The promise of shared prosperity has been fulfilled only in part and only within Israel's pre-1967 borders. Israel's leaders still hold out the prospect of shared prosperity as a key for mitigating hostility, even though identity politics seem to trump the prospect of economic self-interest. Shimon Peres's *Towards a New Middle East* (1993), a widely read book published around the time of the Oslo Accords, is a prime example of a recent version of a Zionist vision. Throughout a long career, Peres reiterated his belief that sharing the opportunities of technology and science and the prospect of material benefit would ultimately induce Palestinians to acknowledge Israel's legitimacy. This hope is apparently being realized by states who are party to the Abraham Accords and forging diplomatic and economic ties to Israel. Yet the motives for these new relationships may be based as much, if not more, on the security benefits most seek as they and Israel confront a potential shared enemy—an aggressive and ambitious Iran.

The issue is more complicated for Arabs who live inside historic Palestine. Economic benefits are important but can only partially satisfy aspirations and deeply felt identities. As one scholar has poignantly written, Zionism's investment in Palestine was economically "irrational."[6] Herzl and the Zionist Organization rejected the few offers for alternative venues, such as the 1903 British offer to settle Jews in what the British then considered Uganda, even in the face of an urgent need for refuge from Russian pogroms.[7] Few Zionists appreciated that the devotion that motivated Jews to invest themselves in a semi-arid land lacking in natural resources was also shared by Palestine's Arabs, who were no less passionately devoted and connected to the land, even though they did not share the Zionist commitment to its potential development.[8] In other words, no less significant than progress and modernity, are value systems rooted in religious traditions, emotions, and shared memory of a history real and imagined. The Holy Land is the patrimony of both peoples. In 1937, the British were the first to propose that the only pragmatic solution was to divide it. That concept is still on the international agenda as even military force will not enable either side to successfully maintain control over the whole of the country. The prism through which individuals and peoples view self-interest have not been, nor likely to be, solely nor perhaps even primarily based on material benefit. That is probably also true elsewhere, but clearly holds for a land sanctified by the contending parties.

Labor and Purchase

Contemporary critics fault Zionism for not employing cheaper, local Arab labor. They overlook or simply dismiss the Jews' commitment to working the land themselves and to a value system that considered labor ethical and moral. Hiring local labor would have been less expensive and would have made sense had they wished to develop, say, a plantation-like agricultural system, as colonial-settlers did elsewhere. The irony is that although they decidedly did not, the same charge is leveled and is an essential part of the colonial-settler accusation. An unbridgeable polarity separates Zionist celebration of Jewish labor and the heroic commitments it embodied, and those who condemn Zionism and its settlement project as insidious.

Ultimately, the method of settlement is less an issue than the religious and national identity of the settler, even when land was purchased. All land—and a great deal was undeveloped and in the public domain—was to remain in "Arab" hands. "Arab land," as it was designated, was not to be owned by Jews. This explicit policy began under the Ottomans and, following a brief period at the beginning of the Mandate, it was reinstated by the British. Had Arabs not sold land to Jews, the Zionist project would certainly have failed. Arab landowners, who included members of the leading Palestinian families, even the Mufti's own kinsmen, protested publicly, but privately pocketed proceeds from sales. The exclusive and parochial view of land is now rampant particularly in the territories where Jewish settlers and their supporters endow land with ethnic, historical, and religious significance. On this basis, struggles over allocation of land and its development by the State of Israel within its internationally recognized borders remain a subject of festering controversy. The creation of international borders is unlikely to sever contending populations from listing their holdings in official state registers and identifying them with collective, emotional associations.

History

Negative characterizations of the other and sympathetic accounts of oneself follow naturally when justice and injustice are represented in dichotomous narratives. Complexity, irony, and paradox are typically absent from such accounts. The use of history was inevitable for both sides as nationalist claims became normative by the twentieth century and because both had access to traditions that could readily illustrate and justify their positions. An Arab majority of long and recent residency was manifestly present even as Jews in increasing numbers claimed the right to return to a homeland, remembered in ancient texts, rituals, and customs, with countless markers of their presence and where the land again resonated with the sounds of their ancient/modern language.

History as validation of the nation is ubiquitous but also inevitably arouses suspicion because, in addition to biased accounts of the self and other, there is, as widely accepted, also a large measure of "invention" or "imagination" in the process. The programmatic and self-serving aspects of historical "narratives" created to advance a political purpose, including claims to territory, have been widely acknowledged from Ernst Renan to Benedict Anderson with many in-between and beyond.[9] This critique may be applied to Zionist and Palestinian writings as well. The use of the term "narrative" itself suggests manipulation, if not fabrication. The question is less whether histories with a political objective are false than the measure of verifiable truth and emotional commitment invested in them.

A crucial and highly contested issue has been the designation of Jews as a "nation" or "people" and their historic connection to the Holy Land/Palestine/Eretz Israel. The Zionist case, based on the Jews' association with the Promised Land is recorded in the Bible, multiple sacred texts in different religious traditions as well as in history, and in the archeological record. The continuity between contemporary Jews and those whose history and ideas are recorded in sources has been maintained for centuries by the Jews themselves, in every generation, but no less by the prejudicial legislation and attitudes of Islamic and Christian societies. That is, wherever they have lived, and even, at times, where they have not, Jews have been and remain an inextricable part of the memory and actuality of these great civilizations. The long and still active history of antisemitism provides a tragic and ironic validation of the real and continuous presence of the Jews as a people in history. It was widely appreciated that Zionism represented an attempt to overcome such historical liabilities, even if the path chosen aroused debate.

This is not to suggest that creating group identities requires ancient lineage. Such constructions are surely taking place in the present world. We have already observed that, initially with the breakup of the Ottoman Empire in the 1920s and, again, following disappointment with Nasser's pan-Arabism and the Arab defeat in the 1967 June War, such reaching back into history for relevant national constructs was occurring throughout the Middle East. As the Palestinian historian Rashid Khalidi has documented, a distinctive Palestinian identity emerged from the musings of Arab notables living in Jerusalem near the outbreak of World War I, began to crystallize in the 1920s, and has grown steadily in subsequent decades to reach its current state of international recognition and legitimacy. This is not exceptional, nor merits objection. Deeply felt identities may be ancient and of long duration or, if recent, also appreciated as genuine. Nevertheless, there are practical consequences for when national identities are formed and recognized. In the crucial period following the Ottoman disintegration and the establishment of new polities in the Middle East to supplant it, the idea of a "Palestinian" people, distinctive within the larger Arab identity, was not widely accepted and rarely claimed. For that matter, the idea that "Palestine" is an independent and discrete political entity was a twentieth century invention formulated by the great imperial powers when disassembling of the Ottoman Empire. The argument in favor of self-determination was initially made on behalf of Palestine's Arab *majority*, not on behalf of a population with a distinctive identity and a recognized place in the historical record. The singularity of a Palestinian people coalesced in the course of the twentieth century as a coherent claim, but too late to forestall recognition of the Jewish state.

It is often maintained that the claims of Arabs on this and other issues have not been heard. Indeed, it is argued that Arab voices have been "silenced."[10] This is far from the case. Certainly, during the crucial early decades of the conflict prior to Israel's establishment, they were insufficiently persuasive to obviate Jewish historical claims. Yet this book testifies to how vigorously, widely, passionately and with so many diverse arguments the anti-Zionist case was made. The categories of rights articulated by Justice Marshall and those that emerged over the following century did not enable uncontested agreement on their application. Importantly, Arabs effectively used them in limiting the initial intentions of British policy and the League of Nations Mandate. It would be more accurate to note that the Palestinian cause was heard but failed to defeat Zionist arguments that referenced the same categories. The Arab case was never extinguished, nor is it likely to be.

Associated with the use of history to construct group identity is the claim of "indigeneity." First used to refer to the presence of a distinctive Arab *majority* that claimed the right of self-determination when the Mandate was established, it effected changes in British policy on Jewish immigration and land purchases. In recent decades, Palestinians use the term "indigenous" to assert their own *first, authentic,* and *continuous* presence, and all the rights that accrue therefrom, whatever the size of the community. This inexact legal concept, supported by previously unheard and highly questionable narratives, has been introduced throughout the post-Ottoman Middle East by nationalist thinkers from Turkey, Lebanon, Syria, and Jordan to Iraq and Iran. Whatever one's views on how far back a discrete Palestinian identity may be observed, denying its vitality in the present, precludes constructive dialogue. Indeed, mutual recognition of the distinctive characteristics of both national identities by the other is a requirement for pragmatic mutual accommodation. That, however, it a daunting challenge.

The foregoing discussions suggest that the categories of analysis I have used to examine how disputes over Palestine were argued prior to 1948 continue to resonate after conclusion of hostilities on the battlefield and the recognition given by the United Nations to Israel as the Jewish state. There was no peace treaty in the aftermath of 1948, only various "armistices"—or temporary suspensions of fighting. On one side there was a "War of Independence." On the other, there was a "Nakba" or "catastrophe." Interpretation over that war and the political conflict of the Mandate continue to rage in the public square and the academy. While I would like to hope that the analysis presented here is correct and persuasive, I have no doubt that it may satisfy only a portion of readers. The application of secular terms whose origins are in the development of legal, political, and historical thought have not brought shared appreciation for the validity of applications of allegedly universal principles. The same holds for attempts to share divergent narratives. In an exercise termed "parallel narratives," contending sides are invited to hear alternative interpretations. These do not produce a single, homogeneous narrative. As in nature, where parallel lines do not meet, so parallel narratives do not become unified into a homogeneous perspective that satisfies all. They remain separate. Nevertheless, considering the other has the value of engendering empathy, an essential quality for enhancing understanding and perhaps accommodation.[11]

Contesting Sacred Land: Internal Debates

I have argued that to understand Israel's ongoing struggle for legitimacy, it is crucial to consider the theological context. Examining this perspective heightens the problem of inherent and enduring dissonance.

The idea of establishing a Jewish state in the twentieth century challenged all three monotheistic religions. Aside from the intermittent control of Christians during the Crusades, Palestine had been in Muslim hands since their conquest in the seventh century. Both Judaism and Christianity sought and hoped for change at some indeterminate time, but Islam's control appeared firm. Muslims certainly expected their hegemony to continue. As a result, theological innovation regarding Jews and the Holy Land was dormant. Ferment began slowly in the nineteenth century among proto-Zionist Christians and pro-Zionist Jews. These were minority movements. By the end of the nineteenth century, with the weakening of the Ottoman Empire, expectations rose, and they were radically elevated to practicality with the dissolution of the Ottoman Empire during World War I. So, it was external events that were the catalyst and stimulated new theological thinking about the Holy Land among adherents of all three faiths. That same effect appears recently to be gaining traction among some Muslims. The question and challenge for those hoping for accommodation is whether the present contest can lead to alternatives or entrenchment of established doxies.

The outcome is far from clear for Judaism. Schisms remain. Aside from increasingly peripheral elements, there is consensus that Jews are not only members of a confessional community but of a historic people who are effectively reconstituting themselves and control large portions of the historic homeland. Living again in the land where seminal and extraordinary events bound the Children of Israel to a role in history, the past reverberates profoundly in the present. As the historian Yosef

Yerushalmi observed in *Zakhor: Jewish History and Jewish Memory*, intensive cultivation of memory is bound up with Jewish identity. The commandment "to remember" [*zakhor*] is given 169 times in the Torah and has been embedded over millennia through recitation and ritual not merely as an individual directive but to Jews as a people.[12] It is noteworthy that this collective historical memory still vividly resonates in the testimonies of the tens of thousands of Jewish Diaspora youth who annually travel to Israel for even a short ten-day visit.[13]

This sense for realization of past promises inevitably results in affirmation of elements of secular discourse that privileges and legitimates contemporary Jewish rights. How this is to be accomplished and whether it must be done immediately produce intense debate. With prophetic significance grafted onto battlefield success, primarily the 1967 War that brought the "entirety" of the Land of Israel [*Eretz Yisrael Hashlema*] under Israeli military control, multiple interpretations have been debated about how that expanded estate should be managed. The previously dominant pragmatic approach has given way to unrestrained mystical yearnings and the conviction the messianic age is at hand. Another significant tradition, originating with the far-reaching proposals for binationalism espoused by Martin Buber and now pressed by his followers, calls for compromise. Others, like the gadfly public intellectual Yeshayahu Leibowitz (1903–1994), warned of the dangers of making present policies based on messianic visions. Still others assign moral precedence to the sacredness of life and the command to protect it over the cost of obtaining sacred land.[14] This debate suggests reflection on a Biblical event. Like the miracle of the "burning bush" that was not consumed, the wonder is that the state has survived the intensity of this dissonance (*Exodus*, ch. 3).

Christianity

Christianity was and remains divided over Israel although the fault lines have shifted in some denominations. Two examples at opposite ends of the spectrum demonstrate this phenomenon: Palestinian Liberation Theology and major elements in Evangelicalism, notably streams of Christian Zionism.

As the term "liberation theology" itself indicates, some Palestinian Christians, located at the core of the conflict, have imported and adapted concepts that originated elsewhere, specifically Central America. This theology is a particular place and time. It explicitly employs Marxist, anti-capitalist, anti-imperialist, and anti-colonialist analyses to call for the liberation of natives who have been exploited by European settlers. And it is noteworthy that as a theology, it draws directly on secular terminology and concepts. Inspired and informed by this precedent, the Palestinian narrative points to perceived parallels between their self-definition as the indigenous people of Palestine to tribes in the Americas and elsewhere. It simultaneously casts Jews as the European invaders. In effect, by denying contemporary Jews are authentically connected to the Holy Land, Palestinian Liberation Theology aligns itself with traditional supersessionism that delegitimates both Jews and the state they created. The claims of illegitimacy are regularly repeated to protest Israel's policies in litanies that include charges of colonialism, apartheid, prejudicial behavior, oppression, and violence.[15] Mainline Protestant churches, receptive to Liberation Theology, are venues for debate over whether to support BDS or take other action, condemning Israel and upholding Palestinian protest. The resulting discourses are amalgamates of secular and theological arguments. A recent telling example is the call by Rev Mitri Raheb (Lutheran) from Bethlehem. As noted earlier, in an essay entitled "Palestine: Time for a Paradigm Shift," he advocates that Christian theology incorporate the widespread secular critique of colonial-settlerism. The explicit syncretism of this approach is captured in the title of the key section of his essay: "The *Theo*politics of Settler Colonialism: The Case of Israel."[16] [my emphasis]

To a lesser but growing extent, criticism is also being voiced by Evangelicals. Since their prime epistemology relies on biblical literalism, they are apparently more distant from secular discourse on the Israel/Palestine conflict and have been the most fervent and active supporters of the reestablishment of a Jewish state. Nevertheless, there are signs that the younger generation is questioning Israel's treatment of Palestinians, and is especially concerned with the fate of a diminishing Christian presence throughout the Middle East. One such movement, called Philos, terms itself the "New" Christian Zionism. The commitment to pluralism may mean less fervent and unequivocal support for Israel, but it does not extend to rejecting it as illegitimate, except perhaps for continuing Israeli control over the West Bank. Identifying itself within the Evangelical tradition, Philos' politics are close to that of Reinhold Niebuhr and James Parkes in being both outspokenly supportive of the Jewish state and critical of its policies regarding Palestine's Arab population and control of the West Bank.[17]

Significant change has taken place in Catholicism. We previously noted Pope Pius X's uncompromising affirmation of supersessionism in his 1904 meeting with Theodor Herzl. The Pope adamantly rejected the notion that Jews should have a state of their own in the Holy Land and be enabled to join the family of nations. Indeed, he warned that, if they tried, the Church would launch an unrelenting effort to convert the returning Jews. Sixty years later, Vatican II formally overturned a theological position that had been maintained for sixteen centuries. Formal relations between the Vatican and Israel were established in 1993. Self-criticism over the role of Catholicism and Catholics leading up to and during the Holocaust as well as a pragmatic need to protect Church interests brought about doctrinal and policy changes. Nevertheless, full acceptance of Israel's sovereignty remains in abeyance, particularly due to reluctance to accept Israel's definition of itself as the "Jewish state."

A majority of Catholics, if not their Church, appear to accept the human condition of living with multiple epistemologies if not two covenants. Numerous Catholic states voted for Jewish statehood well before Vatican II. They did so, in variance rather than in defiance of traditional theology. Claims to territory — the secular and the religious — are not hermetically sealed or necessarily antagonistic to each other. They can coexist. This recalls the dictum of Hugo Grotius referenced in the introduction: *etsi deus non daretur*. That is, one can discern and accept secular truths "*as if* God did not exist" while simultaneously maintaining religious beliefs. In a real way, Church and state have been separated for individuals as well as states and both have influence. Although the Church's residual power is hard to calculate, it would be hazardous for supporters of Israel's legitimacy to discount it.

Schisms therefore remain. The establishment of a Jewish state is an ongoing challenge to theology and whatever realignment may occur will be expressed not only theologically but in those secular positions that best reflect the religious views of the believer.

Islam

Islam presents different and more intransigent challenges to Israel's legitimacy. Unlike western Christian societies in which Israel has achieved formal acceptance, the situation in the Middle East has remained largely hostile when not openly violent. Islam remains a powerful institution and force in the lives of the vast population of the region. In the Middle East, where mosque is so intimately related to government and society, theology remains crucial in driving policy towards Israel.

There are paths to change through alternative interpretations of doctrine expressed through the formulation of *fatwas* that can be applied to relations with Israel even as they have been for interactions with other undesirable entities in the past. Dichotomous views of the world between different "abodes" that produced *jihad* have undergone mitigation. The process that began with Egypt (1978/1979) and Jordan (1994) is making significant headway. This is apparent in the agreement between Israel and the United Arab Emirates in 2020. Officially entitled the *Abraham Accords Peace Agreement: Treaty of Peace, Diplomatic Relations and Full Normalization Between the United Arab Emirates and the State of Israel*, they herald an expansion of relations with other Arab and Muslim states. There are also changes within Israel. In 2021 Mansour Abbas, leader of the Southern Branch of the Islamic Movement is a Hebrew University-trained dentist and author of the Islamic Movement Charter that reinforces Wasatiya Islam, became the first full cabinet minister in a government composed of Zionist parties from the Left to the Right. It appears that at this moment a process of mutual accommodation has begun.

Section B. Modes of Contemporary Criticism

Criminalization

There are also persistent negative indications of attitudes towards the Jewish state. Independence did not end attacks on Israel's legitimacy. Rather it opened a new and wider arena for recycling the arguments that had been persistently raised during the

Mandate. It is not merely old wine in new bottles. There are some new bottles with fresh vintages. Critics continue to charge that the very creation of the Jewish state was an injustice and to press complaints that had already been rejected. However new charges are also leveled. Allegations of illegal and unethical conduct and "crimes against humanity" are pressed not with the intent of correction, but with the expectation that such persistent criminalization will effectively weaken Israel and, in time, contribute to its demise.

A prime and tenacious target is Israel's conduct in the 1948 War. The charge is that the State of Israel was the product of "ethnic cleansing," that the Arab population was expelled, and refugees were not permitted to return. Some Palestinians were indeed forced from their homes during the war and others left of their own accord, particularly members of the middle classes in the conflict's early stages. Where, when, and why mass departures subsequently occurred is a subject of a considerable literature. A range of views explains the departure of Palestinians as a consequence of a bloody civil war or as a result of a pre-meditated Zionist intention that was opportunistically realized in the conflict. It is agreed that after the war, the new state permitted only a small minority to return to their land and to rejoin their families. Suppressed in this view is that the Arab leadership that initiated and carried out the 1948 War had been determined to ensure that a Jewish state would be stillborn and that its population would be thrown into the sea or otherwise removed. There were calls for annihilation by the Mufti and other leaders.[18] It also ignores that the Jewish refugees, who comprised the major element in the population of the "Old City" of Jerusalem since mid-nineteenth century, were clearly expelled and not permitted to return to their homes after the war.[19]

Under these circumstances, allowing Arab refugees to return was unfeasible as well as implausible. The 1948 War did not end with a peace treaty where Arabs in Palestine and the region granted recognition and legitimacy to Israel. As noted above, the fighting subsided in 1949 with "armistice lines" and persistent calls for a "second round." This remained standard policy beyond the 1967 June war. Arab states meeting in September 1967 at Khartoum proclaimed the notorious three Nos: "no peace with Israel, no recognition of Israel, no negotiations with it."[20] Sadat of Egypt paid with his life for challenging these principles.

The insistent accusation that Israel is responsible for the war and for the refugees stems from an incomplete reading of the December 1948 UN General Assembly Resolution 194. Paragraph 11 specifies the terms for the return of refugees:

> Resolves that the refugees wishing to return to their homes and *live at peace* [my emphasis] with their neighbours should be permitted to do so at the earliest practicable date, and that compensation should be paid for the property of those choosing not to return and for loss of or damage to property which, under principles of international law or equity…

The requirement to commit to "live at peace" is crucial. If acceptable for some sectors of the refugee population, it was adamantly rejected by others. Every Arab state voted against a UN resolution that they now embrace since, at the time, they thought it would indicate acquiescence to Israel's legitimacy. In the interim, more than seventy years into the state at the time of this writing, Israel's massive development has accompanied the absorption and resettlement of nearly as many Jewish refugees from Arab countries as Palestinian Arabs who were expelled or left in 1948, as well as nearly an additional two million Jews from other parts of the world. Negotiating terms for compensation and resolution of claims cannot proceed without Palestinian recognition of Israel's legitimacy and its development since 1948. Such a prospect would require substantial change.

Since 1948, anti-Israel rhetoric has remained replete with the charge that a Jewish state is a foreign implant—a colonial-settler society that had usurped the rights of the natives and was in the service of foreign powers. This came to mean that Israel's orientation towards the Western alliance and particularly the United States is proof of its imperialist credentials. This charge places Israel outside the camp of the new states that, like Israel itself, emerged in the post-World War II era of decolonization, but it had real consequences. Israel was isolated and forced to develop in an unremitting hostile environment without the full backing of Western countries, including the United States. The early decades of statehood were marked by such crucial challenges as acquiring armaments, accessing secure financial support, gaining membership in political alliances, providing adequate supplies of fuel and other essentials while simultaneously having to confront enemies actively engaged in planning its destruction.

A detailed history of Israel's foreign relations is found elsewhere. The subtitle of Uri Bialer's recent *Israeli Foreign Policy; A People Shall Not Dwell Alone* (2020) [derived from *Numbers* 23:9] captures the challenge that Israel encountered.[21] A one-time vote established the state and admitted Israel as a member to the United Nations. The long sought-after public recognition of the Jewish state and its full integration into the family of nations has not yet been fully achieved. Formal recognition has not meant full acceptance. The United Nations itself became a key venue for venting explicit and public hostility towards the new state. In other words, with independence, the struggle for legitimacy entered a new phase at a new venue and often with additional arguments.

The United Nations as an Arena of Hostility

When Britain was charged with the Mandate, the public dispute over legitimacy was relatively circumscribed. It was usually conducted within forums that Britain initiated or controlled through the Permanent Mandates Commission of League of Nations in which it had great influence.[22] This changed after World War II. The centers of power moved to Washington and Moscow with the decline of European empires, and the rise of new states across the globe meant the arena of disputation became larger and the contenders more diverse. Postwar decolonization enormously multiplied the number of international actors. In 2023 there are 193 members of the UN. In November 1947, only 57 member states voted on partition. The UN decided in favor by a narrow two-thirds majority of this earlier membership, largely European (both Western and the Soviet Bloc) and American (both North and South.)

It is noteworthy that every member state with a Muslim majority or substantial Muslim population voted against a Jewish state.[23] Resistance continued from the vote on the plan for partition through granting full admittance as a member state. Israel's acceptance was formalized a year later in May 1949 in the General Assembly, and then only after several attempts to block it in the Security Council were overcome. When finally successful in a Security Council vote, the British abstained. Egypt opposed, declaring that Israel's admission would be "an affront to humanity and a sacrilege to the Organization which we are supposed to represent." The use of the term *sacrilege* reflects the blend of the secular and religious that informs the contest at the center of this book.[24]

This hostility presaged continuing objection by a coalition of Arab and Muslim states that have endeavored to isolate Israel in the organization and generate resolutions that deny its legitimacy. The result is that an absurd multitude of anti-Israel resolutions magnify and publicize alleged infringements of Palestinian rights, while the absence of criticism of other states in clear violation of human rights undermines the moral authority of the United Nations.[25]

Israel's isolation became substantially fixed in the aftermath of the 1955 Bandung conference in Indonesia that brought together the emerging African and Asian states created through post-World War II decolonization. The total population represented by Bandung's participants was then 1.5 billion people, or 54 percent of the world's population. Dedicated to fostering economic and cultural cooperation and opposing colonialism, the conference led to the creation of the Non-Aligned Movement. Excluded from both the conference and its aftermath, Israel became an outcast for most states in its region. This set the pattern that Israel still seeks to unravel.

There are many dots between and beyond these points but the persistence of the attack on Israel's legitimacy through the UN is clear. An extensive and insistent torrent of accusations is recorded in the proceedings, documents, and resolutions produced by multiple UN forums such as the General Assembly, the Security Council, the Human Rights Council, UNESCO, and in reports by Special Rapporteurs and others submitted by UNRWA and sympathetic NGOs that become part of the UN's official record. Culpability for the difficult conditions faced by Palestinians and for the consequence of violence between the parties is placed solely on Israel. This does not mean Israel bears no responsibility for the genuine suffering of many Palestinians. It does demonstrate the total imbalance of the indictments that ignore context and distort and exaggerate Israel's culpability while at the same time whitewashing Arab misbehavior and denying any responsibility for the violence and outrages of this protracted conflict. Largely ignored are indiscriminate attacks on Israeli civilian areas emanating from Gaza, an area-controlled by Hamas—widely recognized as a terrorist organization and considered dangerous and hostile even by the Palestinian Authority. The same holds for the plague of terror attacks and suicide bombings against Israeli civilians from diverse Palestinian sources that have required legitimate countermeasures. The unequivocal assertion is that this insistent and violent assault is warranted. It is founded on the contention that Israel, from its inception, is an illegitimate state.[26]

Several salient events demonstrate how such actions through the UN undermine Israel's legitimacy, a member state that it formally recognizes and supports in other facets of its operations.

UNGA Resolution 3379

In November 1975, the United Nations General Assembly voted in favor of a resolution that profoundly undermined Israel's legitimacy. Just 27 years earlier, in 1947, two-thirds of the states that then comprised the United Nations voted for the establishment of a Jewish state. That support was withdrawn by the 1975 vote that proclaimed "that Zionism is a form of racism and racial discrimination" by a vote of 72 in favor, 32 opposed and 35 abstaining. The resolution references an August 1975 statement of the Organization of African Unity that declared "the racist regime in occupied Palestine and the racist regime in Zimbabwe and South Africa have a common imperialist origin, forming a whole and having the same racist structure and being organically linked in their policy aimed at repression of the dignity and integrity of the human being." More than half century after successfully establishing Israel's right to join the family of nations, first before the League of Nations and then the international community including itself, the UN's anti-Israel coalition was still attempting to brand Israel as merely another colonial-settler movement inherently imbued with hostility towards the indigenous population.

Israeli Ambassador to the UN, Chaim Herzog's speech rejecting this position merits repetition here. Herzog dramatically ripped up the printed copy of the UN Resolution as he countered the charge[27]:

> I can point with pride to the Arab ministers who have served in my government; to the Arab deputy speaker of my Parliament; to Arab officers and men serving of their own volition in our border and police defense forces, frequently commanding Jewish troops; to the hundreds of thousands of Arabs from all over the Middle East crowding the cities of Israel every year; to the thousands of Arabs from all over the Middle East coming for medical treatment to Israel; to the peaceful coexistence which has developed; to the fact that Arabic is an official language in Israel on a par with Hebrew; to the fact that it is as natural for an Arab to serve in public office in Israel as it is incongruous to think of a Jew serving in any public office in an Arab country, indeed being admitted to many of them. Is that racism? It is not! That ... is Zionism.

Herzog was joined in indignant opposition by the U.S. Ambassador, Patrick Moynihan, who declared: "The United Nations is about to make anti-Semitism international law."[28] He offered that the "[United States] does not acknowledge, it will not abide by, it will never acquiesce in this infamous act ... A great evil has been loosed upon the world."[29] The pattern of American support in the face of widespread hostility was affirmed in this and on many subsequent occasions.

Not until 1991 did the UN ostensibly change course with a terse statement: "The General Assembly decides to revoke the determination contained in its resolution 3379 of 10 November 1975." The vote for reversal was overwhelming: 111 in favor as opposed to 25 nations against and 13 states that abstained. Nevertheless, lasting damage had already been done. From the 1955 Bandung Conference through the present, a significant portion of the international debate, with echoes in the public square and academy, continues to maintain that Israel's creation was an error; that it caused grave injustice to the Palestinian people; and that Zionism, like Naziism, is a form of racism. The UN abetted programmatic defamation when it granted the PLO Permanent Observer status in 1974, and further institutionalized it by establishing various committees uniquely designed to advance Palestinian causes within the UN Secretariat. Most seriously, the UN has singled out generations of Palestinians from all the millions of twentieth century war refugees, with an institution,—the UNRWA (United Nations Relief and Works Agency) — that provides economic support and a panoply of institutions, including schools, and has maintained their status as refugees for over three generations, while sustaining the promise that they will yet return to Palestine. The qualifiers of the original UN resolution recognizing Israel's right to live in peace are sidestepped. The return of Palestinian refugees is now misrepresented as an absolute right.[30]

Lawfare: NGOS in the Work of the UN

Notable in Israel's criminalization is the mobilization of NGOs that present themselves, and are often thought of, as neutral proponents of human rights but they can also serve as lobbyists for particular causes. The phenomenon of self-appointed, non-elected organizations that are independent of and not responsible to democratically elected governments has grown enormously since the last decades of the twentieth century and into the present. While NGOs have produced an enormous amount of good, they are also mobilized to push problematical political agendas. NGOs have become the main weapon in the campaign of "lawfare" against Israel. As so-called "fact-finding" commissions, they are free to disseminate unsubstantiated claims and unverifiable facts condemning Israel while enjoying the mantle of respectability and support provided by association with UN.

Lawfare was initially defined as a "strategy of using or misusing law as a substitute for traditional military means to achieve military objectives." It has come to refer more broadly to the use of law to undermine an enemy. While this strategy has been applied against the United States, France, and Germany, Israel has been the main target. Under the rubric of defending "human rights," lawfare is used not only as a form of protest, but also as an instrument to obstruct civil and military policy and foreign relations. The record of their work bespeaks the blatant political bias of NGOs in determining what should be the object of protests based in principles of law and justice. Instead, incidences of terrorism and flagrant abuse of human rights by multiple state and non-state actors, many of which are members of the anti-Israel bloc, are regularly ignored.[31]

The UN-initiated 2001 World Conference Against Racism, held in Durban, South Africa, is a prime example of the unrelenting focus on Israel's so-called crimes and repeated attacks on its legitimacy. The conference should have addressed a host of issues that afflict societies in many parts of the world. Instead, it focused on alleged Israeli abuses. Over 8000 participants from 3000 NGOs participated. The event was so extreme and blatant in its abuse of Israel that Israel and the United States walked out. Other western states abstained from voting. The formal chair of the conference, Mary Robinson, appointed by the UN as High Commissioner for Human Rights, came to regret her participation, and resigned her position.[32]

Protest from dissenters succeeded in moderating the final declaration of the Durban Conference. However, many NGOs, under the rubric of the "NGO Forum," issued a parallel document affirming the obnoxious charge expressed in UNGA 3379 that the UN itself had only recently voted to rescind. It described Israel as a "racist, apartheid state" that was guilty of "racist crimes including war crimes, acts of genocide and ethnic cleansing." This was but another instance of NGO's hijacking an international conference avowedly dedicated to the universal agenda of advancing human rights. Instead, led by Arab and Muslim states, the conference insisted on advancing the Palestinian position and, identifying Israel with the Apartheid regime, called for a BDS campaign against Israel like the one used against South Africa. Durban became the point of origin and catalyst for this movement.

The dissemination of "fact finding" reports generated by collaboration between hostile NGOs and the UN itself developed into a pattern. The UN Human Rights Council initiated "Fact Finding Mission on the Gaza Conflict," or the "Goldstone Report" is a prime example. Headed by a noted South African jurist, Richard Goldstone, the mission was officially mandated to investigate improper military tactics and human rights violations in the conflict between Israel and Hamas-held Gaza between 27 December 2008 to 18 January 2009. Israel termed the conflict "Operation Cast Lead." The Muslim world called it "The Gaza Massacre."[33]

The attention given to this conflict by the report was enormous and reflected deeply conflicted positions. At the same time, the declared intention of Hamas to destroy Israel through rockets launched indiscriminately at civilian targets was deemed secondary and largely ignored. The invocation of human rights appears to have been primarily reserved for analyses of Israel's misbehavior, a perspective that ignores context. After much public dispute over the report's faulty methodologies and conclusions, Goldstone disowned his previous conclusion that Israel intentionally targeted civilians and engaged in other war crimes such as causing civilian casualties by using a disproportionate level of force and targeting buildings that were not legitimate military targets. He publicly admitted the report's shortcomings and expressed regret "that our fact-finding mission did not have such evidence explaining the circumstances in which we said civilians in Gaza were targeted, because it probably would have influenced our findings about intentionality and war crimes." He further observed the fact "That comparatively few Israelis have been killed by the unlawful rocket and mortar attacks from Gaza in no way minimizes the criminality [of Hamas]. The U.N. Human Rights Council should condemn these heinous acts in the strongest terms." Finally, he expressed the hope that the "inquiry into all aspects of the Gaza conflict would begin a new era of evenhandedness at the

U.N. Human Rights Council, whose history of bias against Israel cannot be doubted."[34]

Goldstone's public apology for a distorted report is exceptional. His hope for "a new era of evenhandedness at the UN" has not been realized. Issues that hearken back and echo in the debates during the British Mandate that are examined in the first part of this book still resonate in the current discourse of UN resolutions and reports. Among the most flagrant are the repeated resolutions that deny or diminish the connection of Jews to the Holy Land and even exclusively assign Jerusalem and particularly the site of the Temple and of the Al Aqsa Mosque to Palestinians as the sole indigenous people entitled to continued ownership. This rewriting of history is exemplified in the 2016 UNESCO resolution that referred to "Al-Haram al-Sharif" only by its Islamic name, and never as the "Temple Mount." The formulation was consciously framed as an exclusive Muslim narrative. This battle for control of historical narratives and their implications for the present was appreciated by all.[35]

Occupation

The issue of the "occupation" is the most controversial and frequently referenced in the current debate regarding Israel's legitimacy.[36] The very term "occupation" signifies a tangle of diverse meanings. It is commonly used to designate the territories of the West Bank and Gaza occupied by Israel after the 1967 War. But there is a crucial caveat. The "Occupation" is also used to entail the claim that the entire State of Israel is "occupied Palestine" and not just the territories acquired through the 1967 War. As such, it condemns Israel's establishment within any borders as illegitimate. In this way, criticism of the "occupation" gets mixed with a similarly tangled call for boycott, divestment, and sanctions against Israel and the "occupied territories," and demands to negotiate the return of the 1967 territories are conflated with claims that the Jewish state is illegitimate, whether established within the 1948 borders, or anywhere at all.

The sources of this tangled public and academic discourse and the debate over Israel's legitimacy is what much of this book is about. It is an effort to deconstruct the refusal to recognize a Jewish state within any borders. The book traces Arab rejection of the Zionist project from well before 1948, their refusal to accept the UN plan for partition, and their unwillingness and inability to completely normalize relations with Israel since its founding. But importantly, the debate is not limited to criticism of specific policies with differences of opinion as to how competing claims should be adjudicated. From the beginning, it has encompassed arguments rooted in religious doctrines that deny Jews are a living people with a genuine connection to the land and in secular legal and ideological objections to a Jewish nation-state. These fundamental objections to a Jewish state and to the Jews' right to self-determination, remain vital and powerful. Whether or not they are explicitly stated, their roots are deeply embedded in history and culture. They are likely to persist even should, *mirabilis dictu*, a settlement be reached, with a substantial portion of the West Bank and Jerusalem becoming the State of Palestine. Even in that event, the naysayers to a Jewish state are likely to remain in substantial numbers. It stretches the imagination to presume that either the Islamic-based rejection or deeply held secular opposition to Israel will vanish. There is a record of the willingness of some of Israel's leadership over long periods to accept hard pragmatic compromise. Nevertheless, irredentism of all kinds and demands for control over the entire country run deep on both sides.

Disposition of the post-1967 territories is the subject of ongoing debate among Israelis. The partition of Palestine was not intended as absolute justice. It was offered as a pragmatic solution. The willingness of most Zionists to accept such an outcome in 1937 and 1947 enabled Israel to achieve legitimacy through inclusion in the United Nations. Israel's position was further strengthened when it accepted the UN Security Council Resolution 242 in the aftermath of the 1967 War that reaffirmed the principle of negotiations for the division of Palestine. If Israel keeps to that commitment, it may be relatively confident that wide sectors of the international community will affirm its legitimacy. Criticizing the Palestinian Authority for incompetence, corruption, rejectionism, and bad faith, and blaming it for the failure to achieve the two-state solution, does not remove the logic or need for partition. An unwilling and even hostile partner cannot buffer Israel from criticism. Expanding settlements and extending Israeli sovereignty over areas meant to constitute a Palestinian state would be in breach of the partition principle and provoke criticism both at home and abroad. It would most certainly be used as evidence that the Jewish state's territorial ambitions are illegitimate. Achieving agreement to partition and the long-deliberated two state solution will not be possible unless all the parties are willing to compromise. There is nothing simple about this tangle of maximalist positions, contending claims for exclusive control of a patrimony rooted in theology, competing historical narratives, and, for Israel, legitimate security concerns.

Maintaining control of the West Bank exacts a heavy price. Controlling a population that demands to be governed by their own institutions inevitably produces ugly situations that compromise legitimacy. It fuels hostility towards Israel and bolsters the arguments of those who oppose its right to exist. Israel's options are between the less imperfect and the more imperfect. Total acceptance of the Jewish state may not be achievable given the depth of rejection. Nevertheless, legitimacy can be defended and promoted.[37]

In this context the resurfacing of claims based on divine promise pose a great challenge to contemporary Israeli society. The aftermath of the 1967 Six-Day War aroused the aspiration for a return to the pre-1922 view of Palestine as a unitary territory including the entire western bank of the Jordan River and running to the Mediterranean. Supporters have based this idea on secular and on religious grounds, and they have often been intertwined. The solely secular recall the historic presence of ancient Hebrews as depicted in the many books of the Bible in sites held sacred in the hills of Judea and Samaria. They are also keenly aware and vocal about the threats that could emerge from modern Arab states across and even well beyond the Jordan River, especially Iraq. In fact, there was considerable expectation that the 1956 War would be waged not along Egypt's Suez Canal but against a powerful

Iraqi force that could roll across the vulnerable Jordanian Hashemite Kingdom to attack Israel from the west.[38]

A hero of the 1948 War and a prominent Labor leader, Yigal Allon, proposed a response to this threat in an often-discussed plan for post 1967 captured territory. It featured settlements and bases in the valley along the Jordan and on strategic high ground overlooking it was a consequence of this strategic view. Despite rejection of Israel by Arab states and the rise of the Palestine Liberation Organization and even more violent, revanchist groups, his ideas attracted attention. Allon counted on the Kingdom of Jordan to control much of the West Bank as it had since 1949. He expected that this territory would be returned to Arab hands with the restraint of responsible control. On the other hand, Jews with a theological/historical orientation were interested in far more than protection from external threats. They argued for settlement on the whole of the territory, emphasizing the right to return to historic sacred ground wherever it might be, whether amidst large, long-resident Arab populations in or near cities like Hebron in the south or Nablus in the north. In practice, the force, energy, and sense of legitimacy steadily pushed well beyond Allon's initial proposals.[39]

Expansion was initially modest. It began with sympathy for recovering several sites of Jewish settlements that had been forcibly uprooted during the 1948 war and transferred to Arab hands. In the trauma of the post 1973 post Yom Kippur period, religiously motivated settlers identified with Gush Emunim [Bloc of the Faithful] energetically pushed even further, often through flagrant violation of Israeli law and established policy. Yet even these settlements were modest in comparison to a fundamental shift in Israeli politics in the aftermath of the 1977 elections that resulted in the rise of a secular, expansionist rightist Likud supported by a radicalized Religious Zionism suffused with a messianic orientation and the passion for restoration of preeminence in the Holy Land. In the delicate balance of multiple forces that characterizes Zionist politics this combination of intense secular and religious commitment set the course for a major shift in Israeli policy. It contributed to Menachem Begin's ascension to power and the progressive encroachment over succeeding decades by hundreds of thousands of settlers on territory assigned for a Palestinian state.

The alliance between religious and secular supporters of a Greater Israel initially included select portions of the West Bank as well as the Gaza Strip. In 2005 Prime Minister Ariel Sharon engineered a unilateral disengagement from the Gaza Strip and several settlements in Samaria, or the northern West Bank. Long associated with Israeli expansion, his decision for selective withdrawal was pragmatic. Excessive ambition to control a hostile and restive population is costly and too difficult to repress. Withdrawal from Gaza appears to be long-lasting, but how far or long it will be extended to the West Bank is far from certain. The impulse for continual expansion throughout Palestine has no fixed and certain boundaries.

The current moment is thereby fraught with considerable tension. Warnings over taking undue advantage of the 1967 victory were clearly voiced by many quarters in Israeli society, from religious philosophers to secular thinkers. To these voices, practical questions emerged in the 1980s over whether Israel could be both a democratic *and* a Jewish society given the actual and potential size of Palestine and Israel's Arab population. Evidence of the difficulty of maintaining control became evident during the "first" *Intifada* [1987–1993] or uprising by Palestinians unwilling to abide a rapidly growing Jewish population in lands designated for their state. Opposition within Israel developed among political parties as well and among NGOs located in Israel and abroad, even in quarters otherwise generally supportive of Israel. While a respite was in evidence in the aftermath of the Oslo Accords [1993 and 1995] that promised to culminate in mutual Israeli-Palestinian recognition, violence continued during and erupted again in full force in 2000 with the onset of the Second Intifada.

The reality of diminishing prospects for effective partition coexists with another reality. Israel has prospered enormously during these years as an advanced modern country with a vibrant economy, democratic political system, powerful military, and recognition by an ever-increasing number of nations throughout the world, including Arab and Muslim states. Yet, there remains something elusive and tentative in the balance sheet. Numerous indicators demonstrate the antisemitism is on the rise in the West and requires continuing response long after public expression of responsibility and even guilt after the Holocaust under the rubric of "Never Again." However, this unanticipated antisemitism is strongly related to anti-Zionism.

The extent to which Israel is responsible for such hostility and negativism towards itself is an unresolved and contentious issue. Some argue if such antagonism will not be entirely allayed, it might be diminished were different policies adopted enabling improved relationships among the contending populations. To be sure, the failure to achieve an independent Palestinian state rested for many crucial decades on the failure of the Arabs themselves to accept partition and insist on Israel's destruction, but Israel itself has become complicit in foreclosing chances for its implementation. That said, it is still not obvious that the Palestinian side is prepared to accept partition in principle and able to implement it among their own people. Nevertheless, the waning on the Jewish side of the historic restraint on both secular and religious impulses for aggrandizement contributes to eroding the most likely course towards alleviation, let alone resolution, of a century-old confrontation.

Imperfect Paradigm: Binationalism

Meron Benvenisti (1934–2020), a political scientist who served as deputy mayor of Jerusalem, argued in the 1980s that, because of the increasing numbers of Jewish settlers in the West Bank, Israel could not avoid becoming a binational state. His view was based on demographic change that resulted from Israel's policies in the West Bank that prioritized Jewish aspirations while disregarding the rights of Palestinians.[40] This provides the critical justification in the demand to disestablish the Jewish state and replace it with a new entity shared equally by Jews and Arabs.

The first generation to advocate binationalism—Martin Buber and Judah Magness—were concerned that the chauvinism, particularism, and potential aggression to "others" they had witnessed in Europe around World War I could also infect Zionism. Their ideal of a good and proper nationalism was based, in part, on universal values and ideals. But it was also profoundly Jewish and drew on the Jewish prophetic tradition of justice. As theoretically attractive as their understanding of binationalism was for some Zionists, notably Central European intellectuals and members of the left-wing kibbutz movement, almost no Arab partners then supported a binational Palestine. Deviation from an exclusive Arab nationalism hardly existed and was not tolerated when it appeared. Individuals who were attracted to the concept were subject to violence, including murder.[41]

After 1948, a different binational movement appeared. It originated in 1962 and gained traction after the 1967 War as a protest against Israel's expansion into the territory that had been under Jordanian control and exclusively populated by Arabs. This contrary voice did not base its appeal on Jewish values. On the contrary, it was an ideologically deeply left-oriented movement associated with international socialism and communism. Typical of left-wing organizations, it included many divergent and even contradictory elements, but its members shared the objective of ending the Jewish character of the state, and the privileges it inevitably granted to Jewish citizens. Officially termed the Socialist Organization of Israel, it was largely known by the name of its journal, *Matzpen* (*Compass*—a term that resonates with the Hebrew word for "conscience") that was vigorously anti-Zionist and branded Jewish settlement as a colonial-settler movement. This characterization fits with the post-1967 appearance of the colonial-settler paradigm and the demand to create a state that does not privilege one based on national identity, ethnicity, or religion. Given its internationalist and leftist orientation, Matzpen established alliances with New Left-type organizations abroad, including in the Arab world. It held that, by definition, a Jewish state could not be both democratic and Jewish in any form, and that the only solution was to excise Israel's Jewish character.[42]

Such self-criticism has been and continues to be echoed by Jewish intellectuals abroad. Among the most notable was Tony Judt (1946–2010) of New York University who declared in a 2003 essay that Israel was an "anachronism." A one paragraph excerpt merits repetition here:

> The problem with Israel, in short, is not—as is sometimes suggested—that it is a European "enclave" in the Arab world; but rather that it arrived too late. It has imported a characteristically late-nineteenth-century separatist project into a world that has moved on, a world of individual rights, open frontiers, and international law. The very idea of a "Jewish state"—a state in which Jews and the Jewish religion have exclusive privileges from which non-Jewish citizens are forever excluded—is rooted in another time and place. Israel, in short, is an anachronism[43]

Judt's essay spawned an intense debate that continues today especially among Diaspora Jewry who are called upon to desist from traditional support for Israel and to promulgate a range of charges that fit within the category of criminalization. This is not the place to review the extensive criticism of Judt. Suffice to indicate that nationalism is far from passé in the Middle East, among Israeli Jews as well as

Palestinian Arabs, and even among Europeans who served as the model for Judt in conjuring his view of what the future holds for humankind.[44] Moreover, while faulting Israel's Jews for not constructing a properly democratic state, there is no discussion of how well-prepared and experienced Palestinians and others in the Middle East are for creating and managing a democratic society. Success in implementing this model would require the shared commitment and capacity of all sides to its realization.[45]

The first significant and distinctly non-Jewish voices were raised on behalf of binationalism among Israeli Arabs in the 1980s and 1990s. Their position began to take shape after an Israeli Arab protest in March 1976 over the planned expropriation of land owned by Arabs for state purposes. The protest was violent with six Arabs killed and many injured. Commemorated since as "Land Day," it became an annual event.[46] Additional protest against the Jewish state and support for binationalism were stimulated by the 1982 campaign in Lebanon and then the First Intifada (1987–1993) as well as the expanding Jewish settlement on Arab land. The ferment among Israeli Arab intellectuals lead to calls for a "One state" solution that would simultaneously grant enhanced status to the Arab minority and de-emphasize the Jewish identity of the state and the rights of the Jewish population. The first expression of this objective was in 1995 with the organization of *Balad,* a political party [*Brit Leumit Demokratit* in Hebrew or National Democratic Alliance; and *nation* or *country* in Arabic]. The founding leader was Azmi Bishara [1956—], a Christian Arab public intellectual from Nazareth who emerged from the leadership of a student movement born in the aftermath of Land Day and elected to the Knesset four times from 1996 to 2006. He ultimately fled Israel claiming a lack of faith in Israeli justice when he faced charges alleging treason and espionage.[47]

In 2006/2007 several Palestinian manifestoes appeared, advocating binationalism. They appeal to democracy, human rights, and social justice, and call for reducing Jewish national aspirations. The most prominent, the 2006 *Future Vision* document, typically defines Jewish settlement as an illegitimate foreign colonial-settler movement from the outset. In other words, as argued above, the "Occupation" began long before the 1967 War. The coalition of Palestinian intellectuals who authored the *Future Vision* documents held positions in Israeli universities or were professionals, particularly in law, and were established leaders from Arab communities from the Galilee to the Negev. They called for support of their national aspirations within a new polity that would supplant the existing Jewish state with a binational one. The document begins with the pronouncement: "We are the Palestinian Arabs in Israel, the indigenous peoples, the residents of the State of Israel, and an integral part of the Palestinian People and the Arab and Muslim and human Nation." From this beginning, the *Future Vision* reiterates many of the charges that originated during the Mandate to delegitimate the Jewish state that are detailed in Part I of this book. Were it not for the delegitimization of the Jewish state, the authors of these documents would have garnered significant support from Jewish citizens for issues that require correction.[48]

Balad and the *Future Vision* have replaced the original idea of binationalism, rooted in a distinctly Jewish perspective and Jewish sources and sympathetic to

Jewish needs, with a so-called "state of all its citizens," deeply critical of the Jewish state, and despite its purported universalistic perspective, committed to promoting Palestinian interests. Some of its proponents envisage that demography will ultimately result in the emergence of a decidedly Arab Palestinian state. Whether through conscious implementation of an alternative model or through the inevitability of historical processes, the elimination of a Jewish state is predicted, and viewed as desirable.[49]

In all these guises, binationalism is problematic. Paradigms are neat; reality is messy. That surely applies to binationalism in its different and even contradictory formulations. The heading "imperfect paradigm" acknowledges that there is no formulation of a "Jewish" state that can perfectly satisfy all requirements. The same holds for the binational state that is suggested to replace it. Political theorists spin scenarios of a democratic and conflict-free future, but the notion of a binational state has never appealed to most Jews and Arabs. The Palestinian Authority favors a secular Palestinian state and Hamas is committed to an Arab Muslim theocracy. Israeli Jews are unlikely to trust the security of their culture and persons to others in a region where identity politics threaten and subjugates minorities who had until recently been part of the fabric of Middle Eastern society for millennia but lacked the means to protect themselves.

In other words, for all its theoretical attraction, binationalism has not appealed to the wishes and does not correspond to the deep cultural traditions of the peoples the paradigm is intended to benefit and serve. Even if there were a powerful, external intervention in Israel/Palestine, it is difficult to imagine an agreed agenda that would meet the needs of Jewish, Christian, and Muslim, religious and secular citizens, and unify them in a functioning polity.

In theory, binationalism is a scheme for power sharing that respects the fundamental interests of multiple distinctive national groups who inhabit the same territory. The state in which they hold citizenship is meant to maintain unity and centrality through a common government that allocates equally between the two peoples. Note, however, that in this sense, the result is not a "state of all its citizens" because group identity is both recognized and privileged. That is particularly realistic in the case of Israel/Palestine where national, ethnic, and religious identities and allegiances are fundamental to individual identity and group relationships.

One scholar, Uriel Abulof, describes binationalism as "a creature of political fantasy."[50] Another, Michael Walzer, agrees, explaining that "Citizens are never only citizens; they are always something else. They share a culture, or a religious commitment, or an ethnic or national history with some but not all of their fellows, and they attach great value to the sharing and want to express that value in their common life."[51] In effect, a significant school of scholarship argues that binationalism is a utopian ideal, limited by a world in which such states are rare and, in fact, attempts to create them have produced conflict and enduring tension. However attractive binationalism may appear as a panacea for difficult and dangerous communal problems, there is no record of its success. Such societies are typically fraught with tension and instability.

Section B. Modes of Contemporary Criticism

Indeed, the feasibility of binationalism has yet to be demonstrated, and not only in Israel/Palestine. Among the examples are Cyprus, Lebanon, the Indian subcontinent, the Balkans, the former Czechoslovakia and Yugoslavia, Myanmar, Sudan, and Ethiopia, to name a few. It is highly unlikely that the Jews and Arabs of Israel-Palestine will provide a successful precedent any time soon.

Widespread appreciation for this reasoning explains why the formula of two states for two peoples remains the chosen option on the international agenda, however long and difficult its birth pangs are likely to be. For all its deficiencies, partition into two separate but potentially cooperating states remains the most feasible, if imperfect, idea, and the one proposal that has been endorsed by the international community. Alternative scenarios, however generously and innocently proposed, would spell the end of a Jewish state.

Oslo II Map
Outlining Areas A, B, and C

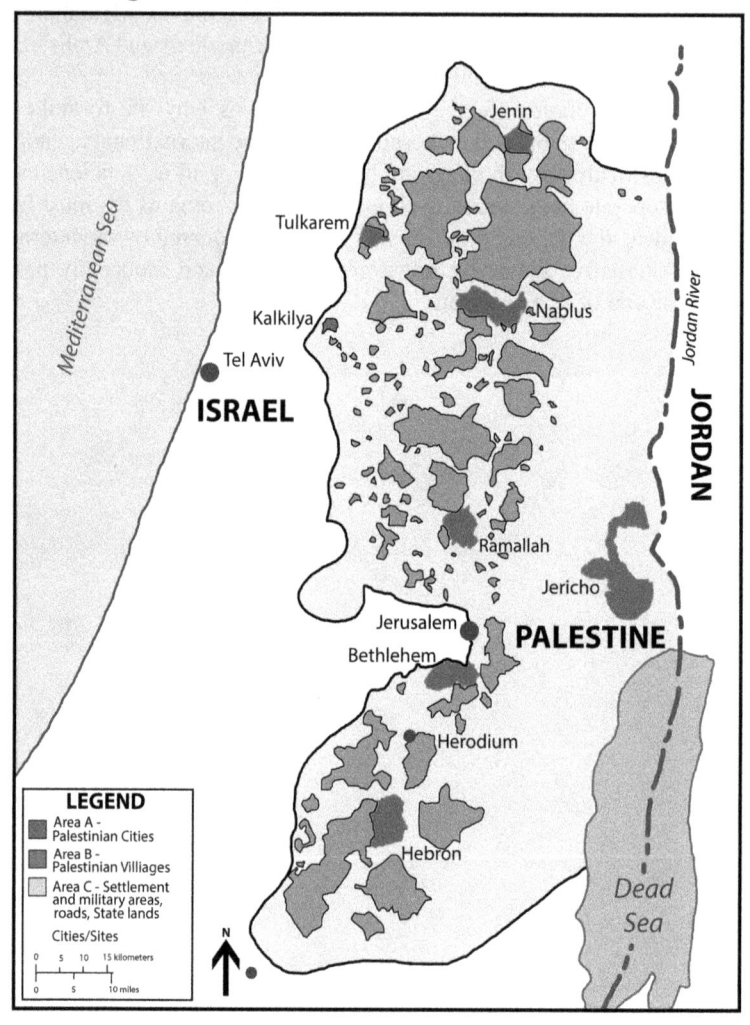

Jewish and Palestinian areas in the West Bank. Map of Palestinian (A and B) and Jewish areas (C) in the West Bank as of 2015. Jewish areas continue to expand steadily, further eroding possibility of establishing a Palestinian state with extensive contiguous areas. The result is that "facts on the ground" threaten to overtake supporters of a two-state solution. Courtesy of Professor Morag M. Kersel, DePaul University

Section C. Towards the Second Century

Complications of the Present

The challenges of the present moment are pressing, dangerous, and sadly familiar. The need for the Jewish state and for its open, public legitimation have become strongly interwoven with a striking upsurge of antisemitism. Criticism of Israel may be entirely independent of antisemitism. On the other hand, antisemitism extends to rejection of the Jewish state and infects and buttresses efforts to delegitimate Israel.

The Arabs' strongly voiced opposition to Zionism and to Israel's establishment after four centuries of Ottoman and Muslim rule was to be expected. It is not surprising that they did not immediately accept Israel's existence as a *fait accompli*. It is also not surprising that Israeli Jews remember that Arab armies launched attacks with the intention of destroying the new Jewish state the day after the state was declared and that their announced mission was to expel them. This brutal rejection and the motivation behind it cannot be ignored. The term "Nakba," the *Disaster* or *Catastrophe*, as originally formulated in 1948, repudiated the failure of the joint Arab forces to achieve their goal. Calls for armed aggression and destruction continue into the present in acts of terror and rhetorical demonization of Israel and Jews.[52]

As a result, in the current debate, criticism of Israel that merits a thoughtful and considered response is tangled up with malicious slogans and slander rooted in seemingly irredeemable hostility toward Jews. This perception impelled thirty governments, including the leading democracies in Europe and North America, to formulate and endorse a *Working Definition of Antisemitism* between 2017 to 2020. The formulation is a non-legally-binding document, produced by the International Holocaust Remembrance Alliance (IHRA). The list of signatories includes Canada, France, Germany the Netherlands, Sweden, and the United States. This document has been endorsed by the Secretary General of the United Nations, the major agencies of the European Union, and the Organization of American States. Many other organizations and institutions, including universities, have also adopted the IHRA statement. No one could have known in 2016 how widely the IHRA working definition of antisemitism would be adopted. It is not a theoretical formulation divorced from reality. It is a response to the reality of rising antisemitism, and this reality helps explain the speed with which it acquired symbolic and canonical status. Such an unusual action is in response to the deeply troubling upsurge on verbal and actual physical attacks on Jewish persons and property—such as buildings, schools, kosher establishments, synagogues, and cemeteries—and inflammatory slogans proliferated in mass demonstrations, speech, and written and visual forms on social media, often in conjunction with demonization of Israel. The statistics are carefully documented and are regularly reported as sensational fare in public and social media. These phenomena are an alarming disavowal of the promise that became current in the post-Holocaust decades: "Never Again."[53]

The IHRA document includes not only such traditional antisemitic tropes as Holocaust denial but accusations about the State of Israel, its actions, and the legitimacy of its existence. It includes denying the Jewish people their right to self-determination and characterizing the State of Israel as an apartheid, racist endeavor that may be compared with Naziism. In effect, it demonstrates how far the demonization expressed in the 1975 UNGA Resolution 3379 and the 2001 Durban conference has infected public discourse. The UN's much belated revocation of UNGA 3379 more than a decade and a half later did not erase its baseless condemnation. The damage had been done. Thus, even as Israel's acceptance has become anchored among most nations, publicly defaming it has also gained traction. An iconic indication of how antisemitism merges with rejection of Israel is the rise and fall of Jeremy Corbyn, the leader of the British Labor party and a serious candidate for prime minister. After a hard-fought campaign within Labor and in the public square, Corbyn was ousted because of personal statements he made, and his deficiencies in handling antisemitism during his leadership (2015–2020). Within that indictment, the central charge was his demonization of Israel and preference for those who would destroy it.[54]

The IHRA document has been challenged by a significant group of primarily Jewish Studies and Israel Studies scholars for its formulations and examples of what constitutes Israel-related antisemitism. Their document, *The Jerusalem Declaration on Antisemitism* (2020), differs primarily in its list of examples of anti-Israel statements and behaviors that may also be considered antisemitic.[55] Nevertheless, both documents are in accord that this pernicious phenomenon exists and requires definition. The Jerusalem Declaration is considerably more restrictive in organizing the list and concerned with protecting the right of academics and other observers to voice legitimate criticism, even though the signers disagree amongst themselves with the positions taken by colleagues. On the other hand, the governments that sponsored the IHRA Declaration are taking responsibility for what happens not only on campus but in society at large where inflammatory language and hate crimes fuse rank antisemitism with demands to eradicate the Jewish state.[56] Moreover, these governments often enact anti-BDS legislation. The 2022 Queen's speech or statement of intended legislation, for example, specifically targets BDS in a proposed "Freedom of Speech Bill" that states: "The Government has zero tolerance for discrimination." It concludes with the assertion that they "contribute to the horrific rise in antisemitism in the UK."[57]

The controversy over the relative appropriateness of the IHRA or the Jerusalem Declaration echoes in opposing arguments in the debates over public policy regarding BDS. They similarly hinge on distinguishing facts from misrepresentations, free speech from hate speech and invective, and legitimate criticism from demonization. In the United States, as of 2021, 35 state legislatures have passed laws or resolutions condemning BDS, typically arguing it is a hate crime and antisemitic in nature. Similar actions have been taken by other western governments, at both the national and local levels. As in the case of the IHRA and the Jerusalem Declaration, commitments to free speech and legitimate criticism are balanced against excess in vilifying the Jewish state that incentivizes and justifies doing actual harm to Jews and

Jewish institutions. Israel's legitimacy is a topic of dispute in the public square and is likely to remain so. One would be hard-pressed to name another state that has had to endure challenges to its legitimacy for so long and in so many different forums.

The issues are not merely rhetorical. Lawfare and criminalization are alternate means to undermine Israel's security. At the same time that Israel is called on to defend its legitimacy, it confronts military challenges to its existence. The threat of formal warfare by massed armies on a field of battle may appear diminished, but incendiary and explosive devices regularly menace the homes and fields of settlements along the border with Gaza; rockets are launched from Gaza targeting kibbutzim, towns, and cities as far north as Tel Aviv; the Hizbullah reportedly has tens of thousands of rockets aimed at Israel from Lebanon; terrorists attack Jewish institutions, citizens, Israelis, and their supporters abroad; and nuclear missiles are threatened by an avowedly antisemitic Iran. Nevertheless, by December 2020, 164 of the other 192 UN member states had formally recognized Israel. Of the 28 that still do not, 15 are members of the Arab league and nearly all the rest are predominantly Muslim states. There are also non-state radical Islamic organizations committed to destroying Israel. At the same time, as of this writing, other Arab and Muslim states are normalizing relations with the Jewish state. In sum, there has been considerable progress along with the upsurge of dangerous phenomena.

Final Observations

Zionism's founders were keenly aware of the pitfalls when they initially sought public approval for their project. The acceptance they hoped for was not realized by the Balfour Declaration; it did not follow from endorsement by the League of Nations or the United Nations. Both secular and theological objections to the Jewish state continued to spawn campaigns to undermine Israel's legitimacy. It is unlikely they could have anticipated such entrenched resistance to a Jewish state in Palestine and the unrelenting denial of its legitimacy. Even formal recognition by numerous states did not necessarily translate into acceptance and cooperation. Substantial pockets of resistance would persist beyond official political institutions. Yet, as the members of the First Zionist Congress ultimately agreed from the outset, the Jewish people's determination to reestablish themselves in a sovereign Jewish state in the Holy Land had to be presented to the world community openly. This intention is explicit in the concise summary of universal justifications that went into the making of Israel's Declaration of Independence. It is a formulation that sums up principles and issues that comprise the first part of this book.

The Declaration of Independence begins with history, the assertion that the "Land of Israel was the birthplace of the Jewish people" where they developed their national culture that has "universal significance." It details the Jews' devotion to their homeland during the long exile, their determination to return and restore the land to its prior productivity and highlights international recognition for that effort. References to the Holocaust further emphasize the existential needs and rights of

Jews to "a life of freedom, dignity and labor." Moreover, the Jews of Palestine shared in the struggle against a common foe in World War II. This, too, supports claims to rights in Palestine. Thus, Israel's declaration addresses the world community invoking what were then universally recognized justifications of claims to land: history, conquest, treaties, purchase, and labor.

In other words, for more than a century, Zionism has been advancing its claims based on the rationale by which modern states have come into being. The phrase that sums up the case for the Jewish people's right to self-determination echoes the American Declaration's much imitated justification for independence—a first in the modern world. It proclaims "these truths" regarding their rights to be "*self-evident*." The Israeli Declaration affirms that it is "the *self-evident* right of the Jewish people to be a nation, like all other nations, in its own sovereign state." The achievement of this historic undertaking was anchored in universal principles "evident" to all mankind and accepted by people of reason and good will.

Yet there is also a particular and unique justification for a Jewish state. Zionist aspirations would result in "reconstituting" the Jewish people in its promised homeland. The cultural, political, economic, and military vitality of the Jewish state can be taken as evidence of success measured in secular terms. It can also be attributed to the fulfillment of Divine promises. On both counts, it has bred opposition and rejection. Allegedly universal principles invoked to justify territorial claims elsewhere have been denied for Jews returning to Palestine. For centuries before colonialism was repudiated, Christianity and Islam repudiated Jewish rights to the Holy Land on theological grounds. This view precluded accepting contemporary Jews as a living "people" or "nation." It insisted they were mere adherents to an ancient faith with no rights to sacred territory. In the more contemporary public square, Zionism has been rejected as a colonial-settler movement, an argument that entails and extends Christian and Islamic theological beliefs in a secular form of supersessionism. So, while theological assertions may appear to be absent from public debate, they continue to influence how secular claims are made and received. Resistance to and acceptance of the State of Israel stem from the admixture of both.

Israel's Declaration of Independence pointedly avoided specific theological references. Two key political leaders who were also rabbis ultimately signed the Declaration after insisting passionately but unsuccessfully that it must include the phrase: "God of Israel" or "the Almighty and Redeemer of Israel." Instead, the Declaration concludes "with trust in the Rock of Israel," an intentionally ambiguous reference to God, the Land of Israel, or some other abstraction.

Here, too, the wording echoes the language of the American Declaration of Independence. Although only Christians drafted and approved it, the framers of the declaration asserted "a firm reliance on the protection of divine Providence...." There is no explicit reference to Christianity or Jesus. The PLO Charter, too, follows in this tradition. The language is not religious. Neither Allah nor any sacred text is referenced. For the last two and a half centuries since the United States was established with a revolutionary reliance on secular authority and sanction, this pattern has been common in foundational documents of new democratic states. It is in striking contrast to the documents of the theologically conservative and fundamentalist

Hamas, that in common with radical Islam invokes traditional religious authority for its legitimation and for its denial to Jews.

I have argued that the reality of the State of Israel has challenged long established systems of belief for Jews, Christians, and Muslims. All have local populations and adherents worldwide with deep and abiding interests in what transpires in the Holy Land. Whatever their religious practices and affiliations in Israel and abroad, many Jews continue to adjust to the unexpected consequences of a Jewish state. For Christians, the idea of multiple covenants addresses concern and even guilt over the consequences of denying the continuing positive presence of Jews in history. For Islam, the practical need to become part of the publicly secular international community based on universal principles has required even more fundamental adjustments. These have begun to include finding ways to accommodate Jewish sovereignty within Islam's traditional domain.

This entails a caveat. The foundational documents of Jewish and Palestinian apparently secular national movements do not include specific religious references. Yet the very absence of theological formulations can obscure the ways religion shapes their national aspirations and policies. Whether overtly expressed or not, theological commitments are real. They cannot be addressed unless their significance is recognized, and their power acknowledged. They are easily identified in the assertions and actions of fundamentalist and extreme nationalist Jewish and Arab groups in Israel and throughout the Middle East. However, their influence is deeply embedded and to whatever degree underlies even secular intellectual, social, and cultural life, and cannot be simply ignored, erased, or uprooted by secular universalist discourse and commitments.

A century is not a long time in the history of the Middle East where contemporary civilizations extend back for centuries and even millennia. The role of religion has been defining and is still vital. The intermixing of secular insights, ideas and justifications is therefore novel, however powerful, persuasive, and significant it appears to moderns. This may explain why fundamentalist nationalist Jewish and Arab groups undertake extreme political programs in total disregard of secular or alternative theological considerations.

The veiled or distanced theological sources underlying the establishment of states may be innovative and provisional. There is ample evidence of reversion to traditional patterns. Ataturk attempted to redefine Turkey beginning in the decade prior to Balfour and his effort often served as a model for Zionists. However, it is now undergoing a reassertion of traditional Islamic influence under Erdogan and the movement he represents. In my introduction, I also noted the tentativeness of the secular revolutions inaugurated by Nehru in India and Ben-Bella in Algeria. Today, theologically based parties have gained public support and wield increasing political power unimaginable in Ben-Gurion's secular Israel. In the Arab world, political parties declare their theologically based policies undisguised. The power of traditional religion is evident in fundamentalist movements such as Hizballah, Hamas, the Islamic Brotherhood, and the Iranian Ayatollahs that call openly for the annihilation of both Israel and Jews.

Sociologists of religion point to a public resurgence of religion across the globe that contradicts the idea that secularization inexorably follows on modernization. The conflict in Israel/Palestine attests to this global phenomenon. Consider what is, in secular terms, the disproportionate attention given the place where Abraham was prepared to sacrifice his son Isaac/Ishmael nearly four millennia ago. Venerated by followers of Abrahamic monotheism, the site is a mere several hundred square meters and although it has no mineral resources or strategic value, it is among the most contentious venues in the world. Today, the Temple Mount or al-Ḥaram al-Sharīf—the focus of threats and conflict on the ground and bitter debates in international, academic, and public forums—may be the most intractable issue in the Arab-Israeli conflict.

This deeply embedded, long-term reality makes current political challenges to Israel's Declaration of Independence even more consequential. This apparently secular document rested on theological ambiguity and served to attract both internal and international support for a Jewish state. The current moves by powerful members in the Israeli polity seem to base Israel's claims and policies primarily, if not solely, on Divine intention. The internal threat is to replace the pluralistic, multiethnic Jewish democratic state with a state anchored in religious principles. The external danger of shifting to a discourse based in theology is even more ominous, as it invites direct confrontation with radical Islam and traditional theological tropes also found in Christianity. Claims of exclusive priority in controlling sacred space readily leads to competition and conflict. Secular discourse can be contentious, but its language can more readily include pragmatic compromise and acceptance.

There was therefore practical wisdom when Zionism centered its claims in secular principles of international law and justice rather than exclusive religious principles. Yet, as I have tried to demonstrate, the secular and theological are tangled. Their complicated connections need to be addressed even if they cannot be entirely unraveled. We must turn our attention to theological claims even if they tend to be underplayed or obscured by the prevailing secular culture. I have argued that unquestioned assumptions rooted in religious doctrine continue to influence how secular claims are made and how they are received. Interrogating this dense weave of religious and secular arguments is essential if we wish to understand why, a century after the international community affirmed the right of Jews to reconstitute themselves in their national homeland, the legitimacy of their achievement is still under attack. And why, in the face of relentless opposition, Jews remain steadfast in their commitment to maintain the State of Israel as their national home even as those who hold alternative beliefs contest their right and this achievement.

Notes

1. The Executive of the Zionist Organization, *The Jubilee of the First Zionist Congress 1897* is conveniently republished and translated in Lawrence J Epstein, *The Dream of Zion; The story of the first Zionist Congress* (Lanham: Roman and Littlefield, 2016), pp. 57–94. The citations referenced here of the deliberations of that first congress are found there.

2. Leo Pinsker, *Auto-Emancipation: An Appeal to His People by a Russian Jew* (1882), see: https://jewishvirtuallibrary.org/quot-auto-emancipation-quot-leon-pinsker
3. Wm. Roger Louis, *Ends of British Imperialism; The Scramble for Empire, Suez and Decolonization* (London: Tauris, 2006); D. K. Fieldhouse, *Western Imperialism in the Middle East* (Oxford: Oxford University Press, 2006), Chaps. 4, 5. The literature of renewed international commitment to a Jewish state through the United Nations vote in 1947 is huge. A recent and masterful review of that decision is found in Jeffrey Herf, *Israel's Moment; International Support for and Opposition to Establishing the Jewish State, 1945–1949* (Cambridge: Cambridge University Press, 2022).
4. Prime minister Levi Eshkol solicited an internal legal opinion that indicated that settling in the conquered territories was illegal. See Gershom Gorenberg, *The Accidental Empire; Israel and the Birth of the Settlements, 1967*-1977 (New York: Henry Holt, 2006), pp. 99–102; The same conclusion is found in an expert opinion submitted by the U.S. State Department Legal Advisor on Israeli Settlement, April 1978, to the House Committee on Foreign Affairs: http://www.fmep.org/resource/u-s-state-department-legal-advisor-on-israeli-settlements/. There are counter arguments. See, for example: Alan Baker, *The Legality of Israel's Settlements: Flaws in the Carter-Era Hansell Memorandum*, Jerusalem Center for Public Affairs, Nov. 19, 2019. https://jcpa.org/publication/jerusalem-issue-briefs/
5. Ben-Arieh, *The Making of Eretz Israel in the Modern Era*, Chap. 3.
6. The conscious, economic irrationality of Zionist settlement is analyzed in Baruch Kimmerling, *Zionism and economy* (Cambridge, MA, 1983) and *Socio-Territorial dimensions of Zionist politics* (Berkeley, 1983). The deep, emotional—even primordial—connection to the land by Jewish pioneers is captured in Boaz Neumann, *Territory and Desire in Early Zionism* (Waltham, MA: Brandeis University Press/University Press of New England, 2011).
7. Gur Alroey, *Zionism without Zion: The Jewish Territorial Organization and Its Conflict with the Zionist Organization* (Detroit: Wayne State University Press, 2016).
8. Dowty, "'A Question That Outweighs All Others', 34–54.
9. On Ernst Renan (1823–1892) see, his 1882 foundational lecture: "What is a Nation." https://web.archive.org/web/20110827065548/http://www.cooper.edu/humanities/core/hss3/e_renan.html; Benedict Anderson, *Imagined Communities: Reflections on the Origin and Spread of Nationalism* (New York: Verso, 2016).
10. The silencing of Palestinian voices is a recurrent theme in Edward Said's writings. See for example, "What they want is my silence," in David Barsamian and Edward Said, *Culture and Resistance; Conversations with Edward W. Said* (Cambridge, MA: South End Press, 2003), pp. 71–102; for purported scholarly evidence of the persistence of the phenomenon see Omar Zahzah, "Digital apartheid: Palestinians being silenced on social media," *Aljazeera*, 13 May 2021. https://www.aljazeera.com/opinions/2021/5/13/social-media-companies-are-trying-to-silence-palestinian-voices#:~:text=Decades%20after%20Edward%20Said%E2%80%99s%20criticism%20of%20the%20US,media%20companies.%20But%20we%20must%20not%20give%20in. Other noteworthy references to Said's charge of a conspiracy of silencing the Palestinian narra-

tive: Keith Whitelam, *The Invention of Ancient Israel; the silencing of Palestinian history* (London: Routledge, 1996) and Nadia Abu El-Haj, *Archaeological Practice and Territorial Self-Fashioning in Israeli Society* (Chicago: University of Chicago, 2001).
11. Robert I. Rotberg, ed., *Israeli and Palestinian Narratives of Conflict: History's Double Helix* (Bloomington: Indiana University Press, 2006).
12. Yosef Yerushalmi, *Zakhor: Jewish History and Jewish Memory* (Seattle: University of Washington Press, 1982). p. 5 and passim.
13. Leonard Saxe, *Ten Days of Birthright Israel: A Journey in Young Adult Identity (Waltham, MA: Brandeis University Press,* 2008).
14. See, for example, Ronald Kronish, ed., *Coexistence and Reconciliation in Israel: Voices for Interreligious Dialogue* (Mahwah, NJ: Paulist Press, 2015).
15. See: https://sabeel.org/category/wave-of-prayers/
16. Mitri Raheb, (2021). "Palestine: Time for a Paradigm Shift," *Academia Letters*, Article 1848, 2021. https://doi.org/10.20935/AL1848
17. *Philos Project*, https://philosproject.org/; Gerald R. McDermott, ed., *The New Christian Zionism; Fresh Perspectives on Israel and the Land* (Downers Grove, IL: IVP Academic, 2016); Philip T. Morrow & Amy Gabriel, "Are Young Evangelicals Experiencing a Change of Heart on Israel?, *Providence*, June 15, 2021: https://providencemag.com/2021/06/are-young-evangelicals-experiencing-change-heart-israel/; Motti Inbari, Kirill M. Bumin, and M. Gordon Byrd, "Why Do Evangelicals Support Israel?" *Politics and Religion* 14:1 (2021), 1–36.
18. Explicit calls by Arab leaders for the total destruction of the Yishuv are recorded in Benny Morris, *1948: a history of the first Arab-Israeli war* (New Haven: Yale University Press, 2008), p. 187 and pp. 407–9.
19. Maoz Azaryahu and Arnon Golan, "Photography, Memory and Ethnic Cleansing: The Fate of the Jewish Quarter of Jerusalem, 1948—John Phillips' Pictorial Record," *Israel Studies*, 17:2, (Summer 2012), 62–76.
20. *Khartoum Resolutions*: https://www.jewishvirtuallibrary.org/the-khartoum-resolutions
21. Uri Bialer, *Israeli Foreign Policy; A People Shall Not Dwell Alone* (Bloomington: Indiana University Press, 2020).
22. Susan Pedersen, <u>*The Guardians, The League of Nations and the Crisis of Empire*</u>, ibid.
23. The total vote was 33 for, 13 against, 10 abstentions and 1 absent. There are 193 member states in the UN as of this writing (2023).
24. https://en.wikipedia.org/wiki/International_recognition_of_Israel
25. See: https://en.wikipedia.org/wiki/List_of_United_Nations_resolutions_concerning_Israel
26. An extensive compilation of Palestinian charges is found at United Nations, *The Question of Palestine*, https://www.un.org/unispal/document-subject/human-rights-and-international-humanitarian-law/
27. Chaim Herzog, "The United Nations: Statement in Response to 'Zionism is Racism" Resolution (November 10, 1975)," https://www.jewishvirtuallibrary.org/israeli-statement-in-response-to-quot-zionism-is-racism-quot-resolution-november-1975
28. Gil Troy, *Moynihan's Moment: America's Fight against Zionism is Racism* (New York: Oxford University Press, 2013), p. 134.

Section C. Towards the Second Century 219

29. Stanley Meisler, *United Nations: A History* (New York: Grove, 2011), p. 215.
30. Particularly pertinent on all these issues is a comprehensive account of the Palestinian refugee issue is Adi Schwartz and Einat Wilf, *The War of Return; How Western Indulgence of the Palestinian Dream Has Obstructed the Path to Peace* (New York: St. Martin's, 2020).
31. Orde F. Kittrie, *Lawfare; Law as a Weapon of* War (Oxford: Oxford 2016) has extensive analyses of the phenomenon includes chapters on Israel. Kittrie assigns the current use of the phrase to an essay by Charles Dunlop, Jr., "Law and Military Interventions: Preserving Humanitarian Values in 21st Conflicts presented at Humanitarian Challenges in Military Interventions Conference (November 29, 2001)," https://scholarship.law.duke.edu/faculty_scholarship/3500/. Although not employed earlier, the phenomenon, if not the term, "lawfare" is directly address in Chap. 2 in the section on Cattan vs. Stone and extensively treated in Steven Zipperstein, *Law and the Arab-Israeli Conflict; The Trials of Palestine* (New York: Routledge, 2020).
32. https://en.wikipedia.org/wiki/Mary_Robinson#High_Commissioner_for_Human_Rights. She ultimately resigned her position under criticism for permitting anti-semitism to play a prominent role and under U.S. pressure. See: Michael Schechter, *United Nations Global Conferences* (London: Taylor and Francis, 2009).
33. Gerald Steinberg and Anne Herzberg, *The Goldstone Report 'Reconsidered': A Critical Analysis* (Jerusalem: NGO Monitor/Jerusalem Center for Public Affairs, 2011); Report of UN Fact-Finding Mission on the Gaza Conflict: https://www.un.org/unispal/document/auto-insert-201780/
34. Richard Goldstone, "Reconsidering the Goldstone Report on Israel and war crimes," *Washington Post,* April 1, 2011. See: https://www.washingtonpost.com/opinions/reconsidering-the-goldstone-report-on-israel-and-war-crimes/2011/04/01/AFgl11JC_story.html. Goldstone wrote: "I have always been clear that Israel, like any other sovereign nation, has the right and obligation to defend itself and its citizens against attacks from abroad and within. Something that has not been recognized often enough is the fact that our report marked the first-time illegal acts of terrorism from Hamas were being investigated and condemned by the United Nations. I had hoped that our inquiry into all aspects of the Gaza conflict would begin a new era of evenhandedness at the U.N. Human Rights Council, whose history of bias against Israel cannot be doubted."
35. Salim Mansour, "The Atrocious Scandal of the UNESCO Vote on Jerusalem," *Gatestone Institute*, 23 November 2016. See: https://www.gatestoneinstitute.org/9402/unesco-jerusalem-scandal; "Israel's anger at UNESCO motion's failure to link holy site to Judaism," *The Guardian*, 13 October 2016. See: https://www.theguardian.com/world/2016/oct/13/israeli-anger-unesco-motion-condemning-aggressions-holy-site-jerusalem
36. Whether or not the areas controlled by Israel since the 1967 War are legal is a hugely controversial subject, including among Israelis. For accessible, direct examples of contending views see Orna Ben-Naftali, Aeyal Gross, and Keren Michaeli Michaeli, Keren, "Illegal Occupation: Framing the Occupied Palestinian Territory," *Berkeley Journal of International Law*, 23: 551 (2005); Dore Gold, "From 'Occupied Territories' to 'Disputed Territories'," *Jerusalem Letter/Viewpoints*, 470:3 (16 January 2002), https://www.jcpa.org/jl/vp470.

htm. An internal, legal memo circulated within Prime Minister's Eshkol's office shortly after the war in September 1967 argued the illegality of civilian settlements but was ignored. Meron left Israel a decade later for an important career as an international judge and legal authority. See: Theodor Meron, "The West Bank and International Humanitarian Law on the Eve of the Fiftieth Anniversary of the Six-Day War," *American Journal of International Law*, 111:2 (10 May 2017), 357–375.

37. There are numerous NGOs that document and protest Israel's activities. Entry into the large literature of criticism can be found at the site maintained by the United Nations: https://news.un.org/en/tags/occupied-palestinian-territories and a leading NGO: B'Tselem. See: https://www.btselem.org/about_btselem

38. The call for expansion was articulated by both secular and religious movements. Many associated with Labor, such as the national poet Natan Alterman, and numerous other intellectuals joined in founding "The Movement for Greater Israel." It also attracted also Revisionist Zionists and Religious Zionists. By the early 1970s, a significant membership that was to create Gush Emunim became prominent. The movement provides an example of how the borders between secular and religious motivations have been blurred. See Amir Goldstein and Elchanan Shilo, "Generational crossover: 'the Movement for the Entire Land of Israel' from the Labour movement to Gush Emunim," *Israel Affairs*, 28:1(2022), 45–59. On the subsequent evolution of this idea through Gush Emuim see Ian Lustick, *For the Land and the Lord; The Evolution of Gush Emunim* (New York: Council on Foreign Relations, 1988), Chap. 3.

39. Although the original concept was published in *Foreign Affairs* in 1976 when he was Foreign Minister, Yigal Allon reanalyzed his proposals in "The West Bank and Gaza within the framework of a Middle East peace settlement," *Middle East Review* 12:2 (Winter 1979–80), 15–18.

40. Meron Benvenisti, *West Bank Data Project: A Survey of Israel's Policies* (Washington: American Enterprise Institute for Public Policy Research, 1984) among many other writings. At the same time, Arnon Sofer, an Israeli demographer offer the same warning about future dangers to Israel should annexation proceed although without the prescription of binationalism. See Larry Derfner, "Sounding the Alarm About Israel's Demographic Crisis," *Forward*, January 9, 2004. https://forward.com/news/israel/6070/sounding-the-alarm-about-israel-s-demographic-cr/

41. Rachel Fish, *Configurations of Bi-nationalism: The Transformation of Bi-nationalism in Palestine/Israel 1920s—Present* (Ph.D. dissertation: Brandeis University, 2013), p. 13, fn. 17.

42. Shaul Magid, "Is Zionism the Problem?" *Tablet*, May 15, 2021. https://www.tabletmag.com/sections/community/articles/is-zionism-the-problem-matzpen

43. Tony Judt, "Israel: The Alternative," *The New York Review*, October 23, 2003: https://www.nybooks.com/articles/2003/10/23/israel-the-alternative/. A more recent article with a similar program that has received much attention is by Peter Beinart, "I No Longer Believe in a Jewish State," *New York* Times, July 8, 2020, https://www.nytimes.com/2020/07/08/opinion/israel-annexation-two-state-solution.html

44. See, for example, Leon Wieseltier, "Israel, Palestine, and the Return of the Bi-National Fantasy: What is not to be Done," *The New Republic*, October 23, 2003. http://www.mafhoum.com/press6/165P51.htm
45. A noteworthy contemporary example is Ian Lustick, *Paradigm Lost: From Two-State Solution to One-State Reality* (Philadelphia: University of Pennsylvania Press, 2021).
46. There are diverse views on the motivation and bias of appropriation of land, particularly Arab owned. See: Yifat. Holzman-Gazit, *Land expropriation in Israel: law, culture, and society* (London: Ashgate Publishing, 2007) and Oren Yiftachel, *Ethnocracy: land and identity politics in Israel/Palestine* (Philadelphia: University of Pennsylvania Press, 2006).
47. My appreciation for the multiple and evolving use of the term, bi-nationalism, derives from Rachel Fish, *Configurations of Bi-nationalism*. On Azmi Bishara see Chap. 5.
48. See Fish, *Configurations of Bi-nationalism*, Chap. 5. A similar view of ultimate replacement is held by Naim Ateek in explaining his acceptance of an Israeli identity in the interim. See Chap. 6.
49. The National Committee for the Heads of the Local Arab Authorities in Israel, *The Future Vision of the Palestinian Arabs in Israel* (Nazareth, 2006). Other significant proposals made at about the same time in which, taken together, reflect the views of Arabs living in Israel are: Mada al-Carmel, *The Haifa Declaration* (Haifa: The Arab Center for Applied Social Research, 2007) and Adalah, *The Democratic Constitution* (Haifa: Adalah, The Legal Center for Arab Minority Rights in Israel, 2007).
50. Uriel Abulof, "Binationalism beyond Israel," in *Nationalism and Binationalism; the Perils of Perfect Structures*, eds. Anita Shapira, Yedidia Z. Stern and Alexander Yakobson (Brighton: Sussex Academic Press, 2013), p. 1.
51. Michael Walzer, "Five Regimes of Coexistence," in Shapira, et al., *Nationalism and Binationalism*, p. 14.
52. Constantin Zureik, *The Meaning of the Disaster* (Beirut: Khayat's College Book Cooperative, 1956) Originally published in August 1948 in Arabic as *Ma'nā al-nakbah*. (Zureik is variously spelled: Zureiq, Zurayk.)
53. International Holocaust Remembrance Alliance, *Working Definition of Antisemitism*, https://www.holocaustremembrance.com/resources/working-definitions-charters/working-definition-antisemitism
54. Clyde Hughes, "Corbyn suspended from British Labor Party over human rights report," *UPI*, Oct. 29, 2020. See: https://www.upi.com/Top_News/World-News/2020/10/29/Corbyn-suspended-from-British-Labor-Party-over-human-rights-report/7891603980281/; https://www.theguardian.com/politics/2020/oct/29/labour-suspends-jeremy-corbyn-over-ehrc-report-comments
55. *The Jerusalem Declaration on Antisemitism*, https://jerusalemdeclaration.org/ A comparison of the relative merits of both is found in a series of debates in the British journal *Fathom*. See the following footnote.
56. Cary Nelson, "Fathom Long Read: Accommodating the New Antisemitism: a Critique of 'The Jerusalem Declaration'," *Fathom*, April 2021. https://fathomjournal.org/fathom-long-read-accommodating-the-new-antisemitism-a-critique-of-the-jerusalem-declaration/. In *Fathom* and other journals there

are extensive analyses and debates over the relative merits and flaws of both the IHRA and Jerusalem Declaration. For a response to Cary Nelson see Derek Penslar, "Why I Signed the Jerusalem Declaration: A Response to Cary Nelson," *Fathom*, April 2021. https://fathomjournal.org/why-i-signed-the-jda-a-response-to-cary-nelson-2/. Pertinent to the debate is Joshua Muravchik, "Anti-Semitic Acts Don't have to Involve Hatred of Jews," *Mosaic,* July 30, 2021: https://mosaicmagazine.com/response/politics-current-affairs/2021/07/anti-semitic-acts-dont-have-to-involve-hatred-of-jews/

57. https://www.gov.uk/government/speeches/queens-speech-2022

Selective Glossary

This glossary elaborates on a selection of concepts and names mentioned in the essays. Items are listed alphabetically but are explained under category headings where readers could find such grouping useful. For example, rather than being listed separately, such items as Arab Leaders, Israeli Political Leaders, and U.N. Resolutions can be viewed together.

Some items are referred to by different names. For example, the 1967 War is referred to also as the Six-Day War, the 1967 War, and occasionally just 1967. In such cases I list the item with its various names and occasionally variant spellings separated by commas.

Arab Leaders

Mansour Abbas (1935–) Born in al-Maghar, a town in the Galilee with a mixed population of Druze, Christians and Muslims. He studied dentistry at the Hebrew University of Jerusalem where he was elected chair of the Arab Students Committee and joined the Islamic Movement under the leadership of Abdullah Nimar Darwish. In 2007 Abbas became Secretary General of the United Arab List, and in 2010 was elected Deputy Chairman of the Southern Branch of the Islamic Movement. He has served multiple terms as a Member of Knesset and became the first Arab Minister in an Israeli government. He is appreciated as an Arab leader who accepts that Israel is a Jewish state and supports policies that improve the situation of the country's Arab populations.

Arafat, Yasser (1929–2004) Born in Cairo, Egypt, Arafat was a founder and later chairman of Fatah (1968–2004), which after the 1967 War emerged as the most powerful faction of the Palestine Liberation Organization (PLO). Arafat advocated and directed armed struggle against Israel. He was PLO chairman from 1969 and elected President of the Palestine Authority (PA) in 1996 elections that followed the Oslo Accords in which he participated along with Israeli Prime Minister Yitzchak Rabin and for which he was awarded a Nobel Prize. Arafat held both positions until his death.

Husseini, Haj Amin al (1893–1974) Born in Jerusalem, Al-Husseini was a Palestinian nationalist appointed in 1921 by Herbert Samuel, the High Commissioner for Palestine, as Mufti and later Grand Mufti of Jerusalem, a title given Islamic scholars whose learning gives them authority to issue religious rulings. Samuel forgave al Husseini's 10-year prison sentence for instigating the 1920 riot in Jerusalem against Zionist settlement. Despite his promise to maintain order, the Mufti was instrumental in fomenting the bloody 1929 and 1936 attacks on Jewish settlements, and his position was revoked in 1936. He attempted to mobilize Muslim support for Nazi Germany during World War II when he met with Nazi leadership in 1941 that assured him of German intentions to destroy Jews residing in the Arab world.

Hussein bin Talal, King of Jordan, (1935–1999) Born in Amman, Jordan, reportedly a direct descendant of the Prophet Muhammad (40th generation), Hussein became King of the Hashemite Kingdom of Jordan in 1952 following the assassination of his grandfather, King Abdullah in 1951. He called for resolving conflicts between Israel and Arabs and among Arab states, helped draft UNSC Resolution 242 following the 1967 War supporting land for peace, and participated in the Madrid Peace Conference (1991), eventually signing a Peace Treaty with Israel in 1994.

Nasser, Gamal Abdel (1918–1970) Born in Egypt, Nasser was instrumental in the 1952 coup that deposed King Farouk I. He secretly ran Egypt until he named himself Prime Minister following a 1954 assassination attempt instigated by the Muslim Brotherhood. Nasser refused to recognize Israel, advocated pan-Arabism, and in 1958, joined by Syria, changed the name of Egypt to the United Arab Republic. With Soviet support he built the Aswan High Dam (1968).

Sadat, Anwar (1918–1981) Born in Egypt, Sadat is remembered in Israel and the West for his courageous and path-breaking visit to Jerusalem in 1977 and speech before the Knesset calling for peace between Egypt and Israel. Vice-President Anwar Sadat became President of Egypt after the death of President Gamal Abdel Nasser. He repealed some of the repressive measures put in place by Nasser, abandoned pan-Arabism, and focused instead on Egypt's needs, changing its name to The Arab Republic of Egypt. Sadat led Egypt in the surprise attack on Israel of the 1973 Yom Kippur War, hoping to win back the Sinai Peninsula conquered by Israel in the 1967 War. Later, he initiated moves to resolve the conflict including rapprochement with the U.S. and a break with the Soviets, and disengagement agreements with Israel that ultimately led to an Egypt-Israel Peace Treaty/Camp David Accords in 1978. Sadat served as President from 1970 until his assassination at the hands of an Islamist group in 1981.

Israeli Political Leaders

Begin, Menachem (1913–1992) Born in Brest-Litovsk, Poland, Begin became head of Betar Poland in 1938 and, after fleeing Poland at the start of World War II, joined the Free Polish Army and eventually made his way to Palestine. A Revisionist Zionist who led the Irgun, one of several military groups of the pre-State period, Begin was founder and leader of Herut and later the Likud. He was elected Prime Minister in 1977. Characterized as a hawk, it was nevertheless Begin who entered into agreements with Egypt on Israeli withdrawal from Sinai and ultimately, on the basis of a return of territory, signed the 1979 peace treaty with Egypt. He resigned in 1983 in the wake of popular opposition and negative outcomes of the 1982 Lebanon War.

Ben-Gurion, David (1886–1973) Born David Green (Grun) in Plonsk, Poland, Ben-Gurion came to Palestine in 1906 and spearheaded Labor Zionism's efforts to lay both the moral foundations and infrastructure for the Jewish State. A leader of Ahdut Ha'avoda , he helped establish the Histadrut (1920) and served as General Secretary from 1921–1935, and was chairman of the Jewish Agency's executive committee from 1935–1948. In this role, Ben-Gurion declared Israel's independence in May, 1948. Widely appreciated as a pragmatic, determined and decisive leader, he was elected Prime Minister in Israel's first national election in 1949 as the head of Mapai (Labor), and with the exception of 1954–1955, he was Prime Minister until 1963, a position he usually held together with that of Minister of Defence.

Herzl, Theodor (1860–1904) The originator of Political Zionism, Herzl was an assimilated Austro-Hungarian journalist and playwright. His encounters with anti-semitism in Vienna and later in Paris, where he reported on the Dreyfus trial, caused him to reject the idea that enlightenment secular education and assimilation or even conversion would solve the "Jewish problem" and allow Jews to integrate as equal citizens in Europe. He convened the First Zionist Congress in Basle, Switzerland in 1897, and began a movement demanding a Jewish national home for the Jewish people in Palestine. His novel, *Altneuland* (1902) describes the near utopian state he imagined founded on modern technology and science. His statement "If you will it, it isn't a fable" became a watchword of the Zionist movement.

Herzog, Chaim (1918–1997) The son of Ireland's Chief Rabbi, Chaim Herzog was born in Belfast, UK, and emigrated to Mandatory Palestine in 1935 where he rose in the ranks of the Haganah and Israeli army to Major General. He was Israel's Permanent Representative to the U.N. from 1975 to 1978, and when the General Assembly passed Resolution 3379, equating Zionism with racism, Herzog firmly rejected the resolution, publicly tearing it up. He served two terms as Israel's sixth President, from 1983 to 1993.

Peres, Shimon (1923–2016) Born in Belarus, Peres emigrated to Palestine with his family in 1934. During Israel's first decade, as Director-General of the Ministry of Defense he helped forge Israel's relationship with France, negotiated its acquisition of arms, notably French Mirage III jet fighters, and establishment of the nuclear reactor in Dimona. Nonetheless, he played a crucial role in negotiating the Oslo Accords, for which he was awarded the Noble Peace Prize (1994) along with Yitzchak Rabin and Yasser Arafat. He twice served as Prime Minister and served as Israel's 9th President from 2007 to 2014.

Rabin, Yitzhak (1922–1995) Born in Jerusalem, Rabin served in the Palmach before and during the 1948 War, and in 1962 was appointed Chief of the General Staff. Following a highly successful military career, he was Israel's Ambassador to the United States from 1968 to 1973, and was Israel's first native son to be elected Prime Minister in 1974. Leader of the Labor party, Rabin was defeated by Menachem Begin at the head of the Likud in the 1977 elections, in what is known as "Hamahapach" (the upheaval), when, for the first time since the establishment of the State, the Labor party was deposed. In his second term as Prime Minister (1992–1995) Rabin negotiated the 1993 Oslo Agreements with the PLO, was instrumental in the Declaration of Principles that, in an historic move, he signed together with PLO leader Yasser Arafat, and in 1994, reached a peace treaty with Jordan. He was awarded a Nobel Peace Prize together with Shimon Peres and Yasser Arafat for these achievements in 1994. Yitzchak Rabin was assassinated by a right-wing Jewish extremist at a peace rally in Tel Aviv in November 1995.

Sharon, Ariel (1928–2014) Born in Kfar Malal, Sharon was known as a brilliant military strategist and field commander and fought in all of Israel's wars from 1948 through the 1973 Yom Kippur War. As Minister of Defense under Menachem Begin, he directed the 1982 Lebanon War. He was criticized for Israel's engagement in Lebanon, and was held responsible for failing to prevent the massacre of Palestinians by Lebanese Phalangist militias at Sabra and Shatila, two refugee camps. After joining the Likud, he served in a variety of positions and led the party from 2001. Although Sharon strongly advocated Jewish settlement of the West Bank and Gaza following the 1967 War, as Prime Minister from 2002 to 2006 he left Likud to form Kadima (Forward) and in the face of fierce opposition, carried out Israeli military and civilian disengagement from Gaza in 2005. Following a massive stroke in January 2006, Sharon remained in a coma for eight years until his death.

Weizmann, Chaim (1874–1952) Born in Motal, a village near Pinsk in Russia, Weizmann was awarded a Ph.D. in organic chemistry from the University of Fribourg in Switzerland, and became a British citizen in 1910. An ardent Zionist, he was instrumental in persuading Lord Balfour to issue the 1917 declaration that bears his name. Weizmann was an effective advocate of a Jewish national homeland in Palestine, and became President of the World Zionist Organization in 1920. He laid the foundation stone for the establishment of the Hebrew University in Jerusalem and the Institute of Science, later the Weizmann Institute in Rehovot, Palestine. Chaim Weizmann was Israel's first President for 4 years, from 1948 until his death.

Israeli Political Parties

Agudat Yisrael (the Union of Israel) Established in Poland in 1912 as an organization of ultra-Orthodox (Haredi) Jews who opposed Political Zionism, since the establishment of the State Agudat Yisrael has participated in Israel's governments despite being avowedly Non-Zionist, preferring to await the arrival of the Messiah to bring about the promised Return to the Holy Land.

Labor Since it was established in 1968 by a union of Mapai, Ahdut Ha'avoda and Rafi, Labor has been Israel's major left of center party emphasizing social and economic needs and democratic values. Under different names and with evolving ideologies, its pragmatic approach to domestic issues and the conflict with the Arabs was voted a majority from Ben-Gurion in 1948 to 1977 when Menachem Begin was elected and the right of center Likud party came to power.

Likud (**Consolidation**) Like Labor, Likud was initially a merging of distinct political groups. It was founded by Menachem Begin who united the right wing Herut which he led with the Liberal party and others in 1973 around a platform that emphasized social equality and Jewish culture and promised a free market economy in opposition to Labor's traditionally socialist leanings and greater government control. Likud heads Israel's present government under Benjamin Netanyahu and has formed the government 7 times beginning in 1977.

Mapai (acronym for Workers' Party of Eretz Yisrael) Founded in 1930 with a social democratic ideology, Mapai was the dominant party of Labor Zionism. It was instrumental in laying the social foundations of the Yishuv and later of social welfare in the State, and in assembling its first defense forces, Hashomer and the Hagana. Ben-Gurion was General Secretary of Mapai from 1930 to 1953, and again from 1955 to 1963. In 1968 Mapai was subsumed by the Labor Party.

Mizrahi (Spiritual Center) A movement founded in 1902 in Vilnius, the name Mizrachi is an acronym for the Hebrew *Merkaz Ruchani* (Spiritual Center). It became a Religious Zionist political party in Mandatory Palestine, and in 1956 joined with Hapoel Hamizrahi, a religious labor party, to form the National Religious Party.

Poalei Zion (Laborers of Zion) Groups of Jewish Marxist-Zionist workers organized in the Diaspora around the start of the twentieth century. In Palestine, as a political party, Poalei Zion split into left and right factions. The right joined in with Ahdut Ha'avoda, the party led by Ben-Gurion which became Mapai, while the left joined Hashomer Hatza'ir and became Mapam.

Islam
Al-Aqsa Mosque; Temple Mount, Haram al-Sharif, the Noble Sanctuary; and the Dome of the Rock

- **The Al-Aqsa Mosque** of Omar ("the Farthest Mosque"), distinguished by a silver dome, is located in the area called by Muslims *Haram al -Sharif* (The Noble Sanctuary) and *Har Habayit* (the Temple Mount) by Jews. The mosque is under the protection of the Hashemite King of Jordan, and together with the surrounding area is administered as a Jordanian and Palestinian led Islamic Waqf (religious benevolence), held in trust in perpetuity.
- **Haram al Sharif** (Arabic: The Noble Sanctuary), also *Har Habayit* (Hebrew: The Temple Mount) This area, surrounded by a wall, is located in the Southeast corner of the Old City of Jerusalem, and includes more than five and a half acres. According to the Jewish tradition, this was the site of Solomon's Temple (The First Temple) some 3000 years ago and the remains of the Second Temple, including the Holy of Holies. Both Jews and Muslims identify this site with Mount Moriah, the place where Abraham came to sacrifice his son (Isaac or Ishmael, depending on the tradition).
- **The Dome of the Rock** with its golden dome is a Muslim shrine built over the stone from which the Prophet Muhammad is believed to have ascended to heaven.

Dhimmi literally means "protected person" and is applied to a non-Muslim subject, initially Jews and Christians as fellow "Peoples of the Covenant" and "Peoples of the Book." Dhimmitude was later extended to other major religious groups. As such, dhimmis enjoy official membership in Islamic societies and its protection but are assigned to inferior status and limitations such a not serving in the military, residence restrictions, and obligated to special taxes. In some areas, such as the Ottoman Empire, they were subject to their own courts in matters that affected only members of their communities.

Dar al-Islam literally means the "home" or "abode" of Islam. In such countries, Islam is the law of the land and governments abide by the state's religion. On the other hand, *Dar al-harb*, refers to the "house of war" that are governed by non-Islamic law and rulers. In some versions, a natural antipathy exists between these two abodes that may be expressed in inevitable conflict although this view, certainly in practice, has diminished in modern times.

Fatwa is a legal ruling on a point of Islamic law (*sharia*) given by a qualified jurist, usually a *mufti*. Fatwas have played an important role throughout Islamic history with their widespread use in Islamic states assuming particular significance in the modern period.

Hashemite is the name a family that dates from the time of the Prophet Muhammad and associated with responsibilities for ruling the holy city of Mecca. Rooted in the Hejaz, or Arabian Peninsula, modern descendants were accorded thrones by Britain in Iraq and Syria as well as in Transjordan in the aftermath of World War I. The name of its kingdom changed to Jordan since it conquered the West Bank of the River Jordan in the 1948 War. They have claimed entitlement to continuing their role as protectors of Islamic holy sites, especially Jerusalem.

Khaybar is an oasis, rich in agricultural produce that served caravans, north of the city of Medina that had been inhabited by Jewish tribes prior to its conquest by Muhammad's armies in 628 C.E. The justification for subjugating and ultimately expelling Jewish inhabitants is alleged in accounts of their rejection of the Prophet. Their defeat and fate have long been a trope in Islamic lore but has been given special prominence by Hamas and other contemporary opponents of the Jewish state as an admonition regarding Israel's fate.

Intifada is an uprising or rebellion indicating resistance. It derives from an Arabic word meaning "to shake", "shake off", or "get rid of" as one might shake off the undesirable aspects of oppression. It has been used throughout the contemporary Arabic world from North Africa through Middle East. In the Palestinian context, it refers to attempts to "shake off" the Israeli occupation of the West Bank and Gaza Strip since the 1980s in the *First Intifada* (1987–1993) and *Second Intifada* (2000–2005).

Ottoman Empire, often termed the Turkish Empire, became a transcontinental entity ruling significant regions in Europe, Asia and Africa with the central core emanating out from the Mediterranean basin. Originating in Anatolia in the fourteenth century, it spread over six centuries through southeastern, Central Europe, around the Mediterranean through North Africa and across the Middle East and Persian Gulf to Western Asia until its demise in the course of World War I. Its capital was located in Constantinople (now Istanbul), the capital of the Byzantine Empire, since its conquest in 1453 by Mehmed II. The Ottoman Caliphate or political-religious state was officially terminated in March 1924 by the secular rulers of the modern state of Turkey.

Palestinian and Arab Movements and Organizations

al-Qā'ida, al-Qaeda is a militant Sunni Islamist terrorist network founded in 1988 by Osama bin-Laden that came to world public attention when it carried out the notorious attacks on the Twin Towers in Manhattan and other locations in the U.S., now remembered as "9/11".

Fatah Founded in 1964 by Yasser Arafat as the Palestinian National Liberation Movement in opposition to the PLO, Fatah is headed today by Palestinian Authority President Mahmoud Abbas (Abu Mazen) and is the PLO's major political faction.

Fedayeen (self-sacrificers) Palestinian militants who from the early 1950s carried out raids across Israel's borders from Syria, Jordan, and Egypt, hitting both military and civilian targets.

Hamas Founded in 1987 in conjunction with the First Intifada, Hamas is a Palestinian Sunni Islamic organization associated with Egypt's Muslim Brotherhood. According to the Hamas Charter (1988), it is the Islamic Resistance Movement, one of the wings of the Moslem Brotherhood in Palestine. Opposed to Fatah and the PLO, which are secular, Hamas defeated Fatah in parliamentary elections in 2006, winning a decisive majority. Their rivalry culminated in violence in 2007, when Hamas took over control of Gaza and forced the PLO leadership to retreat to the West Bank which is now under the control of the Palestinian Authority (PA).

Hezbollah, Hezballah, Ḥizbollāh (the Party of Allah) Hezbollah is a militant Islamist Shia political party and well-armed military organization that operates out of Lebanon and is supported by and allied with Iran.

Muslim Brotherhood Founded in Egypt in 1928 to encourage an Islamic revival in response to the dissolution of the Ottoman Empire and the ban imposed on the Caliphate, this movement espouses terrorist methods in the name of jihad, a holy war, typically to bring territories under Muslim control by military means.

Palestine Liberation Organization (PLO) Founded in 1964 under the leadership of Ahmad Shuqari to liberate Palestine through armed struggle. In 1969 Yasser Arafat, leader of Fatah, was named the PLO's chairman. The PLO was endorsed by the 1974 Arab Summit and recognized by some 100 U.N. member nations as the "sole and legitimate representative of the Palestinian people". Because of its terrorist activities it was labeled a terrorist organization, and both the U.S. and Israel denied its authority until the U.S. brokered negotiations between Israel and the PLO at the 1991 Madrid Conference. In 1993 the PLO recognized Israel's right to exist and in accordance with U.N. Resolutions 242 and 338 rejected violence, while Israel accepted the PLO as the legitimate representative of the Palestinian people.

Palestine Authority (PA) Following the 1993 Oslo Accords, the Palestinian (National) Authority became the interim governing body of the West Bank and Gaza Strip of a future autonomous Palestinian state (1994). The PA lost control of Gaza when Hamas defeated Fatah, the major PLO party, in the 2006 elections, and its leadership was forced to retreat to the West Bank where it has authority over Areas A and B and shares responsibility for maintaining security with the Israel-governed Area C. See also under West Bank.

Pan-Arabism This ideological movement originated around World War I and was influenced by socialist and Marxist ideology. Associated with early Arab nationalism, it imagined an transnational union of all Arab countries making up the

"Arab World." Egyptian President Gamal Abdel Nasser became a strong proponent in the 1950s and this lead to renaming Egypt when he joined it with Syria in 1958 to establish the "United Arab Republic".

Christianity

Catholicism or **Roman Catholicism** is the most numerous Christian Church with more than two and a half billion adherents in its various divisions that comprehend churches in Western and Eastern Europe, the Middle East and across the globe. The bishop of Rome, also identified as the Pope residing in the Vatican, is the acknowledged head of this immense assembly. His authority, viewed in terms of infallibility, derives from the belief that he is the successor to Saint Peter who, together with other apostles, were granted authority as successors to Jesus Christ. Church teachings have been defined and elaborated over many centuries at Church councils. Their role has been crucial in defining the place of Judaism in Christian societies and in history at large.

Crusades were a series of campaigns initiated and supported between 1095 and 1291 primarily by Latin or Western Christian Church to wrest control of the Holy Land from Muslim rule with control over Jerusalem as a key target. Beginning with the First Crusade that achieved the conquest of Jerusalem in 1099, numerous successive campaigns were organised with intermittent and varying success. This period of intense confrontation may also be viewed as part of a political and military competition between Islam and Christianity that began in the seventh century with the rise of Islam. A particularly significant earlier confrontation is the 732 Battle of Tours in southern France where Charlemagne defeated Muslim armies moving up from Spain and in 1683 at Vienna where Ottoman expansion ended, followed by an extended period of retrenchment towards the Turkish homeland.

Evangelicalism is a movement within Protestantism whose origins are usually located in the early eighteenth century with the term derived from the Greek term for "good news." Central beliefs include individual, personal conversion and being "born again," the literal authority of the Bible in both the Old and New Testaments as God's revelation to humanity, and the imperative to disseminate the Christian message. Among the many denominations that may be associated with this movement are Quakerism, Presbyterianism, Moravianism, Pietism especially within Lutheranism, and Puritanism. While originating in the English-speaking world, it spread to Germany and far beyond to number today more than 600 million adherents across the world. About one in four American Christians are classified as Evangelicals.

Liberation Theology A movement originating in Latin American Roman Catholicism in the second half of the twentieth century, and dedicated to actively addressing the immediate needs of poor parishioners. Its ideological repudiation of the "sinful" socioeconomic arrangements leading to inequalities and call for political engagement have been used by Palestinian Christians to delegitimize the Zionist project.

Nostra Aetate (Latin for "In our time"), or the **Declaration on the Relation of the Church with Non-Christian Religions**, is the official document promulgated in October 1965 by a vote of the vast majority of more than two thousand bishops of the Second Vatican Council under the sponsorship of Pope Paul VI. One of its final documents succinctly redefines the relationship between the Catholicism and Jews even as others relate to Muslims and other major faiths in attempting to encourage harmony among divergent religious traditions. Specifically, it attempted to undo what could be considered Christian antisemitism. It renounced "hatred and persecutions of Jews, whether they arose in former or in our own days," affirmed the validity of Judaism as a religious way of life with which Catholics must establish relations of "mutual knowledge and respect," and repudiated the idea of "the Jewish people as one rejected, cursed, or guilty of deicide." In so stating Church doctrine, it departed from hostile supersessionism to a new relationship with Jews and the Jewish state.

Judaism

Haredim This is the name given to communities of religious Jews who, in opposition to the secularization invited by emancipation and the Enlightenment, reject modern culture and live separately, strictly adhering to Jewish religious law, or *Halakha*. Often referred to as ultra-Orthodox in English, a term some object to as derogatory, the Hebrew term denotes those who serve the Divine with fervor and anxiety. Initially opposed to the Zionist project, many have come to participate in the State's political life, and in recent years are slowly taking advantage of carefully crafted educational options that will allow them some degree of integration and opportunities for work in fields such as law and computers and even participation in the military.

Haskalah (Jewish Enlightenment) In the context of the more general European Enlightenment, for approximately a century from the 1770s to the 1880s, the Haskalah movement induced Jews to partake of secular culture and learn European languages rather than limiting themselves to Yiddish. The movement that began in Galicia and later spread to Eastern Europe, stimulated the revival of Hebrew language and gave rise to a rich literature in both Hebrew and Yiddish. Whereas especially Western European Jews frequently assimilated in response to their encounter with secular culture and the emancipation, the resurgence of European antisemitism eventually led many to view Zionism as the solution to the "Jewish problem."

Columbus Platform (1937) In significant measure a response to the alarming spread of virulent antisemitism in Europe, the Reform movement adopted the revolutionary Columbus Platform and its new ideological guidelines that "embraced Jewish peoplehood and leaned toward support of political Zionism."

Pre-State Palestine

Balfour Declaration (1917) The first recognition of the Zionist aim of reestablishing the Jewish national homeland in Eretz Yisrael/Palestine by a world power (United Kingdom), the declaration was in a letter by Foreign Secretary Arthur James Lord Balfour to Lord Walter Rothschild. It states "His Majesty's Government view with favour the establishment in Palestine of a national home for the Jewish people, and will use their best endeavours to facilitate the achievement of this object, it being clearly understood that nothing shall be done which may prejudice the civil and religious rights of existing non-Jewish communities in Palestine, or the rights and political status enjoyed by Jews in any other country."

British Mandate for Palestine (1918–1948) was a consequence of World War I. The British were made trustees and administrators of the territory they conquered between the Jordan River and the Mediterranean Sea by the Mandate for Palestine. The Mandate is a legal document, unanimously affirmed by the 51 member countries of the League of Nations in 1922, that recognized "the historic connection of the Jewish People with Palestine and ...the grounds for reconstituting their national home in that country."

Peel Commission Report (1937) This document was issued by a royal commission of inquiry into Arab-Jewish violence (1936–39) headed by Lord Robert Peel. The commission recommended ending the Mandate and partitioning Palestine into Jewish and Arab states and an international zone centered around Jerusalem. The proposal was endorsed by the British Parliament, hotly debated but accepted by Zionists, and rejected by the Arabs.

Partition plan (1947) Resolution 181 was put forward by the United Nations Special Committee on Palestine (UNSCOP) convened after the British declared their intention to end the Mandate. It recommended partition into two independent states, a Jewish and an Arab state "joined by economic union," with Jerusalem and Bethlehem as an international zone. The vote on November 29, 1947 in the United Nations General Assembly approved partition 33 to 13, with 10 abstentions. The plan was accepted by the Jews and roundly rejected by Arabs who countered it by invading the area designated for Jews. The UN partition plan was never implemented.

Two-state solution found in Peel and Resolution 181 has become the widely accepted paradigm for resolving the Arab-Israeli conflict. Numerous U.N. Resolutions, beginning in 1947, have proposed two states with recognized borders, but so far, repeated diplomatic efforts including contemporary efforts commencing with the Madrid Conference in 1991 have not led to progress.

White Papers

This is the generic term for a series of official British reports authored by various commission to investigate the Jewish-Arab conflict during the 1920s and 1930s. The most significant are three:

(1) The 1922 White Paper that subsequent to the Arab riots of 1921, affirmed the Balfour Declaration and asserted that Jews were in Palestine by right. It nevertheless reduced the original area marked as Palestine by assigning the East side of the Jordan River for an Arab political entity to be ruled by the Emir Abdullah, a member of the Hashemite family.

(2) The Passfield White Paper of 1930 was issued subsequent to the Arab riots of 1929 and the Hope-Simpson Report on Immigration, Land Settlement and Development that first investigated their causes. This White Paper restricted Jewish immigration and purchase of land due to presumed reduction of opportunities for resident Arabs. Quotas were slightly reduced in 1931 through a decision of Prime Minister Ramsay MacDonald but the policy set a precedent

that had serious impact during a decade of intense pressure on European Jews who desired to emigrate to Palestine.

(3) The White Paper of 1939 was the most severe of all, effectively assigning Jews to permanent minority status with limitations on their ability to settle in Palestine and thereby reversed the 1937 Peel Commission Report that proposed partition of Palestine as a pragmatic path to both maintain fidelity to the promise of establishing a Jewish national homeland and recognizing Arab claims. Restrictions on Jewish immigration and development resulted in massive attempts to bypass this policy during and after WWII when Jewish aspirations in Palestine grew intense and desparate by the realities of the war.

Zionism

Cultural Zionism Promulgated by Ahad Ha'am in contrast to Herzl's Political Zionism, cultural Zionism assumed most Jews would remain in the Diaspora, but that Jewish cultural and linguistic renewal in Eretz Yisrael were fundamental and would strengthen Jewish spiritual and ethical identity everywhere.

General Zionism Initially this designation referred to the general commitment to a Jewish homeland without affiliation to any particular faction or political party. In 1922 it was institutionalized as the Organization of General Zionists, splitting into two factions in 1931 over issues relating to Palestine including social affairs and attitudes to the Histadrut, and reuniting in 1945. A majority of Israel's Liberal movements and parties originated within General Zionism and resulted from mergers in and secessions from the movement.

Hibbat Zion, Hovevei Zion, Chibat Zion, Chovevei Zion (Lovers of Zion or Love of Zion) was a pre-Zionist movement organized in response to Russian pogroms in 1881, and became an official entity at an 1884 conference led by Leon Pinsker, author and advocate of Jewish "Auto-Emancipation." Members founded Rishon Lezion, the first Zionist settlement, in 1882.

Labor Zionism, Socialist Zionism, founded by Nachum Syrkin, sought to fuse Zionism with Socialism, and held that "the Jewish problem" would not be solved by a Socialist revolution in the Diaspora, but by Jewish emigration to their own homeland. Only Zionism would allow for restructuring the class system to liberate the people and the Jewish Proletariat. David Ben-Gurion, Yitzchak Ben-Zvi and Berl Katznelson were all important leaders of Labor Zionism in the pre-State years, a movement that later gave rise to the Labor Party.

Political Zionism, associated with Theodor Herzl, this faction emphasized the political means necessary for gaining international recognition for the Zionist program and support for Jewish sovereignty.

Religious Zionism When the Fifth Zionist Congress (1902) included cultural activity in the Zionist Program, Merkaz Ruchani (Spiritual Center) with the acronym Mizrachi organized and focused its 1904 platform on the observance of commandments and Jewish religious life in Zion. While ultra-Orthodoxy considered Zionist activity blasphemous and a misguided human effort to undertake Divine prerogative, Rabbi Abraham Yitzhak Hacohen Kook endorsed the program, declaring Jewish "settlement in the Land of Israel as the beginning of Redemption."

Revisionist Zionism began as an effort, led by Vladimir Zeev Jabotinsky (1925) to revise Herzl's Political Zionism, taking a more assertive stance toward Great Britain with demands for open immigration and a Jewish majority in Palestine, a state on both sides of the Jordan and military training. Leaving the ZO to form their own organization, Revisionist Zionism rejoined in 1946 since the Biltmore Program had declared Zionist commitment to a Jewish Commonwealth in Palestine. Members of the more militant Revisionist Zionism joined the pre-State military organizations Etzel and Lehi and the Revisionist movement merged with the Herut movement in the Herut party, later part of the Likud.

Zionist Terms

First Aliya (1882–1903). *Aliya* literally "going up" or "ascent", this Hebrew term refers to immigration to Israel. Mainly from Eastern Europe and fleeing pogroms but also from Yemen, in all around 35,000 immigrants made up the First Aliya. About half remained in Ottoman Palestine, establishing small rural settlements of independent farmers called moshavot.

Second Aliya (1904–1914) Of some 40,000 young idealists from Eastern Europe who made up the Second Aliya, about half remained. They set the tone for the nascent state, reviving Hebrew, initiating collective settlement experiments that became the kibbutz and moshav, and setting up organizational structures that underlay the Yishuv.

Third Aliya (1919–1923) Like their predecessors, most of the 40,000 young halutzim or pioneers of the Third Aliya were fleeing antisemitism. The majority remained in then Mandatory Palestine, encouraged by the Balfour Declaration (1917) to plan for and begin creating the infrastructure for the Jewish National homeland.

Aliyah Bet (1939–1948; a shortened form of *Aliya Bilty Legalit*) refers to the illegal immigration intended to circumvent British blockades of Palestine to Jews that began in the 1930s with the promulgation of White Papers, particularly from 1939 when in the face of dire threats and war in Europe the need of Jews for safe haven became extreme. Only the establishment of Israel finally terminated British restrictions. By then, approximately 110,000 Jews safely eluded the blockade to enter Palestine.

Yishuv The Hebrew term which comes from the root that means to sit and to settle, refers to communities of Jewish immigrants who settled pre-State Palestine with the intention of building and being rebuilt in the land, reconstituting a Jewish homeland and reviving the Hebrew language and culture. The **Old Yishuv** refers to pre-Zionist, pre- 1881 Jewish communities in Palestine.

United Nations Resolutions

Resolution 181(November 29, 1947) Also known as the Partition Plan, Resolution 181 calls for Palestine, then under British Mandate, to be partitioned into three parts: a Jewish and an Arab State, and an international condominium under UN control around Jerusalem and Bethlehem. The date in 1947 when the General Assembly voted to pass the Resolution 33 to 13 is still memorialized in Israel.

Resolution 242, United Nations Security Council (UNSC) Resolution 242 (November 1967) This Resolution, adopted following the 1967 War, affirms that "a just and lasting peace" should include both Israeli withdrawal from the territories it occupied and "respect for and acknowledgement of the sovereignty, territorial integrity and political independence of every State in the area and their right to live in peace within secure and recognized boundaries free from threats or acts of force." This Resolution is still referenced in diplomatic efforts to implement the conditions it sets forth.

Security Council Resolution 338, UNSC Resolution 338 In the later days of the 1973 War, after Israel had succeeded in pushing back the Syrian assault on the Golan Heights and occupied a bridgehead on the Egyptian side of the Suez Canal, Resolution 338 called for a cease fire and for negotiations to begin immediately based on Resolution 242.

Resolution 3376 (November 1975) This Resolution of the U.N. General Assembly expresses concern for the lack of progress by the Palestinian people to achieve its "inalienable rights in Palestine" including "their inalienable right to self-determination without external interference and the right to national independence and sovereignty…and their inalienable right to return to their homes and property from which they have been displaced and uprooted." The resolution ends with the decision "to include the item entitled 'Question of Palestine' in the provisional agenda of its thirty-first session."

Resolution 3379 (November 1975) Sharply and unequivocally rejected and denied by American Ambassador to the United Nations Daniel Patrick Moynahan, Resolution 3379 defined Zionism as racism and a form of racial discrimination. 72 states voted in favor, 35 against, and 32 abstained. Despite sustained objection, the Resolution was not revoked until 1991.

UN Related Initiatives

Bandung Conference (1955) This meeting of 29 newly independent Asian and African countries excluded Israel when the Arab states threatened a boycott. An effort to unify and ensure cooperation and peaceful coexistence, the conference condemned colonialism in all of its manifestations thus implicitly including the Soviet Union along with the West, and adopted a 10-point declaration. However, the unity was short-lived. In 2015, organizers of the conference on the 60th anniversary announced that all U.N. recognized Asian and African countries had been invited to attend except Israel, and on the last day of the conference issued a declaration that linked anti-colonialism and justice for Palestine.

Goldstone Report or the **United Nations Fact Finding Mission on the Gaza Conflict** was established in April 2009 following the war in between Palestinians in Gaza, particularly those associated with Hamas, and Israel concerning abuses of human rights. South African jurist Richard Goldstone headed the mission. Although initially and superficially finding against both Israel and Hamas for committing war crimes and crimes against humanity, it was widely read as a condemnation primarily of Israel. The report aroused enormous controversy with critics claiming bias, lack of balance and inaccuracies. In April 2011, Goldstone retracted many claims particularly that Israel deliberately targeted civilians although other participants in formulating the report stood by the document. The same divisions were expressed in the international community with largely western democracies faulting the report and supporters of Palestinians remaining adamant. The controversy was typical of divisions on similar issues that came before the UN in recent decades.

Other Relevant Terms
West Bank, Judea and Samaria, Area C

The West Bank is the area West of the Jordan River. After the 1948 War the West Bank including East Jerusalem fell to Transjordan, which occupied and administered the territory, annexing it in 1950. The 1947 U.N. Partition Plan designated "the hill country of Samaria and Judea" including the territory now known as "the West Bank" to be included in the new Arab-Palestinian state. The "East" Bank was then part of Jordan. Since the 1967 War, when Israel captured the territory on the other side of the Jordan, including East Jerusalem, the West Bank has been used to refer to the area that is supposed to become an important part of a future Palestinian state, with rural villages, towns and cities such as Ramallah and the new planned Palestinian city of Rawabi, and Israeli settlements and cities, like Ariel. The territory was divided by Oslo II into Area A (18%) and Area B (22%) that include about 2.8 million Palestinians and are primarily administered by the Palestinian Authority. In 2023, about 300,000 Palestinians live in 532 residential areas located partially or fully in Area C, along with some 400,000 Israeli settlers residing in approximately 230 settlements in 2022. Area C is under full Israeli control. https://www.anera.org/who-we-are/

Select Bibliography[1]

Chapter 1: From Theological to Secular Claims

Arneil, Barbara, *John Locke and America* (Oxford: Oxford University Press, 1996).
Banner, Stuart, *How the Indians Lost Their Land: Law and Power on the Frontier* (Cambridge: Harvard University Press, 2005).
Berger, Peter, *The Many Altars of Modernity: Toward a Paradigm for Religion in a Pluralist Age* (Boston/Berlin: De Gruyter Mouton, 2014).
Epstein, Lawrence J., *The Dream of Zion; The story of the first Zionist Congress* (Lanham, MD: Roman and Littlefield, 2016a).
Frankel, David, *The Land of Canaan and the Destiny of Israel; Theologies of Territory in the Hebrew Bible* (Winona Lake, Indiana: Eisenbrauns, 2011).
Havelock, Rachel, *The Joshua Generation; Israeli Occupation and the Bible* (Princeton: Princeton University Press, 2020).
Liebman, Charles and Eliezer Don-Yehiya, *Civil Religion in Israel; Traditional Judaism and Political Culture in the Jewish State* (Berkeley: University of California Press, 1983).
Lipset, Seymour M., *The First New Nation: The United States in Historical and Comparative Perspective* (New York: Basic Books, 1963).
Louis, Wm. Roger, *The British Empire in the Middle East 1941-1951; Arab Nationalism, The United States, and Postwar Imperialism* (Oxford: Oxford University Press, 1984).
Robertson, Lindsay G., *How the Discovery of America Dispossessed Indigenous Peoples of Their Lands* (Oxford: Oxford University Press, 2005).
Russel, Peter, *Recognizing Aboriginal Title: The Mabo Case and Indigenous Resistance to English Settler Colonialism* (Toronto: University of Toronto Press, 2005).
Shimoni, Gideon, *The Zionist Ideology* (Hanover, NH: UPNE, 1995a).
Shneer, Jonathan, *The Balfour Declaration: The Origins of the Arab-Israeli Conflict* (New York: Random House, 2010).
Stein, Leonard, *The Balfour Declaration* (New York: Simon & Schuster, 1961).
The Executive of the Zionist Organization, *The Jubilee of the First Zionist Congress 1897-1947* (Jerusalem, 1947).
Tuchman, Barabara, *The Proud Tower: A Portrait of the World Before the War, 1890-1914* (New York: Random House, 1996).
Walzer, Michael, *The Paradox of Liberation; Secular Revolutions and Religious Counterrevolutions* (New Haven: Yale University Press, 2015).

Wazana, Nili, *All the Boundaries of the Land; The Promised Land in Biblical Thought in Light of the Ancient Near East* (Winona Lake, Indiana: Eisenbrauns, 2013).
Weinfeld, Moshe, *The Promise of the Land: The Inheritance of the Land of Canaan by the Israelites* (Berkeley: University of California Press, 1993).

Chapter 2: Conquest, Treaties and Self-Determination

Antonius, George, *The Arab Awakening; The Story of the Arab National Movement* (Beirut: Libraire Du Liban, 1969).
Cattan, Henry, *Palestine, the Arabs and Israel; The Search for Justice* (New York: Longmans, 1969a).
Cattan, Henry, *To Whom Does Palestine Belong?* (Beirut: Institute for Palestine Studies, 1969b).
Cattan, Henry, *Palestine and International Law* (New York: Longman, 1973).
Cattan, Henry, *The Status of Jerusalem* (New York: St. Martin's Press, 1981).
Cleveland, William L., *A History of the Modern Middle East* (Boulder: Westview, 1994).
Friedman, Isaiah, *Germany, Turkey, and Zionism 1897-1918* (Oxford: Clarendon Press, 1977).
Friedman, Isaiah, *Palestine: A Twice Promised Land? The British, the Arabs and Zionism 1915-1920* (New Brunswick: Transaction, 2000).
Keren, Michael and Shlomit Keren, *We Are Coming, Unafraid: The Jewish Legions and the Promised Land in the First World War* (Landham, Md: Rowman & Littlefield, 2010).
Khalidi, Rashid, *Palestinian Identity: The Construction of Modern National Consciousness* (New York: Columbia University Press, 1997a).
Klorman, Sharon, *The Right of Conquest: The Acquisition of Territory by Force in International Law and Practice* (Oxford: Oxford University Press, 1996).
Lawrence, T. E., *Seven Pillars of Wisdom* (London: John Cape, 1935).
Louis, Wm. Roger, *Ends of British Imperialism; The Scramble for Empire, Suez and Decolonization* (London: Tauris, 2006a).
Pedersen, Susan, *The Guardians: The League of Nations and the Crisis of Empire* (Oxford: Oxford University Press, 2015).
Quigley, John, *The Legality of a Jewish State: A Century of Debates over Rights in Palestine* (Cambridge: Cambridge University Press, 2022).
Star, Leonie, *Julius Stone: An Intellectual Life* (Oxford: Oxford University Press, 1992).
Stone, Julius, *Israel and Palestine – Assault on the Law of Nations* (Baltimore: Johns Hopkins, 1981).
Walzer, Michael, *Just and Unjust Wars; A Moral Argument with Historical Illustrations* (New York: Basic Books, 2000).
Watts, Martin, *The Jewish Legion and the First World War* (New York: Palgrave Macmillan, 2004).

Chapter 3: From Discovery to Rediscovery: The Economic Absorptive Capacity of Palestine

Albright, William F., *The archaeology of Palestine and the Bible* (Cambridge, MA: American Schools of Oriental Research, 1974).
Alroey, Gur, *An Unpromising Land; Jewish Migration to Palestine in the Early Twentieth Century* (Stanford: Stanford University Press, 2014).
Ben-Arieh, Yehoshua, *The Making of Eretz Israel in the Modern Era; A Historical-Geographical Study, 1799-1949* (Berlin: De Gruyter, 2020).
Ben-Gurion, David and Izhak Ben-Zvi, *Eretz Israel in the past and in the present*, [Hebrew] trans. from Yiddish by David Niv (Jerusalem, Yad Ben-Zvi, 1979).

Select Bibliography   239

Boorstin, Daniel, *The Discoverers: A History of Man's Search to Know His World and Himself* (New York: Vintage, 1985).
Brutzkus, Eliezer, *Physical Planning in Israel; problems and achievements* (Jerusalem: 1964).
Dunbar-Ortiz, Roxanne, An Indigenous Peoples' History of the United States (Boston: Beacon Press, 2014).
Glueck, Nelson, *Rivers in the Desert: a history of the Negev* (New York: Norton, 1968).
Gottmann, Jean, *Études sur L'état d'Isräel et le Moyen Orient, 1935-1938* (Paris, 1959).
Gruenbaum, Abraham, *Four-year development plan of Israel 1950-1953* (Hebrew) (Tel-Aviv, 1950).
Huntington, Ellsworth, *Palestine and its transformation* (Boston: Houghton Mifflin, 1911).
Lamb, Hubert, *Climate: present, past and future* (London: Methuen, 1972).
Lowdermilk, Walter C., *Palestine: Land of Promise* (London: Harper and Bros, 1944).
MacKenzie, John M., *Orientalism: History, theory and the arts* (Manchester: Manchester University Press, 1995).
Macalister, Robert A., *A century of excavation in Palestine* (London: The Religious Tract Society, 1925).
McCarthy, Justin, *The Population of Palestine: Population History and Statistics of the Late Ottoman Period and the* Mandate (New York: Columbia University Press, 1990).
Mossek, Moshe, *Palestine immigration policy under Sir Herbert Samuel: British, Zionist and Arab attitudes* (London: Frank Cass, 1978).
Nathan, Robert, Oscar Gass, and Daniel Creamer, *Palestine: problem and promise, an economic study* (Washington: American Council on Public Affairs, 1946).
Or-Ner, Ran, *Tide below sea level; Jews, English, Palestinians, and Jordanians in the Potash Factories* (Tel-Aviv: Riesling, 2022) [Hebrew].
Reifenberg, Adolf , "The struggle between the "Desert and the Sown,"" in *Desert research: proceedings, international symposium held in Jerusalem, May 7-14, 1952* (Jerusalem: Research Council of Israel, 1953).
Ruppin, Arthur, *Three Decades of Palestine; speeches and papers on the upbuilding of the Jewish national home* (Jerusalem: Schocken, 1936).
Ruppin, Arthur, *Arthur Ruppin: memoirs, diaries, letters* (London; Weidenfeld and Nicolson, 1971).
Said, Edward W., *Culture and Imperialism* (New York: Random House, 1994).
Sharon, Aryeh, *Planning in Israel* (Jerusalem:1951).
Spiegel, Erika, *New Towns in Israel*; urban and regional planning and development urban and (New York: Praeger, 1967).
Tal, Alon, *The Land is Full; Addressing Overpopulation in Israel* (New Haven: Yale University, 2016).
Warren, Charles, *The land of promise* (London, 1875)

Chapter 4: Possession and Dispossession Through Labor and Purchase

Avneri, Arieh L., *The Claim of Dispossession: Jewish Land Settlement and the Arabs* (Bew Brunswick, New Jersey: Transaction Books, 2006).
Beska, Emanuel, *From Ambivalence to Hostility: The Arabic Newspaper Filastin and Zionism, 1911–1914* (Bratislava: Slovak Academic Press, 2016).
Esco Foundation for Palestine, *Palestine; A Study of Jewish, Arab, and British Policies* (New Haven: Yale University Press, 1947a).
Fields, Gary, *Enclosure; Palestinian Landscapes in a Historical Mirror* (Berkeley: University of California Press, 2017).
Granott, Abraham. *The Land System in Palestine; History and Structure* (London: Eyre and Spottiswood, 1952).

Hertzberg, Arthur, *The Zionist Idea; A Historical Analysis and Reader* (Philadelphia: Jewish Publication Society, 1997).
Horowitz, David, *Economic trends of Jewish development* (Jerusalem, 1947).
Hurewitz, J. C., *The Struggle for Palestine* (New York: Norton, 1950).
Karlinsky, Nahum, *California Dreaming: Ideology, Society and Technology in the Citrus Industry of Palestine, 1890-1939* (Albany: SUNY, 2005).
Kedar, Ben-Zion, *The Changing Land between the Jordan and the Sea: Aerial photographs from 1917 to the Present* (Jerusalem and Tel Aviv: Yad Ben-Zvi and Israel Ministry of Defense, 1999).
Khalidi, Walid, *Before Their Diaspora: A Photographic History of the Palestinians, 1876-*1948 (Washington, D.C. : Institute for Palestine Studies, 1984).
Khalidi, Walid, *All That Remains: The Palestinian Villages Occupied and Depopulated by Israel in 1948* (Washington, D.C. : Institute for Palestine Studies, 1992).
Metzer, Jacob, *The divided economy of Mandatory Palestine* (New York: Cambridge University Press, 1998).
Owen, Roger, ed., *Studies in the Economic and Social History of Palestine in the Nineteenth and Twentieth Century* (Carbondale, IL: Southern Illinois Press, 1982).
Porath, Yehoshua, *From Riots to Rebellion: The Palestinian-Arab National Movement, 1929-1929* (London: Frank Cass, 1974a).
Shimoni, Gideon, *The Zionist Ideology* (Hanover, NH: University Press of New England, 1995b).
Stein, Kenneth, *Land Question in Palestine, 1917-1939* (Chapel Hill, N.C.: University of North Carolina Press, 1984).
Sternhell, Zeev, *The Founding Myths of Israel: Nationalism, Socialism, and the Making of the Jewish State* (Princeton: Princeton University Press, 1999).
Tristam, H. B., *The Land of Israel: A Journal of Travels in Palestine* (London: Society for Promoting Christian Knowledge, 1865).
Troen, S. Ilan, *Imagining Zion; dreams, designs, and realities in a century of Jewish settlement* (New Haven: Yale University Press, 2003).

Chapter 5: History as Legitimacy

Aharoni, Reuven, *The Pasha's Bedouin; tribes and states in the Egypt of Mehemet Ali, 1805-1848* (New York: Routledge, 2007).
Ashkenazi, Toviyah, *The Bedouin in the Land of Israel* (Jerusalem, Mass, 1957) [Hebrew]
Ateek, Naim, *Justice and Only Justice: A Palestinian Theology of Liberation* (Maryknoll, NY: Orbis,1989a).
Davies, Philip, *In search of ancient Israel* (Sheffield, JSOT Press, 1992)
Engerman, Stanley L. and Jacob Metzer, eds., *Land Rights, Ethno-Nationality, and Sovereignty in History* (London: Routledge, 2004).
Fieldhouse, Dennis K., *The colonial empires: a comparative survey from the eighteenth century* (London: Macmillan, 1966).
Fieldhouse, Dennis K., *Western Imperialism in the Middle East 1914-1958* (Oxford: Oxford University Press. 2008).
Finkelstein, Israel and Neil Silberman, *Archaeology's New Vision of Ancient Israel and the Origin of Its Sacred Texts* (New York: Simon & Schuster, 2002).
Gans, Chaim, *A political theory for the Jewish people: three Zionist narratives* (New York: Oxford University Press, 2016).
Gribetz, Jonathan, *Defining Neighbors: Religion, Race, and the Early Zionist-Arab Encounter* (Princeton: Princeton University Press, 2014).
Inbari, Motti, *Jewish Fundamentalism and the Temple Mount; Who Will Build the Third Temple?* (Albany: SUNY Press, 2009a).

Jacobson, Abigail and Moshe Naor, *Oriental Neighbors: Middle Eastern Jews and Arabs in Mandatory Palestine* (Waltham, MA: Brandeis University Press, 2016).
Kalmar, Ivan D. and Derek Penslar, eds., *Orientalism and the Jews* (Hanover, NH: University Press of New England, 2005).
Katriel, Tamar, *Talking Straight: Dugri Speech in Israeli Sabra Culture* (Cambridge, UK: Cambridge University Press, 1986).
Kaufman, Asher, *Reviving Phoenicia: The Search for Identity in Lebanon* (London: Tauris, 2004).
Kedar, Alexandre, Ahmad Amara, and Oren Yiftachel, *Emptied Lands; A Legal Geography of Bedouin Rights in the Negev* (Stanford: Stanford University Press, 2018).
Kittrie, Orde, *Law as a Weapon of War* (Oxford: Oxford University Press, 2016a).
Khalidi, Rashid, *Palestinian Identity: The Construction of Modern National Consciousness* (New York: Columbia University Press, 1997b).
Kimmerling, Baruch, *Zionism and territory: the socio-territorial dimensions of Zionist politics* (Berkeley: University of California Press, 1983a).
Koestler, Arthur, *The Thirteenth Tribe: The Khazar Empire and Its Heritage* (New York: Random House, 1976).
Kressel, Gideon and Reuven Aharoni, *Egyptian Emigres in the Levant in the 19th and 20th Centuries* (Jerusalem: Jerusalem Center for Public Affairs, 2013).
Lassner, Jacob and S. Ilan Troen, *Jews and Muslims in the Arab World; Haunted by Pasts Real and Imagined* (Lanham, MD: Rowman & Littlefield, 2007a).
Malkawi, Fakhry, and Michele Piccirillo, and Hasan ibn ʻAlī Saqqāf, *The Holy Sites of Jordan* (Amman: Turab, 1996).
National Committee for the Heads of the Arab Local Authorities in Israel, *The Future Vision of the Palestinian Arabs in Israel* (Nazareth: National Committee for the Heads of the Arab Local Authorities in Israel, 2006).
Porath, Yehoshua, *The Emergence of the Palestinian-Arab National Movement, 1918–1929* (London: Cass, 1974b).
Reiter, Yitzhak, *Contested Holy Places in Israel-Palestine: Sharing and Conflict Resolution* (New York: Routledge, 2017).
Reiter, Yitzhak, *Jerusalem and its Role in Islamic Solidarity* (New York: Palgrave Macmillan, 2008a).
Rodinson, Maxime. *Israel: A Colonial Settler-State?* (New York, Monad Press, 1973.
Salameh, Franck, *Charles Corm; An Intellectual Biography of a Twentieth Century Lebanese "Young Phoenician"* (Lanham, MD: Lexington Books, 2015).
Sand, Shlomo, *The Invention of the Jewish People* (London: Verso, 2009).
Saposnik, Arieh, *Becoming Hebrew: The Creation of a Jewish Culture in Ottoman Palestine* (Oxford: Oxford University Press, 2008).
Schama, Simon, *Two Rothschilds and the land of Israel* (New York: Knopf, 1978).
Shafir, Gershon, *Land, Labor and the Origins of the Israeli-Palestinian Conflict 1882-1914* (Berkeley, University of California Press, 1996).
Silberman, Neil Asher and Israel Finkelstein, *The Bible Unearthed: Archaeology's New Vision of Ancient Israel and the Origins of Its Sacred Texts* (New York: Touchstone, 2002).
Shlomo Sand, *The Invention of the Land of Israel; From Holy Land to Homeland* (London: Verso, 2012).
Thompson, Thomas L., *Early History of the Israelite people from the written and archaeological sources* (Leiden: Brill, 1992).
Uzer, Umut, An Intellectual History of Turkish Nationalism (Salt Lake City: University of Utah, 2016).
Whitlam, Keith, *The Invention of ancient Israel; the silencing of Palestinian history* (London: Routledge, 1996).

Chapter 6: Judaism's Claims: A Multiplicity of Interpretations

Barak-Gorodetzky, David, *Judah Magnes: The Prophetic Politics of a Religious Binationalist* (Philadelphia: Jewish Publication Society, 2021).

Bentwich, Norman, *For Zion's Sake. A Biography of Judah L. Magnes. First Chancellor and First President of the Hebrew University of Jerusalem* (Philadelphia: Jewish Publication Society of America, Philadelphia, 1954).

Biale, David, and David Assaf, Benjamin Brown, Uriel Gellman, Samuel Heilman, Moshe Droyanov, Alter and Shulamit Laskov, *Documents on the history of Hibbat-Zion and the settlement of Eretz Israel* [Hebrew], comp. and ed., 7 vols. (Tel-Aviv, 1982-1993).

Efron, Noah, *Real Jews; Secular Versus Ultra-Orthodox and the Struggle for Jewish Identity in Israel* (New York: Basic Books, 2003).

Feige, Michael, *Settling in the Hearts: Jewish Fundamentalism in the Occupied* Territories (Detroit: Wayne State, 2008).

Firestone, Reuven, *Holy War in Judaism; the Fall and Rise of a Controversial Idea* (Oxford: Oxford University Press, 2012),

Galnoor, Itzhak, *The Partition of Palestine: Decision Crossroads in the Zionist Movement* (Albany: SUNY, 1994).

Goren, Arthur, ed., *Dissenter in Zion: From the Writings of Judah L. Magnes* (Cambridge, MA: Harvard University Press, 1982).

Gorenberg, Gershom, *The Accidental Empire; Israel and the Birth of the Settlements, 1967-1977* (New York: Henry Holt, 2006a).

Hattis, Susan Lee *The Bi-National Idea in Palestine During Mandatory Times* (Haifa: Shikmona, 1970).

Hirschhorn, Sarah, *City on a Hilltop: American Jews and the Israeli Settler Movement* (Cambridge, MA: Harvard University Press, 2017).

Inbari, Motti, *Jewish fundamentalism and the Temple Mount :who will build the Third Temple?* (Abany: SUNY, 2009b).

Inbari, Motti, *Messianic religious Zionism confronts Israeli territorial compromises* (New York: Cambridge University Press, 2012).

Kaplan, Kimmy, *Amiram Blau; The World of Neturei Karta's Leader* (Jerusalem: Yad Ben-Zvi and Ben-Gurion U of the Negev, 2017) [Hebrew].

Kaye, Alexander, *The Invention of Jewish Theocracy; The struggle for legal authority in Israel* (Oxford: Oxford University Press).

Lustick, Ian, *For the Land and the Lord: Jewish Fundamentalism in* Israel (New York: Council on Foreign Relations, 1988).

Mendes-Flohr, Paul, ed., *A land of two peoples: Martin Buber on Jews and Arabs* (Chicago: University of Chicago Press, 2005).

Myers, Jody, *Seeking Zion: Modernity and Messianic Activism in the Writings of Tsevi Hirsch Kalischer* (Oxford: Littman Library of Jewish Civilization, 2003).

Mirsky, Yehudah, *Rav Kook; Mystic in a time of revolutions* (New Haven: Yale University Press, 2014).

Pianko, Noam, *Zionism and the Roads Not Taken; Rawidowicz, Kaplan, Kohn* (Bloomington: Indiana University Press, 2010).

Ravitzky, Aviezer, *Messianism, Zionism, and Jewish Religious Radicalism*, (Chicago: University of Chicago, 1995).

Rosman, Gadi Sagiv, and Marcin Wodzinki, *Hasidism; A New History* (Princeton: Princeton University Press, 2018).

Sarna, Jonathan, *American Judaism; A History* (New Haven: Yale University Press, 2019)

Shaul, Michal, *Holocaust Memory in Ultraothodox Society in Israel* (Bloomington, Indiana University, 2020).

Sprinzak, Ehud, *Brother against Brother: violence and extremism in Israeli politics from Altalena to the Rabin assassination* (New York: Free Press, 1999).

Select Bibliography 243

Troen, S. Ilan and Noah Lucas, eds., *Israel; The First Decade of Independence* (Albany: SUNY, 1995).

Chapter 7: Christianity's Claims: A Kaleidoscope of Theologies

Ariel, Yaakov, *An Unusual Relationship: Evangelical Christians and Jews* (New York: NYU Press, 2013).
Ateek, Naim, *Justice, and only Justice, a Palestinian Theology of Liberation* (Maryknoll, NY: Orbis, 1989b).
Bialer, Uri, *Cross on the Star of David: The Christian World in Israel's Foreign Policy, 1948-1967* (Bloomington: Indiana University Press. 2005).
Caitlin Carenen, Caitlin, *The Fervent Embrace: Liberal Protestants, Evangelicals, and Israel* (New York: NYU Press, 2012).
Carroll, James, *Constantine's Sword; The Church and the Jews* (New York: Houghton Mifflin, 2001).
Chacour, Elias, *Blood Brothers; the dramatic story of a Palestinian Christian working for peace in Israel* (Grand Rapids, Mich: Chosen Books, 1984).
Chacour, Elias, *We Belong to the Land; The story of a Palestinian Israeli who lives for peace and reconciliation* (Notre Dame, Indiana: University of Notre Dame Press. 2003).
Chaim Chertok, *He Also Spoke as a Jew; The Life of the Reverend James Parkes* (London: Valentine Mitchell, 2006).
Ciani, Adriano E., *A Study of Cold War Roman Catholic Transnationalism* (Ph. Thesis, University of Western Ontario (2011).
Cunningham, Philip, Ruth Langer, and Jesper Svartvik, *Enabling Dialogue About the Land* (New York: Paulist Press, 2020).
Eibner, Jon, *The Future of Religious Minorities in the Middle East* (Lanham, Md: Lexington, 2018).
Elath [Epstein], Eliahu, *Through the Mist of Time* (Jerusalem: Yad Ben-Zvi, 1989) [Hebrew].
Farah, Rimah, *A Predicament of the National Identity of Arabic-Speaking Christians in Israel: 1980-2014* (unpublished Ph.D. dissertation, Brandeis University, 2022).
Geller, Randall S., *Minorities in the Israeli Military, 1948-58* (Lanham, MD: Lexington, 2017).
Goldman, Samuel, *God's Country; Christian Zionism in America* (Philadelphia: University of Pennsylvania, 2018).
Hummel, Daniel, *Covenant Brothers Evangelicals, Jews and U.S. Israeli Relations* (Philadelphia: University of Pennsylvania, 2019).
Lindsay, Mark R., *Barth, Israel, and Jesus: Karl Barth's Theology of Israel* (London: Routledge, 2007).
Lindsey, Hal, *The Late Great Planet Earth* (Grand Rapids, MI: Zondervan, 1970)
Long, Burke O., *Imagining the Holy Land: Maps, Models, and Fantasy Travels* (Bloomington. IN: Indiana University Press, 2003).
McDermott, Gary R., ed., *The New Christian Zionism; Fresh Perspectives on Israel and the Land*, (Downers Grove: IL: InterVarsity Press, 2016a).
Meotti, Giulio, *The Vatican Against Israel; J'Accuse* (Canada: Mantua Books, 2013).
Merkeley, Paul Charles, *Christian Attitudes towards the State of Israel* (Montreal: McGill-Queen's University Press, 2001).
McGahern, Una, *Palestinian Christians in Israel; State Attitude towards Non-Muslims in a Jewish State* (London: Routledge, 2011).
Moseley, Carys, *Nationhood, providence, and witness: Israel in modern theology and social theory* (Cambridge: Cambridge [England]: James Clarke & Co, 2013).
Nirenberg, David, *Anti-Judaism; The History of a Way of Thinking* (New York: Norton, 2013).
Olson, Jason M., *America's Road to Jerusalem*)Lanham, MD: Lexington, 2018).
Pawlikowski, John T., *Restating the Catholic Church's Relationship with the Jewish People: The Challenge of Super-Sessionary Theology* (Lewiston, New York: Edwin Mellen Press, 2013).

Presbyterian Church (USA), *Zionism Unsettled: a congregational study guide* (Israel/Palestine Mission Network of the Presbyterian Church (U.S.A), 2014).
Sennott, Charles, *The Body and the Blood: The Holy Land at the Turn of a New Millennium: A Reporter's Journey* (New York: Public Affairs, 2001).
Valkenberg, Pim and Anthony Cirelli, ed., *Nostra Aetate* (Washington, D.C.: Catholic University of America Press, 2016).

Chapter 8: Islam: Encountering a Contemporary Challenge

Cohen, Hillel, *Year Zero of the Arab-Israeli Conflict 1929* (Waltham: Brandeis University Press, 2015).
Dowty, Alan, *Arabs and Jews in Ottoman Palestine; two worlds collide* (Bloomington: Indiana University Press, 2019).
ESCO Foundation for Palestine, *Palestine; A Study of Jewish, Arab, and British Policies* (New Haven: Yale University Press, 1947b).
Hurevitz, J. C., *The Struggle for Palestine* (New York: Norton, 1950).
Lassner, Jacob and S. Ilan Troen, *Jews and Muslims in the Arab World: Haunted by Pasts Real and Imagined* (Lanham, MD: Rowman and Littlefield, 2007b).
Lewis, Bernard, *Semites and Anti-Semites; An Inquiry into Conflict and Prejudice* (London: Weidenfeld and Nicolson, 1986).
Lewis, Bernard *The Political Language of Islam* (Chicago: U of Chicago Press, 1988).
Braude, Benjamin and Bernard Lewis, eds., *Christians and Jews in the Ottoman Empire; the functioning of a plural society* (New York: Holmes & Meier. 1982).
Levy, Avigdor, ed., *Jews, Turks, Ottomans; A Shared History, Fifteenth Through the Twentieth Century* (Syracuse: Syracuse University Press, 2002).
Khadduri, Majid, *War and Peace in the Law of Islam* (Baltimore: The Johns Hopkins University Press, 1955).
Jankowski, James and Israel Gershoni, eds., *Rethinking Nationalism in the Arab Middle East* (New York: Columbia University Press, 1997).
Mandel, Neville, *The Arabs and Zionism before World War* (Berkeley: University of California Press, 1976).
Ohana, David, *The Origins of Israeli Mythology; Neither Canaanites nor Crusaders* (Cambridge: Cambridge University Press, 2012).
Piscatori, James P., *Islam in a World of Nation-States* (Cambridge: Cambridge University Press, 1986).
Porath, Yehoshua, *The Palestinian Arab National Movement, 1929-1939; From Riots to Rebellion* (London: Cass, 1977).
Yitzhak Reiter, *Jerusalem and Its Role in Islamic Solidarity* (New York: Palgrave Macmillan, 2008b).
Reiter, Yitzhak, *War, Peace and International Relations in Islam; Muslim Scholars on Peace Accords with Israel* (Brighton: Sussex Academic Press, 2011).
Sivan, Emmanuel, *Radical Islam: Medieval Theology and Modern Politics* (New Haven: Yale, 1990, enlarged edition).
Shaham, Ron, ed., *Law, Custom, and Statute in the Muslim World; Studies in honor of Aharon Layish* (Leiden: Brill: 2007).
Wiktorowicz, Quintan (ed.), *Islamic Activism: A Social Movement Theory Approach* (Bloomington: Indiana University Press, 2004).

Chapter 9: Concluding Reflections

Abu El-Haj, Nadia, *Archaeological Practice and Territorial Self-Fashioning in Israeli Society* (Chicago: University of Chicago, 2001).

Adalah, *The Democratic Constitution* (Haifa: Adalah, The Legal Center for Arab Minority Rights in Israel, 2007).

Alroey, Gur, *Zionism without Zion: The Jewish Territorial Organization and Its Conflict with the Zionist Organization* (Detroit: Wayne State U Press, 2016).

Anderson, Benedict, *Imagined Communities: Reflections on the Origin and Spread of Nationalism* (New York: Verso, 2016).

Barsamian, David and Edward Said, *Culture and Resistance; Conversations with Edward W. Said* (Cambridge, MA: South End Press, 2003).

Benvenisti, Meron, *West Bank Data Project: A Survey of Israel's Policies* (Washington: American Enterprise Institute for Public Policy Research, 1984).

Bialer, Uri, *Israeli Foreign Policy; A People Shall Not Dwell Alone* (Bloomington: Indiana University Press, 2020).

Epstein, Lawrence J, *The Dream of Zion; The story of the first Zionist Congress* (Lanham, MD: Rowman and Littlefield, 2016b).

Fieldhouse, D. K., *Western Imperialism in the Middle East* (Oxford: Oxford University Press, 2006).

Fish, Rachel, *Configurations of Bi-nationalism: The Transformation of Bi-nationalism in Palestine/Israel 1920s—Present* (Ph.D. dissertation: Brandeis University, 2013).

Gorenberg, Gershom, *The Accidental Empire; Israel and the Birth of the Settlements, 1967-1977* (New York: Times Books, 2006b).

Holzman-Gazit, Yifat, *Land expropriation in Israel: law, culture, and* society (London: Ashgate Publishing, 2007).

Kimmerling, Baruch, *Zionism and territory*: the *socio-territorial dimensions of Zionist politics* (Berkeley, 1983b).

Kittrie, Orde F., *Lawfare; Law as a Weapon of War* (Oxford: Oxford University Press, 2016b)

Kronish, Ronald, ed., *Coexistence and Reconciliation in Israel: Voices for Interreligious Dialogue* (Mahwah, NJ: Paulist Press, 2015).

Louis, Wm. Roger *Ends of British Imperialism; The Scramble for Empire, Suez and Decolonization* (London: Tauris, 2006b).

Lustick, Ian, *Paradigm Lost: From Two-State Solution to One-State Reality* (Philadelphia: University of Pennsylvania Press, 2021).

Mada al-Carmel, *The Haifa Declaration* (Haifa: The Arab Center for Applied Social Research, 2007).

McDermott, Gerald R., ed., *The New Christian Zionism; Fresh Perspectives on Israel and the Land* (Downers Grove, IL: IVP Academic, 2016b).

Meisler, Stanley, *United Nations: A History* (New York: Grove, 2011).

Morris, Benny, *1948: a history of the first Arab Israeli war* (New Haven: Yale University Press, 2008).

Nelson, Cary, *Israel Denial: Anti-Zionism, Anti-Semitism, & the Faculty Campaign Against the Jewish State* (Bloomington: Indiana University Press, 2019).

Neumann, Boaz, *Territory and Desire in Early Zionism* (Waltham, Massachusetts: Brandeis University Press/University Press of New England, 2011).

Oren, Michael, *Power, faith, and fantasy: America in the Middle East, 1776 to the* present (New York: Norton, 2007).

Rotberg, Robert I., ed., *Israeli and Palestinian Narratives of Conflict: History's Double Helix* (Bloomington: Indiana University Press, 2006).

Saxe, Leonard, *Ten Days of Birthright Israel: A Journey in Young Adult Identity (Waltham, MA: Brandeis University Press,* 2008).

Schwartz, Adi and Einat Wilf, *The War of Return; How Western Indulgence of the Palestinian Dream Has Obstructed the Path to Peace* (New York: St. Martin's, 2020).

Schechter, Michael, *United Nations Global Conferences* (London: Taylor and Francis, 2009).
Shapira, Anita, Yedidia Z. Stern and Alexander Yakobson, eds., *Nationalism and Binationalism; the Perils of Perfect Structures* (Brighton: Sussex Academic Press, 2013).
Steinberg, Gerald and Anne Herzberg, *The Goldstone Report 'Reconsidered': A Critical Analysis* (Jerusalem: NGO Monitor/Jerusalem Center for Public Affairs, 2011).
The National Committee for the Heads of the Local Arab Authorities in Israel, *The Future Vision of the Palestinian Arabs in Israel* (Nazareth, 2006).
Troy, Gil, *Moynihan's Moment: America's Fight against Zionism is Racism* (New York: Oxford University Press, 2013).
Wasserstein, Bernard. *Divided Jerusalem: the struggle for the holy city* (New Haven: Yale University Press, 2008).
Whitelam, Keith, *The Invention of Ancient Israel; the silencing of Palestinian history* (London: Routledge, 1996).
Yerushalmi, Yosef, *Zakhor: Jewish History and Jewish Memory* (Seattle: University of Washington Press, 1982).
Yiftachel, Oren, *Ethnocracy: land and identity politics in Israel/Palestine* (Philadelphia: University of Pennsylvania Press, 2006).
Zipperstein, Steven, *Law and the Arab-Israeli Conflict; The Trials of Palestine* (New York: Routledge, 2020).
Zureik, Constantin, *The Meaning of the Disaster* (Beirut: Khayat's College Book Cooperative, 1956) Originally published in August 1948 in Arabic as *Ma'nā al-nakbah*. (Zureik is variously spelled: Zureiq, Zurayk).

Note

1. Each chapter has extensive footnotes to sources often with bibliographic commentary. Rather than a combined alphabetical list of all the books, academic articles, newspaper accounts, official reports and other items referenced or discussed in footnotes, the following bibliography lists only books that are relevant for the topics treated in the chapters. Wherever possible, the English edition rather than the Hebrew is indicated. Although many items are relevant for multiple chapters, only the first citation is provided.

Index[1]

A
Abbas, Mansour, 178, 195, 223
Abraham Accords, 174, 188
Adams, John Quincy, 7
Agudat Israel, 113–115, 117, 119, 226
Al-Aqsa Mosque, 95, 121, 167, 169, 170, 176, 202, 227
Albright, William, 53, 54
Alkalai, Yehudah, 116, 117
Allenby, Edmund, 22, 28, 29, 31
American Council for Judaism, 123
Antonius, George, 31, 40n15, 147, 150, 160
Arab land, 37, 39, 48, 189, 207
Arab Peace Initiative (API), 173, 175
Arafat, Yasser, 5, 15, 147, 167–169, 223, 225, 226, 229
Ataturk, Kemal, 94, 215
Ateek, Naim, 96, 97, 145–147, 154n32, 221n48
Augustine (Saint), 13, 133, 135, 141

B
Balfour Declaration, 1, 2, 8, 24, 25, 27, 29, 34, 35, 37–39, 42n36, 48, 50, 51, 54, 58, 67, 75, 88–90, 92, 100, 105n20, 138, 157, 160, 186, 187, 213, 231, 232, 234
Bandung Conference, 198, 200, 235
Bedouin, 9, 28, 29, 54, 79, 90–92, 97–99, 106n36, 106n38

Begin, Menachem (1913-1992), 121, 173, 174, 204, 224–226
Ben-Gurion, David, 5, 26, 30, 53, 54, 57, 61n20, 75, 116, 119, 125–127, 158, 215, 225–227, 233
Ben-Zvi, Yitzhak, 26, 30, 53, 54, 57, 233
Berger, Elmer, 123
Berger, Peter, 5
Bialik, Nahman, 66
Binationalism, 127, 193, 205–209, 220n40
Borochov, Ber, 68
British Mandate (for Palestine), x, 1, 3, 24, 27, 34, 49, 51, 73, 90, 92, 98, 125, 168, 186, 187, 202, 232, 234
Brit Shalom, 122, 125
Buber, Martin, 125–127, 193, 206

C
Capitulations, 21, 22, 24, 134, 175
Catholic/Catholicism, vii, 13, 134–137, 143, 144, 149, 162, 165, 194, 230, 231
Cattan, Henry, 33–37
Chacour, Elias, 147, 148
Christian Arabs, 147–150, 161, 165, 207
Christian Aramaic Nationality, 150
Christianity, vii, ix, x, 3, 4, 6, 9, 13, 53, 61n22, 82, 95, 97, 128, 131–151, 157, 158, 161, 164, 167, 178, 192–195, 214, 216, 230–231
Churchill, Winston, 38, 75

---

[1] Note: Page numbers followed by 'n' refer to notes.

© The Author(s), under exclusive license to Springer Nature Switzerland AG 2024
S. I. Troen, *Israel/Palestine in World Religions*,
https://doi.org/10.1007/978-3-031-50914-8

247

Colonial-settler, ix, 11, 90, 93, 98–102, 127, 143, 189, 197, 199, 206, 207, 214
Columbus Platform, 123, 231
Conder, Claude R., 51–53
Conquest, vii, 2, 8–10, 21–40, 43, 59, 75, 95, 97, 103, 112, 150, 159–161, 169, 186–188, 192, 214, 228
Constantine, 13, 132
Crusader, 2, 14, 141, 167–168
Crusades, 133, 159, 167, 192, 230

D

Dar al-Islam, 14, 36, 159, 171, 175, 177, 228
Declaration of Independence (Israel), 30, 88, 112, 115, 119, 213, 214, 216
Declaration of Independence (United States), 6, 214
Dhimmi, 13, 14, 92, 93, 101, 151, 160, 161, 164, 227
Discovery, 8–10, 43–59, 91, 103
Durban (World Conference Against Racism), 200, 201, 212

E

Economic absorptive capacity, viii, 11, 43–59, 99, 102, 186, 188–189
Enlightenment, 3, 6, 8, 14, 66, 87, 113, 114, 133, 141, 157, 225, 231
Evangelical, 13, 137–139, 144, 147, 194, 230

F

Fatwa, 15, 174–177, 182n39, 195, 228
Fedayeen, 229
Fellahin, 65, 78–81
Fieldhouse, D. K., 100, 101, 107n48
Future Vision (of the Arabs in Palestine), 91, 92, 207

G

Goldstone Report, x, 201, 235
Gordon, Aaron David, 68, 69
Grotius, Hugo, 5, 6, 10, 194

H

Hamas, ix, x, 171–174, 177, 178, 198, 201, 208, 215, 219n34, 228, 229, 235
Hashemite, 30, 31, 39, 94, 95, 160, 187, 228, 232

Hasidism, 128n2
Haskalah, 114, 231
Herzl, Theodor, 23, 46, 101, 117, 122, 125, 134, 138, 143, 186, 188, 194, 225, 233, 234
Herzog, Chaim, 199, 225
Hezbollah, 171, 177, 229
Hibbat Zion, 117, 233
Husseini, Haj Amin al, *see* Mufti Palestine, ix

I

Identity, viii, 1, 13, 27, 31, 37, 39, 41n32, 46, 65, 82, 83, 88, 89, 92–95, 97, 101, 105n20, 147, 150, 151, 160, 161, 170, 188–191, 193, 206–208, 221n48, 233
Indigeneity, vii, 9, 12, 15, 88, 90–94, 98, 99, 106n38, 146, 158, 191
International Holocaust Remembrance Alliance (IHRA), 211, 212, 222n56
Intifada, 171, 205, 228

J

Jabotinsky, Vladamir, 26–28, 234
Jerusalem Declaration on Antisemitism, 212, 222n56
Jewish land, 25, 36, 65, 77, 78, 81–83
Jewish Legion, 26–28, 30, 73
Jihad, ix, 15, 75, 159, 168, 172, 175, 176, 195, 229
Jordan (Transjordan), 2, 3, 15, 17n3, 24, 28, 31, 94, 95, 98, 119, 160, 161, 171, 173, 177, 187, 191, 195, 204, 224, 226, 228, 229, 234, 236

K

Kalischer, Zvi Hirsch, 116, 117
Khaybar, 165–167, 180n20, 228
Khazar, 90, 104n6
Kitchener, Herbert, 47, 51
Kook, Rabbi Abraham, 118–120, 129n15, 233
Kook, Rabbi Zvi Yehuda, 120, 121

L

Labor (concept), 66–67, 69, 189
Labor (political party), 226
Lawfare, 16, 200–202, 213, 219n31
Lawrence, T. E., 28, 29, 47

Index 249

League of Nations, 1, 2, 21, 22, 24, 25, 32, 35, 37, 48–50, 57, 81, 88, 90, 93, 94, 112, 170, 186, 199, 213, 232

Legitimacy, viii, 1, 3, 4, 7, 9, 10, 12, 13, 15, 16, 23, 32–34, 37–40, 43, 50, 59, 87–103, 123, 124, 128, 134, 137, 138, 140, 141, 148, 149, 157, 158, 163, 170, 173, 177, 178, 185–188, 191, 192, 195–199, 201–204, 212, 213, 216

Liberation Theology, 97, 102, 145–149, 193, 194, 230

Locke, John, 6–8, 11, 66

M

Magnes, Judah, 124, 125, 127, 206
Marshall, John, 8–11, 18n16, 39, 43, 83, 191
Matzpen, 206
Mufti (of Egypt), 176
Mufti (of Jerusalem), 31, 158, 165, 169, 174
Mufti Palestine, ix, 31, 78, 168, 169, 224
Muslim Brotherhood, 168, 171, 224, 229

N

Nakba, 80, 192, 211
Nasser, Gamal Abdel, 94, 95, 167, 190, 224, 230
Nathan, Robert, 55, 56
Neturei Karta, 114
Niebuhr, Reinhold, 139, 141–151, 153n16, 153n21, 154n22, 154n23, 154n30, 194
Nostra Aetate, 13, 135, 136, 149, 230
Nusseibah, Sari, 58, 59

O

Occupation, 35, 39, 46, 79, 97, 146–148, 160, 202–205, 207, 228
Oslo Accords, 147, 169, 173, 177, 178, 188, 205, 223, 225, 229
Ottoman Empire (Turkish Empire), vii, 1–3, 10, 14, 21–24, 32, 35–39, 47, 76, 79, 83, 92, 94, 97, 100, 101, 105n23, 116, 160, 161, 164, 171, 175, 190–192, 228, 229

P

Palestine Authority (PA), 18n18, 152n3, 223, 229
Palestine Exploration Fund (PEF), 47, 51, 52

Palestine Liberation Organization (PLO), 35, 36, 38, 93, 96, 114, 124, 162, 167, 171–173, 204, 223, 226, 229

Palestine National Charter, 35
Pan-Arabism, 94, 95, 190, 224, 229
Parkes, James, 139–142, 153n17, 153n18, 153n19, 153n21, 194
Partition, x, 22, 31, 32, 37, 39, 55, 65, 74, 82, 89, 116, 119, 125, 141–144, 147, 176, 187, 197, 198, 202, 203, 205, 209, 232, 233
Pawlikowski, John, 136, 137, 153n18
Peel Commission, 76, 79, 116, 119, 159
Peres, Shimon, 133, 188, 225, 226
Philos, 194
Pope Francis, 133
Pope Paul VI, 134, 231
Pope Pius X, 134, 143, 194
Pope Pius XII, 134
Protestantism, 13, 139, 141, 143, 230

Q

Qur'an, 148, 159, 162–165, 172, 176–178, 179n12

R

Rabin, Yitzhak, 121, 223, 225, 226
Radical Islam, 171–173, 177, 178, 215, 216
Raheb, Mitri, 147, 154n35, 194
Rashi (Rabbi Shlomo Itzhaki), 4
Reconstitution, 102
Reform Judaism, 122–125
Replacement theology, *see* Supersessionism, ix
Revisionist Zionism, 27, 234
Rodinson, Maxine, 99
Ruppin, Arthur, 56, 57

S

Sadat, Anwar, 173–176, 196, 224
Sand, Shlomo, 99, 100
Satmar, 113, 114
Second Vatican Council, 135, 231
Self-determination, vii, 9, 10, 21–40, 59, 90, 91, 103, 146, 158, 169, 186, 191, 202, 212, 214, 235

Settler-colonialism, *see* Colonial-settler
Stone, Julius, 33, 37–40, 219n31
Supersessionism, ix, 13, 95, 97, 132–136, 138, 140, 141, 146, 148, 162, 175, 193, 194, 214, 231
Sykes-Picot Agreement, 24

T

Temple Mount, 95, 120, 169, 170, 202, 216, 227
Terra nullius, 9
Treaties, vii, 8–10, 21–40, 43, 59, 91, 103, 159, 166, 167, 169, 175–177, 182n40, 182n41, 185, 186, 191, 196, 214, 225, 226
Truman, Harry, 50, 142
Trumpeldor, Josef, 26
Two-state solution, 2, 59, 187, 203, 210, 232

U

Ultraorthodoxy, 113–118, 121, 125, 233
United Nations Secretariat, 157
United Nations Security Council (UNSC) Resolution
   Resolution 181, 143, 232, 234
   Resolution 242, 120, 203, 224, 234, 235
   Resolution 338, 235
   Resolution 3376, 235
   Resolution 3379, 199–200, 235

UNSCOP, *see* UN Special Commission on Palestine
UN Special Commission on Palestine (UNSCOP), 144

V

Vatican, 134–136, 143, 152n3, 194, 230

W

Walzer, Michael, 5, 208
Waqf, 76, 78, 172, 173
Warren, Charles, 51, 52
Weizmann, Chaim, 50, 226
West Bank (Judea and Samaria), 12, 120, 236
White Papers
   of 1922, 232
   of 1939, 9, 65, 74, 94, 233
   Hope-Simpson Report, 74, 232
   Passfield White Paper of 1930, 74, 232
World Zionist Organization (WZO), 23, 134, 226

Y

Yishuv, 39, 57, 66, 69, 75, 80, 115, 118, 218n18, 227, 234

Z

Zionism Unsettled (a congregational study guide), 97, 143, 145–147
Zion Mule Corps, 26

Printed in the USA
CPSIA information can be obtained
at www.ICGtesting.com
CBHW050252041124
16857CB00004B/127